Debating Critical Theory

Essex Studies in Contemporary Critical Theory

Series Editors: Peter Dews, Emeritus Professor of Philosophy at the University of Essex; Lorna Finlayson, Lecturer in Philosophy at the University of Essex; Fabian Freyenhagen, Professor of Philosophy at the University of Essex; Timo Jütten, Professor of Philosophy at the University of Essex; and Jörg Schaub, Senior Lecturer in Philosophy at the University of Essex

Essex Studies in Contemporary Critical Theory. This series aims to develop the critical analysis of contemporary societies. The series publishes both substantive critical analyses of recent and current developments in society and culture and studies dealing with methodological/conceptual problems in the critical theory tradition, intended to further enhance its ability to address the problems of contemporary society.

The Political Is Political, Lorna Finlayson
The Spell of Responsibility, Frieder Vogelmann; translated by Daniel Steuer
Social Suffering: Sociology, Psychology, Politics, Emmanuel Renault; translated by Maude Dews
Critical Theory and Social Self-Understanding, Robin Celikates; translated by Naomi van Steenbergen

Debating Critical Theory

Engagements with Axel Honneth

Edited by
Julia Christ
Kristina Lepold
Daniel Loick
Titus Stahl

ROWMAN & LITTLEFIELD
Lanham • Boulder • New York • London

Published by Rowman & Littlefield
An imprint of The Rowman & Littlefield Publishing Group, Inc.
4501 Forbes Boulevard, Suite 200, Lanham, Maryland 20706
www.rowman.com

6 Tinworth Street, London, SE11 5AL, United Kingdom

Copyright © 2020 by Julia Christ, Kristina Lepold, Daniel Loick, and Titus Stahl

This publication is part of the DFG-funded Cluster of Excellence (2007–2019) "The Formation of Normative Orders" at Goethe University Frankfurt am Main.

All rights reserved. No part of this book may be reproduced in any form or by any electronic or mechanical means, including information storage and retrieval systems, without written permission from the publisher, except by a reviewer who may quote passages in a review.

British Library Cataloguing in Publication Information Available

Library of Congress Cataloging-in-Publication Data

Names: Christ, Julia, editor.
Title: Debating critical theory : engagements with Axel Honneth / edited by Julia Christ, Kristina Lepold, Daniel Loick, Titus Stahl.
Description: Lanham : Rowman & Littlefield, 2020. | Series: Essex studies in contemporary critical theory | Includes bibliographical references and index. | Summary: "Bringing together leading scholars in contemporary social and political philosophy, this volume takes up the central themes of Axel Honneth's work as a starting point for debating the present and future of critical theory, as a form of socially grounded philosophy for analyzing and critiquing society today"— Provided by publisher.
Identifiers: LCCN 2020010332 (print) | LCCN 2020010333 (ebook) | ISBN 9781786614780 (cloth) | ISBN 9781786614797 (paperback) | ISBN 9781786614803 (epub)
Subjects: LCSH: Honneth, Axel, 1949- | Critical theory. | Criticism (Philosophy) | Social sciences—Philosophy.
Classification: LCC B3279.H84574 D43 2020 (print) | LCC B3279.H84574 (ebook) | DDC 142—dc23
LC record available at https://lccn.loc.gov/2020010332
LC ebook record available at https://lccn.loc.gov/2020010333

Contents

Debating Critical Theory: An Introduction   vii
Julia Christ, Kristina Lepold, Daniel Loick, and Titus Stahl

SECTION I: CRITIQUE   1

1. Realism, Yet Again   3
   Raymond Geuss

2. Kantian Republicanism versus the Neo-Republican Machine: The Meaning and Practice of Political Autonomy   17
   Rainer Forst

3. Taking a Stand: Second-Order Social Pathologies or First-Order Critique   35
   Sally Haslanger

4. Immanent Normativity and the Fact of Domination: Notes on "Immanent Critique"   51
   Martin Saar

5. Moral Economy: A Critical Reappraisal   67
   Didier Fassin

6. Radical Civility: Social Struggles and the Domestication of Dissent   83
   Robin Celikates

SECTION II: RECOGNITION — 95

7 Rousseau on the Nature of Social Inequality — 97
Frederick Neuhouser

8 Repressive Empathy? A Plea for Contextualization — 113
Martin Hartmann

9 On Human Sociability — 129
Joel Whitebook

SECTION III: SOCIAL FREEDOM — 149

10 Ethical Life and Anomie: From Social Philosophy to Sociology of the State — 151
Bruno Karsenti

11 Socialism and the Nation-State — 173
David Miller

12 Hegel's Concept of the Person and International Human Rights — 187
Seyla Benhabib

13 Fashioning Our Selves? On Understanding and Criticizing the Digitized Society — 205
Beate Roessler

14 The Crisis of Liberalism: The Dialectic of Politics and Police — 225
Christoph Menke

SECTION IV: PROGRESS — 245

15 John Dewey Goes to Frankfurt: Pragmatism, Critical Theory, and the Invisibility of Moral/Social Problems — 247
Philip Kitcher

16 Political Progress: Piecemeal, Pragmatic, and Processual — 269
Christopher F. Zurn

17 Psychoanalysis and the Critique of Progress — 287
Amy Allen

About the Contributors and Editors — 305

Debating Critical Theory

An Introduction

Julia Christ, Kristina Lepold,
Daniel Loick, and Titus Stahl

One of the distinctive features of a critical theory of society in the tradition of the Frankfurt School is the fact that it conceives of itself not as investigating timeless truths, but as historically embedded and as engaging with the "struggles and wishes of the age." It is thus entirely appropriate, and indeed necessary, for critical theorists to reflect about their work in terms of its own contemporary context.

At the beginning of the third decade of the twenty-first century, few theorists are as influential in debates in critical theory as Axel Honneth. Even though critical theory today can be understood less as forming a coherent "school" than it could have been at times in the twentieth century, and even though a robust pluralism of methods, concepts, and political commitments is now one of the defining features of this tradition, there can be no doubt that Honneth's work represents a central point of reference for countless contemporary contributions to critical theory (see, among many others, Fraser and Honneth 2003; Cooke 2006; Deranty et al. 2007; van den Brink and Owen 2007; Petherbridge 2011; Stahl 2013; Honneth and Rancière 2016; Christ 2017; Celikates [2009] 2018; Jaeggi [2014] 2018). This is because Honneth's work has not only shaped debates about the very idea of a critical theory, but in doing so also proposed a new way to link critical theory and the social sciences as well as theory and social struggles (in other words, practice).

Among the key concepts that Honneth has redefined and which are at the heart of ongoing debates in critical theory are "critique," "recognition," "social freedom," and "progress." Given the importance of Axel Honneth's work for contemporary critical theory, we decided to invite leading political theorists, sociologists, and philosophers not to write *about* Honneth's work, but to reflect on the significance of the questions that Honneth's work raises for a critical theory of society from the perspective of their own research. Specifically, we asked our contributors to reflect on one of these four concepts – "critique," "recognition," "social freedom," and "progress." This book thus presents engagements with important themes from the work of Axel Honneth from a range of contemporary perspectives.

By way of introduction, we would like to contextualize Honneth's contributions to critical theory to show how those four concepts are developed in Honneth's work and why it is therefore appropriate to focus on them.

Honneth's contributions to critical theory can perhaps best be understood by starting from a number of methodological commitments that Honneth inherits from Horkheimer, Adorno, and Habermas; all of whom distinguish critical theorizing from established or traditional forms of theorizing social and political life (see Horkheimer [1937] 2002; Adorno [1963] 2005; Habermas [1965] 1966, [1968] 1987). What emerges from their reflections are three particular features of theories that are to be called "critical": firstly, critical theories are self-conscious of their social embeddedness, more particularly, of their connection to social practices and struggles. Secondly, critical theories give up the pretence of neutrality and are committed to a particular goal, namely the emancipation of all human beings from exploitation, oppression, and domination. Last but not least, they see the theoretical enlightenment that they aim to bring about (i.e. "the self-clarification of the struggles and wishes of the age," as Marx ([1843] 1975, 209) so famously put it) as itself a contribution to achieving this goal. Honneth's first major intervention into critical theory in *Critique of Power* ([1985] 1993) takes place against this backdrop. From very early on, Honneth is thus committed to a particular notion of "critique" which can be distinguished most notably from the idea of social criticism we find in liberal theories of justice (see, despite important differences, Rawls 1971; Cohen 2008), but also from the one that can be found in theories of so-called communitarian thinkers (see especially Walzer 1987, 1988).

In his dissertation *Critique of Power*, Honneth examines more specifically both the theories of the first generation of the Frankfurt School and of Habermas (as well as of Foucault) with regard to their conceptualization of social conflict and finds them deficient (see the overview in Lepold 2019, 251–53). While Horkheimer first unsuccessfully attempts to locate social struggles in the activity of work, Adorno and Horkheimer ultimately assimilate social integration to domination (of both human beings and nature) and thereby lose sight of the constant social struggles around the organization of social life. According to Honneth, Habermas' theory of communicative action provides a way out of this impasse; as Honneth puts it in a later text, Habermas "re-established access to an emancipatory sphere of action" (Honneth 1994, 257). However, in Habermas' social theory, communicative action is limited to only one sphere of social life, namely the lifeworld, leaving untouched the sphere of economic production and political administration. Moreover, in the context of Habermas' social theory, communicative action is conceived of as the site of a process of rationalization that is the unintentional by-product of what individuals do, and not as the site of emancipatory struggles of social groups. In the light of this, Honneth identifies the need for a theoretical framework that goes beyond Habermas and is capable of making visible that the organization of the whole of social life is subject to constant social struggles which are morally motivated (see Honneth [1985] 1993, 303). This interest in the moral grammar of social life will eventually lead Honneth to renew the concept of critique. Unlike Habermas, Honneth comes to focus on the normative structure of *all* social spheres constitutive of bourgeois society. He aims at criticizing practices within these spheres by taking their own normative structure as the basis for identifying deviations or unrealized promises (see Zurn 2015, 92–126). It is in the context of this renewal of critical theory that the concept of "recognition" appears.

Honneth's subsequent work *Struggle for Recognition* ([1992] 1996) develops an original account of social conflicts and their basic moral grammar. Drawing on Hegel's early "Jena" work as well as on insights from sociology and psychoanalysis, Honneth argues that social struggles must be understood as motivated not merely by material interests, but by moral experiences, more specifically, by experiences of disrespect. According to Honneth, such moral experiences of disrespect point to the basic need of individuals for recognition. Individuals need recognition because it is only in virtue of the recognition by others that individuals are capable of developing a "practical relation-to-self" (see, for example, Honneth [1992] 1996, 92) on the basis of which they can realize themselves, that is, be truly free. Honneth claims that individuals need more specifically three forms of recognition which enable them to develop three distinct self-relations: first, on an anthropological level, the care for individual needs in the context of intimate relationships, family life, and friendships which provides the basis for developing self-confidence; second, specific to modern societies, the respect for individual autonomy through rights in the context of modern constitutional and democratic arrangements which provides the basis for developing self-respect; and third, the social esteem for the particular contributions of individuals to society which provides the basis for developing self-esteem (see Honneth [1992] 1996, ch. 5). By laying out this basic conceptual framework, Honneth is less interested in a mere empirical thesis about the contribution of institutions and practices to the psychological development of individuals than in uncovering the normative dynamics within modern societies. As he puts it, it is his "intention […] to explain processes of social change by referring to the normative demands that are […] internal to the relationship of mutual recognition" (Honneth [1992] 1996, 92). It is not difficult to see how such social change is supposed to come about. If recognition is vital for developing a practical relation-to-self and for being really free, experiences of disrespect with regard to one's needs, one's capacity as an autonomous being, as well as one's contributions to society represent obstacles to individual freedom. Therefore, according to Honneth, such experiences provide the motivational basis for social struggles in which recognition (or more appropriate recognition) is demanded – initially, only in the spheres of respect and esteem, in Honneth's later work in all three domains, which, as he clarifies there, are all domains of modern social life. Such struggles for recognition are what drives emancipatory social change.

Struggle for Recognition provides Honneth's first systematic answer to the methodological desideratum that critical theories must be seen as giving voice to the struggles of their present, and the concept of "recognition" plays a key role in this. Honneth's theory of recognition specifies the three features of critical theories described above in a particular manner: first of all, critical theory in the form of the theory of recognition is linked directly to social struggles, namely struggles for recognition which emerge on the basis of experiences of disrespect. Secondly, the critical theory of recognition is partisan insofar as it binds the idea of freedom to a social and historical context and takes side with struggles for recognition which are supposed to enable greater freedom. Finally, the critical theory of recognition attempts to contribute to the self-understanding of these struggles and can hence be understood as a means to theoretical enlightenment.

It should be noted, however, that in the context of his recognition-theoretic renewal of Frankfurt School critical theory Honneth has also further elaborated on the concept of "critique." Especially in his exchange with Nancy Fraser in 2003, Honneth has made it clear that the kind of critique he envisions within the recognition-theoretic framework is "immanent" not only in the sense that it is based on ongoing struggles in actual social reality, but that it relies on norms that are already realized in social reality, albeit imperfectly. Indeed, according to Honneth, demands for recognition which are made on the basis of experiences of disrespect do not express universal expectations of recognition that all persons share qua human beings – an impression that *Struggle for Recognition* may leave readers with (Zurn 2015, 207; Stahl 2013, 167). "Rather," as Honneth clarifies in his exchange with Fraser, "such expectations are the product of the social forming of a deep-seated claim-making potential, in the sense that they always owe their normative justification to principles [or norms — the editors] institutionally anchored in the historically established recognition order" (Honneth 2003, 137). In other words, individuals have the expectation to be recognized in their needs, their capacity for autonomy, and their particular contributions to society – and make corresponding demands – by virtue of participating in institutions and practices which promise these three forms of recognition and whose existence is characteristic of modern societies. In Honneth's view, against the backdrop of new interpretations of their needs, their claims as autonomous beings and their contributions, individuals and social groups will again and again reach the conclusion that their expectations of recognition are presently not or not fully met. The given institutions and practices thus continuously fail to grant the recognition they promise. Because of this, it can be argued that the underlying norm of recognition needs to be practiced differently so as to better realize its promise. Honneth refers to this as "surplus of validity" (Honneth 2003, 151).

Importantly, the methodological background here is no longer provided only by critical theory in the tradition of the Frankfurt School, but centrally by Hegel's mature social philosophy, too. Already in his 1999 Spinoza lectures *Suffering from Indeterminacy* (Honneth 2000), Honneth turns to Hegel's *Philosophy of Right* in an attempt to "reactualize" it. Honneth discovers here the idea he draws on in his exchange with Fraser, namely that the ethical life of a society is based on shared value commitments or the adherence to norms which not only animate citizens' loyalty to social institutions but also enable a critical reflection on these institutions. In his opus magnum *Freedom's Right* ([2011] 2014), Honneth builds on this reading of the mature Hegel. However, rather than merely outlining the idea of an immanent critique of social life, Honneth now engages in the ambitious undertaking of actually developing an immanent critique of the present organization of social life; and he seeks to do this through a historical reconstruction of "the struggles that have been fought on the normative foundation of modernity" (Honneth [2011] 2014, viii). The aim of this reconstruction is to lay open which "promises" (ibid.) have yet to be fulfilled today.

In this context, the concept of "social freedom" becomes central in Honneth's work. Following Hegel, Honneth argues that the only norm that can command any allegiance in modernity is the norm of individual freedom (see Honneth [2011] 2014, 15–19). At closer inspection, Honneth finds that the overarching norm of individual freedom can be disaggregated into different norms of freedom which all play a role in modern ethical life. In *Freedom's Right*, he discusses the familiar idea of negative freedom, which is institutionalized in the legal sphere (see ibid., chs. 1 and 4), as well as ideas of positive freedom and reflexive or procedural freedom, which are at the heart of modern morality (see ibid., chs. 2 and 5). However, it should come as no surprise that Honneth is of the view that neither the legal sphere, in which individuals merely enjoy negative freedom (for a follow-up on this idea, see Loick 2017), nor modern morality, in the context of which individuals in principle enjoy reflexive freedom, constitute the essence of modern ethical life. In his earlier work, Honneth describes social life in modern societies as being characterized above all by three forms of recognition. In the present context he stays faithful to this assertion and defines these three forms of recognition as love, solidarity, and democratic respect. Moreover, he now interprets these three forms of recognition as realizing in different ways an idea of freedom not yet explored by social and political philosophy, namely what he calls following Hegel "social freedom" (see also Neuhouser 2000). According to Honneth, even though the concept of "social freedom" has received little attention by philosophers, it is impossible to understand modern ethical life without it. Social freedom is a "kind of freedom that results from our purposes being promoted by those of others" (Honneth [2011] 2014, 61). It is generated in contexts of recognition in which the agency of others is not seen as a limitation of one's own freedom, but as its very condition.

This idea provides for a clear and distinct philosophical definition of "social freedom." However, it does not entail that social reality already offers many unambiguous instances of such freedom being realized. Rather, Honneth's historical reconstruction of the three forms of recognition through which it has been realized in modern societies yields mixed results. While he endorses a quite optimistic picture of the changes that have taken place with regard to personal relationships, his analysis of the developments in the economic and political spheres is much more sceptical. Honneth identifies for each of these two spheres a normative promise emerging from the practices themselves which constitutes them. Concerning the market, this is the concept of "solidarity," specific to the division of social labour (Durkheim [1893] 2013). Concerning the political sphere, this is the concept of "collective formation of the law." However, naming the immanent normative promises to these spheres of action does not mean that the historical reconstruction of these spheres testifies to the realization of these promises. For the market sphere, Honneth fully acknowledges that competitive practices, referring individuals to their personal interests and the subjective rights that protect them, have taken precedence over solidarity practices; and for the political sphere Honneth is well aware of the dangers of oppression of the citizens by the most important modern political institution, that is, the state. Honneth's own critical gesture here is not to declare these two institutions – market and state – unfit for the promotion of social freedom, but to proceed to their immanent critique on the basis of the normative promises they do not keep and which are nevertheless inherent to them.

Recently, Honneth has built on this immanent critique developed in *Freedom's Right* and offered a new interpretation of the political ideal of socialism. According to Honneth, socialism properly understood is the name for the realization of social freedom in all three domains of modern social life ([2015] 2016). Therefore, in accordance with his program of a reconstructive normative philosophy, he seeks in all social practices essential to the production and reproduction of society (family, economy, and political action) the idea of socialism, understood as collective search for social freedom.

This rather optimistic view of modern social life according to which social freedom is already an active normative ideal in various social domains and represents therefore either a real motivation in social interaction and social change or at least the basis for an immanent critique obviously implies a strong concept of progress (see Honneth [2011] 2014, 335). This concept has been present in Honneth's work all along. Since any critical theory takes sides with emancipatory social struggles, it is clear that critical theories are generally committed to social and political progress; Honneth's theory is no exception to this. As Honneth believes himself to have found a convincing answer to the question of what drives progressive social change, namely struggles for recognition, he sketches an unstoppable moral dynamic (see Honneth [1992] 1996, 143–44): members of previously excluded or subordinated social groups can draw on promises of recognition and social freedom made by current institutions and practices and demand a fuller realization of these promises. Arguably, however, the concept of "progress" has gained new importance in the context of his recent writings. This is because his project of an immanent critique of the present organization of social life in *Freedom's Right* makes the idea of freedom that is realized in different ways in modern institutions the starting point of his analysis. Claims about progress, at least as a "regulative" ideal, are necessary in this framework, because the choice of taking these institutions as a starting point only supplies critical theory with a foundation, if we can reasonably assume that they are best understood as the result of historical processes of learning in which the results of past struggles for recognition have been conserved (Honneth [2011] 2014, 335; for a critical assessment, see Allen 2016). To be sure, Honneth does not assume that there is a transcendent standard for progress. However, he is of the view that for those involved in struggles (or in the activity of critique), such a concept of progress is a necessary hermeneutic tool to understand their historical location (Honneth 2007b, 16).

As this short outline shows, Honneth's work not only offers a highly complex response to the fundamental questions of critical theory, but in doing so also introduces a number of important concepts to contemporary critical theory that will animate the discussion for years to come. For the purpose of this book, we have collected contributions of some of the most prominent voices in contemporary social and political theory on the four main themes that we have identified in Honneth's work.

CRITIQUE

The contributions in the first section of the volume all engage with questions of critique that are raised by Honneth's renewal of critical theory. Essential for this renewal is the rejection of the idea of a social critique rooted in practice-independent insights into the nature of social justice or moral obligations of individuals. As an alternative to this idea, which is still prevalent in liberal philosophical discourse, Honneth presents a version of immanent and historical social critique which takes as its point of departure social institutions and practices of recognition and the conflicts they generate. Critique is, in this picture, not a neutral arbiter above the messy social reality, but a partisan for its progressive potentials. Of course, this model prompts the questions: how we can distinguish progressive from regressive developments without an outside standpoint, how critique relates to ideology and whether there is any systematic place for an ideal vision of society. Finally, it also invites reflection on the practices of critique itself. When Honneth follows Hegel in conceiving of critics as always operating from the inside of institutionalized social consciousness, does this leave room for more oppositional practices and even forms of radical social change?

Over the past decade, *Raymond Geuss*' work has become the anchoring point for a radical "realist" critique of liberal "ideal theory" approaches in political philosophy. While the criticism of the ahistorical and individualistic presuppositions of these accounts is widespread in the history of Frankfurt School criticism, Geuss argues for an even more radical departure from the premise of human rationality in his chapter "Realism, Yet Again" that has wide-ranging implications for the project of social critique. Distinguishing his realism from more vulgar forms, Geuss argues for a conjunction of two claims: first, that an adequate political understanding must depart from a reformulation of the Hegelian claim that the true is the concrete whole; second, that all political speech or action is located in a context structured by relations of power and that the manner in which it is so located is not up to the acting or speaking subject to determine. This puts limits on any normative project that claims to be able to abstract from power – a project which Geuss considers to be deeply flawed.

Rainer Forst takes up the debate between "Hegelian" and "Kantian" approaches of generating critical norms (which, in some respects, could also be read as a dialogue between the so-called second and third generations of the Frankfurt School). Forst, who has long aligned himself with the Kantian side of this quarrel, insists that only by incorporating a "transcendental" moment can critical theory go beyond established normative justifications – and thus can remain truly critical. He interrogates Philip Pettit's concept of freedom as non-domination as a possible interpretation of the recognition-theoretical ideal that acknowledges persons not only as legal subjects but as law-makers. However, according to Forst, Pettit's notion of "non-domination" needs to be radically reinterpreted as the fulfilment of what Forst calls an undeniable subjective claim to a "right to justification." This way, Forst hopes to take a first step towards reconciling the insights of both the recognition-theoretical and the autonomy-based traditions.

Sally Haslanger's contribution interprets Frankfurt School critical theory in general and Honneth's theory in particular as being primarily interested in the critique of ideology. Her main worry is that ideology critique, especially in Honneth, takes an overly rationalistic form. For Haslanger, this rationalism is particularly evident in considering how the critical theorist is supposed to motivate their addressees and achieve social change. She reads Honneth as relying on an "enlightenment model," which she contrasts with a "contestation model" of ideology critique. The latter model she deems at once more realistic, more methodologically sound and capable of addressing a variety of injustices. The remainder of her contribution is devoted to fleshing out the theoretical presuppositions of the contestation model by drawing on poststructuralist and feminist thinkers.

In his contribution, *Martin Saar* homes in on an aspect of critique that has been prominent in recent discussions within Frankfurt School critical theory over methodology, thanks largely to the work of Honneth, namely critique's immanent character. Specifically, Saar is interested in how Honneth conceives of the immanence of critique by tying it to social norms and their failure. While Saar thinks that this model of immanent critique has a lot to it, he believes that there is an important ontological insight into the workings of norms that Honneth sometimes touches on, but that is far more prominent in the poststructuralist tradition that critical theory therefore should take more seriously. This, according to Saar, is the fact that norms also dominate and exclude and that they do this by constituting subjects. Saar concludes his contribution by making the plea that critique should become immanent in another sense and address the entanglements of norms and subjects.

Didier Fassin undertakes a review of approaches to the concept of moral economy. He traces its history from Edward P. Thompson to Lorraine Daston in order to identify the different normative and epistemological dimensions of the concept. This historical overview is necessary in order to clarify and reopen the concept. Against Thompson and Daston who both insist on the stability of moral economies – whether that of traditional peasants or that of modern science – Fassin sees them as historically grounded, politically related, and therefore permanently changing, sometimes in dramatic ways. He therefore proposes a concept of moral economy that takes into account the ways in which values and affects related to social issues are produced, circulated, are appropriated, as well as how they decline. Fassin's aim is to use the concept of moral economy in a more heuristic than operational perspective in order to focus on the evaluative and emotional traits of the public construction of social problems, revealing or highlighting the moral norms and sentiments as well as moral tensions and contradictions driving ideological discourses, political decisions, and social mobilizations. In doing so, Fassin deepens the concept of immanent critique by focusing on the affective relations of the actors to social norms, which in this perspective are much less stabilized by the social institutions than Honneth's approach allows us to think.

Robin Celikates explores the political contestation around the concept of "civility." Following Honneth's insight that it is sometimes by means of cultural dominance that moral outrage and indignation of oppressed and marginalized groups are being rendered illegible, Celikates investigates how calls for civility often serve to pacify and domesticate radical dissent. However, this should not lead us to give up the notion of civility altogether, he argues, as it can also be used as a tool to mobilize unruly political practices, since it refers to a political bond between people beyond state-based concepts of citizenship. Rather than simply rejecting the idea, Celikates proposes that critical theory should reconceptualize it along the lines of a "radical civility."

RECOGNITION

Honneth's account of recognition has faced questions from different directions. One concerns the degree to which it is connected to an account of human nature. While he takes the concept of recognition from Hegel, Honneth tries to sidestep many of the metaphysical commitments connected to this philosophical tradition, and partly grounds his notion of recognition in a thinly anthropological view, partly in a view about the requirements of social integration that are irreducible to individual psychology. This prompts the question whether the Hegelian framework is actually the most adequate one or whether other models available in the history of philosophy offer us more adequate conceptions of recognition. Second, it is clear that the philosophical concept of recognition does not immediately translate to an empirical psychological level but incorporates normative assumptions. Not all desires for social affirmation are socially embedded in a necessary way, nor do all such desires carry with them the potential for emancipation. It is therefore an interesting question to consider whether the very identification of the normatively relevant forms of recognition does not lead us to some universal normative standard after all. Honneth's reliance on a certain paradigm of psychoanalysis, that is, a psychoanalysis that has abandoned "instinct" as the main driving force of human action, replacing this Freudian concept by "need", and therefore focuses on intersubjectivity, has similarly led many of his interlocutors to question whether that tradition really provides evidence for an unambiguously progressive role of recognition or whether we need rather to consider recognition as a more ambivalent phenomenon, describing situations of vital psychic dependence.

Frederick Neuhouser seeks to reconstruct Rousseau's account of social inequality. In doing so, Neuhouser is especially interested in the kind of thing that social inequality is, according to Rousseau. Neuhouser argues that Rousseau conceives of social inequalities on the one hand as privileges and on the other hand as human made. According to Neuhouser's reconstruction, social inequalities are privileges because they are enjoyed by some members of society to the detriment of others. Furthermore, social inequalities are human made because they rely in their existence on human activity, although, as Neuhouser stresses, this often goes unnoticed by the participants themselves. But while the latter can in principle be revealed to them by means of denaturalizing genealogies, Neuhouser thinks that Rousseau identified another obstacle to diminishing social inequalities that could prove more difficult to overcome, namely *amour propre* or the search for recognition by others which can motivate persons to create and maintain social inequalities.

In his contribution, *Martin Hartmann* ponders the question of whether empathy is morally problematic per se, as a number of publications have argued in recent years. Specifically, Hartmann addresses what he calls the "limitation charge" and the "partiality charge." While it is relatively easy to dismiss the limitation charge, that is, the charge that because we can only empathize with a few people at the same time empathy is morally corrosive, the partiality charge, that is, the charge that because our empathy is biased it is morally corrosive, is more tricky to deal with. Hartmann admits that our empathy can be biased. However, he argues that it is important to see that this is always about empathy in context. Whether or not empathy is biased depends on social, cultural, economic, and political structures. In the light of this, Hartmann concludes by suggesting that empathy could and probably does play a positive moral role in our social life too.

Joel Whitebook reviews the dominant reading of Donald Winnicott's work within the debates in social philosophy that rely on Honneth's concept of recognition. The latter, as well as Honneth himself, often use Winnicott to support psychoanalytically the claim that sociability is based on intersubjectivity and that consequently the major pathology of social life is the misrecognition of the other. Whitebook points out that while it is true that the relational dimension plays a primordial role in Winnicott's refoundation of psychoanalytic theory, Winnicott does not abandon central theses of Freud, including that of primary narcissism, that is, the sentiment of omnipotence of the child, who hates the world that constantly objects to this illusion of omnipotence. Whitebook thus proposes to put the focus in the theory of sociability on the desire to destroy the other and to recode social pathologies by taking into account this "hatred of the other." The theoretical gain of this approach is not only a more accurate and correct reading of Winnicott's work, Whitebook claims, but also a more nuanced understanding of social pathologies that are not just the effects of misrecognition. According to Whitebook, indeed, racism, tribalism, religious hatred, nationalism, misogyny, and xenophobia cannot be understood by means of the concept of "misrecognition of the other." These phenomena rather attempt to destroy the "not-me" and cannot be explained by the disrespect the actors may have suffered. Whitebook concludes that in order to be effective, a psychoanalytically well-founded social theory must be guided by political realism rather than wishful thinking.

SOCIAL FREEDOM

In his theory of social freedom as the dominant ideal of modernity that is already embedded – albeit not always realized – in the institutions of modern social life, Honneth takes up a large argumentative burden. Not only must he argue that his theory of social freedom offers us a more adequate understanding of the normative self-image of the "ethical life" of modern societies than most of the dominant political theories, he also wants to show that, in the major institutional spheres, the ideal of social freedom can serve as a yardstick for both the diagnosis of pathologies and the identification of normative potentials. This close connection between normative theorizing and social analysis of the existing social institutions has raised a number of questions, concerning the role of the political that Honneth mainly discusses in regard to the liberal nation-state, which he must recognize on the one hand as the primary social political institution, but criticizes on the other hand as containing the danger of an over-institutionalization of social relations. If Honneth can convincingly show that solidarity forms the moral structure of the private sphere and even the economic sphere, it is much more difficult for him to find a form of equal exchange aiming a relationship of solidarity with respect to the relation between the citizens and state institutions. The state simply seems to be too powerful to be interested in such equality. Even if Honneth tries to overcome this problem by focusing on the democratic political debate in the public sphere, he also argues that the institutions of the liberal nation-state are institutions of social freedom.

Bruno Karsenti proposes a solution for this problem, claiming that only a sociological concept of the modern nation-state can understand this institution as an institution of social freedom. He shows that sociology can indeed produce a concept of the state, rather than reducing it to a repressive organ, if sociology pushes the analysis of modern political society far enough to discover that individuals' practical experience of their freedom is an effect of their socialization in the state. According to Karsenti, it is at this point that Durkheim-inspired political sociology and neo-Hegelianism translated into social philosophy are linked. He claims that the whole of Honneth's normative reconstruction of modern society leans in this direction. However, Karsenti criticizes Honneth's approach of the state as being too much anchored in Hegelianism, leading Honneth to consider the state as an excess of institutionalism that democratic ethical life can only resolve by enfranchising itself. According to Karsenti, this critique of the state depends on Honneth's conception of the state as a philosophical problem and not as the sociological problem that it actually is. From a sociological point of view, however, the state is not the crowning achievement or self-confined and disconnected head of the institutional system, but rather the ever-reopened possibility of social life.

While Honneth engages the question of politics by focusing on the democratic public sphere as the place where the citizens can question and correct state institutions, and therefore minimizes the active role of the nation-state for social freedom, *David Miller* offers an unreserved defence of the idea that the realization of social freedom cannot do without the nation-state. Miller argues that the model of market socialism preferred by him and by Honneth can only emerge as a result of a process of large-scale historical experimentation; and that such experimentation requires both large-scale solidarity and political control over economic organization, two conditions that, he argues, are for the foreseeable future only met within nation-states, concluding that the cosmopolitan aspirations of the socialist tradition which are associated with the concept of a "democratic public sphere" stand in deep tension with the project of feasible socialism.

While Karsenti and Miller follow Honneth in considering the role of rights in the realization of social freedom largely at the level of both subjective and social rights guarantees established within the modern nation-state, many philosophers have recently turned their critical attention to the issue of international human rights. This is also the focus of *Seyla Benhabib*'s contribution. Benhabib shares with Honneth the strategy of critically appropriating Hegel's *Philosophy of Right*. While Hegel is famously critical of the idea of "abstract right," that is, of a legal regime which is not embedded in institutions of ethical life, and of transcendental and ahistorical conceptions of natural rights, Benhabib argues that his account is nevertheless sympathetic to a well-understood idea of human rights. She cites both his insistence that the right of the state to its citizens' loyalty is limited and convergences between Hegel and Arendt on the idea of "a right to have rights." This leads her to the conclusion that the international regime of human rights protection should be considered an essential part of modern social freedom.

Beate Roessler tackles another aspect of the institutional conditions of social freedom that has recently found increased attention: the move towards a digitized society. She argues that this move involves a reconfiguration not only of our self-relation, but also our relation to technology and society that poses important risks to social freedom, especially as surveillance, commodification, and manipulation threaten to undermine social relationships. Roessler argues that critical theory itself has the basic conceptual resources to deal with these problems, but often suffers from phenomenological and analytical blind spots, and that it therefore has to draw on the insights of research in surveillance studies, phenomenology, and current analytical philosophy.

Christoph Menke's contribution delivers a biting critique of political liberalism. The liberal understanding of freedom cannot but presuppose freedom as "natural," mostly due to its dependency on individual "rights." This naturalization of freedom, Menke argues, leads to a depoliticization of the social processes that create individual freedom, consequently fabricating illiberal subjectivities as well as illiberal policies. Political liberalism, according to Menke, thus constantly produces its own opposite, namely authoritarianism – with potentially catastrophic consequences. Only by resolutely breaking with the liberal paradigm theoretically as well as politically can critical theory therefore escape the circle of the self-negation of bourgeois society.

PROGRESS

The notion of progress often evokes one of two critical responses. On the one hand, the question arises whether we need any such notion for social critique. Is it not sufficient to apply the best normative standards that we have, without introducing the assumption that these standards are already realized in some form of historical tendency, thereby relieving ourselves from an argumentative burden that has become more and more problematic thanks to the interventions especially of feminist and post- and decolonial scholars? On the other hand, one can ask, even if we might need to rely on that notion, whether there is any plausible conception of progress available that avoids a simplification of actual history. If we rid ourselves of the presuppositions of a Hegelian view, is there any hope for a philosophical theory of progress that is both defensible and suitable for the purposes of a critical theory?

Philip Kitcher explores the similarities and differences between Honneth's Hegelian account of critical theory and his own Deweyan pragmatism. The differences between the two approaches, according to Kitcher, are mostly based on a different understanding of progress as problem-solving. While recent critical theorists such as Honneth and Rahel Jaeggi have made attempts at answering the important ontological question of what exactly a "problem" is, pragmatists have largely focused on methodological questions. But without a robust notion of social critique – that several generations of the Frankfurt School have provided – Kitcher argues, the pragmatist method remains at a too superficial level to really address the deep normative structure of society – reason enough for Kitcher to propose that John Dewey take a trip to Frankfurt.

Christopher Zurn explores the question of how we can adjudicate the issue of political progress specifically in relation to populist movements that describe themselves as restoring or deepening democracy. He both defends an appropriately constrained conception of political progress of a type that seems to be compatible with Honneth's reliance on the idea and can be defended against recent criticism, and argues that such a conception has practical value in guiding us in political matters. While some versions of the concept of "progress" have been rightfully criticized for often hiding ideological content, committing its adherents to downplaying the moral catastrophes of modernity, or incorporating Eurocentric perspectives, Zurn argues that the idea of progress is not only ineliminable, but that there is another version available that rejects grand-scale narratives for piecemeal evaluations, understanding progress not as goal-driven, but as a description of learning processes and as incorporating processual standards. Using this conception of progress, one can arrive at a convincing critique of populist narratives that actually undermine learning processes in favour of abstract ideals with an ideological content.

Amy Allen discusses the theory of progress that can be found in Freud's late writings. Following Joel Whitebook, she identifies an unofficial position of the *Aufklärer* Freud regarding his faith in the idea of progress. But contrary to the usual readings of *Civilization and Its Discontents* which see a pessimistic Freud at work, demonstrating the harmful effects of the internalization of domination, Allen defends a much more nuanced methodological thesis concerning the consequences that can be drawn from Freud's late position. According to Allen, Freud remains impartial regarding the "correct" reading of the history of civilization. Freud's profession of impartiality on the question of whether civilization is the best thing that ever happened to us or not worth the effort suggests that any attempt to read history as having a clear normative direction, whether that direction is construed progressively or regressively, constitutes an attempt to support one's own illusions – be they optimistic or pessimistic. Therefore, she concludes, Freud's unofficial position provides the resources for a powerful psychoanalytic critique of the pernicious racialized legacy of the notion of historical progress.

*

The occasion for this book was Axel Honneth's seventieth birthday in July 2019. With this gift, the editors and contributors wish to express their deep gratitude for many years of inspiration, mentorship, and friendship.

BIBLIOGRAPHY

Adorno, Theodor W. (1963) 2005. "Critique." In *Critical Models: Interventions and Catchwords*. Translated by Henry W. Pickford, 281–88. New York: Columbia University Press.

Allen, Amy. 2016. *The End of Progress. Decolonizing the Normative Foundations of Critical Theory*. New York: Columbia University Press.

Celikates, Robin. (2009) 2018. *Critique as Social Practice: Critical Theory and Social Self-Understanding*. Translated by Naomi van Steenbergen. Lanham: Rowman & Littlefield International.

Christ, Julia. 2017. *Kritik des Spiels – Spiel als Kritik: Adornos Sozialphilosophie heute*. Baden-Baden: Nomos.

Cohen, Gerald A. 2008. *Rescuing Justice and Equality*. Cambridge, MA: Harvard University Press.

Cooke, Maeve. 2006. *Re-Presenting the Good Society*. Cambridge, MA: MIT Press.

Deranty, Jean-Philippe, Danielle Petherbridge, John Rundell, and Robert Sinnerbrink (eds.). 2007. *Recognition, Work, Politics: New Directions in French Critical Theory*. Leiden and Boston: Brill.

Durkheim, Emile. (1893) 2013. *The Division of Labour in Society*. Edited by Steven Lukes. Houndmills: Palgrave Macmillan.

Fraser, Nancy and Axel Honneth. 2003. *Redistribution Or Recognition?: A Political-Philosophical Exchange*. London and New York: Verso.

Habermas, Jürgen. (1965) 1966. "Knowledge and Interest." *Inquiry* 9, no. 1–4: 285–300.

Habermas, Jürgen. (1968) 1987. *Knowledge and Human Interests*. Translated by Jeremy J. Shapiro. Cambridge, UK: Polity Press.

Honneth, Axel. (1985) 1993. *The Critique of Power: Reflective Stages in a Critical Social Theory*. Translated by Kenneth Baynes. Cambridge, MA: MIT Press.

Honneth, Axel. 1994. "The Social Dynamics of Disrespect: On the Location of Critical Theory Today." *Constellations. An International Journal of Critical and Democratic Theory* 1, no. 2: 255–69.

Honneth, Axel. (1992) 1996. *The Struggle for Recognition*. Translated by Joel Anderson. Cambridge, UK: Polity.

Honneth, Axel. 2000. *Suffering from Indeterminacy*. Translated by Jack Ben-Levi. Spinoza Lectures. Amsterdam: Van Gorcum.

Honneth, Axel. (1994) 2007. "Pathologies of the Social: The Past and Present of Social Philosophy." In *Disrespect. The Normative Foundations of Critical Theory*, 3–48. Cambridge, UK: Polity.

Honneth, Axel. 2007b. "The Irreducibility of Progress: Kant's Account of the Relationship between Morality and History." *Critical Horizons* 8, no. 1: 1–17. https://doi.org/10.1558/crit.v8i1.1.

Honneth, Axel. 2008. *Reification: A New Look at an Old Idea*. Oxford: Oxford University Press.

Honneth, Axel. (2011) 2014. *Freedom's Right. The Social Foundations of Democratic Life*. Translated by Joseph Ganahl. Cambridge, UK: Polity.

Honneth, Axel and Jacques Rancière. 2016. *Recognition or Disagreement: A Critical Encounter on the Politics of Freedom, Equality, and Identity*. Edited by Katia Genel and Jean-Philippe Deranty. New York: Columbia University Press.

Horkheimer, Max. (1937) 2002. "Traditional and Critical Theory." *Critical Theory: Selected Essays*. Translated by Matthew J. O'Connell and others, 188–243. New York: Continuum.

Jaeggi, Rahel. (2014) 2018. *Critique of Forms of Life*. Cambridge, MA: Belknap Press of Harvard University Press.

Lepold, Kristina. 2019. "Examining Honneth's Positive Theory of Recognition." *Critical Horizons* 20, no. 3: 246–61.

Loick, Daniel. 2017. *Juridismus. Konturen einer kritischen Theorie des Rechts*. Berlin: Suhrkamp.

Marx, Karl. (1843) 1975. "Letter to A. Ruge, September 1943." *Karl Marx: Early Writings*. Edited by Rodney Livingstone and Gregor Benton. New York: Vintage Books.

Neuhouser, Frederick. 2000. *Foundations of Hegel's Social Theory. Actualizing Freedom*. Cambridge, MA, and London: Harvard University Press.

Petherbridge, Danielle (ed.). 2011. *Axel Honneth: Critical Essays*. Leiden and Boston: Brill.

Stahl, Titus. 2013. *Immanente Kritik. Elemente einer Theorie Sozialer Praktiken*. Frankfurt a. M.: Campus.

Rawls, John. 1971. *A Theory of Justice*. Cambridge, MA: Belknap Press of Harvard University Press.

van den Brink, Bert and David Owen (eds.). 2007. *Recognition and Power. Axel Honneth and the Tradition of Critical Social Theory*. Cambridge, UK: Cambridge University Press.

Walzer, Michael. 1987. *Interpretation and Social Criticism*. Cambridge, MA, and London: Harvard University Press.

Walzer, Michael. 1988. *The Company of Critics. Social Criticism and Political Commitment in the Twentieth Century*. New York: Basic Books.

Zurn, Christopher F. 2011. "Social Pathologies as Second-Order Disorders." In *Axel Honneth. Critical Essays*, edited by Danielle Petherbridge, 345–70. Leiden: Brill.

Zurn, Christopher F. 2015. *Axel Honneth*. Cambridge, UK: Polity.

Section I

CRITIQUE

Chapter 1

Realism, Yet Again

Raymond Geuss

What does it mean to have an orientation in politics or indeed in life? First, I can be said to have or lack "orientation" in a spatial, in an expectational or in a moral sense. If I am standing in the middle of Paris, I may know where I am and where relevant landmarks are, or not. In the first case, I am said to be oriented, in the second not. This will obviously admit of degrees. I can be said to be oriented in an "anticipatory or expectational" sense if I know what kind of things I can expect to happen in my surroundings (and what kinds of things are unlikely to happen). I can expect most people to be speaking French (or nowadays Arabic or English), I will not expect to see people in chain mail, togas, or leopard-skins, and I expect the pavements to bear my weight if I walk on them. This too is something that will admit of degrees, depending on how certain and how detailed my expectations are. Finally, I may have or lack orientation in a moral sense, to the extent to which I know or fail to know which way I "ought" to go. What "ought" means in this context is, of course, open to interpretation. It could mean "Do I have enough time to go back to one of my favourite bookshops before I need to go to the *Gare du Nord* to catch my train back to London?" or "Ought I really to go over to that man who looks destitute and give him some money?" or "Should I join in this demonstration against racism that is just passing?," "Would it be a good idea to go over to that kiosk and buy some magazines?"

There is a traditional view which proposes that the basic task of philosophy is to give us an orientation in life, and that having any kind of orientation in life at all requires having a full and complete orientation, that is, always knowing where we are, no matter where we might be placed, knowing correctly the basic way in which the world around us functions, and always knowing what it is best for me to do in all situations. One might, of course, have strong reservations about the demand for completeness. As has already been mentioned, one might, for instance, say that if, standing on a bridge, I know that the *Gare du Nord* is to my right, and I need to get there, then that is sufficient. One might equally think that if I know I *ought* as a matter of urgency to help this man who has fallen over in front of me, unless I have some absolutely overwhelming reason not to, then I have all the orientation I need or could reasonably want, despite the fact that in some abstract sense I might not be doing the world a favour to save this man – he might own a bank or be a major investor in the arms trade, or even a lawyer. To return, though, to the traditional view, having the requisite full and complete orientation in the world is thought to require one to have a definitive overview of the world as a whole. Originally, for instance in Plato, this doctrine was connected with the idea that there would be a single theory that would put together and formulate the essential properties and the relations between the most important features of the world, in such a way that knowledge of that theory would give sure and universal orientation in the spatial and anticipational senses. In Plato, there is a further assumption at work which we can "anachronistically" call "naturalism," that is, his view is that because the "good" is an objective feature of the world just like other objective features, the universal theory – because it would tell us about the nature of the world – would also give us orientation in the moral sense. Knowing about the world and knowing what is good (including what is good for us) are intertwined enterprises.

There is one more qualification that needs to be added here, which concerns the role of abstraction in coming to a final orientation in the world. The traditional view implies a basically optimistic and uncomplicated attitude towards the whole phenomenon of abstraction. If one wants to make sense of the great confusion of the world, the welter of apparently utterly different and disconnected phenomena it exhibits, one must use the marvellous human capacity to abstract. I see lots of small creatures running around, some grey, some black and white, some with reddish hair, some with spots, some with stripes, but I get a grip on this situation and overcome my confusion by subsuming all these creatures under a "concept": the concept "cat." The concept gives me what is essential to all the animals in question, and thereby permits me to abstract from, that is, neglect, overlook, pay no special attention to, the manifold potentially confusing differences in phenomenal appearance. I can focus on what is truly important or even essential and ignore everything else. My tabby has stripes but no spots, she is a fifth the size of a leopard, and she purrs rather than emitting a raucous coughing cry, but she and the leopard are both "cats" and for certain purposes and in certain contexts (nutrition, reproduction, mode of locomotion) their differences can be neglected. For the traditional philosopher, one must glory in abstraction, because it is a necessary concomitant to conceptualization; and without conceptualization where would humans be?

Where, indeed? However, in the nineteenth century there came to be a school of philosophers who had grave reservations about the unbridled use of abstraction. Hegel spoke of the powers of the understanding as absolute, but he added a qualification "the true is the whole" (Hegel [1807] 1977, 11) and Lenin added a second "truth is always concrete" (Lenin [1905] 1962, 86).[1] The concrete whole which Hegel envisaged as the truth was itself a speculative object, but if your main interest was a fully disenchanted theory of human politics rather than theology and metaphysics, it might seem just a step to thinking of the relevant "totality" not as "the Absolute," but as the human species historically constituting itself through time in a series of sociopolitical configurations. The only real truth was thus the singular story of that object through time, and the truth about anything less extensive than that human history as a whole was its place in that story.[2] The truth about the laws governing the sale by auction of slaves in the late Roman Republic was, eventually, the whole story of how that law functioned in the institution of slavery as a whole, what place Roman slavery had in Roman social history, and eventually what place slavery in general had in human history. To say that the true is the concrete whole is not to say that no abstraction is ever possible or desirable. It is perfectly true that if you live in late Republican Rome and your interest is merely in becoming an adequate practitioner of the law, not in philosophical understanding or radical political action, then you can make the appropriate abstractions and ignore the wider social and historical context into which slavery fits. To be sure, you won't get much real understanding of what you are studying, and your study will have strictly limited value if you imagine yourself called upon to justify in some general way what you are doing or if it is to guide you in political action. All you will be able to say is that this is the way auctions of slaves are conducted here; this is what you need to do to avoid legal sanction; this is how you need to proceed with a sale for it to be valid. Of course all of this holds only on condition that the social structure as a whole remains essentially unchanged. This limited kind of study does not make it impossible to introduce slightly more conceptual order into the way we understand the laws covering the auctioning of slaves, by cleaning up and clarifying the underlying assumptions one can find in the existing practice, proposing ways of resolving difficulties, tying up loose ends. This will be a proposed theory of Roman legal practice in the matter of the sale of slaves, and there might be alternative ways of conceptualizing what happens, and disagreement about which one fits the facts better.

As far as action is concerned, knowledge of the type just described may help you to act, provided the system as a whole remains intact and unchanged, although you are unlikely to know exactly what the conditions for remaining intact are, but it will be of no use if what needs to be done is action of a more far-reaching sort, or potentially action that would change things. It may not be an inherent internal part of the law of slave auctions that the system of slavery must and will always exist, but if the study is pursued "abstractly," without reference to a larger whole, then it will be natural that those who study it will make that assumption. Furthermore, to propagate such an abstract theory will be likely to entrench the central concepts in it ("slave," "freeman," "emancipation") used more and more deeply in actual practice, thus rendering them more difficult to dislodge. This could obviously have political effects. Context, though, is of the greatest importance: it is conceivable that an abstract theory of the law governing Roman slave auctions, presented in an advanced history seminar nowadays, might not have any significant effect of embedding concepts like "slave" in everyday discourse. Whether or not that was the case would depend on the circumstances. However, the situation would be completely different if such a theory was being advanced in ancient Rome itself or indeed in a contemporary society in which slavery is still a live option.

What, one might ask, does all of this have to do with realism? Rather a lot, I think, since I take "realism" in political philosophy to be best understood as a successor of the type of Hegelian-Marxist political philosophy I mentioned above. Let me explain and begin by calling, for purposes of discussion, the opponents of "realism" defenders of an "ideal theory" approach to politics.

As far as I can tell, there are three ways in which "realism" has been used, and I wish to use the term in yet a fourth sense. "Realism" can refer to

a) an ontological claim about the priority of the real as contrasted with the imaginary, the merely theoretical, or the non-existent.
b) an epistemological claim which emphasizes the importance of direct sensory experience as against the use of reason, the imagination, or construction.
c) a specific theory about human motivation.

"Realism" in the first sense is a kind of ontological theory, essentially a claim about what kinds of objects exist and what importance different kinds of object have and about what kinds of entities can figure in serious theories. One might, in fact, formulate it as comprising two sub-theses. First, only those things that are objects in the external world are real (so no mental, psychological, or theoretical construct is real). For this to be true some version of a reductivist programme would seem to need to have been completed, but no plausible version of that is available at the present time. Second, only objects that are "real" in this sense are relevant for politics; only they can be appealed to for the purposes of explanation and justification, and only they are appropriate landmarks for orientation in action. Phrased in this bald way, the position is clearly daft because humans do not always respond merely to objective features of their environment; rather their perception of their environment is a crucial factor in how they act. If I don't see the tiger, he may really eat me, but I shall not move to avoid him. If I think I see a tiger, even if there is none, that perception (or misperception) may move me to act. So obviously perception (and misperception), that is, some form of mental processing, must play some role in explaining human action. No one, not even the most dyed-in-the-wool realist in political philosophy, is foolish enough to fail to have noted these trivial truths.

So, perhaps one should revise the account of "realism" so that the second sub-thesis reads: Only real objects and simple (or direct) perceptions (or misperceptions) of such real objects are relevant for politics. Here the focus shifts from the ontology to epistemology. "Realism" now seems to turn on what counts as "simple" perception. However, if the "realism" in question is supposed to be a position held in political philosophy, this sense of "realism" is also a non-starter because much of the basic stock-in-trade of all traditional forms of political realism has been to the effect that power relations and interests (rather than moral theories) are central to politics, and however one might fiddle with the notion of "simple and direct perception," it is exceedingly hard to see how it can be construed as giving one access to either relations of power or interests – we do not in any sense "see" these, they are artificially construed entities, visible only through the lens provided by complex theories. Any serious theory of politics must recognize more than direct sensory perception as a mode of access to the phenomena it studies, so to take "realism" seriously is to admit that it, too, must allow *some* role for human cognitive powers that go beyond direct perception.

In a third sense one can distinguish between realism and some form of "idealism" as alternative theses about human motivation. In this sense the realist might assert, for instance, some variant of the claim that all political motivation is, in the final analysis, a form of the pursuit of our interests or of power. An idealist (in this sense) would deny this, and assert, for instance, that in some cases ideal entities, ideals, norms, principles, rules, results of pure ratiocination, and so on motivate people to political action.

This looks like a clear contrast, but the more one thinks about it, I submit, the less clear it becomes. Take the idea that people always pursue power because they always pursue their own interests. "People always pursue their own interests" is one of those formulae that shifts back and forth in a demonically ambiguous way between an apparent vacuous and tautological truth, on the one hand, and palpable empirical falsehood, on the other. Such formulae are veritable breeding-grounds for ideological confusion. "Interests" is just the most recent variant concept used in a similar structure.

Thus, in the ancient world philosophers like Plato started from the apparent tautology:[3]

a) All humans desire what seems to them to be good because if they did not take whatever they pursue to be good in some sense at least for them, why would they pursue it? This means roughly what(ever) they desire, they take to be good.

They then shifted from (a) to a completely different interpretation of the statement that all humans desire the good:

b) All humans desire the good, that is, there is an objective good, which is identifiable independently of human desire and prior to it which all humans in fact desire.

Into the gap between these could be maneuvred the philosopher-kings.

c) I/we *know* what is objectively good.
d) Therefore we know what others really desire (even if they are confused about it).

However, the original statement has whatever plausibility it has because it does *not* depend on an antecedent specification of what the content of the "good" (or the "seeming good") is. In fact, it seems explicitly to leave it open, as in Sappho:

οἱ μὲν ἰππήων στρότον, οἱ δὲ πέσδων,
οἱ δὲ νάων φαῖσ ἐπὶ γᾶν μέλαιναν
ἔμμεναι κάλλιστον, ἔγω δὲ κῆν' ὅτ-
τω τις ἔραται[4]

[Some people say a troop of horsemen, some
a troop of foot-soldiers, some a fleet of ships
is the most beautiful thing on the black earth,
but I say it is that thing, whatever it is, that one
wants]

If that is true, an inference to (c) and (d) is not possible. In addition, for the sake of discussion I have assumed that "all humans want the seeming good" in the first version is true, is even something like a tautology, but both the Roman poet Ovid ("*Video meliora proboque deteriora sequor*" (Ovidius 1998, l. VII: 20–21)) and following him St. Paul (Rom. 7: 15–19) see clearly that this is in fact false. The difference between the two is simply that Ovid thought he was describing a pathological state ("*si possem, sanior essem*" (Ovidius 1998, l. VII: 18)) although one which befell humans frequently, just as we might think that the flu was a state of ill-health, but nonetheless a recurrent and recognizable feature of human life, whereas Paul thought that this was the ineluctable and universal state of fallen humanity from which only the supernatural action of divine grace and faith in Jesus could raise us. If either of these is at all correct, one must wonder what to make of the whole platonic form of argumentation about the human desire for the good.

In the early modern period, however, there was a successor argument that had a very similar structure to the above:

a) All humans desire what they think to be rational (to do what they think is rational) and to be what they take to be rational = what they want, they will take to be rational.

This then gets transformed into:

b) All humans desire what is rational = there are some things that are objectively rational (e.g. being consistent) and all humans want them.

Through this gap, the Jacobins march. One does not, however, have to go to Dostoyevsky (particularly, for instance, to his *Notes from Underground*) to see that this whole enterprise won't work (*und damit ist Kant erledigt*). Not even palpable contradiction, the *non plus ultra* of irrationality, is necessarily a motivation turn-off. "Have our cake and eat it too" is not the description of the UK Brexit policy by an opponent, but by a (very articulate and university educated) supporter.

The modern version of this old *canard* is: people always pursue their interests. The apparently tautological form of this suffers from Dostoyevski's observation that it simply is not true – people act against even what they clearly know to be their own interest all the time. If one adds to this the further assumption that we know antecedently what those interests are, or even must be, and can formulate them independently of observing how people really act, this just compounds the absurdity. So if there is a form of realism – I'll call it "vulgar realism" – which is committed to a view like this and which identifies "interest" with, say money, or prestige, or power, or any well-defined concrete magnitude, this *is* an alternative to "ideal theories." Then it is the case that the (vulgar) realist says people pursue, say money, power, and prestige, whereas the ideal theorist says that they occasionally pursue, say, consistency or morality, or human decency or some other ideal, and that these things are something different from money and power. Of course, this depends absolutely on being able to give plausible and more or less sharp distinctions between the objects which the realist recognizes and those which the idealist recognizes. That would seem to be no very significant restriction, because what could be clearer than that prestige and consistency are two very different things. I simply flag this at the moment, and will return to it later.

There is, though, I wish to claim, a possible form of realism which is different from all three of those just mentioned. In particular, it is not, like the vulgar realism described above, committed to the view that people never act on principle or to realize ideals. Rather, it affirms that political speech or action – and speech, of course, is a kind of action – is action considered as located within the context of power, and that whether or not your action is to be considered as located in a context of power is not necessarily for you to say. That, of course, is not just a completely different thing from the claim of the vulgar realist that the object or motivation of people is maximization of their power, but it is a different *kind* of claim. And at that point, this line of argument reconnects with the discussion of whole and part and of abstraction from that which is more concrete.

The realism I wish to propound is a position in political philosophy. If what one is talking about is *politics*, rather than various other things (aesthetics, efficiency, positive legality) the dimension of power and the pursuit of interests in a context structured by relations of power is always relevant, nor can one abstract from it insouciantly. Furthermore, this view asserts that, whatever objections one might have in principle about the project of getting a final, conclusive, and all-exhaustive overview of things, it makes sense to retain from the traditional project of philosophy, the idea that arbitrarily limiting one's field of vision is a mistake.

If anyone thinks that politics has nothing inherently to do with relations of power and its exercise, then I probably don't know what to say to that, but that is because I simply do not understand what such a person could possibly mean by saying this; they must, unless they have much more to say to me, mean something completely different by the word "politics" than I do. If someone says that political philosophy should have nothing to do with politics, then equally it is hard to see how discussion with such a person could continue. If anyone were to say that ideals, norms, principles, and so on actually cannot in any way be conceivably be construed as having anything to do with relations of power, then that seems clearly and demonstrably false. If such a person says that ideals, norms, and principles *ought not* to be so construed, does "ought not to be so construed" mean "ought never and not for any reason or in any context whatever to be brought into any cognitive relation with structures of power"? What kind of argument could one give for this extraordinary claim? If "ought not to be construed" is not intended as a blanket denial of legitimacy in any case whatever, then in which kinds of contexts is it legitimate and in which is it not to refer to power? The argument here would, of course, refer to various facts, but it would not be couched exclusively in terms of factual truths, rather in terms of expediency, usefulness, acceptability, and other properties that belong to the domain of potential human action.

To the extent, then, to which such ideals did actually motivate people or have an effect on the way in which they acted, they were as much a part of the domain of politics (in particular politics studied in a "realist" way) as anything else that really motivated people to act. So there is a disagreement between realists and ideal theory approaches only if the ideal theorists have some view to the effect that ideals do not actually motivate people (in which case why is one studying them as a part of *politics*) or that they have a wholly non-empirical standing or origin, or finally, that there was no point in investigating or thinking about their origin or function in society: this could be abstracted from without loss.

But surely, one must claim, it is possible and legitimate to abstract from power relations in some contexts. That is, of course, true, if only because without abstraction there would be no thinking at all, but not relevant. The question is not abstraction versus total absence of abstraction. That is a non-starter of an issue. Rather it is between controlled abstraction, an action which is capable of giving an account of why and how it is performed, and uncontrolled and arbitrary abstracting. If one is engaged in a philosophical investigation, that means that one should be prepared to try to give *some* reason for whatever abstractions one makes – one must make some, but one must be able to cite reasons for abstracting in *this* way (only aesthetic properties) rather than *that* way (only compatibility with the Papal *magisterium*). There is, of course, a general philosophical point, made by a number of philosophers, each in his own way, that "reasons" do not in fact ever either continue ad infinitum or *ad indefinitum,* nor do they stop when they arrive at something which is, as it were, the self-grounding Reason of all Reasons. The Wittgensteinean version of this runs that, as we dig further and further down into the soil of reasons, we eventually hit a rock, and our "spade is turned" (Wittgenstein 1958, para. 217). The question is, what do we say about that rock? Is it just some accidental feature of *our* social life? The Nietzschean version of the same thought seems to me slightly more sophisticated. It compares the space of reasons with the space of the visual field: as one moves out towards the edges one loses sharpness and focus gradually, and eventually nothing is visible, even though there will not be any determinate point which constitutes a fixed boundary between "reason" and "absence of reason" (Nietzsche [1881] 1988, §117, 3: 110). This general point seems completely correct, but is also irrelevant. The request to locate abstract moralizing conceptions in existing contexts of power and action is not a request to go on forever. Take the example of someone who develops an ideal theory of politics based on some (abstract) conception of freedom or of equality. If I then request that you think again about why you wish us to ignore the institutional context within which *this* theory has arisen, the assumptions it makes about human agency, and the systemic effects of developing, propounding, and acting on the abstractive theory in question, you cannot reasonably respond to this particular request or objection by referring to the general impossibility of ever coming to an end with reasons. To return to the example, it is highly implausible that our spade turns when it encounters the concept of "equality" and we simply have to take a step back from the excavation and admire this huge boulder. It is equally implausible that our vision and the grip of our concepts simply peter out when we get to this concept. We know, in fact, that "equality" can't in itself be an immovable obstacle because we have historical knowledge of lots of societies which have done very well without the assumption of universal human equality, and also societies in which equality was construed in very different ways. In such circumstances, it seems perfectly reasonable to say that a form of "abstraction" which simply isolates the concept of equality, makes some assumptions about its necessary universality, and then ratiocinates about it, is arbitrary, and a person who treats it simply as a given, an ideal entity to be defined, and analysed perhaps, but not located in action contexts, is not acting as a philosopher, but as something else.

I have emphasized the "arbitrary" and non-philosophical nature of certain forms of absolutized abstraction, but there is another side to that. What seems "arbitrary" from one point of view may and will usually turn out to be only too well motivated from another. To abstract so as to isolate our concept of universal equality, to extract it from its context and consider it by itself, is *in fact* to act in a certain way. Why should that action not itself be subject to political evaluation, that is, to analysis of the way in which it functions in existing contexts of power? Is it always politically neutral to ignore or even divert attention from this context? If we cannot antecedently know that it is *always* politically neutral, and it seems difficult to see how one could reasonably assert that we could know that, then the realist's question is always relevant.

After all, it would not be at all surprising that societies secrete around themselves conceptions that keep them going and reproduce existing structures, that a certain conservatism or tacit commitment to the *status quo* is the default position. If that is the case, then failure explicitly to reflect on the context of action is tantamount to allowing it to maintain itself, if not endorsing it.

Now there is a deeply misguided reaction to this to the effect that the deficiencies of this kind of naive empiricism can be remedied by yet more empiricism. This is misguided because it overlooks the partial malleability of social reality to the concepts we ourselves use. Put bluntly, think of the self-validating prophecies originally analysed by Merton (1968): labour unions exclude blacks because they are strike-breakers, or, in a more sophisticated form "undercut wages," but because the labour unions exclude them, black workers have no possibilities of employment except at an exceedingly low wage or outside the union system. Similarly, if everyone in the society actually believes that all relations between people can be modelled on commercial transactions, then this will increasingly come to be the case. In neither of these cases is it obvious that an increase in further close empirical observation will lead to enlightenment.

To say that some ideal theory which is derived from generalized observation of basic features of our society, but which does not specifically thematize relations of power, *may occasionally* be used in such a way as to have emancipatory effect, is irrelevant, because, by virtue of the way the situation envisaged is defined, this effect is accidental. The traditional idea behind having an orientation, though, was not that what was supposed to give orientation might accidentally point you in the right direction. I don't give you orientation in the appropriate sense if, never having been to Paris in my life and having no clue where anything is, I suggest to you that you go straight ahead to the *Gare du Nord*, even if in some cases it might happen that (accidentally) by going straight ahead you would come to the *Gare du Nord*. If that counts as "orientation," then what is disorientation?

The "realist's" objection to ideal theories is not a denial of them altogether nor an objection to abstraction or idealization per se. In fact, it would be completely self-defeating to object to "abstraction," because all thought is of necessity an abstraction. Rather the realist wishes to make two points. First, if these ideal theories are simply presented abstractly as objects to contemplate, there seem to be more interesting, complex, and shapely ones around than the theories of Bentham or Rawls. Try thinking about Euler's identity or one of Gödel's theorems and you will find that much more rewarding. Why choose these to study? They also seem to contain peculiar, and arbitrary, specific provisions for which there seems no obvious motivation except if what is at issue is some kind of attempt to map the real world of politics. Why bother with these features, if the point is aesthetic or formalistic? If the point is capturing something about a real political world, why employ such imaginative effort in trying to abstract from that?

Second, abstract purity does not exist in itself, come from, and go to nowhere. Things *are* not pure, neither are thoughts, concepts, theories, or ideals; in some cases, they can be made or kept pure. They are made into something isolated and pure by real processes of abstraction and isolation, and the price one pays for that is the maintenance of an apparatus of surveillance and enforcement of boundaries that requires the mobilization of power. This power may be highly soft and take the form of gentle ostracism for the conversation, being ignored, not taken seriously, marginalized, but then it is a major mistake to think that *all* power relations are like that which exists between the bound victim and the man wielding the knout. With the knout in the cupboard (and the police at the end of a telephone line), more subtle, complex, and etherialized, but arguably even more effective, forms of power may be developed.

To put the point I have been trying to make in slightly more Hegelian terms: Realism, as I have been presenting it, has nothing against abstraction in itself, if only because without abstraction there is no thought, but it does object to the absolutization of abstractions. Absolutization is the explicit denial or tacit claim that it is not ever relevant to look back at the larger context from which the abstraction is made or the potential total context of power, interests, and institutions within which it will be applied or have effects.

There is what may seem to some a paradoxical outcome to this, which is that what is sometimes called "contextualism" is not the natural opposite, but the natural associate of "holism." If one thinks that "really" only the concrete whole is the true, and one also holds, as one would have to do following Hegel, that this concrete whole is not expressible in a detachable theory, but only through the enactment of a complicated series of movements of thought, which for humans can take place only in time, in, in fact, a rather long period of time, then it follows that in everyday life one will in general use relatively simple formulae that are in fact abstractions. As one moves out of the realm of immediate action to reflect on these, one will see them as, at best, only contextually meaningful. It was an idea of a certain form of socialism in the nineteenth century to replace "politics" with "mere administration," but that was an aspiration that was to be realized only in a fully free society in a utopian future. Since "politics" as we know it is not, or at any rate is not always and ought not to be, a matter of mere and fully routinized action, but always has within it the possibility of novelty, any real understanding even of routines will require putting them in their context.

Ideal theories always stand in a context which it is relevant to study. Absolutizing them limits human understanding and the possibilities of human action. Of course, in *one* sense it is very easy to find a theory that gives you "orientation": just adopt one and stick to it through thick or thin. "Giving an orientation" presumably means giving us some direction in the world based on how that world really is, not on some fantasy, and some set of conceptions of what is valuable and how we should act that are in some sense "satisfactory," even if the notion of "satisfactory" itself is up for grabs and continual renegotiation. Ideal theories may play some role in providing orientation in particular contexts, but they cannot be anything like the final answer they present themselves as being. If one objects that a realistic analysis itself will not give one a final, definitive and complete form of orientation of the type we all are supposed to aspire to, then I submit that this is an objection to human life itself, not to realism.[5]

NOTES

1. "The truth is concrete" was also one of Bert Brecht's favourite philosophical principles.
2. Marx thought that in the final analysis the only science was (a philosophically grasped) history. See the *German Ideology* (Marx and Engels [1846] 1976).
3. Perhaps most easily visible in *Gorgias*.
4. Fragment 195; text from Page (1968, 101).
5. I owe a great debt of gratitude to two philosophers, both of whom warned me about my use of the term "realism." Richard Raatzsch (EBS/Wiesbaden) who read the manuscript of *Philosophy and Real Politics* in draft and recommended, indeed warned me, to avoid using the word "realism." I ignored this good advice, although I would have been wise to have taken it. I believe that Christoph Menke (Exzellenzcluster "Normative Ordnungen," Frankfurt/M.) was trying to make some of the points I make in this essay in a comment at a symposium on *Philosophy and Real Politics* in Frankfurt/M. in about 2011, but I was too slow on the uptake immediately to see what he was saying, and have only retrospectively begun to appreciate its force.

BIBLIOGRAPHY

Hegel, Georg. (1807) 1977. *Phenomenology of Spirit*. Translated by A. V. Miller. Oxford: Oxford University Press.
Lenin, Vladimir Ilitch. (1905) 1962. "Two Tactics of Social-Democracy in the Democratic Revolution." In *June–November 1905*, translated by Abraham Fineberg and Julius Katzer, 15–140. Collected Works 9. Moscow: Progress Publishers.
Marx, Karl and Friedrich Engels. (1846) 1976. "The German Ideology." In *Collected Works: 1845–47*, 19–539. Collected Works 5. New York: International Publishers.
Merton, Robert K. 1968. "The Self-Fulfilling Prophecy." In *Social Theory and Social Structure*, 473–86. New York: Free Press.
Nietzsche, Friedrich Wilhelm. (1881) 1988. "Morgenröthe." In *Morgenröthe. Idyllen aus Messina. Die fröhliche Wissenschaft*, edited by Giorgio Colli, 9–331. Kritische Studienausgabe Vol. 3. Berlin: De Gruyter. https://doi.org/10.1515/9783110859850.
Ovidius, Naso Publius. 1998. *Metamorphoses*. Edited by William S. Anderson. Reprint of the 2nd updated ed. 1982. Berlin, Boston: De Gruyter. https://doi.org/10.1515/9783110948547.
Page, Denys Lionel. 1968. *Lyrica Graeca selecta*. Clarendon Press.
Wittgenstein, Ludwig. 1958. *Philosophical Investigations*. Oxford: Blackwell.

Chapter 2

Kantian Republicanism versus the Neo-Republican Machine

The Meaning and Practice of Political Autonomy[1]

Rainer Forst

NORMATIVE AUTHORITY

Social and political philosophy reflects on us as social and political beings; but such reflection must include, at a fundamental level, an idea of us as moral beings. More precisely, when dealing with the question of how social or political power should be exercised, we need to develop an understanding of the authority and legitimacy of such exercises, and that leads us to the basic question regarding our nature as normative beings: Who has the justified authority to rule over us?

In his magisterial reconstruction of the history of the idea of recognition, as in his work generally, Axel Honneth shows us that we must turn to the tradition of German Idealism after Kant in order to answer that question. For it was Kant who first formulated the revolutionary idea that in the realm of morality (and hence in all other normative realms) it is ultimately "we" as human beings guided by reason who are the ultimate normative authority. As Honneth shows, there is a complex system of interrelated concepts, such as reason, freedom, and mutual recognition, at work here to develop the essential notion of autonomy as crucial to the question of authority; but the basic thought is as simple as it is liberating – namely, that in the normative realm, ideally speaking, we are all equals and ought to follow no other or higher authority than ourselves as equals who construct the moral and political norms that will rule over us together. As Honneth argues, the foundational form of recognition is "that the subjects have recognized each other reciprocally as co-authors of the norms they practice [*dass die Subjekte sich reziprok als Koautoren der von ihnen praktizierten Normen anerkannt haben]*" (Honneth 2018, 200, my translation, RF). Somewhat contrary to the stark contrast between the French and the German traditions of thought about recognition highlighted by Honneth, I think we should credit Spinoza, and especially Rousseau, when it comes to the genealogy of that notion of autonomy, especially in the political realm.[2] However, I agree with Honneth that the way in which Hegel in particular tried to mediate that notion of autonomy with certain social forms of recognition and institutional forms of life is essential for contextualizing the idea that we are the co-authors of the norms that bind us (Honneth 2014).

Still, it is I think a Kantian reminder that alerts Honneth to the "blind spot" (Honneth 2018, 223) in Hegel's theory of recognition, one that leads Hegel to interpret a given order of recognition as *constraining* the realm of normative reasons in such a way that certain critical questions regarding its exclusions and asymmetries cannot be asked. In such a situation of constraining noumenal power, as I would call it (Forst 2017a, ch. 2), in which certain social forms that should in principle be questioned and rejected are accepted as natural, our "nature" as free noumenal equals materializes in the form of critique that is both situated and transcends given orders of recognition. At such moments, the right to and the faculty of justification as a rejection of given forms of justification find expression. And herein lies the *Kantian moment* – in reclaiming one's status as a normative authority equal to all others who should not be dominated by an established but unjustifiable order of recognition and power. That liberating moment consists in breaking up a fixed order of justification and reconstructing it along the lines of normative co-authorship. It is the moral moment of political and social autonomy, a moment of non-domination.

It is in the light of this liberating moment and its political implications that I would like to develop a Kantian form of republicanism and contrast it with contemporary neo-republicanism, especially with Philip Pettit's important theory. Recent interpretations of Kant, such as that of Arthur Ripstein, which focus on the "innate right" to freedom as independence, have injected new life into the debates about Kant's political philosophy, as have neo-republican accounts of non-domination like Pettit's. I regard Kant as a theorist of independence as well as of non-domination. But I think that a particular version of Kantian republicanism needs to be added to this conversation because we misunderstand Kant and fail to appreciate what republicanism contributes to contemporary political philosophy if we conceive of the freedom of persons primarily as consisting in "using" or "receiving" legal rights that protect their individual freedom of choice. For we must bear in mind what Honneth's reading brings out, namely that Kant insists on the freedom of persons as *law-givers*, as producers and guarantors of freedom – in short, as politically autonomous citizens. The dignity – to use a recognition-related term that has special importance here – of a free person can never be understood only as that of someone who "enjoys" freedom or certain liberties; it is also always the freedom to give laws to oneself, the freedom of self-determination or autonomy. This is what it means to be a normative authority on an equal footing with others; Kantian dignity is that of equal authors of norms and law-makers. This kind of freedom comes in two modes, one moral and one political-legal; but, despite the difference between them, the basic *modus operandi* is the same in both cases, namely a practice of reciprocal and general justification or a practice of practical reason among normative equals, one moral and one political (but both intertwined). The laws that constitute that practice and those generated within it do not just protect freedom; rather, they *express* it.

In what follows, I will explain the moral grounds of such an approach and its political and legal implications, before I draw a comparison to neo-republicanism. In doing so, I will not dwell too much on "Kant's republicanism" as such but on my own version of "Kantian republicanism," which creates a certain distance to Kant's original account while remaining true, I think, to the major ideas in his work. Thus, the approach that I suggest is a neo-Kantian one.

MORAL GROUNDWORK

Both parts of the *Metaphysics of Morals*, the doctrine of right and the doctrine of virtue, deal with laws of freedom, generally called "moral laws" by Kant (Kant 1996a, 375). Those that regulate external action are called "juridical," those that are at the same time reason and motive for moral action are called "ethical." Hence, they differ not so much in their content as in their respective modes of lawgiving and motivational structures: "The doctrine of right and the doctrine of virtue are therefore distinguished not so much by their different duties as by the difference in their lawgiving, which connects one incentive or the other with the law" (ibid., 384). Both doctrines explain the relation between freedom, law, and reason (the latter being the faculty of justification) in such a way that moral freedom is the freedom determined by practical reason, and legal and political freedom is the freedom within a system of positive law that can be generally and reciprocally justified through an exercise of the public use of reason and with appropriate law-making institutions. Hence at the core of the Kantian view lies this particular connection between freedom, law, and the practice of reason-giving, which can be best understood through a reflection on what it means to be an autonomous agent of practical justification in different contexts, one moral and one legal-political.

In order to gain a better understanding of this connection, let us take a closer look at Kant's notion of moral autonomy. Kant's key idea is that the capacity for moral judgement and action must be located exclusively in the faculty of practical reason and that moral action not only presupposes *moral autonomy*, the freedom to determine one's will in accordance with self-imposed laws, but also the *autonomy of morality* from heteronomous determinations of its principle and "incentives," be they doctrines of earthly happiness or heavenly blessedness (see Forst 2012, ch. 2). A "pure moral philosophy" must be explained in terms of principles of practical reason alone and its imperatives must be justifiable *without exception* because they claim *unconditional* validity for each and every person. Thus, Kant links the question of which actions are morally justifiable with a procedure which tests their universalizability in such a way that no moral person serves "merely as a means" to someone else's end, whatever it might be: each person is and remains a free and equal moral authority in the realm of the justification of moral norms. For, as Kant explains using the example of a false promise, "he whom I want to use for my purposes by such a promise cannot possibly agree to my way of behaving towards him, and so himself contain the end of this action" (Kant 1998, 38). Thus, not only must happiness not serve as a motive for acting morally so as not to lead to heteronomous actions, but the happiness of a (responsible adult) person must not be made the end of the action (which affects this person in a relevant way) against his or her will either. Happiness is an object of irresolvable conflicts of opinion, "not an ideal of reason but of imagination" and experience and thus not a reliable guide for moral reflection (ibid., 29). Hence, the obligation to promote the happiness of others must take its cue from *their* conception of happiness, even though this need not be accepted as binding or represent the reason for moral action. Neither the imposition of my notions of happiness on them nor, conversely, of theirs on me would be reconcilable with the dignity of a moral person endowed with reason and capable of self-determination. The core of the idea of being an end in itself is that autonomous persons have a "worth" that must not be subsumed under or dominated by other ends, because they are the rational authorities over practical ends in the first place. They are not just end-seekers; they are end-definers and, in this capacity, superior ends in themselves. The only ends worth pursuing are those that such persons adopt and can adopt as justifiable towards others. Justifiability comes first, and with it the person as the highest authority of justification on an equal footing with all others.

The dignity of the person can accordingly be understood in such a way that every moral person has a basic moral *right to reciprocal and general justification* of all action-legitimating norms that claim reciprocal and general validity.[3] In my interpretation, this notion of a basic moral right corresponds to the duty expressed by the categorical imperative, although Kant himself does not use the notion of a moral right in this way except when he speaks of the "innate" or "original" right to independence or freedom as non-domination (which I discuss below). The decisive point, contrary to a "liberal-ethical" reading, is that the respect for the autonomy of the other person is *not* grounded in the fact that this enables him or her to lead a "good life," for then a specific conception of the good life would once again be guiding. Rather, it consists in respect for the dignity of the other person as a morally self-determining reasonable being and normative authority who uses, offers, and receives reasons, whom one encounters *as an equal* (in that noumenal capacity) and to whom one owes reasons for morally relevant actions. This is the substance of the requirement of respect for maturity [*Mündigkeit*] and the right to make an independent use of one's reason – not just in "religious matters" – which for Kant is the hallmark of an enlightened morality that is not in need of any further ethical or religious grounding. The autonomous person as an agent of justification, and the right to it as an equal normative authority, is the very ground of morality.

The respect that persons owe to each other as autonomous members of a "Kingdom of Ends," a kingdom in which they mutually recognize and uphold each other's freedom by acting in conformity with laws that they could have given themselves as moral equals, is an unrestricted respect subject to no further qualifications (Kant 1998, 41–42). Hence, the essential point of the Kantian conception of morality is precisely that other persons must be respected unconditionally as moral persons *without* any need of a further reason that refers to one's own well-being or that of others or to the will of God, and thereby imports a relativizing element into moral respect. Someone who asks for a further reason of this kind fails to understand the point of morality, according to Kant, as does someone who thinks that moral respect in a Kantian scheme must be proportionate to the cognitive capacities or moral virtue of others. On the contrary, such empirical qualifications deny the noumenal equality between us and commit a category mistake. The Kingdom of Ends contains all human beings independently of their empirical characteristics.

I express the idea of the basic respect for autonomous persons in the language of a moral "right to justification" because, as pointed out above, according to the Kantian conception there is a categorically undeniable subjective claim to be respected as a normative authority who is free and equal to all others – and such a claim I call a moral right, one which is binding on every other moral person. It is not a right to some good or a right based on some interest; rather, it is based on being a person as a reason-giving and reason-receiving entity and an authority in the space of reasons.[4] It is therefore the ground of all further claims to moral respect and to the validity of more specific moral norms, which must be justified by appeal to reciprocally and generally non-rejectable reasons. I call this form of justification *moral constructivism* (Forst 2012, pt. I; Forst 2017a, ch. 1). It is both a discursive and a recursive enterprise; discursive, because justification needs to be a practice between free and equal persons, even if it is only counterfactually possible,[5] and recursive, because no content or value is given except that of the agents and criteria of construction.[6] This is what the autonomy of morality really means: its substance is constituted by principles and agents of practical reason. In other words, we can only find out what is morally justified by reconstructing the principles and agents of moral justification and using these principles in the right way.

My discourse-theoretical reconstruction of the moral point of view locates the practice of justification in two worlds, the world of actual and that of possible justification. Moral action here and now needs to take the actual claims of others adequately into account, since this is what moral respect demands. Yet at the same time the criteria of generality and reciprocity require us to transcend concrete justification situations and ask a generalized validity question, so that we are not held captive by particular perspectives. The two criteria allow for such a two-worldswitch, because my discourse-theoretical view is not based on the idea of consensus but on that of reasonable non-rejectability. Reciprocity means that no one may make a normative claim that he or she denies to others (call that reciprocity of content) and that no one may simply project his or her own perspective, values, interests, or needs onto others so that one claims to speak in their "true" interests or in the name of some truth beyond mutual justification (reciprocity of reasons). Generality means that the reasons that are supposed to ground general normative validity have to be shareable by all affected persons, given their (reciprocally) legitimate interests and claims. Thus, even where no consensus – or, classically speaking, "general will" – can be found, these criteria help to filter out reasons that are reciprocally and generally rejectable. In such discourses, the right to justification gives individuals a right to veto rejectable reasons.

THE RIGHT TO JUSTIFICATION IN POLITICAL AND LEGAL CONTEXTS

It would be mysterious if Kant thought that the moral idea of a Kingdom of Ends could easily be projected into legal and political contexts; but it would be equally mysterious if it had no or very little bearing on it either. Why should the normative order of the law and of the state follow principles and ideas that are completely independent from the notion of autonomy? It is at this point that the *Rechtslehre* comes in. It provides the principles for understanding the justifiable forms of freedom under law as well as the political justification of law that establishes that kind of freedom.

As for Kant's conception of morality, it is essential for his understanding of the moral law that it must remain free from notions of and aspirations to happiness. Kant contrasts law as regards its content with all ethical doctrines of happiness and as regards its form with moral imperatives, because positive law refers only to external actions and not to inner motivation. As I said above, the essential difference between legality and morality resides less in the content of the respective laws than in the "incentives": positive law is external coercive law and constrains freedom of choice, whereas moral laws determine the moral will (Kant 1996a, 384–85). Thus, the moral prohibition on unjustifiable restrictions on freedom between autonomous moral persons is enshrined in law in such a way that the supreme principle of law specifies that restrictions on freedom are in need of universal justification: "Right is therefore the sum of the conditions under which the choice of one can be united with the choice of another in accordance with a universal law of freedom" (ibid., 387). The foundation of this definition of law, according to which all forms of legal coercion are in need of reciprocal and general justification among free and equal persons, is a moral human right to *lawful* freedom prior to any positive law: "*Freedom* (independence from being constrained by another's choice), insofar as it can coexist with the freedom of every other in accordance with a universal law, is the only original right belonging to every man by virtue of his humanity" (ibid., 393). Note here that in my reading freedom as independence is not the central term – rather, "universal law" is. Kant's "innate right" is the strict implication for law of the (in my terminology) basic moral right to justification, that is, of the universal right to be respected as an "end in oneself," as a person (representing humanity) whose human dignity is the unconditional basis of morality *and law*. Here once more it becomes apparent that the protection of individual freedom in no way rests on a conception of the good life for which, on a certain liberal conception, legally protected and socially enabled forms of autonomy would be necessary. Kant's conception is rather that it is already the inviolability of the person, that is, his or her dignity, that excludes interference by others – whether this helps the non-"violated" person to achieve a good life is a completely different matter. The barrier posed by the need to justify restrictions on freedom is raised earlier, according to Kant, and it is stricter than that allowed for by such an alternative conception of ethical autonomy:

> But the concept of an external right as such proceeds entirely from the concept of *freedom* in the external relation of people to one another and has nothing at all to do with the end that all of them naturally have (their aim of happiness) and with the prescribing of means for attaining it; hence too the latter absolutely

must not intrude in the laws of the former as their determining ground. (Kant 1996b, 290)

Against the background of the original right of human beings and the corresponding definition of law, Kant proceeds to formulate different conceptions of the "person."[7] For in addition to the autonomous *moral person* who acts in accordance with the categorical imperative and is owed moral respect, Kant distinguishes three "a priori principles" in the "civil condition," and correspondingly three further conceptions of the person, namely an ethical, a legal, and a political conception. The three principles are as follows: "1. The *freedom* of every member of the society as a human being. 2. His *equality* with every other as a *subject*. 3. The *independence* of every member of a commonwealth as a *citizen*" (Kant 1996b, 291; see also Kant 1996a, 457–58). The first means: "No one can coerce me to be happy in his way (as he thinks of the welfare of other human beings); instead, each may seek his happiness in the way that seems good to him" (Kant 1996b, 291). According to Kant, this excludes a "paternalistic government" in which the subjects are treated as "minor children." The legal autonomy of the person is thus protected from outside interference, and law functions on the inside as a "protective cover" for the *ethical person* to live her life in accordance with the conceptions of the good that seem right to her, whatever her reasons may be. Thus, the freedom of the ethical person is secured, and with it the possibility of living an autonomous and possibly good life, through a law which is agnostic with regard to the good life and is based exclusively on the principle of reciprocal and public justification. Correspondingly, the second principle, equality, signifies that persons as *legal persons*, as "subjects" who are subjected to the law, are bound by laws which hold in the same way for everyone and place the same restrictions on everyone's freedom of choice regardless of their social status.

Finally, the third principle spells out the role of the person as a citizen, as a "colegislator" (ibid., 294). This follows from the fact that, according to the principle of right, only "general laws" can be laws of freedom, and they can be general only if they are in accordance with the "united will of the people" (Kant 1996a, 457). The citizen can be politically autonomous – and here Kant takes up Rousseau's notion of autonomy – only in this role because, as a matter of principle, he obeys only laws that he has given himself, that is, no other law "than that to which he has given his consent" (ibid.) – "for it is only to oneself that one can never do wrong" (Kant 1996b, 295). As an active member of the polity, as a voting citizen, the person is a *citoyen*, not just a *bourgeois* (though Kant, in arguing against feudal privileges, at the same time restricts political rights to men who have a certain economic independence, which servants and labourers, as well as women, lack). The citizen is simultaneously author and addressee of the law. Hence, generally and reciprocally binding law can be legitimate only if it was or could have been – to add the counterfactual justificatory realm that sheds a critical light on real procedures (and exclusions) – agreed upon in procedures of general and reciprocal justification. The "mere idea of reason," "which, however, has its undoubted practical reality," states that "the touchstone of any public law's conformity with right" is its ability to command general agreement (ibid., 297). In short, just as the moral principle which makes it a duty to justify morally relevant actions and norms in a particular way becomes the foundation of the original right to freedom, in the same way it here becomes the foundation of the requirement to justify coercive laws in the medium of "public reason." All forms of coercion are in need of justification before those who are subjected to coercion as normative equals, and it depends on the nature of the norms in question whether the form of justification required is a moral or a political one.

This shows how the right to justification is situated within legal and political contexts. It appears as the "innate right" of human beings who are ends in themselves and have to regard themselves as such, as the first duty of right requires them to. The imperative of *honeste vive* on Kant's interpretation states that every person ought to assert his or her "worth as a human being in relation to others, a duty expressed by the saying, 'Do not make yourself a mere means for others but be at the same time an end for them'" (Kant 1996a, 392; see Forst 2017b). And he affirms that this is a duty implied by the "right of humanity in our own person," which specifies what kind of freedom free and equal persons can claim from each other (in the strictly relational picture Kant presents), namely only those forms of freedom that can be reciprocally and generally justified between free and equal justificatory beings. If we ignored the nature of persons as justificatory authorities and only focused on the "independence" aspect as one secured by law, we would only get half the picture; for freedom according to the "general law" is as much a part of the first human right as is the right to be the justificatory authority in practically co-determining this general law.

Let us clarify this idea by using a thought-experiment. Imagine a perfect freedom-regulating computing machine that could properly process all justifiable freedom claims and calculate a right, generally justifiable measure that only needed to be secured by law afterwards. Would that be a Kantian regime of freedom? No, it would not, for in such a regime freedom would have come about in a heteronomous way. Legal freedom cannot be thought of or exist without the exercise of political liberty in the form of justificatory autonomy as a co-legislator. The freedom of a subject in the legal state is the freedom "of obeying no other law than that to which he has given his consent" (Kant 1996a, 457). This is the real meaning of legal independence or political-legal non-domination: you are only independent or not dominated if you are at the same time subject *and* author of the law, for otherwise your right to freedom or to justification is only half realized. You might *receive* freedom or some justification, but if you cannot be the *co-author* of the laws of freedom, it is not real freedom that you are being offered, only a dependent or possibly dominated and in any case heteronomous scope for action. The laws securing freedom must be reciprocally and generally justifiable; but no one, not even a perfect machine, has the authority to fabricate these justifications for you, because you are an autonomous agent of justification.

I consider this to be the essence of Kantian republicanism, in line with Ripstein's interpretation, which stresses independence as a basic moral principle of right for rational, end-setting beings who coexist in social space (Ripstein 2009, 16–17 and 371). It is, in my words, the right to have all other rights (and duties) justified reciprocally and generally, and thus it is the right that grounds all other rights – in a discursive, reflexive way, not by way of a deduction. In the mode of moral constructivism, this leads to a conception of moral rights, and in the mode of *political constructivism*, it leads to a conception of human rights as well as to a conception of democratic political and social justice (Forst 2016a). Human rights are all the rights that persons who respect each other as free and equal cannot deny each other within a normative order of legal, political, and social life (Forst 2016b). Here again the main point is a reflexive one, namely that no one must be subjected to a normative order that cannot be adequately justified to him or her. This is the basic human right and the basic claim of justice. Thus, basic rights have no other ground than the practice of democracy has, since the aim of basic rights is to secure the status of persons as non-dominated legal, political, and social equals.

A comprehensive theory of political and social justice can be constructed on this basis, something at which I can only hint here (see Forst 2012). First we must make a conceptual distinction between *fundamental (minimal)* and *full (maximal) justice*. Whereas the task of fundamental justice is to construct a *basic structure of justification*, the task of full justice is to democratically construct a *justified basic structure*. The former is necessary in order to pursue the latter, that is, a "putting-into-effect" of justification through constructive, discursive democratic procedures in which the "justificatory power" is distributed as evenly as possible among the citizens. In spite of the appearance of paradox, this means that fundamental justice is a substantive starting point of procedural justice. Based on a moral right to justification, arguments are presented for the basic structure in which those who are part of it have real opportunities to co-determine the institutions of this structure, including economic and social institutions, in a reciprocal and general manner. Fundamental justice guarantees all citizens an effective status "as equals" in this sense. Again, the freedom of being protected in one's liberties and the freedom to co-determine that structure of liberties go hand in hand.

The democratic institutions of a normative order have to be arranged in such a way that the reasons that guide laws and political decisions are not only publicly justified and justifiable, but that vulnerable minorities have sufficient justificatory power, whether parliamentary, plebiscitary, or juridical, to veto unjustifiable majority decisions. Democracy is an arrangement for the public realization of the force "towards the better argument" within a political order.

TWO CONCEPTIONS OF NON-DOMINATION AND THE REPUBLICAN MACHINE

The Kantian republican conception I sketched suggests a discourse-theoretical notion of non-domination. Domination in the political sphere has two aspects, namely being subjected to a normative order that cannot be properly justified to you and being subjected to a normative order in which no proper institutions and possibilities of justification are in place to begin with. The second is the more grievous form of domination because it removes the structural possibility of co-determining the normative order.

How does this compare with Philip Pettit's version of neo-republicanism (see Forst 2013)? According to Pettit, republicanism is essentially a theory of legitimate government based on a particular idea of freedom as "non-domination," as "the social status of being relatively proof against arbitrary interference by others, and of being able to enjoy a sense of security and standing among them" (Pettit 1997, vii). In contrast to freedom as mere "non-interference," non-domination is tied to being and seeing oneself as someone who is not at the mercy of others' arbitrary will, even if these others were to leave you alone most of the time. It is the *potential* of arbitrary interference against which the republican notion of self-respect and freedom is directed (ibid., 5 and 22–23). Hence the importance of the rule of law and of a legal status protecting persons against social and political vulnerability to the possibility of private or public arbitrary interference. The notion of freedom at work here has as its counterpart the condition of a slave, who represents the extreme case of a dominated person.

Still, even though Pettit is right to stress the difference between freedom as non-interference and freedom as non-domination, a negative conception of liberty remains normatively essential in his view, for the argument for non-domination ultimately serves to secure the realm of freedom of choice of persons against arbitrary interference (Pettit 2002, 340). This is why I call it *negative republicanism*: the republican infrastructure is mainly a sheltering mechanism for individual liberty thus understood. In his republican theory, citizens are "law-checkers" interested in the security of their freedom of choice, not "law-makers" as on a Rousseauian or Kantian conception (Pettit

2012, 15). The value of democracy is essentially the instrumental value of a control mechanism to ensure the robust protection of individual freedom of choice.

This seems to establish a huge distance between my Kantian conception of republican justice as non-domination and Pettit's conception of republican freedom as non-domination. However, I would like to propose a reading – or, if you prefer, an immanent critique – of Pettit that brings him closer to the Kantian family. I think that the real force of freedom as non-domination, even in Pettit's view (correctly understood), derives from a notion of justice as justification that both grounds and defines it. Justificatory justice grounds freedom as non-domination because the basic claim of republican citizens is not one to freedom of choice generally, but to be free from *arbitrary* – that is, *unjust* and *unjustifiable* – rule, that is, domination; thus, the claim is ultimately based on one's standing as a free and equal agent of justification and it is a claim to a kind of liberty (and liberties) defined by what oneself and others can justifiably and justly ask from one another in a basic social structure. Justifiable rule, as Pettit explains in his discussion of Quentin Skinner's view championing non-interference, is *not* seen as domination, which compromises freedom (Pettit 2002); only *arbitrary* rule is seen as domination, and that means *unjustifiable* rule over others which denies their standing as free and equal agents with (what I call) a "right to justification." To be denied that right leads to the "grievance [...] of having to live at the mercy of another" which Pettit identifies as the main social and political evil (Pettit 1997, 4–5); and given that interference or rule by others is not seen as an infringement of freedom if it is justifiable between equals, the notion of *justice* referring to the quality of the relations between free and equal participants in a justifiable political structure is central and *normatively prior* to that of freedom of choice.

Interpreting Pettit in this way might seem to be reading a Kantian notion of freedom into his approach, but only if one overlooks the implications of his distinction between domination, which compromises freedom, and the non-arbitrary rule of law, which does not; rather, that rule is seen as "conditioning" or shaping justifiable forms of freedom, which is close to Kant's view (Pettit 2002, 342). This shows that the point of republican freedom is the "full standing of a person among persons" (ibid., 350), and with explicit reference to Kant Pettit goes on to explain: "The terrible evil brought about by domination, over and beyond the evil of restricting choice, and inducing a distinctive uncertainty is that it deprives a person of the ability to command attention and respect and so of his or her standing among persons" (ibid., 351). Pettit not only introduces a Kantian notion of respect here, he also gives it priority over mere freedom of choice, because a "conditioning" of that freedom by reciprocally justifiable laws is not seen as an evil, while a huge space of freedom possibly granted by a mild dictator is. Thus, the main evil, I take it, is that of not being regarded as "a voice worth hearing and an ear worth addressing" (ibid., 350) – that is, in my words, as a person with a right to justification. As Pettit formulates it: "To be a person is to be a voice that cannot properly be ignored, a voice which speaks to issues raised in common with others and which speaks with a certain authority: enough authority, certainly, for discord with that voice to give others reason to pause and think" (Pettit 1997, 91). Every person is to be respected as such a justificatory authority, and this is the essential meaning of freedom as autonomy: having a *categorical* right not to be subjected to norms that cannot be reciprocally justified and thus having the positive right to co-determine these norms. Contrary to Pettit's view, however, I do not see how that kind of moral-political status can be explained in non-deontological terms. For can we imagine a value that could trump that kind of right and status? Or a higher value or notion of the good that this status serves?[8]

One might disagree with this interpretation and hold that for Pettit individual freedom of choice, robustly secured, really is the most important value in political life and that democratic legitimacy and justice only find their place starting from there. So if – to remind you of my thought-experiment above – there were a perfectly reliable *neo-republican machine* of non-arbitrariness that could compute, determine, and robustly secure spaces of reciprocal freedom of choice that pass the "eyeball test," and maybe more determinate tests, would something be missing in a Pettitian scheme? For a Kantian republican there would, and for the Pettit who stresses "voice" and "authority" as in the quotations above I think there would be, too, but maybe not for the Pettit who emphasizes the supreme importance of the secure private "enjoyment" of freedom of choice. Then it would remain a purely negative form of republicanism for which political self-determination had a purely instrumental value as long as the perfect machine does not work reliably.

In a recent paper, Pettit responds to this challenge, arguing that such a "robot would have to be installed by will and if this will does not operate under a suitable system of popular control, it is a dominating presence" (Pettit 2019, 30, fn. 18). This seems to leave open the possibility of being ruled by such a machine, provided that its installation and operation can be "suitably" controlled by a public agent, thus denying the value of autonomous agency expressing itself through democratic lawmaking (since the machine produces the laws). But if the popular control that is meant here implies that any subjection to such a consequentialist machine producing the right metric of freedom of choice would amount to heteronomous and thus arbitrary rule and domination, then it relies on a notion of non-domination along the Kantian lines I suggest.

In my view and in my preferred Kantian reading of Pettit, we have gone beyond a negative conception of freedom without at the same time adopting a controversial "positive" one based on some notion of the ethical good of leading an autonomous life. Rather, it is freedom as autonomy as a form of freedom *from* unjustifiable subjection or coercion and freedom *as* a self-determining agent of (moral as well as political) justification which matters in a Kantian account of non-domination. There is no idea of the good life at work here. Politically speaking, this means freedom within a just(ifiable) regime, and thus it is justice as justifiability that counts – not merely as an idea but as a real practice. Freedom as non-domination is only guaranteed where democratic practices of justification exist that prevent some from dominating others. Rather than focusing on the "robust" state of not being dominated in our freedom of choice, we should focus on the *relational* freedom of being a co-determining agent of justification within the normative order that binds you. And we should do so not because the practice of justification is the only valuable practice of freedom, but because it is only through this practice that we can bring about a society in which freedom, equality, and justice are autonomously and justly arrived at. Only here are we not at the mercy of masters. This is a society that honours the dignity of its members – or better, that expresses their dignity as law-makers.

REPUBLICANISM AND RECOGNITION

In a note on his debate with Rawls, Habermas briefly characterizes his own understanding of Kantian republicanism, stressing the central importance of "the collective exercise of giving laws to oneself" (*gemeinsam ausgeübte Selbstgesetzgebung*). For the spheres of liberty to be justly delineated, only the public use of reason in appropriate democratic and discursive institutions is the proper medium: "In an association of free and equal persons, all members must be able to understand themselves as joint authors of laws to which they feel themselves bound individually as addressees." And a bit more emphatically: "Nobody can be free at the expense of anybody else's freedom" (Habermas 1998, 101). From such a perspective, there is no other just way to determine and realize personal independence or non-domination than through a republican system of law *and* democratic law-making based on the right to justification of agents who have a basic claim to enjoy all the rights that can be mutually and generally justified among themselves, including, first of all, the right to produce, contest, and reject normative justifications. In a Kantian scheme, the structure of rights is reflexive and recursive: you have the "innate" right not to be subjected to a normative order of rights and duties that is not justifiable to you as an autonomous person and citizen. It is not that you are only "truly free" if you use that right actively, as older republican theories had it, but that you are only free if you enjoy that right as the right of rights, so to speak. And at the social and political level, having that right presupposes not just appropriate collective ways of exercising it, but membership in a community of political respect and equality.

It is at this point that Kantian reflections on the deontological nature of "having" basic rights that cannot be reasonably rejected among normative equals need to be combined with Hegelian considerations of the social conditions required to realize such rights. Axel Honneth's work is exemplary for connecting these two dimensions of social and political philosophy, thus remaining true to the legacy of German Idealism as this is continued in a left-Hegelian tradition. In all of his works, he shows that freedom must be realized in *sittliche* ["ethical"] social and political forms; but the dynamics of recognition he reconstructs at the core of such forms never accept that a social horizon of recognition limits the possibilities of establishing more egalitarian, more democratic, and more culturally sensitive forms of mutual recognition – in short, more justifiable forms of recognition. This is why he argues that "only in the political-democratic sphere does interaction consist in an exchange of arguments, i.e. a reflexive process." And this is why the democratic sphere needs to be enlarged and strengthened as the "sphere of reflexive self-thematization" essential for the autonomous progress of freedom (Honneth 2014, 331).

In all of this, the main insight interpreted by Habermas in a Kantian way and by Honneth in a Hegelian way is that genuine political and social freedom can never be attained at the expense of the other's unfreedom. It can only be realized as a practice of mutual recognition and reciprocal justification, as a practice of autonomy.

NOTES

1. Earlier versions of this chapter were presented at the conference "Kant and Republicanism," which was organized by Peter Niesen and Marcus Willaschek in Hamburg in 2014, and at a panel organized by Volker Gerhardt at the 12th International Kant Congress in Vienna in 2015. A German version was published in the proceedings of the congress under the title "Die neorepublikanische Maschine: Zur Unabdingbarkeit des kantischen Republikanismus," in *Natur und Freiheit: Akten des XII. Internationalen Kant-Kongresses*, ed. Violetta Waibel, Margit Ruffing and David Wagner (Berlin: de Gruyter, 2018). I owe special thanks for their commentaries to the colleagues just mentioned, as well as to Pauline Kleingeld, Bernd Ludwig, George Pavlakos, Philip Pettit, Arthur Ripstein, and Lea Ypi. Ciaran Cronin kindly corrected my English. My greatest debt, however, is to Axel Honneth. For without his constant reminders of the blind spots in Kant that Hegel saw and our endless discussions of the issues they raise, I would have remained in a dogmatic slumber.

2. On Rousseau and Kant in particular, see my article Forst (2017b); for a more general treatment, see Schneewind (1998).

3. For a detailed account, see Forst (2012), part I.

4. For my critique of interest-based notions of rights, see Forst (2016a).

5. For the idea of discursive justification, see Habermas (1990).

6. For the idea of recursive justification, see O'Neill (1989).

7. On the following fourfold differentiation of conceptions of the person and conceptions of autonomy, see Forst (2002), esp. chs. V.2 and V.3, and Forst (2012), ch. 5.

8. I must leave a discussion of the full version of Pettit's moral philosophy aside here, for which, see Pettit (2015).

BIBLIOGRAPHY

Forst, Rainer. 2002. *Contexts of Justice: Political Philosophy beyond Liberalism and Communitarianism*. Berkeley and Los Angeles: University of California Press.

Forst, Rainer. 2012. *The Right to Justification: Elements of a Constructivist Theory of Justice*. New York: Columbia University Press.

Forst, Rainer. 2013. "A Kantian Republican Conception of Justice as Nondomination." In *Republican Democracy: Liberty, Law and Politics*. Ed. Andreas Niederberger and Philipp Schink. Edinburgh: Edinburgh University Press, 154–168.

Forst, Rainer. 2016a. "The Justification of Basic Rights: A Discourse-Theoretical Approach." In *Netherlands Journal of Legal Philosophy* 45, no. 3, 7–28.

Forst, Rainer. 2016b. "The Point and Ground of Human Rights: A Kantian Constructivist View." In *Global Political Theory*. Ed. David Held and Pietro Maffettone. Cambridge, UK: Polity, 22–39.

Forst, Rainer. 2017a. *Normativity and Power: Analyzing Social Orders of Justification*. Oxford: Oxford University Press.

Forst, Rainer. 2017b. "Noumenal Alienation: Rousseau, Kant and Marx on the Dialectics of Self-Determination." In *Kantian Review* 22, no. 4, 523–551.

Habermas, Jürgen. 1990. "Discourse Ethics: Notes on a Program of Philosophical Justification." In *Moral Consciousness and Communicative Action*. Cambridge, MA: MIT Press, 43–151.

Habermas, Jürgen. 1998. *The Inclusion of the Other: Studies in Political Theory*. Cambridge, MA: MIT Press.

Honneth, Axel. 2014. *Freedom's Right: The Social Foundations of Democratic Life*. Cambridge, UK: Polity.

Honneth, Axel. 2018. *Anerkennung: Eine europäische Ideengeschichte*. Berlin: Suhrkamp.

Kant, Immanuel. 1996a. "The Metaphysics of Morals." In *Practical Philosophy*. Ed. and trs. Mary J. Gregor. Cambridge, UK: Cambridge University Press, 353–603.

Kant, Immanuel. 1996b. "On the Common Saying: That May Be Correct in Theory, But It Is of No Use in Practice." In *Practical Philosophy*. Ed. and trs. Mary J. Gregor. Cambridge, UK: Cambridge University Press, 273–309.

Kant, Immanuel. 1998. *Groundwork of the Metaphysics of Morals*. Ed. and trs. Mary J. Gregor. Cambridge, UK: Cambridge University Press.

O'Neill, Onora. 1989. *Constructions of Reason: Explorations of Kant's Practical Philosophy*. Cambridge, UK: Cambridge University Press.
Pettit, Philip. 1997. *Republicanism: A Theory of Freedom and Government.* Oxford: Oxford University Press.
Pettit, Philip. 2002. "Keeping Republican Freedom Simple: On a Difference with Quentin Skinner." In *Political Theory* 30, no. 3, 339–356.
Pettit, Philip. 2012. *On the People's Terms: A Republican Theory and Model of Democracy*. Cambridge, UK: Cambridge University Press.
Pettit, Philip. 2015. *The Robust Demands of the Good: Ethics with Attachment, Virtue, and Respect*. Oxford: Oxford University Press.
Pettit, Philip. 2019. "The General Will, the Common Good, and a Democracy of Standards." In *Republicanism and the Future of Democracy*. Ed. Yiftah Elazar and Geneviève Rousselière. Cambridge, UK: Cambridge University Press, 13–40.
Ripstein, Arthur. 2009. *Force and Freedom: Kant's Legal and Political Philosophy*. Cambridge, MA: Harvard University Press.
Schneewind, Jerome B. 1998. *The Invention of Autonomy: A History of Modern Moral Philosophy*. Cambridge, UK: Cambridge University Press.

Chapter 3

Taking a Stand

Second-Order Social Pathologies or First-Order Critique

Sally Haslanger

INTRODUCTION[1]

We live in an unjust world. The injustice takes many forms and is upheld in a variety of ways, many of them coercive. Resistance to injustice is not hard to explain or defend in contexts where institutions violate explicit principles that have formed the basis of the polity. In democratic countries, there are plenty of resources to critique authoritarian rulers; we can expect uprisings against violations of specified rights – due process, religious freedom, universal franchise, and so on – in societies where such rights are constitutionally protected. There is no guarantee that injustice will be recognized or corrected, but resistance has a foothold.

However, injustice is also maintained by ideology. Such injustice is harder to identify and critique. It structures our everyday lives and shapes our experience. It functions as "doxa" that is taken for granted as common sense. Political and legal theorists and judges are as subject to ideology as anyone else, and because power relations grant them status as authorities, their insights may simply reinforce the background unjust social structure.

The Critical Theory tradition is shaped by the goal of ideology critique.[2] A central idea is that society suffers from "social pathologies of reason." The emancipatory goal of critique is to free us from epistemic distortions and illusions so that we are able to realize a rational form of life, both individually and collectively. In this chapter, I consider Axel Honneth's approach to critique. After offering an interpretation of Honneth's version of the Critical Theory model, I argue that his view rests on a set of background ideas about social change that are implausible and overly rationalistic. Moreover, although Honneth's approach is free of some of the more worrisome elements of twentieth-century Critical Theory that he himself notes, there is an alternative that better meets the methodological commitments of critical theory. I will then sketch a conception of ideology, inspired by Althusser and Foucault, and offer an alternative model of critique.

CRITIQUE IN FRANKFURT SCHOOL CRITICAL THEORY

Traditionally, critical theory begins in a sceptical moment. The critic is positioned as a social theorist facing entrenched injustice. The task is to illuminate the injustice in ways that provide a basis for resistance. However, ideology sustains injustice by masking or distorting what's good, right, just. But it is more than this, for ideology also distorts what is taken to be possible by making the current social formations appear natural, inevitable, desirable. Even worse, because ideology is enacted in our practices, we make it true. If our practices interpret the flesh of dead cows and pigs as food, it becomes food; if the hobbled walk of women in high heels is interpreted as sexy, it becomes sexy. We want it.

Ideology fails us both morally and epistemically, and fails us morally *by* failing us epistemically. The goal of critical theory is not just to provide a true description of social reality. Truth is not enough. Critical theory has a practical and political aim: it should reveal injustice in a way that informs action. And because, as I have just suggested, the world itself can become distorted, we need a critical vantage point not just on what we believe, but on what is. As Danielle Allen puts it, "In dark times what is wrong is the world" (2001, 877). But embedded as we are in a society shaped by ideology, how do we proceed?

It would appear that we need a peephole to see through the distortions of ideology so that we recognize them as distortions. Mostly, they are modal distortions: distortions of what is possible, natural, desirable, good, known. What we see on the other side of the peephole should also be motivating so that we are prepared to act in order to reconstruct our current social reality. Of course, as is typical of sceptical scenarios, we must be prepared that what appears to be a peephole cutting through ideological distortions has a lens that is also distorting and that the appeal of what we see is a further illusion.

Critical Theory aims to address this cluster of problems: to provide a vantage point that reveals existing social pathologies and provides a basis for collective resistance. In his essay, "A Social Pathology of Reason: On the Intellectual Legacy of Critical Theory" (2009), Axel Honneth sketches what he takes to be three central commitments of critical theory. They include "the normative motif of a rational universal, the idea of a social pathology of reason, and the concept of an emancipatory interest" (2009, 42). Very roughly, humans have an "emancipatory interest" in the full exercise of their rational capacities; this can be achieved only through engaging together in a collective project of self-actualization (an ideal referred to as "the rational universal"). Social pathologies prevent us from achieving this good. Critical Theory draws on our emancipatory interest in the rational universal to reveal and disrupt the social pathologies. Honneth argues that these core ideas "require conceptual reformulation if they are still to fulfil the function that was once intended" (2009, 42) and undertakes to do so. I am in no position to evaluate Honneth's interpretive claims about the commitments of the Frankfurt School. However, in order to explore the possibilities of ideology critique, it is useful to begin with Honneth's reformulation of the tradition.

Because Critical Theory aims to motivate and guide social change, it cannot rely on a set of "external" imported values: "any 'strong,' context-transcending form of social criticism necessarily brings the risk of paternalism or even despotism" (2009, 44). Of course, the correlative problem is that if one can only rely on the locally entrenched value horizon, then it is unclear that one will have the resources to break through the grip of ideology (2017, 2). Consequently, the goal is to find resources for critique within the unjust social order whose warrant does not depend on their acceptance in that very order.

> It was considered self-evident that a theory of society could engage in critique only insofar as it was able to rediscover an element of its own critical viewpoint within social reality; for this reason, these theorists continually called for a diagnosis of society that could bring to light a degree of immanent intramundane transcendence. (Honneth 1994, 256)

"Immanent intramundane transcendence"? What exactly does this involve? Honneth suggests that the challenge is to find "a pretheoretical sphere of emancipation to which critique can refer in order to confirm its normative standpoint within social reality" (Honneth 1994, 260). As I read him, the "pretheoretical sphere of emancipation" is our peephole. It enables us to locate – in our current social reality – the basis for a warranted critique of the existing social order. This normative ground is, in principle, accessible to all of us, but is hidden or distorted by our current practices. We find it, and we are motivated by it, because it speaks to an "emancipatory interest" that is, in principle, shared by all humans and gives us a (rational) motivation to promote social change. According to Honneth, members of the Frankfurt School fill in this schema by offering different specifications of Hegel's idea that

> a successful, undistorted life together is only possible if all [members of society] orient themselves according to principles or institutions that they can understand

as rational ends for self-actualization. Any deviation from the ideal outlined here must lead to a social pathology insofar as subjects are recognizably suffering from a loss of universal, communal ends. (Honneth 2009, 24)

This ideal is something humans respond to or, perhaps more plausibly, we respond to its lack. Given this characterization of the ideal, our emancipatory interest lies, at base, in our rationality:

In the end, this idea comes down to the strong and frankly anthropological thesis that human subjects cannot be indifferent about the restriction of their rational capacities. Because their self-actualization is tied to the presupposition of cooperative rational activity, they cannot avoid suffering psychologically under its deformation. (Honneth 2009, 39)

As a result, we are capable of judging a particular social formation as defective (or unjust) because "social pathologies must always express themselves in a type of suffering that keeps alive the interest in the emancipatory power of reason" (Honneth 2009, 36). Reason sets us free.

But why do we go so wrong? It seems that the social pathologies of our current social order exploit our non-rational capacities, for example, our desire for esteem (or, in the work of other critical theorists, our desire for meaningful work, or for commodities), so it can rely on our heteronomy to recruit us into relations of domination and subordination. ("The idea that human beings have a deep-seated interest in overcoming dependencies and heteronomy has always been a hallmark of the tradition of critical social theory deriving from Marx" [Honneth 2017, 908].) Reason, however, is resilient; it gives us the capacity to transcend our immediate circumstances and to overcome heteronomy (cf. Honneth 2014a, 4). We are fundamentally motivated to live a rational life – this is not only an exercise of our cognitive capacities, but includes the realization of our full moral agency – and, importantly, we *ought* to do so. This provides an immanent, historically situated, and warranted basis for critique: morally acceptable social conditions must allow the full exercise of our rational capacities, both individually and collectively (e.g. Honneth 2009, 50). On this broad approach, the challenge of ideology critique is to locate the socially imposed irrationality that we, as rational beings, are warranted in resisting.

Recall that under conditions of ideological oppression (in contrast to repression), agents are willingly engaged in the practices that oppress them and may even identify with the practices and find value in them. (The task of explaining the wrong of repression is important, but not the focus here.) Our social conditions are pathological because they prevent agents from being fully autonomous, that is, of fully realizing their capacities for a rational life.[3]

This happens because their agency is not transparent: ideology masks the fact that they are engaging in self-destructive practices whose promised rewards will never be realized. On Honneth's view, the specific social pathology that we currently face concerns the economy of esteem, that is, the distribution of recognition and its lack.[4] We continually seek what we will never obtain. However, agents are wrong about what they do and why they are doing it, not by accident, or because we are self-deceived, but because the social conditions undermine us and block such understanding. This point is sometimes made by saying that ideology blocks reflexivity: our capacity to know what we are doing and why is systematically disrupted (Zurn 2015, ch. 4; 2011). However, our autonomy cannot simply be an individual achievement because we are social beings. Ideology is pernicious because it prevents us from living together democratically, and so rationally.

How do we judge a social formation to be ideological on this account? If agents are denied the opportunity "to conceive of him or herself as an equal and, at the same time, unique member of society ... then this must be taken as an indication of the pathological development of a society" (1994, 265). Social protests serve as evidence of recognition failures and reveal that "the normative core of such notions of justice is continuously constituted by expectations connected to respect for one's own dignity, honor, or integrity" (1994, 262). The experience of disrespect by itself is not a sufficient basis for social critique; we can conclude that a system is pathological when and only when we can establish that "there is a systematic connection between specific experiences of disrespect and the structural development of society" (1994, 265; cf. Zurn 2015, ch. 4).

So, at the individual level, in undertaking critique one is protesting a kind of heteronomy: I cannot endorse the reasons that are offered to me as a basis for action for they are incompatible with my dignity, honour, or integrity. At the social level, for me to make a claim against others for greater respect or recognition is to refuse to endorse the collective terms of association that I am assumed to be party to: my engagement in the community does not meet standards that are rational for me individually and for all of us collectively.

CRITICAL THEORY AS A POLITICAL PROJECT

Does Honneth's analysis give us an adequate model for achieving social justice under conditions of ideological oppression? A hallmark of critical theory is that it aims to be emancipatory (Geuss 1981). On Honneth's account, pathologies of reason shape us to live under conditions that prevent reflexivity. Some individuals, however, become aware of this through the experience of disrespect; they resist and demand recognition and esteem that the system denies them. The critical theorist's task is to reveal to these agents ways in which they are *structurally* denied the recognition and esteem they desire.

However, we must also reveal to those still in the grip of ideology how society is failing them so that we can coordinate to create a fully rational life together. Of course, some members of society are likely to be recalcitrant – perhaps they can't understand the critical theorist's analysis, or they are so deeply in the grip of the ideology they can't believe the alternative, or they are secure where they are and are afraid of change. What then? Presumably, Honneth's emancipatory interest must be very, very compelling; the theorist somehow has to motivate all agents to act on it, for society, and the agents who compose it, cannot be fully rational unless and until we are all reflexively coordinating our desires, habits, and expectations. Let's call this the *enlightenment model* of social change.

Here is another. Let's call it the *contestation model*. On the contestation model, it is a basic fact of life that agents have conflicting interests and there are insufficient resources to satisfy everyone's interests simultaneously. Ideology manages this problem by shaping people's interests and distorting their understanding so that they coordinate on terms that are less than fair, just, ethical, reasonable (include your favourite normative term here) because they see no other alternative, or think it is the best they can get, that is, they are "disciplined" to coordinate. As on Honneth's model, there comes a moment when this becomes intolerable and individual resistance is collectivized and becomes a movement. The movement's members are not in the grip of the ideology; they don't need to be convinced of anything by theorists (in fact, they usually understand the situation better than theorists). The goal is to gain sufficient power to force renegotiation of the terms of association so they are more fair, just, and so on. The values at issue evolve over time, across cultures, in response to material conditions, so the demands and the normative basis for critique will reflect this. Renegotiation is a political process, and there will be winners and losers. There is no utopian solution.

I believe that the contestation model is more realistic, is more in keeping with the methodological commitments of critical theory, and is more apt for addressing the broad range of ideological oppression.

More realistic: Is it really plausible that there is a universal "emancipatory interest"? Honneth characterizes this as "a self-standing epistemic interest in emancipation rooted in invariant features of a specific human practice" (2017, 909; also 1996, 39) that is needed as "an epistemological foundation for critical theory itself" (2017, 909). He ultimately discovers this in a "conceptual explanation of the essential properties of social norms" (2017, 914). But the search for an invariant feature of social life that provides a universal foundation for critique is, to my mind, neither necessary nor desirable. Different ideologies or pathologies may structure society in ways that demand quite different forms of critique, justified in different ways. And, arguably, the desire to unify all critique, however formally, by rooting it in a shared universal interest echoes the grand narratives that Honneth sought to rework (2009).

Moreover, the history of social movements supports the idea that (a) not all social justice movements are identity-based (e.g. Mansbridge et al. 2001, 34–48); (b) that contestation rather than rational argumentation is what generates pressure against the powerful to renegotiate (Tilly and Tarrow 2015); and (c) that attempts to shape citizens so that they live together harmoniously, that is, ignoring their conflicting interests, is a threat to justice and is anti-democratic. On this last point, Danielle Allen (2001) argues that a democracy that fails to acknowledge that it is an imperfect way of managing conflicting interests causes the less powerful groups to become socially invisible. We are so concerned to affirm that democracy establishes the "common good" that we demonize who resist the results as not "really" one of us. Democracy inevitably requires sacrifices on the part of those whose interests are not fulfilled in the collective bargain, and these sacrifices are constitutive of a genuinely democratic community:

> Those who ask for sacrifices without acknowledging the nature of their requests generate invisibility. Not only are particular sacrifices and sacrificers rendered invisible but so too is the basic logic of democratic decision-making: If democratic decisions are to rest on full consent, then those citizens who lose political arguments, whose interests are defeated in the public forum, must consent to their losses; democratic consent and legitimacy, in other words, depend on sacrifice. To ignore sacrifice, to avoid talking about it directly, is to turn away from a fundamental feature of democracy. (Allen 2001, 872–73)

Methodologically more sound: Where does the critical theorist stand to diagnose the social pathologies that block emancipation? Recall that the critic faces a sceptical moment; the task is to find a basis for critique that is neither external to the social order nor merely an expression of its internal values. Honneth finds it in the normative structure of human agency. This move to a "formal" basis for critique is common in the Critical Theory tradition. The suggestion is that substantive first-order critique must be either external or internal critique and so flawed; the only alternative is second-order critique grounded in the norms of rationality. But this is wrong. Critique need not be merely formal and it need not be morally neutral.

Note that Marx describes the project of critical theory as "the self-clarification ... of the struggles and wishes of the age" (1844). Note that in this passage Marx characterizes the theoretical task as a *self-clarification*: the theorist's struggles and wishes are the struggles and wishes of the movement.

In my experience, the struggles are substantive, first order. In the same text, Marx makes this explicit:

> Nothing prevents us, therefore, from lining our criticism with a criticism of politics, from taking sides in politics, i.e., from entering into real struggles and identifying ourselves with them. (Marx 1844)

Of course, this does not mean that the theorist is dogmatically committed to whatever others in the movement enjoin. But the critical theorist is a participant in the movement and is helping to articulate, motivate, and explain its demands. These demands are her demands. She is not (or need not be) neutral on the first-order struggles (cf. Celikates 2018; Jaeggi 2018). On the contestation model, the theorists efforts are derivative from the values and demands of the movement as a whole. Moreover, the critical theorist, *qua theorist*, is not positioned as having privileged access to the defects of the social order; her task is parasitic on the insights of the social critic (who may be herself).

But, you might ask, on what basis does the theorist (or the movement) claim that *these* are the right values, when they too might be ideologically biased? The point of anti-utopian theorizing is made clear in the contestation model: the goal of a movement is not, in the first instance, to realize an encompassing vision of the fully rational life, but instead to articulate claims against the existing social order and to mobilize power behind them, so that these can be taken up for renegotiation. It is *negative*. We focus on what is not working, what we see to be damaging, and go from there. We generate proposals, but there is no utopia in mind, no promises. We only know that this is intolerable. This is more in keeping with the anti-utopian and open-ended commitments of critical theory.

Alert to many varieties of social injustice produced ideologically: Honneth suggests that social protest is grounded in identity violations. For example, he claims that humans perceive something as "morally unjust in everyday social life ... whenever, contrary to their expectations, they are denied the recognition they feel they deserve" (1994, 263). Of course it is true that people often perceive something as morally wrong or unjust if they are targets of disrespect. But this isn't the only occasion for protest or moral outrage. I am outraged by the treatment of non-human animals. It would be insulting to suggest that this moral outrage should be understood as my feeling of a lack of social recognition for my animal welfarist values. My outrage isn't about me. I am outraged by the treatment of African Americans, disabled people, violations of LGBTQ rights; I am outraged by attempts to curtail voting rights, corporate power over the government, and a million other things. I am also outraged by the *excess* of esteem I receive due to the ideologies of white supremacy, ableism, meritocracy, and capitalism. The wrong of ideological oppression isn't all about recognition, or even about being subordinated; it is also about being positioned as dominant. My outrage is that we are hailed into social practices that undermine efforts to live together on morally acceptable terms and to fully appreciate the plurality of values.

IDEOLOGY AND SUBJECTION[5]

I've outlined several concerns about Honneth's model of social critique and social change. But is there a plausible account of social agency and social critique underlying the contestation model? My starting point for understanding ideology is Althusser. In his essay, "Ideology and Ideological State Apparatuses" (1971 [2014]), Althusser distinguishes *repressive state apparatuses* (RSAs) and *ideological state apparatuses* (ISAs). RSAs include the "government, administration, army, courts, prisons" that "function by violence" or, "massively and predominantly by repression." ISAs, including religion, education, the family, the legal system, the political system, trade unions, communications/media, and culture ("literature, the arts, sports, etc.") "function massively and predominantly by ideology." (RSAs and ISAs depend crucially on each other, though in modern society, the ISAs are the dominant mode of social management.)

On Althusser's view, the role of ISAs and RSAs, together, is to reproduce the productive forces within specific relations of production. Althusser highlights the educational system (or the "school-family") as the primary contemporary ISA. Learning technical "know-how" at school is not enough:

> Children at school also learn the "rules" of good behaviour, i.e. the attitude that should be observed by every agent in the division of labour, according to the job he is "destined" for: rules of morality, civic and professional conscience, which actually means rules of respect for the socio-technical division of labour and ultimately the rules of the order established by class domination. They also learn to "speak proper French," to "handle" the workers correctly, i.e. actually (for the future capitalists and their servants) to "order them about" properly, i.e. (ideally) to "speak to them" in the right way, etc. (235–36)

A crucial difference between an ISA and an RSA is that individuals are hailed into a subject position by an ISA, rather than violently forced into it; and it is characteristic of those "good subjects" who respond to the hailing that they take up the norms as binding on themselves. As a result, they don't need to be coercively managed, they work "all by themselves" (269)!

This interpretation of modern power is developed in Foucault: "The perfection of power should tend to render its actual exercise unnecessary" (Foucault

1979, 201). In *Discipline and Punish*, Foucault meticulously chronicles the ways in which modern power is exercised by discipline: the crafting of subjects who monitor and manage themselves, their bodies, to conform to the demands of social position. For example, as Sandra Bartky points out, women's bodies are constrained by norms specifying shape, size, motility, and appearance; "A woman's skin must be soft, supple, hairless, and smooth; ideally, it should betray no sign of wear, experience, age, or deep thought" (Bartky 69). This is not usually achieved directly by coercion. We do it to ourselves, voluntarily. "The absence of a formal institutional structure and of authorities invested with the power to carry out institutional directives creates the impression that the production of femininity is either entirely voluntary or natural" (Bartky 75).

Leaving aside many complexities of interpretation and details of Althusser, Foucault, and Bartky, two ideas from this tradition are relevant to a discussion of critique. First, self-knowledge and self-mastery are not politically innocent. What I know about myself is not necessarily an adequate starting point for critique or liberation. First-person experience, or even the shared experiences of a group, may only be evidence of the effects of ideology. Second, ideology is not simply a matter of beliefs, but acts on and trains our bodies, our perception, our desires, our emotions, through our engagement in practices (Haslanger forthcoming). To consistently conform to social norms, it is much easier to identify with them, than to fake it and only go through the motions.

My conception of ideology is Althusserian in the following sense (Haslanger 2017). We participate in social practices guided by a set of public meanings, scripts, norms, assumptions, and so on – a complex *cultural technē*. Practices organize us around things taken to have +/− value; let's call these (assumed or constructed) *resources*, or, alternatively, *sources* of value and disvalue. Some sources are material (such as medicine, traffic, toxic waste), and others not (such as time, knowledge, boredom). We are "hailed" into practices in a variety of ways, for example, we are hailed into speaking English by having English spoken to us; we are hailed into the role of student by being sent to school and finding ourselves responding to the teacher as an authority (nudged by threat of punishment); we are hailed into adulthood by having to pay the rent (with threat of legal coercion in the background). We then develop ways of being and thinking so that we are (more or less) fluent English speakers, fluent students, fluent rent-paying adults. Ideology is not a set of beliefs, though it may produce belief. As Althusser says, "Ideology always exists in an apparatus and its practice or practices. Its existence is material" (1971 [2014], 259).

Our social practices and the corresponding cultural technēs are a mixed bag. Discipline, the hailing of social subjects, is inevitable in society. Some forms of discipline are empowering and valuable; some are efficient and practical; but others function to sustain an unjust (capitalist, racist, sexist, etc.) system. I use the term "ideology" in the pejorative sense. An ideology is a cultural technē "gone wrong" in at least two ways: it guides practices and structures that organize us in unjust or harmful ways, or it prevents us from aptly recognizing different kinds of value, and what's of value and what's not.

Ideology is pernicious. We – both the dominant and the subordinate – are enlisted in unjust practices; at least many of us internalize the norms and perspective on the world they demand. Again we must ask: if we are constituted as embodied social subjects through ideological practices, then where do we stand to critique them? We cannot trust our experience of meaning to be a reliable guide to justice (Scott 1991). What source of knowledge is resilient even under conditions of ideological discipline?

SOCIAL AGENCY AND SOCIAL CHANGE

Practices afford spaces for deliberation; they have choice points. But the choice points occur against a backdrop of routine, habit, and skill. This is inevitable, and I would say, desirable. To live a life in which every action is reflectively considered and chosen would be hell. Full reflexivity is not really an option. But heteronomy is not as bad as it is made out to be. Our affective system has evolved "for efficient and effective collection and utilization of information to generate an expectation-based evaluative landscape that implicitly guides thought and action as the individual navigates its way through its physical and social environment" (Railton 2014, 836).

On an Althusserian view, the problem with ideology is not that we are disciplined to become social agents who act mindlessly, without reflexivity, or to only see reason to do what we are supposed to do. The problem is that the practices we are hailed into are damaging – to our sensibilities, to our bodies, to our relationships, to distant others, to the planet. It is, of course, a further problem that we are prevented from seeing this and so, not only do nothing to stop it, but actively, even enthusiastically, continue. But the epistemic problem is a secondary problem; it arises because we want change, and to bring about change we have to recognize what is wrong. Ideology makes this difficult.

Note, however, that I speak of ideological social practices being "damaging." What normative basis for critique am I presupposing? Instead of seeking a universal and unquestionable basis, we should resist the demand for a unified ground. Such a demand assumes a foundationalist model of justification. I reject foundationalist assumptions according to which all knowledge must be grounded in experience or a "pre-theoretical" anchor (see also Quine

1953 [1980]; Antony 2018; Haslanger 2019). Both epistemic and moral foundationalism are unsupportable. This is not to deny that justification is required. But forms of justification may be diverse, holistic, context-sensitive, and path-dependent.

Ideology is not thoroughly hegemonic; subjection is, in the first instance, role and practice specific. Our lives involve participation in multiple practices that are open-ended and often in tension with each other; as a result, cultural technēs are not internally consistent. Moreover, discipline is not all-controlling; there is always an excess that surpasses the presumed "closure" of the dominant ideology.[6] Some part of the excess may be material, bodily, "pre-theoretical." But even if the body "speaks," understanding it requires interpretation. And finally, the workings of micro-power are unstable and contested.

A standpoint begins, as Honneth suggests, in pain, struggle, alienation, and disaffection. Suffering is a sign that something is going wrong, but it is not necessarily a sign of a pathology of *reason* or a failure of *self-actualization*. The initial impulse to resist may arise from being embedded in multiple – perhaps conflicting – practices, from adjusting to new practices, or from facing circumstances or conditions that render the existing practice questionable (perhaps through the development of new technologies or climate change). Moral and cognitive estrangement is valuable here, for estrangement allows one to gain critical perspective (Kapusta forthcoming). However, a standpoint is not achieved simply by having a recalcitrant experience or "outlaw" emotion. A standpoint is a position occupied by a group, not an individual. The process of consciousness raising alters our perspective on the world in a way that what before seemed certain is called into question. The ground shifts. What we took for granted before is now in question. Oppositional consciousness and the norms it invokes are not justified by reference to a secure and universal foundation. A critical standpoint is achieved through collective reflection on and evaluation of the testimony and insights of others in spaces open to heterodox ideas and feelings, together with empirical investigation and experimentation with new tools. A paradigm shift does not mean that anything goes. Consistency and empirical adequacy remain epistemic constraints. Political uptake is necessary. And the results must be tested by living them.[7]

An adequate standpoint will illuminate injustice in the current social order. The justification of critique goes along with the epistemic credentials of the standpoint from which it arises; however, the project is holistic rather than foundational, and not merely doxastic. So the standpoint of a regressive social movement can be tested and shown to be inadequate, for example, if it fails to satisfy constitutive epistemic norms – including empirical adequacy; if it is closed to reflective review and critique; if it silences or undermines the credibility of stakeholders; and if its social meanings and other cultural tools fail to provide a basis for meaningful coordination.

ACKNOWLEDGEMENTS

Thanks to Ásta, Louise Antony, Susan Brison, Robin Celikates, Stefan Gosepath, Hilkje Hänel, Daniel James, Tamara Jugov, Kristina Lepold, Mirjam Müller, Katja Stoppenbrink, Jeffrey Stout, Robin Zheng, and other participants at the workshop on Structural Injustice and Ideology at the Freie Universität, Berlin, 14 June 2019 for helpful discussion and comments. Special thanks to Kristina Lepold who has convinced me that engaging more fully with the Critical Theory tradition is deeply worthwhile and has been invaluable in helping me understand it.

NOTES

1. Some parts of §1 and §4 draw on Haslanger (2019).

2. I use the term 'critical theory' in lower case to refer to the project of social critique broadly (including ideology critique), and the term 'Critical Theory' in upper case to refer to Frankfurt School Critical Theory.

3. My primary training is in the Anglophone tradition, so the terminology I use may be somewhat distorting of Honneth's view. In particular, Honneth doesn't use the term 'autonomy' or the idea that acting autonomously involves acting from reasons that one can reflectively endorse; nor does he usually use the language of ideology or ideological oppression.

4. There are multiple forms of recognition that include objective (and material) conditions, including: "…emotional concern in an intimate social relationship such as love or friendship, rights-based recognition as a morally accountable member of society, and, finally, the social esteem of individual achievements and abilities" (Honneth 1994, 266).

5. The terms "subject," "subjectivity," "subjection," and "subjectivation" (or "subjevctivization") are used in multiple ways in the literature on Althusser and Foucault. Two sets of issues are relevant (1) how ISAs/power/knowledge construct subjects and how they construct subjectivity (understood psychologically), and (2) how and to what extent the construction is subjugating, endured passively (as opposed to taken up actively), and politically suspect. I will use the term "subjection" for the construction of subjects (and only derivatively subjectivity), will assume (as should be clear) that one is active in becoming a subject, and that subjection happens in both subordinate and dominant positions. See also Lepold (2018).

6. This is a significant theme in Derrida's work; see, for example, Balkin (1990).

7. Elizabeth Anderson has developed a pragmatist moral epistemology that relies on evidence from experiments in living. See, for example, Anderson (2014).

BIBLIOGRAPHY

Althusser, Louis. 1971 [2014]. "Ideology and Ideological State Apparatuses." In *On the Reproduction of Capitalism*. Trans. Ben Brewster. London: Verso. https://www.marxists.org/reference/archive/althusser/1970/ideology.htm.

Anderson, Elizabeth. 2014. "Social Movements, Experiments in Living and Moral Progress: Case Studies from Britain's Abolition of Slavery." The Lindley Lecture, University of Kansas.

Antony, Louise. 2018. "Finding the Truth." *Duquesne Law Review* 56(2): 7–19.

Balkin, J. M. 1990. "Nested Oppositions." *The Yale Law Journal* 99(7): 1669–705.

Bartky, Sandra. 1990. *Femininity and Domination: Studies in the Phenomenology of Oppression*. New York: Routledge.

Celikates, Robin. 2018. *Critique as Social Practice: Critical Theory and Social Self-Understanding*. London: Rowman and Littlefield International.

Foucault, Michel. 1979. *Discipline and Punish: The Birth of the Prison*. Trans. Alan Sheridan. New York: Random House (Vintage Editions).

Fraser, Nancy and Axel Honneth. 2003. *Redistribution or Recognition? A Political-Philosophical Exchange*. New York: Verso.

Geuss, Raymond. 1981. *The Idea of a Critical Theory*. Cambridge: Cambridge University Press.

Haslanger, Sally. 2017. *Critical Theory and Practice*. Amsterdam: Koninklijke Van Gorcum.

———. 2019. "Disciplined Bodies and Ideology Critique." *Glass Bead*. https://www.glass-bead.org/article/disciplined-bodies-and-ideology-critique/?lang=enview.

———. Forthcoming. "Cognition as a Social Skill." *Australasian Philosophical Review*.

Honneth, Axel. 1994. "The Social Dynamics of Disrespect: On the Location of Critical Theory Today." Trans. John Farrell. *Constellations* 1(2): 255–69.

———. 1996. "Postmodernism, Critique, and the Pathology of the Social." In David M. Rasmussen (ed.), *Handbook of Critical Theory*. Oxford: Blackwell, 369–396.

———. 2009. *Pathologies of Reason: On the Legacy of Critical Theory*. Trans. James Ingram and Others. New York: Columbia University Press.

———. 2014. "The Normativity of Ethical Life." Trans. Felix Koch. *Philosophy and Social Criticism* 40(8): 817–26. doi: 10.1177/0191453714541538.

———. 2017. "Is There an Emancipatory Interest? An Attempt to Answer Critical Theory's Most Fundamental Question." *European Journal of Philosophy* 25: 908–20.

Jaeggi, Rahel. 2018. *Critique of Forms of Life*. Trans Ciaran Cronin. Cambridge, MA: Harvard University Press.

Kapusta, Stephanie. Forthcoming. "The Social Practice of Cognitive Estrangement." *Australasian Philosophy Review*.

Lepold, Kristina. 2018. "An Ideology Critique of Recognition: Judith Butler in the Context of the Contemporary Debate on Recognition." *Constellations* 25: 474–84.

Mansbridge, Jane and Aldon Morris. 2001. *Oppositional Consciousness: The Subjective Roots of Social Protest*. Chicago: University of Chicago Press.

Marx, Karl. 1844. Letter to Ruge. https://www.marxists.org/archive/marx/works/1843/letters/43_09-alt.htm.
Quine, W. V. O. 1953 [1980]. "Two Dogmas of Empiricism." In *From a Logical Point of View*. Cambridge, MA: Harvard University Press, 20–46.
Scott, Joan W. 1991. "The Evidence of Experience." *Critical Inquiry* 17(4): 773–97.
Tilly, Charles and Sidney Tarrow. 2015. *Contentious Politics*. 2nd Edition. Oxford: Oxford University Press.
Zurn, Christopher. 2011. "Social Pathologies as Second-Order Disorders." In Danielle Petherbridge (ed.), *Axel Honneth: Critical Essays*. Leiden: Koninklijke Brill NV, pp. 345–70.
———. 2015. *Axel Honneth: A Critical Theory of the Social*. Cambridge: Polity Press.

Chapter 4

Immanent Normativity and the Fact of Domination

Notes on "Immanent Critique"

Martin Saar

INTRODUCTION: THE QUESTION OF CRITIQUE

Current social philosophy in general and critical theory in the Frankfurt School tradition in particular have increasingly reflected on their own modus operandi or methodology. Indeed, asking "what is critique?" has become a major theoretical concern in a way that would have seemed hardly intelligible a couple of decades ago. While Max Horkheimer's famous essay on the form and function of critical theory from 1937 had already opened up this discourse, for quite some time it seemed obvious that any theoretical analysis tackling relations of domination was, one might say, in itself critical, by being critical of domination. For quite some time, a roughly speaking Marxist or late-Marxist theoretical framework was understood to provide this very foundation by pointing out the exact forms or figures of domination in a more or less articulated social-theoretical fashion. Critique, as it were, seemed to be nothing more than an implication of a sound social diagnosis, grounded in the very nature of a given social constellation. Given this background, on the one hand it seemed obvious that the question of critique could not be severed from questions about the scope, strength, and plausibility of the social theory that was meant to be its very precondition and context. On the other hand, at the very moment when the theoretical tools and supports of this conception of the social became fragile, critique itself became dislocated and in need of a new articulation or reflection.

Speaking in terms of intellectual history, one might assume that the theoretical discourses in the 1970s and 1980s on the Left were introducing exactly this sense of dislocation and the need for re-grounding, that led to a new urgency of both new theories of the social and a new sense for the site, form, and function of critique. In the particular tradition of the (never homogenous) Frankfurt School, several attempts to rethink both society and critique were made, and it is in the work of Jürgen Habermas that this development found its most prominent and exemplary expression. What in the beginning could still announce itself as a "reconstruction" of historical materialism was evolving into a new – one might say "Post-Marxist" – social-theoretical synthesis that later became a general theory of communicative action, not disloyal to the earlier programme of critical theory but highly innovative and different on the conceptual and systematic level.[1]

It is against the background of this theoretical situation that the early work of Axel Honneth should be placed. The attempt to bring into conversation the early enterprise of Horkheimer and Adorno with Foucault's historical analysis and alternative theory of modernity was the ambition of his doctoral thesis, submitted at the Free University of Berlin in 1983. For the publication in 1986, however, Honneth added three new substantial chapters on Habermas. It is this theoretical constellation for which *Critique of Power* rather quickly became famous. Honneth had succeeded in showing that there is a certain line running from the dark or negativistic philosophy of history of the first generation of the Frankfurt School to the sceptical and conflict-oriented thought of Foucault, but also to the more revisionary and conciliatory social theory of Habermas. Both paradigms, Honneth seemed to contend, contribute indispensable elements for a comprehensive framework, but ultimately, and in isolation, both fail to grasp the specificity of social relations. Foucault's quasi-functionalist conception of human action and his refusal to account for his own moral standards and the convictions that guide his historical analyses for Honneth are proof of a methodological misunderstanding. Similarly, Habermas's reliance on functionalist arguments from systems theory for Honneth testifies to the former's misguided attempt to conceive of crucial areas of the social as "norm-free domains of social interaction" (Honneth 1991, 288, cf. Petherbridge 2013, pt. 1).

These two critical stances are related: Honneth sees Foucault and Habermas as bound up in a comparable abstraction from the inherent normative dynamism of social processes; this, in Honneth's eyes, should not be understood in abstraction from real subjects' interests, values, and normative investments in their own actions because it is a constitutive part of the social itself. Neither Horkheimer and Adorno nor Foucault nor Habermas, Honneth seemed to say in the mid-1980s, had found a language and an articulation of the immanent normativity of the social; but therefore, one might conclude, none of them had convincingly shown how modern subjects can be capable of criticizing their own society, namely by holding it to standards or norms it is already replete or diffused with.

These formulations already make use of exactly the sort of Hegelian vocabulary and assumptions that Honneth later presented as a way to a theoretical solution in the decade after *Critique of Power*. His magisterial book *Struggle for Recognition*, submitted as a *Habilitation* in 1990 and published in 1992, offered a reading and congenial interpretation of Hegel and provided a social theory built on the normative expectations and capacities of social subjects. Giving and taking, granting and receiving recognition in this framework was offered as the key practice constituting the social; being social could be read as living in a web of relationships (and their concomitant institutions) in which personal selfhood and autonomy can be realized in a process of mutual value-based ascriptions of status. These processes are conflictual, even antagonistic to the extent that nothing outside of these practices decides on the very terms in which value can be assessed and status should be granted (cf. Bertram and Celikates 2015.).

While *Struggle for Recognition* had not yet fully draw this systematic intersubjectivist conclusion and allows for non-social sources of interpersonal appreciation, a more radical thesis is already implied: social subjects enter into a process of open-ended negotiation about what should count as a valuable contribution (i.e. something to be recognized) or who should count as a valuable contributor to social life (i.e. someone to be recognized) by its different scales of assessment and how this might be processed. However, none of these expectations or demands is unrelated to the very society they are addressed to; all of them articulate a sense of belonging to it. The very dynamics driving social cooperation, communication and contestation within a given social community, could therefore be regarded as purely immanent, as arising out of the very nature of the social bond or out of the very communality that *is* the social.

With these conceptual moves, Honneth had secured a ground from which in the following years he could build an encompassing social theory which is inherently critical. This allowed actually making good on the ambition to continue or update the original programme as set out by Horkheimer by providing an analysis that can both assess the pathologies of the social and account for the dynamics of the desire to overcome them. Since the mutual granting and receiving of normative status is the systematic function but also an intentional stance constitutive of the social, reflecting on the grammar and structure of recognition in a given social configuration appeals to the first (or participant's) and the third (or observer's) point of view at the same time. Social critique, accordingly, is no outsider game let alone a view on society from nowhere. It is part of social life itself, arising from the recurring non-congruence of demands for recognition and their actualization. Social critique, based on this vision of the social, is immanent to social life; there is no gap and no motivational deficit. Critique is, as it were, natural to society.

In the following, I will focus on this conception that brings normativity, society, and critique into a close relationship, or, put differently, that conceives of normativity in the social as immanent normativity. As I said, this is an assumption characterizing critical theory as such, but of which Axel Honneth has provided an original and particularly strong interpretation. Therefore, understanding it better also opens the way for reflecting on the stakes and possibilities of a critical theory for our time. In order to contribute to this debate, I will first comment on the specific neo-Hegelian version this idea has taken in Honneth's later work, namely in *Freedom's Right*, and I will argue that the neo-Hegelian framing of this thought prioritizes methodological aspects over ontological ones. I will then contrast this version with a slightly different conception of a critique based on the immanence of normativity that takes more cues from Spinoza than Hegel, and some more from Foucault than the later Honneth. Finally, I will offer some thoughts on a possible critical theory following this alternative route and will try to sketch the horizon of a form of immanent critique that will definitely not, as it is so often accused of doing, acquiesce in the very powers it appeals and refers to.[2]

RECONSTRUCTION AS CRITICAL METHOD

In a series of publications, Honneth has engaged with the question of the form and methodology of critique within the framework of a critical social theory or, more broadly, critical social philosophy. In most cases, he uses the term "reconstructive" to refer to a methodological topos familiar from Hegel.[3] It sees in "determinate negation" a dynamic principle leading the way from a content to its negation to its overcoming. Negating something means starting from there (and not from nowhere) and means distancing oneself from it (and not positing something completely different). Famously, Hegel in *Phenomenology of Spirit* had projected an entire conceptual trajectory out of such a vision of the conceptual development of particular concepts' negation and revision. This vision in his metatheoretical reflections in *Science of Logic* then became the basis for an entire conceptual system of interrelated conceptual elements, forming a systematic whole in movement and constant internal contradiction.[4]

Honneth has always expressed some scepticism concerning the metaphysical side of this Hegelian picture but has wholeheartedly endorsed its methodological implications for a material description of social realities.[5] Societies can be treated as social totalities with different elements (namely individuals) that are integrated and interconnected. The social analyst or critic can assess and reconstruct the common points of reference binding these elements together. Such an endeavour will reveal the "moral grammar" (Honneth

1996a) of a given society and can point to differences, divergences, and tensions within a system of shared values or norms. Methodologically speaking, such an operation works immanently because it is reconstructive: It refers to nothing else than the values and norms already in play or circulation in, indeed constituting this very society. In his essays on critique, therefore, Honneth could refer to his and other critical theory forms of critique as "reconstructive," implying that its mode is one of immanent critique (as opposed to external critique). This conceptualization was meant to clarify that such a critique is not "constructive" in the Kantian sense of creating normative standards by rational means; but it is neither "deconstructive" in the Nietzschean sense of subverting the normative orientation as such (cf. Honneth 2000b, and for context McCarthy 1993; Forst 2017; Iser forthcoming).

In *Freedom's Right*, Honneth gives the strongest affirmation of this methodological enterprise to date but largely leaves aside the terminology of "immanent critique" in favour of the methodological title "normative reconstruction" (cf. Schaub 2015). But its contours remain the same: against the trend in moral and political philosophy to think that the principles of justice "stand alone" (Honneth 2014, 1), Honneth aims to "develop the principles of social justice by means of an analysis of society" (ibid., vii.). In explicating the different "premises" of such an approach, he asserts (echoing Talcott Parsons) "that social reproduction hinges on a certain set of shared fundamental ideals and values" (ibid., 3). This means that society as a whole can be treated as the institutionalization of these very norms. In this sense he is opting for an "immanent analysis" (ibid., 5), "taking immanently justified values as a criterion for processing and sorting out the empirical material" (ibid., 6). Against the common criticism that this ties social analysis too closely to the very structures it is meant to criticize, he affirms that such an analysis can still also aim "to correct and transform them" (ibid., 8). It becomes possible to "draw on these same values in order to criticize given practices as being unsuited to what it is they are supposed to represent" (ibid., 9). But there is no other way than "picking up on values and ideas already institutionalized in society" (ibid., 63).

Leaving aside many interesting and controversial implications of this systematic proposal opening up the rich material argumentation in the later parts of *Freedom's Right*, I want to focus exclusively on its methodological structure. Critique, we might say, in this picture is reconstructive in a strong sense, since its object, a given society, can be understood as an object that is normatively structured, it already consists of the very elements a critique is meant to bring in: values, norms, promises, expectations, and their failure. Critique, we might say, will essentially consist in revealing how societies fail to live up to their own norms which are the norms shared by its members. In the background of this conception, for sure, there is a strong reliance on the binding force of accepted norms which indeed are the cement of society and for whose totality Hegel had coined the term *"Sittlichkeit"* which Honneth also adopts as a name for his own object of inquiry.

The most fascinating feature of this approach consists in the fact that it does not presuppose or import specific normative concepts or criteria but can claim to derive them exclusively from its analysis or description of a given form of social life. If modern societies, as Honneth claims, are constituted by a deep-seated commitment to freedom and autonomy, it becomes possible to read them as landscapes and institutionalizations of these values. Such a freedom-based or freedom-oriented *Sittlichkeit* justifies itself and can be justified by an observer in terms of this meta-value, and the different institutional forms it has invented can be read as responses to demands for freedom.[6] The normativity, as it were, does not reside in the critic's perspective but is already expressed in her object.

The term "immanent normativity" seems apt to describe this very configuration. Against the impression that the critic brings her own standards and criteria to the table, this critical social theory advances a complex view of the very object a society is and sees its own role as one operating from within a given cosmos of norms. The critic does not (in general or *in toto*) step outside the social context she tries to elucidate, since it is also her own. It is this topos that, as already mentioned, places Honneth's recent writings firmly in the horizon of classical critical theory. It was one of the most fundamental arguments of Horkheimer to criticize the missing reflection on embeddedness in what he had termed "traditional theory." Mistaking its object (namely society) as something the critic (or social scientist) is isolated from is the crucial failure only another form of thinking can overcome. Only a (more or less strictly) dialectical reflection on the interaction and interdependence between the individual researcher and its social context (as materialized in the academic system, the social division of labour, the political embeddedness of research, etc.) allows for a controlled, non-naïve epistemic stance towards the social world that does not just reproduce the ideological structures already in force.

In a fascinating recent commentary on the core idea of critical theory discussing both Horkheimer's fundamental text and Habermas' conception of an "emancipatory interest" as advanced in *Knowledge and Human Interest* from 1968, Honneth highlights a related, but slightly different, key idea from the original programmatic. Horkheimer had spoken of a "critical activity [*kritisches Verhalten*] which has society itself for its object" (Horkheimer 1986, 206) already existing in society as a necessary condition for any critical perspective on it in the realm of theory. Habermas had – unsuccessfully, as Honneth contends – tried to account for this precondition in his conception of the practical interests implied in any theoretical perspective. Honneth offers his own take on this problem by asserting that the critique of domination meant to be supported by critical theory must be informed by the point of view of those subjected to this domination. It is only this motivation that gives rise to the critical insight that the current order of things, values, rights, and status serves some more than others, and is indeed a situation of domination, that generates substantial and radical critique.

Given that Honneth subscribes to the rather rich normative view of social life outlined above, he is inclined to account for the fact of "domination" not in terms of the absence or outright violation of the shared norms but as a conflict over their interpretation. The general structure of a social struggle therefore has the following form: "Previously disadvantaged groups regularly and recurrently rely on the interpretative openness of social norms in attempts to win recognition for their own neglected interests by way of re-interpretation. [...] their only recourse will normally be to call into question the established interpretations of those norms by articulating creative and more inclusive re-interpretations guided by their own particular concerns" (Honneth 2017, 915).

The basis, as it were, of social discontent or critique also in this description resides in the realm of norms, and the criticism also here emerges from a given normative structure: "It needs to be shown that the norms regulating social interaction do in fact always lend themselves to being called into question by pointing to their one-sided interpretation" (ibid., 914). An act of rebellion or revolt at the same time refers to the norms already existing *and* questions their existing application and interpretation: "It must be shown that groups who experience exclusion or discrimination due to hegemonic interpretations of norms do in fact tend to call these interpretations into question and to rebel against existing social orders" (ibid.). Such a perspective can indeed locate the power and the motivation of critique in a particular social experience (of domination) that comes with a particular consciousness or knowledge (an insight into the dominating character of the hegemonic interpretation of norms). Social critique therefore generally takes the form of "the transformative re-interpretation of established social norms" by "oppressed social groups in all societies" (ibid., 915).

Let me just highlight one feature of this picture, closely related to the observations in the first part of this section. Honneth reaffirms in another key his view of an immanent normative process and reaffirms his reliance on the constitutive normative structure of a society. The interesting emphasis here is the one on the disunity, or even discord, at the very heart of the social. Even a society integrated by the common reference to shared norms (making it an instance of *Sittlichkeit*) can be (or will be) torn by forces and privileges among those who are thought to be equal – and equally worthy – members of this society. Being a member of a society subscribing to certain norms does not protect from discrimination and, to a certain degree, exclusion. What is called "interpretation" or "application" of norms here indeed refers to a wide range of actions and processes that potentially distribute status and value unevenly among social subjects.[7] With this conception, Honneth indeed comes again closer to a Foucaultian perspective on norms and the working of norms than the more strictly Hegelian formulations seemed to allow for.

To say that critique and contestation arise immanently and refer to norms and values already given, shared, and justified, here acquires another meaning. It not only means that the critic is in general in accord with what the society already deems valuable and worthy of recognition, it also means that the very social problems and separations arise from a basis that is normative and already agreed-upon, namely certain conceptions and values that are impossible not to appeal to in order to be recognizable as a social subject in this society at all. But this meaning of "being immanent," it seems to me, is stronger than the more methodological meaning discussed above. Now it is not only a question of which norms to use or turn to in order to criticize certain pathologies as injustices. Now it means acknowledging that even the agreed-upon, supposedly general norms will not save anyone from discrimination or exclusion, since it will be in their very application or interpretation that pathologies and injustices can arise.

Or, put differently, it seems that Honneth is using the schema of immanent critique in two different senses or ways. While the first looks purely methodological and just seems to elucidate the formal features of an act of critique in a given social situation, the second seems more radical, or at least to go one step further. In the second sense, immanent critique will be inescapably bound up with the norms of a given society, because these norms (or their application and interpretation) will be the source and cause of the wrong the critique is meant to address. We might call this second model "ontological" in the sense that it points to a constitutive relation between norm and domination, norm and power, norm and exclusion. It is more radical in its focus on the norm as a source of the problem, not only of the remedy. Honneth, to my mind, at least in the last article referred to here, seems to touch on this second, more radical schema, but to follow it more thoroughly might have led Honneth astray from of the more Hegelian-Parsonian path his official account so energetically affirms.

THE ONTOLOGY OF NORMS AND POWER

In a current social-theoretical discourse that draws on rather different sources than Honneth, the very idea that norms, power, and society need to be thought closely together has gained a new systematic articulation. In a theoretical development combining concerns from poststructuralist thought and a rediscovery of ontological theorizing, the conception that norms regulate societal life and the lives of subjects has been cast in a new form. Its first element is the Foucaultian thesis that the life of modern subjects is increasingly bound up with not only ethical, but also scientific, medical, and epistemic norms determining the range of normality, health, and social desirability. To be a modern subject is to be subjected to these (and other) norms and to acquire agency and social status through the active commitment to, even dispositional investment in these norms. The second element is to interpret, following Judith Butler, this condition as one of "the psychic life of power" (Butler 1997) in the sense that this entanglement of norm and subject accounts for the effective transmission of powerful social structures into subjectivities. Given that social subjects desire to exist, to be heard and seen, indeed that they need to be recognized in order to acquire a status as social subjects at all, desiring the norms of recognition and acceptance becomes an existential necessity. The third element, implied in the second, is to account for this mechanism of a paradoxical love of power or "wounded attachments" to the norms that subject (cf. Brown 1995; Butler 1997, 6–18) in an affect-theoretical way. Taking some cues from neo-Spinozism and Deleuzianism, one can model these paradoxical subjectivations where norms become internalized even in the face of harm, as an affective economy in which the impulse to survive, that is the Spinozian *conatus* or the "'desire to persist in one's being" (cf. Spinoza 1994, pt. III, proposition 6), translates into an active, positive investment in the ruling social norms and laws.

Let me comment on each of these steps in turn a little more explicitly, just in order to mark the theoretical difference to the framework used to far. Regarding the first step, which builds on Foucault's historical thesis about the "biopolitical" nature of modern society, it seems necessary to remark that the very term "norm" here has a different meaning.[8] It does not refer to the abstract moral or ethical value used to articulate the desirability of an action or to assess the legitimacy of an institution, but more generally to frameworks of evaluation in all kinds or ways and embodied in discourse across different social spheres. In Foucaultian terms, it is less obvious that modern societies should be characterized by their general commitment to freedom and equality as the master political categories than that they should be interpreted along the lines of the expectations they establish (and make obligatory) about the shape, form, and performance of "normal" subjects. Modern "biopolitical" society therefore, in a sense, is "normative" through and through (cf. Foucault 1990). It is, one might say, an integrated and interconnected system of norms arising from different social spheres and institutions constructing a vision of the healthy, legitimate, able subject. The norms in question here are less objects of conscious reflection and deliberation than elements that circulate in the social sphere and that are implied and effectively operating in its core institutions that educate and teach, sanction and reward, advise and correct modern subjects.

While this account seems to abstract from the subject's own point of view in favour of a seemingly functionalist description from above, the Foucaultian picture is turned inwards in the second step. The position of the subject vis-à-vis the social norms regulating her life in a society cannot be one of neutrality or indifference. Since the norms in question govern what is valuable and acceptable and what is expected from subjects in order to even appear as worthy members, there is an existential need to display compliance with but also internalize the social standards and expectations imposed on subjects (cf. Butler 1997 and Lepold 2018). Wanting to be, the desire to gain a status as a visible and respectable social being requires the commitment to a way of being, or to being in a certain way. But when (human) being realizes itself in a certain conative structure, as a constellation or hierarchy of desires, projections and psychic investments, the transmission of social norms into individual subjects is a translation of the social into the individual, a social modulation of subjectivity. This description of normativity has shifted from the evaluative level to an ontological register. Norms are here seen as constitutive of subjectivity, via the mechanism of psychic or affective investment.

To substantiate such a – broadly speaking, ontological – vision of subjectivity produced by normativity, in a third step the recourse to overtly ontological and affect-theoretical arguments has proven promising. A wide range of authors following Althusser and Deleuze have acknowledged the power of proposals originally rooted in the metaphysical debates of the seventeenth century when Spinoza was defending an anti-dualistic ontological conception of man in nature against his predecessors Hobbes and Descartes.[9] Especially promising is the idea of a fundamental striving or essential vital force colouring all human dispositions that might help explicate the wide range of human affective reactions. Contemporary affect theory has taken up this proposal and has tried to account for the variety of affective patterns in relation to their objects. Specific desires can then be read not as purely functional (oriented towards the objects for the satisfaction of needs) but as expressive of a subject's internal dispositions and its "desire to live" (and therefore oriented towards those objects that will secure survival). And since, as Spinoza and his readers contend, the subject's ideas about what will be productive and meaningful will rely heavily on social interaction, ideological offerings, and other imaginings, this will be less a question about the hard facts of human flourishing than about the socially mediated visions and fantasies of a good life.[10] The norms of society, again, appear as fundamental elements in a subject's inner life and orientations.

This rough sketch of a complex and multifaceted position concerning the relation between subjectivity and normativity was just meant to provide an outline for a different form of immanent critique. Because in all three steps, the connection between norms, the social, and the life of subjects appears as fundamental, in all three steps the capacity to relate to the social is inescapably bound up with the norms already in force in a given social situation. If Foucault is right and modern subjectivity can only be understood as an effect of a varieties of powerfully established and imposed norms, every act of critique of the modern subject will have to attack these very norms. If Butler is right and the social is translated into the inner life of subjects, there will be no outside from which to claim agency and social status; any rebellion against given norms will have to take the form of a risky, life-threatening form of self-critique (cf. Butler 1997, 27–30). If (neo-)Spinozism is right in its postulation of an inner economy of affective life, norms will have to be seen as essential elements in a dynamics of desire, identification, and the will to survive. Criticizing a given social institution, practice, or value will involve addressing the subject's very conditions of life.

In this sense, the fundamental implications and complications of subjectivity, normativity, and sociality pointed to here justify calling the form of critique apt to address them "immanent." However, this is not meant to evoke the methodological meaning of this term as expressed in the neo-Hegelian mode. Rather, it points to ontological implications and the ontological entanglements of the subject (of critique) with its objects, namely the social norms.[11] Ontologically speaking, in this picture the norms constitute the subject, or put differently, the subject constitutes itself through social norms. The object of critique is not outside but inside the very instance or site of critique. This, to me, seems to appeal to the heavily ontological resonances the topos of "immanence" has had in many usages (and in its origins).[12] Moreover, despite the heavy systematic costs the introduction of ontological vocabulary into critical theory might have, I believe that this alternative version has great heuristic value.

CONCLUSION: THE FUTURE OF CRITIQUE

The sketch just given of an alternative model of immanent critique bears only a faint resemblance to the neo-Hegelian conception Axel Honneth has advanced so forcefully in recent years. The latter was a major contribution to the reactualization of critical theory whose first generation, as one should not forget, was deeply rooted in Hegelian thought and Marxist theory, dialecticians to the bone. The alternative model draws on other sources and references, and its scope and *modus operandi* are definitely different. In my concluding remarks, I want to briefly argue that these differences notwithstanding, this model refers and contributes to critical theory too and even shares some major goals with Honneth's project. Obviously, shifting the ground to a different conception of norms and normativity and redefining the form of critique leads to huge theoretical and methodological differences, but some common general traits and shared ambitions remain.

First, both models share an investment in understanding normativity in its material social contexts, as social facts in social environments. Both try to break away from a more abstract or free-standing conception of norms and both are sceptical about philosophy's ability to rationally construct or fully rationalize norms. This, one might say, anti-Kantian reservation leads to different theoretical gestures. While Honneth's methodological conception emphasizes the historical and social specificity of any deliberation about norms, the second, more ontological conception, emphasizes the material existence and concrete operations of given regimes of normativity. Since a more Foucaultian perspective will see norms embedded in classifications, regulatory institutions, and techniques of subject formation, the realm of the normative ceases to appear as a noumenal or abstractly evaluative domain, but as a matter of rather mundane, material facts about the very set-up of modern societies. In a sense, the second model, with its implied methodological monism about the social, remains in closer contact to the more materialist legacy of critical theory. It might be more attentive to the technological, institutional, and economic factors framing and structuring the cognitive and normative attitudes and dispositions subjects in certain contexts are able to develop. Arguably, within such a framework, the classical concept of ideology might easily reappear as a name for point of conjunction between the social and the individual, the factual and the normative.[13]

Second, both models have a place for discord and conflict, indeed the very fact of domination and division that characterizes modern societies. But this aspect tends, as we have seen, to retreat into the background story of Honneth's official theory, at least in *Freedom's Right*. The second, more ontological account places it centre stage. It understands the working of (modern) norms at both integrating societies and dividing them by setting up ever new lines of differentiation, with class, race, and gender being the most obvious. This means that a powerful division, that is, domination in the strong sense, is built into the very fabric of society.[14] In this sense, the second model radicalizes the conflict-theoretical line that was an integral part of the critical theory tradition from Marx onwards but that became weakened by other theoretical developments. Rethinking this topos along the lines of a constitutive conflictuality within the normative structure of any society itself might clear the way also for more conflict-oriented empirical analyses of current social arrangements. Far from being lost on the way to late modernity, domination has never waned, but has just transformed itself and morphed into new *Gestalten*, the diagnosis of which remains the urgent task of critical social philosophy (cf. Saar forthcoming b).

Third, both models remain deeply philosophical and refer to high-level conceptual questions that combine empirical observations with categorical theorizing as the tradition of critical theory has always done. However, while Honneth's more dialectical approach tends to create the impression that normative progress can be generated out of an inner development of norms and their criticism that then plays out in history, the second approach insists on the world-creating, society-shaping power of norms. To account for this working of norms, a mere methodological reflection on which meta-norms to use in order to judge them is not enough. Normativity is revealed as a battleground, but not only on the level of consciousness or competing attitudes but on the level of social reality itself. Tensions and contradictions and a play of forces are therefore located in the realm of actually existing social identities, social structures, and social totalities. Critique, as it were, is nothing that refers to the reality of the social from somewhere else; it is part of the real.

Hence, critical social philosophy can take a different form and express itself as a full-fledged social or political ontology.[15] While this might sound unfamiliar given the methodological shape of most current critical theory, it should not appear too surprising given the recent prominence of contemporary "post-foundationalist" political theories and the rich legacy of ontological theorizing within older critical theory (from Bloch to Marcuse). Any critical assessment of society will necessarily involve ontological statements about the very constitution and emergence of certain social forms, identities, and relationships (and not others). If power, domination, and antagonism are essential, ontological features of society, any critique will have to place itself in relation to, and not outside of, them. Critique is immanent in that it is part of the current struggles and the desires for emancipation today.

NOTES

1. For a *tour d'horizon* of these developments, cf. McCarthy (1993), Baynes (1993), Lepold (2019), and Iser (forthcoming).

2. This chapter is a follow-up to "Power and Critique" (Saar 2013b), which was originally published in a volume on the occasion of Axel Honneth's sixtieth birthday. What was there discussed in terms of two different conceptions of the critique of power reappears here in terms of two different paradigms of normativity and immanent critique. I have first tried out this idea, which is implicit in my recent work on critical theory after the ontological turn, in an essay on Foucault's mode of critique (Saar 2017).

3. For prominent examples, cf. Honneth (1996b, 2000b, 2000c, 2002).

4. For a state of the art account of Hegel's conception of immanent critique, cf. Särkelä (2018), for the state of the current methodological discussion, see Stahl (2013) and Romero (2014).

5. Cf. also the opening remarks in Honneth's first book on the mature Hegel (Honneth 2000a).

6. On this methodological level, it becomes obvious how closely related Rahel Jaeggi's recent proposal of a *Critique of Forms of Life* (2018) is to this approach, except that hers remains more formal and not already committed to one specific image of modern culture as freedom-oriented.

7. See Menke (2000) for a dialectical account of equality dependent on criteria and standards that make differences and therefore always potentially create exclusions.

8. Cf. Genel (2019) for an excellent elaboration of this point.

9. For references and introductions, cf. Montag and Stolze (1998), Balibar (1998), Gatens and Lloyd (1999), and Sharp (2011).

10. For discussions and interpretations, cf. Saar (2013a, ch. VI), Andermann (2018), and Mühlhoff (2018).

11. For variants of this model, cf. Fischbach (2005), Lordon (2014), Macherey (2014), and Saar (forthcoming a).

12. For this rich intellectual history, cf. Yovel (1992) and Rölli (2018), for its connection to critical theory from Marx to the Althusserians, see Norris (1990).

13. For a general discussion of this point, cf. Saar (2018).

14. Jaquet (2014) provides a fascinating model of social class division building on Spinoza and Bourdieu.

15. Cf. Sharp (2011) and Saar (2013a, conclusion).

BIBLIOGRAPHY

Andermann, Kerstin. 2018. *Die Macht der Affekte. Spinozas Theorie immanenter Individuation*. Unpublished Habilitation (Philosophy). Leuphana Universität Lüneburg.

Balibar, Etienne. 1998. *Spinoza and Politics*. Transl. Peter Snowdon. London: Verso.

Baynes, Kenneth. 1993. *The Normative Grounds of Social Criticism: Kant, Rawls, and Habermas*. Albany: SUNY Press.

Bertram, Georg W. and Robin Celikates. 2015. "Towards a Conflict Theory of Recognition: On the Constitution of Relations of Recognition in Conflict." In *European Journal of Philosophy* 23, no. 4, 838–861.

Brown, Wendy. 1995. "Wounded Attachments." In *States of Injury: Power and Freedom in Late Modernity*. Princeton: Princeton University Press, 52–76.

Butler, Judith. 1997. *The Psychic Life of Power: Theories in Subjection*. Stanford: Stanford University Press.

Fischbach, Franck. 2005. *La production des hommes. Marx avec Spinoza*. Paris: PUF.

Forst, Rainer. 2017. *Normativity and Power: Analyzing Social Orders of Justification*. Transl. Ciaran Cronin. Oxford: Oxford University Press.

Foucault, Michel. 1990 [1976]. *The History of Sexuality, Volume I: An Introduction*. Transl. Robert Hurley. New York: Vintage.

Gatens, Moira and Genevieve Lloyd. 1999. *Collective Imaginings: Spinoza, Past and Present*. London: Routledge.

Genel, Katia. 2019. "The Norm, the Normal and the Pathological: Articulating Honneth's Account of Normativity with a French Philosophy of the Norm (Foucault and Canguilhem)." In *Critical Horizons*, online 20 June. doi: 10.1080/14409917.2019.1616482.

Honneth, Axel. 1991. *The Critique of Power: Reflective Stages in a Critical Social Theory*. Transl. Kenneth Baynes. Cambridge, MA: MIT Press.

Honneth, Axel. 1996a. *Struggle for Recognition: The Moral Grammar of Social Conflicts*. Transl. Joel Anderson. Cambridge, MA: MIT Press.

Honneth, Axel. 1996b. "Pathologies of the Social: The Past and Present of Social Philosophy." In *Handbook of Critical Theory*. Ed. David M. Rasmussen. London: Blackwell, 369–398.

Honneth, Axel. 2000a. *Suffering from Indeterminacy: An Attempt at a Reactualization of Hegel's Philosophy of Right*. Trans. Jack Ben-Levi. Amsterdam: Van Gorcum.

Honneth, Axel. 2000b. "Reconstructive Social Critique with a Genealogical Reservation: On the Idea of Critique in the Frankfurt School." Transl. Jeff Seitzer. In *Graduate Faculty Philosophy Journal* 22, no. 2, 3–12.

Honneth, Axel. 2000c. "The Possibility of a Disclosing Critique of Society: The Dialectic of Enlightenment in Light of Current Debates in Social Criticism." Transl. John Farrell and Siobhan Kattago. In *Constellations* 7, no. 1, 116–127.

Honneth, Axel. 2002. "Idiosynkrasie als Erkenntnismittel. Gesellschaftskritik im Zeitalter des normalisierten Intellektuellen." In *Der kritische Blick. Über intellektuelle Tätigkeiten und Tugenden*. Ed. Uwe Justus Wenzel. Frankfurt am Main: Fischer, 61–79.

Honneth, Axel. 2014. *Freedom's Right: The Social Foundations of Democratic Life*. Transl. Joseph Ganahl. Cambridge, UK: Polity.

Honneth, Axel. 2017. "Is There an Emancipatory Interest? An Attempt to Answer Critical Theory's Most Fundamental Question." In *European Journal of Philosophy* 25, no. 4, 908–920.

Horkheimer, Max. 1986 [1937]. "Traditional and Critical Theory." In *Critical Theory: Selected Essays*. Transl. Matthew O'Connell. New York: Continuum, 188–243.

Iser, Mattias. Forthcoming. *Indignation and Progress: Foundations of a Critical Theory of Society*. Transl. Ciaran Cronin. New York: Oxford University Press.

Jaeggi, Rahel. 2018. *Critique of Forms of Life*. Transl. Ciaran Cronin. Cambridge, MA: Harvard University Press.

Jaquet, Chantal. 2014. *Les Transclasses ou La non-reproduction*. Paris: PUF.

Lepold, Kristina. 2018. "An Ideology Critique of Recognition: Judith Butler in the Context of the Contemporary Debate on Recognition." In *Constellations* 25, no. 3, 246–261.

Lepold, Kristina. 2019. "Examining Honneth's Positive Theory of Recognition." In *Critical Horizons* 20, no. 3.

Lordon, Frédéric. 2014. *Willing Slaves of Capital: Spinoza and Marx on Desire*. Transl. Gabriel Ash. London: Verso.

Macherey, Pierre. 2014. *Le sujet des norms*. Paris: Ed. Amsterdam.

McCarthy, Thomas. 1993. *Ideals and Illusions: On Reconstruction and Deconstruction in Contemporary Critical Theory*. Cambridge, MA: MIT Press.

Menke, Christoph. 2000. "The Self-Reflection of Equality." In *Reflections of Equality*. Transl. Howard Rouse and Andrei Denejkine. Stanford: Stanford University Press, 1–48.

Montag, Warren and Ted Stolze. 1998. *The New Spinoza*. Minneapolis: Minnesota University Press.

Mühlhoff, Rainer. 2018: *Immersive Macht. Affekttheorie nach Spinoza und Foucault*. Frankfurt am Main and New York: Campus.

Norris, Christopher. 1990. *Spinoza and the Origins of Modern Critical Theory*. Oxford: Blackwell.

Petherbridge, Danielle. 2013. *The Critical Theory of Axel Honneth*. New York: Lexington Books.

Rölli, Marc. 2018. *Immanent denken. Deleuze – Spinoza – Leibniz*. Wien: Turia + Kant.

Romero, José M. Ed. 2014. *Immanente Kritik heute. Grundlagen und Aktualität eines sozialphilosophischen Begriffs*. Bielefeld: Transcript.

Saar, Martin. 2013a. *Die Immanenz der Macht. Politische Theorie nach Spinoza*. Berlin: Suhrkamp.

Saar, Martin. 2013b. "Power and Critique." In *Journal of Power* 3, no. 1, 7–20.

Saar, Martin. 2017. "Die Form der Macht. Immanenz und Kritik." In *Vierzig Jahre "Überwachen und Strafen". Zur Aktualität der Foucault'schen Machtanalyse*. Ed. Marc Rölli and Roberto Nigro. Bielefeld: Transcript, 157–173.

Saar, Martin. 2018. "What is Social Philosophy? Or, Order, Practice, Subject." In *Proceedings of the Aristotelian Society* 118, no. 2, 207–223.

Saar, Martin. Forthcoming a. "Power, Affect, Matter: Critical Theory and the Challenges of Neo-Spinozism." In *Critical Theory and New Materialisms*. Ed. Arthur Bueno, Hartmut Rosa, and Christoph Henning. London: Routledge.

Saar, Martin. Forthcoming b. "Rethinking Resistance: Critical Theory before and after Deleuze." In *Coils of the Serpent: Journal for the Study of Contemporary Power* 5, no. 2.

Särkelä, Arvi. 2018. *Immanente Kritik und soziales Leben. Selbsttransformative Praxis nach Hegel und Dewey*. Frankfurt am Main: Klostermann.

Schaub, Jörg. 2015. "Misdevelopments, Pathologies, and Normative Revolutions: Normative Reconstruction as Method of Critical Theory." In *Critical Horizons* 16, no. 2, 107–130.

Sharp, Hasana. 2011. *Spinoza and the Politics of Renaturalization*. Chicago: Chicago University Press.

Spinoza, Baruch de. 1994 [1677]. *A Spinoza Reader: The Ethics and other Works*. Transl. and ed. by Edwin Curley. Princeton: Princeton University Press.

Stahl, Titus. 2013. *Immanente Kritik. Elemente einer Theorie sozialer Praktiken*. Frankfurt am Main and New York: Campus.

Yovel, Yirmiyahu. 1992. *Spinoza and Other Heretics*. Princeton: Princeton University Press.

Chapter 5

Moral Economy
A Critical Reappraisal
Didier Fassin

> *If I did father the term "moral economy" upon current academic discourse, the term has long forgotten its paternity. I will not disown it, but it has come of age and I am no longer answerable for its actions. It will be interesting to see how it goes on.*
>
> E. P. Thompson, "Moral Economy Reviewed" (1991, 351)

In the first footnote to an influential essay "The Moral Economy of Science," Lorraine Daston (1995, 3) expresses her gratitude to two of her colleagues "for pointing out that my use of the term *moral economy* diverges significantly from E. P. Thompson's in 'The Moral Economy of the English Crowd in the Eighteenth Century.'" Two decades later, it remains remarkable that two concepts born a quarter of a century apart using the same terms would have followed two parallel trajectories, their users generally displaying a complete and lasting mutual ignorance. While Thompson's original idea has fostered abundant research and intense debates among social historians, cultural anthropologists, and political scientists, Daston's reinvention of it has inspired the work of numerous historians of science and medical anthropologists. This is by no means a unique example of a term's parallel trajectory in the social sciences, and one could evoke, for instance, the concept of "social capital," initially created by Pierre Bourdieu (1980), later developed by James Coleman (1988) and popularized by Robert Putnam (1993): neither of the latter two referred to their French predecessor, and each of them gave the term a distinct meaning (Fassin 2003). However, the case of "moral economy" seems unique in that it independently emerged from two different fields and spread through multiple disciplines and domains, thus creating two discrete and prolific paradigms.

Indeed, both versions of the concept have produced their own intellectual legacy. On the one hand, following Thompson's analysis of peasants' revolts in eighteenth-century Britain (1971), social scientists have studied the moral economy of food riots in Chile (Orlove 1997), labour protests in Egypt (Posusney 1993), popular disturbances in India (Arnold 2000), the Mau Mau revolt in colonial Kenya (Lonsdale 1992), and even the hungering mobs in Shakespeare's *Coriolanus* (Cheng 2010) as well as the moral economy of entrepreneurship in Highland Nepal (Parker 1988), tobacco in the United States (Griffith 2009), corruption in Africa (Olivier de Sardan 1999), cultural identity in Tibet (Saxer 2012), and witchcraft in comparative perspective (Austen 1993). These authors use Thompson's concept, sometimes criticizing it or distorting it, but always considering the word "economy" in its common meaning of human activities related to the production, distribution, and consumption of goods and services. On the other hand, adopting Daston's redefinition and application of the term to the scientific realm (1995), historians and anthropologists have analysed the moral economy of the daguerreotype in nineteenth-century France (Tresch 2007), drosophila genetics in early twentieth-century United States (Kohler 1999), and contemporary human embryonic stem cell science (Salter and Salter 2007) as well as the moral economy of the psychiatry of trauma (Young 1995) or the neurology of brain-death (Lock 2001), thus expanding the model to medicine. Such works refer to Daston's concept, using the word "economy" in the older sense of the ordering of the various parts of a system. Finally, as a testament to the success and even trivialization of "moral economy" in the social sciences, some authors do not refer to any literature or suggest any definition, as if it could be taken for granted. They often consider it an equivalent of local morality (Howell 1997) to explore, for instance, the moral economy of ancestor worship among Singapore's Chinese (Kuah 1999) or of drinking practices among the Navajos (Quintero 2002). This abundance confirms the recent thriving interest for moral issues in sociology (Hitlin and Vaisey 2010) and anthropology (Fassin 2012) as well as in psychology and the cognitive sciences (Sinnott-Armstrong 2008). Yet, the heterogeneity of the corpus makes the use of the phrase problematic and calls for a reappraisal of the concept. Paraphrasing Ian Hacking's incisive question regarding "social construction" (1999), one could ask: The moral economy of what?

Prima facie, the two moral economy paradigms are not only distinct but also incompatible. For Thompson, the term pertains to a form of production and circulation of goods based on traditional rights and obligations that precedes and contrasts with the modern market economy, whereas for Daston, it regards a set of values and emotions that underlies and determines scientific work. In other words, for the former, the defining term in the expression is "economy," while for the latter it is "moral." Not without a sense of provocation, Thompson (1991, 271) even writes, twenty years after his pioneering essay: "Maybe the trouble lies with the word 'moral'. 'Moral' is a signal which brings on a rush of polemical blood to the academic head. Nothing has made my critics angrier than the notion that a food rioter might have more 'morals' than a disciple of Dr Adam Smith. ... I could perhaps have called this a sociological economy." For her part, Daston (1995, 4) makes it clear that she is not referring to what most people have in mind: "Here *economy* has a deliberately old-fashioned ring: it refers not to money, markets, labor, production, and distribution of material resources, but rather to an organized system that displays certain regularities, regularities that are explicable but not always predictable in their details. A moral economy is a balanced system of emotional forces, with equilibrium points and constraints." Thus, Thompson dismisses the adjective "moral," whereas Daston distances herself from the substantive "economy." Most social scientists have adopted one stance, rarely even acknowledging the existence of the other, still less discussing their differences.

The object of this chapter is twofold: first, to analyse and compare the two paradigms, showing their strengths and limitations; second, to propose an alternate definition, drawing on these models but trying to move beyond their respective weaknesses. In the final words of his review of the concept written two years before his death and quoted in the epigraph of this chapter, Thompson invites his readers to resume the inquiry, adding that "it will be interesting to see how it goes on." Reopening the case: This is what I will try to do in the following pages by questioning a phrase that too often seems to be taken for granted.

E. P. THOMPSON AND THE MORAL ECONOMY OF THE POOR

It is generally and correctly assumed that the term "moral economy" in Edward Palmer Thompson's work has its first occurrence in his monumental *The Making of the English Working Class* in 1963. Discussing the "more or less spontaneous popular direct action" of the eighteenth and nineteenth centuries, Thompson observes that "it rested upon more articulate popular sanctions and was validated by more sophisticated traditions than the word 'riots' suggests" (1968/1963, 67–68). According to him, "this was rarely a mere uproar which culminated in the breaking open of barns or the looting of shops," but "it was legitimized by the assumption of an older moral economy, which taught the immorality of any unfair method of forcing up the price of provisions by profiteering upon the necessities of the people." However, in this book, the term "moral economy" is simply mentioned in passing and, considering retrospectively its later success, it is worth noting that it does not even appear in the index of the volume. Actually, in spite of the importance granted by the author to values and morals to explain the conflicts, revolts, and strikes, both in the eighteenth-century peasant world and the nineteenth-century working class, neither of these words is cited in the long list provided at the end of the volume. This absence can be interpreted in two possible ways: either Thompson was not entirely aware of the revision of the Marxist doxa he proposed by shifting from the material to the moral in the interpretation of class struggle or he was somewhat hesitant to confront his orthodox Marxist colleagues too directly by putting forward his new conceptualization. From what is known of the boldness of the author, I tend to favour the first option. It is only eight years later that he seems to have taken stock of his theoretical breakthrough.

Indeed, the most substantial discussion of the term "moral economy" appears in the famous article from *Past and Present*. This is where Thompson proposes what seems to be the only real definition he provides for it in his entire writings: "A consistent traditional view of social norms and obligations, of the proper economic functions of several parties within the community, which taken together, can be said to constitute the moral economy of the poor" (1971, 79). The rest of the sixty pages of the essay is essentially dedicated to multiple illustrations of this general statement. The contrast between the brief conceptual moment and the long empirical development reveals a paradox noted by Charles Tilly (2000, 259): "Given his outspoken opposition to Theory, it comes as a shock to recognize what a great theorist was Edward P. Thompson. He had a talent for redefining a problem with a striking phrase." Let us consider how he redefines the problem of the food riots by introducing the concept of moral economy.

According to Thompson, the common description of peasants' disorders by historians suggests "a spasmodic view of popular history," which denies those involved their status as "historical agents" and regards their actions as "compulsive rather than self-conscious" (1971, 76). It is even more true when these disturbances correspond to so-called food riots, caused by sudden rises of grain prices and easily assimilated to "rebellions of the belly," that is, physiological responses to the stimulus of hunger (1971, 77). To this representation, the British historian opposes a more political perspective, which he claims to be simply more historically relevant. Riots are not instinctive reactions to material conditions, but "crowd actions" that find their source in "some legitimizing notion," which is, for the men and women who participated in them, "the belief that they were defending traditional rights or customs," a belief endorsed by a "wide consensus of the community" (1971,

78). Rather than values, which Thompson deliberately refuses to include in his definition, this common ground thus comprises "social norms and obligations." In other words, the moral economy of the peasant, as he conceives it, is an economy based on mores rather than morality and resting on a form of implicit social contract. Its articulation within the market economy functions as long as the older paternalist model works, guaranteeing local protection for the poor when they face hard times due to soaring prices and scarce resources. Riots occur when this relation disintegrates, as was increasingly the case in the eighteenth century. In this paradigm, which strikingly resembles, although this author is never mentioned, Karl Polanyi's 1944 theory of the "great transformation," with the opposition between the "embedded economy" of traditional societies and the "disembedded economy" of market societies (Polanyi 2001/1944), the tension resides between a traditional moral economy and a modern political economy.

Logically, Thompson's theoretical model has been influential among historians who study social movements and popular rebellions, such as John Bohstedt (1983), but it has also been appropriated by anthropologists working on contemporary peasantry and peasant revolts in the Third World in the wake of Eric Wolf (1969) and, following William James Booth (1993), by political scientists examining the tensions between the traditional farmer economy and the growing market economy in rural areas of the United States. In the latter two cases, however, Thompson's influence was not direct, and Marc Edelman (2012) goes so far as to speak of the "neglect" of this pioneering work by his colleagues from other disciplinary fields. Actually, one author was instrumental in translating the concept from history to social anthropology and political science: James Scott. Much of the importation of the concept of moral economy in these two disciplines is indeed due to the work of this scholar who served as intellectual broker. Thus, *The Moral Economy of the Peasant* (1976) has become a major reference for those studying not so much food riots and popular protests as the moral values embedded in traditional agrarian economy. Conspicuously, in his monograph, Scott barely discusses Thompson, whose name appears incidentally in three footnotes and is absent from the index. The reason for this surprising treatment, especially considering the title of the book, is probably to be found in the use Scott makes of the concept: in fact, he borrows the phrase more than the original concept. He is more interested in the "subsistence ethic" (Scott 1976, 13) in the rural world of Southeast Asia than in the moral economy of the peasant in a strict sense and contrary to his predecessor emphasizes the values that underlie it. Besides, he is already more focused on what will become in later works what he calls the "weapons of the weak" (Scott 1987, xvi), in other words the everyday adaptation and resistance to domination and exploitation, than in the occasional insurrections, to which he only dedicates one chapter.

Most authors who, following Thompson, have used the concept of moral economy in its "economic" sense have struggled to extend it beyond and sometimes distort its initial meaning. For instance, Thomas Clay Arnold (2001, 85) in his study of water politics in the arid American West asserts: "The traditional conception of moral economy in political science (1) rests too heavily on the distinction between nonmarket and market-based societies and (2) reduces to the unduly narrow claim that economic incorporation of a nonmarket people is the basis for the moral indignation that leads to resistance and rebellion." He proposes instead to reconceptualize moral economies in terms of social goods, so as to account for various historical or contemporary situations of moral indignation, including within market-structured contexts.

Central to these various attempts to criticize and redefine the concept of moral economy are four main elements that are present in Thompson's original work: first, "economy" refers to the production, distribution, and utilization of goods and services; second, "moral" connotes the role of traditional norms, obligations, and expectations in the unfolding of action; third, tensions or conflicts between groups always arise, revealing forms of domination; fourth, moral economies exclusively concern those who are on the weak side of power relations and at the bottom of the inequality scale, whether peasants, workers, or poor communities. Historians of science take a completely opposite stance.

LORRAINE DASTON AND
THE MORAL ECONOMY OF SCIENCE

Indeed, if Thompson's and Scott's philosophical background as well as that of many promoters of the moral economy model in history, anthropology, and to a lesser degree political science was to be found in Karl Marx, Lorraine Daston (1995) gets her inspiration in the intellectual world of Gaston Bachelard who, in *La Formation de l'esprit scientifique* (2002/1938), pleads for a psychoanalysis of the scientific unconscious that focuses on the sentiments more or less related to the libido. It is in this line that Daston proposes to analyse the moral economy of science, which she defines in the following way: "What I mean by a moral economy is a web of affect-saturated values that stand and function in well-defined relationship to one another. In this usage, 'moral' carries its full complement of eighteenth- and nineteenth-century resonances: it refers at once to the psychological and the normative" (1995, 4). In other words, values and affects are intimately linked: "To imbue objects or actions with emotion is almost always thereby to valorize them, and vice versa." Whereas moral philosophers in the past and cognitive psychologists today engage in endless discussions of whether reason or sentiment comes first, Daston considers them to be intricately and irreducibly associated. Both are decisive for the production of science. And she insists that the psychology she is after is not concerned with individuals but rather with collectives: "This is a psychology at the level of whole cultures, or at least subcultures, one that takes root within and is shaped by quite particular historical circumstances" (1995, 5). Moral economies of science describe the scientists' mental and emotional states of time and place, the values they believe in, and the affects that move them.

As was the case for the historian of the English working class when he introduced the concept, Daston's intention in proposing to study science from the perspective of its moral economy is to oppose previous theoretical models. Two main types of interpretation have been provided to account for how values enter the world of scientists: One insists on their internality, the other on their externality. In Robert Merton's classic essay (1942), the "ethos of science" is governed by internal norms of universalism, communism, disinterestedness, and organized scepticism, which form the "superego" of the scientist. By contrast, according to critical approaches, scientific activity is determined by external factors, whether ideology, as examined by G. E. R. Lloyd's study (1983) of life sciences in ancient Greece, or broader social expectations, as explored by Norton Wise (1995) in his work on the values of precision in the age of steam and telegraphy. To the former idealist view, Daston (1995, 6–7) opposes the historical and cultural character of values as well as their inscription in the very act of knowing, and with the latter constructivist perspective, she contrasts the singularity and specificity of scientific values independently of the scientists' interactions with society at large. More specifically, she analyses how quantification, empiricism, and objectivity came to define the scientific mentality in seventeenth- and eighteenth-century Europe. In a later book published with Peter Galison (2007, 363), she pushes the theory further, this time into Aristotelian ethics, speaking of "epistemic virtues" that contribute to the making of a "scientific self." A significant shift is thus perceptible from moral economies as a set of values and affects within science to ethical subjectivities as the result of a process of self-transformation or, in other words, from an almost Durkheimian perspective to an overtly Foucauldian interpretation.

The relatively broad definition provided by Daston invited historians of science and medical anthropologists to adopt and apply it to their domain of research rather than reformulating or contesting it. Most of the time, they did so in a relatively loose way, often emphasizing the values at the expense of the affects, whether to describe the emergence of collaborations between drug companies and medical researchers (Rasmussen 2004) or to explore the current ethical procedures in animal engineering (Harvey and Salter 2012).

A potential risk here is to produce a form of culturalist analysis. If a moral economy simply corresponds to "the unwritten expectations and traditions that regulate and structure a community," as Patrick McCray (2000) proposes in his inquiry into the changes brought about by large telescopes in astronomy, or, even more explicitly, to a "system of values that underlies the exchange of scientific knowledge," as Bruno Strasser (2011, 63) writes in his study of the evolution of life sciences with the appearance of DNA sequence databases, then it is not so different from what one usually names "culture." Interestingly, such works conducted on scientific domains that have necessitated in recent years heavy investments for new and costly technologies reintroduce the material dimension of scientific activity as well as its economic and political stakes and pose questions of resource allocation and power control. In this same vein, Janet Atkinson-Grosjean and Cory Fairley (2009, 150 and 167) suggest that the moral economy of science as defined by Daston pertains to a somewhat too pure and homogeneous realm of values and affects. On the one hand, the material conditions "demarcate the bounds of the possible" and consequently favour one moral community with its values and affects over another, especially when scarce resources must be allocated to expensive projects, rendering choices necessary. On the other hand, the contemporary transformations of science imply a "constant questioning of what we know and how we know it" and therefore a multiplicity of possible values and affects mobilized by scientists. According to this pragmatist approach, competing scientific agents, disciplines, and epistemes ultimately produce more fluid and transient moral economies than Daston suggests.

Beyond these variations, however, the introduction of the concept in the social studies of science and medicine involves several common elements: first, "moral" is the defining term of the phrase, introducing a dimension of intellectual work until then overlooked; second, "economy" does not cover the activities usually investigated by economists, but instead a given arrangement of values and affects; third, even when divergent views are present, their interaction resembles more a conversation or sometimes a competition than a confrontation, still less a conflict; fourth, agents seem to inhabit a somewhat pacified world without relations of power or domination. These four features sharply contrast with those derived from the Thompsonian tradition.

A MODEST PROPOSAL FOR REDEFINING THE CONCEPT

Ultimately, do we have to decide between the two meanings of the concept? Are they not, rather than contradictory, merely incommensurable? Indeed, following Carol Greenhouse's observation (2005, 356) that, for phrases that have become keywords in the social sciences, the "question of the emphasis" is crucial, we may have to choose between moral *economy*, as in Thompson's usage, and *moral* economy, as implied in Daston's definition. In other words, do we consider moral economies to be about exchanges of goods and services or about webs of values and affects? The tendency among most social scientists over the past decade or so has been to overlook the profound differences I underlined between the two meanings. For social anthropologists and political scientists, the term serves to call attention to the social norms and obligations and to the moral assumptions and expectations which underlie economic relations within traditional societies or even market contexts. They thereby oppose strictly materialist as well as rational-actor approaches. For historians or anthropologists of science and medicine, the idea is to pay heed to values and affects at work in these domains, which are usually saturated with expertise and technologies. This does not exclude, however, a possible concern for the economic dimension of science and medicine.

One could certainly be satisfied by the relative vagueness of "moral economy," which allows for a wealth of interpretations. After all, as André Lalande (1993, 261) wrote almost a century ago in his *Technical and Critical Vocabulary of Philosophy*, even "the phrase 'political economy' is poorly constructed." Is it then really necessary to have a coherent, if not consensual, definition of moral economy? Recently reappraising the success of the concept, Marc Edelman (2012, 63–64) affirms that "the first job of any historian or social scientist is to indicate the sense in which he or she is employing a particular term, a specification that involves genealogical scrutiny of the category itself," but regrets that, in this specific case, "Thompson's signal contribution to theories of moral economies has of late often been obscured" since the phrase turned into "an overly capacious, catchall" notion that is "simultaneously clever and meaningless." Having already outlined the genealogy of the category in the two previous parts, I now wish to address the two other aspects of Edelman's comment, that is, to clarify its sense for future use while recovering something of its original critical edge.

The strengths of Thompson's theoretical innovation can be analysed on three levels: moral, historical, and political. First, it acknowledges a genuine perspective of the agents, who are not only driven by biological needs or relations of production but also act according to logics deeply embedded in local moralities of norms and obligations. Second, it captures the role of historical forces, whether inscribed in long-term changes or sudden outbursts of protest. Third, by incorporating the questions of power and inequality as well as the dynamics of resistance or emancipation, it entails a political dimension. Yet at the same time it suffers from two major defects. On the one hand, it implies a normative stance, moral economies and their protagonists being regarded as good, while market economies and their agents are viewed negatively: but should social scientists "moralize" their object? On the other hand, it only involves one segment of society, that of the oppressed, dominated, or poor, failing to recognize the possible moral justifications of the other actors: but do capitalists not have values and affects? In fact, both aspects are intimately related since the decision to choose the side of the weak supports – and is reciprocally supported – by the appreciation of the traditional form of exchange based on solidarity rather than interest. Finally, although this should not be seen as a defect but rather as a limitation, it is restricted to the domain of goods and services, in other words to economy in its common sense, when a broader meaning would potentially be more heuristic.

The perspective adopted in Daston's moral economies can be regarded as symmetrical. Its strengths respond to the British historian's weaknesses. First, it avoids the normative pitfall: it neutrally reflects the values and affects at work in the realm of science. Second, it does not presume the a priori exclusion of certain social groups: scientists cannot be described as a dominated group. Third, it does not limit its social scope to economy in a strict sense: it can be applied to any domains of human activity. However, it loses some of the critical edge of the Marxist concept on two fronts: historical and political. On the one hand, although it is historically situated, it emphasizes stability more than change: the moral economy of seventeenth- and eighteenth-century scientists appears somewhat enduring. On the other hand, although a politics of science is at stake, it relies on the production of knowledge: power relations, interests, and conflicts are notably absent.

As opposed as these concepts may seem, I suggest that it is possible and heuristic to draw from their merits. Paraphrasing Jean-Baptiste Say's classical definition of political economy (1832), I therefore propose that a moral economy corresponds to the production, distribution, appropriation, and use of values and affects in society (Fassin 2009). According to this definition, values and affects are produced, distributed, appropriated, and used just as goods and services are. They are more than the timeless result of the mind's work that moral philosophy and the cognitive sciences explore: they also have a social life inscribed in an historical temporality. Their emergence and circulation in the public sphere as well as their transformation and eventual disappearance are linked with and shaped by the often conflicting concerns, sensibilities, and representations of a given moment: they are thus embedded in the political realm. Whereas the emphasis on values and affects borrows from Daston's definition, the importance given to the production, distribution, appropriation and use of them follows Thompson's approach. In other words, the social significance of the moral realm is acknowledged as well as its dynamic nature. Moral economies characterize a time and place.

But moral economies of what – or whom? For Thompson, a moral economy refers to a social group: peasants, workers, or the poor. For Daston, it describes a social field: science and, by extension, biomedicine. The risk, in both cases, is to view moral economies as subcultures or even cultures. The moral economy of the peasant refers to a traditional material subculture. The moral economy of science relates to a modern intellectual culture. But do we need this concept then, if it is only a modified version of culture? And by attributing this culture to a group or a field, does it not essentialize the qualities of the group or the field? The risk of both Thompson's and Daston's readings is a subtle form of culturalism. In the definition I propose, moral economies instead crystallize around social issues, that is, social facts which are often construed as social problems: crime, violence, addiction, justice, welfare, taxation, for instance. This is a crucial difference with previous significations. By associating moral economies with social issues, we avoid the culturalist bias and focus instead on historical dynamics. Just as social issues are constructed, moral economies are produced. They result from interactions and competitions between values and affects as well as between those who defend or experience them. They are temporary configurations, which are modified by the course of events and the action of agents, but also by more profound evolutions in society, both symbolic and material. Considered together, these moral economies provide a sense of the broader moral climate that typifies a given time and given place, reflecting how moral sentiments are legitimized and expressed publicly, revealing the moral foundations of social life regarding inequality and solidarity, deviance and policing, and so on. Rather than isolating values and affects in a sort of cultural bubble, the study of moral economies establishes a connection between morality, history, and politics.

Towards the end of his life, Michel Foucault stated in an interview that "the notion which serves as a common thread for all the studies" he had conducted since his *History of Madness* was that of "problematization," as he realized in retrospect: "Problematization does not mean representation of a preexisting object or creation through discourse of a non-existing object. It consists in the discursive or non-discursive practices that make something enter into the game of true and false and constitute it as an object of thought" (Foucault 2001, 1488). The example he proposes is that of "the transformations of the relationship between delinquency and punishment via penal practices and penitentiary institutions at the end of the eighteenth and the beginning of the nineteenth century," which are the subject-matter of *Discipline and Punish*. Moral economies pertain to this sort of problematization.

More precisely, they correspond to the values and affects underlying the way in which society "problematizes" such issues in a given time. From a genealogical perspective, the response to crime can thus be analysed in terms of a shift from a moral economy of the debt to a moral economy of suffering (Fassin 2018). In ancient as well as pre-colonial societies, the social treatment of violations of the law, such as thefts or murders, was a compensation of the loss, which involved the family or the clan. This tradition is still documented in the early Middle Ages in various European countries as wergild. Under the influence of the church, the collective debt was replaced by an individual fault interpreted as a sin to be redressed via the infliction of pain. The secularization of the justice system by the state, which was never complete, transformed the fault into a liability but maintained the imposition of an affliction, the most common form of which is imprisonment. From a historical perspective, changes in the moral economy of punishment can be visible within a shorter temporal scale. This is particularly remarkable in the United States and Great Britain in the past half-century (Garland 2001). Whereas until the 1970s, the so-called penal welfare state was based on moral reform and social re-entry, the punitive turn was marked in these countries by "tough on crime" policies leading to an unprecedented phenomenon of "mass incarceration," which is often considered to be the contemporary structural equivalent of chattel slavery and Jim Crow laws. The shift from repair to punishment or from rehabilitation to retribution, in these two examples, relies on a modification of the values underlying social responses to transgressions, and of the affects related to their assessment. It is a change in moral economies.

The concept of moral economy allows for the comprehension of the evaluative and emotional dimensions of social issues and of the political response they elicit. This comprehension is often hindered by the fact that the values and emotions in question are taken for granted and therefore invisible to analysis. Thinking in terms of moral economy exposes them to the light.

CONCLUSION

The concept of moral economy stems from two intellectual lineages. For E. P. Thompson, it meant the recognition of a traditional set of norms and obligations among the poor and the dominated, against purely materialist readings. For Lorraine Daston, it implied the acknowledgement of a particular network of values and affects that defined the work of science, against approaches emphasizing idealized principles or sociological determinations. The former was interested in economy and the latter in morality. Their concept referred to a social group in the first case and to a human activity in the second case. Both have given rise to an abundant literature on the "moral economy of" with little concern for the disparity and even incommensurability of the two paradigms.

This chapter is an attempt both at conceptual clarification and at theoretical reopening. Whereas both Thompson and Daston insisted on the stability of moral economies – whether that of traditional peasants or that of modern science – I see them as historically grounded, politically related, and therefore permanently changing, sometimes in dramatic ways. Indeed, the definition I propose accounts for the way in which values and affects related to social issues are produced, circulate, are appropriated, and decline. The heuristic potential of the concept is that it captures the evaluative and emotional traits of the public construction of social problems, revealing or highlighting the moral norms and sentiments as well as moral tensions and contradictions driving ideological discourses, political decisions, and social mobilizations. Accounting for sympathy and resentment, compassion and mistrust, admiration and contempt, indifference and concern, sense of fairness or impulse of vengeance is crucial in apprehending the way in which social issues are addressed and debated, and which response and solution they receive.

In a recent review essay titled "Moral Economy as Critique," Andrew Sayer affirms that "any critique presupposes critical standpoints, from which it can be argued that certain phenomena may be problematic in some respect" (2007, 261). The concept of moral economy definitely has such a critical edge. It highlights aspects of social life which we tend to consider uncritically both because they are deeply grounded in our values and because they intensely mobilize our affects. For the social sciences, incorporating these values and affects into the analysis, situating them within their historical context, and discussing their political dimension makes the concept of moral economy a critical instrument to comprehend profound social change often rendered imperceptible, precisely because they are morally invested.

POST-SCRIPTUM

This chapter is an attempt to clarify the terms of a discussion I had with Axel during one of the sessions of the seminar that we organized at the Institute for Advanced Study during the academic year 2018–2019. The session was on moral economy, a notion which I thought should be re-conceptualized so as to liberate it from both the modern definition of economy and the normative approach to morality. While I am not certain to convince him with the argument developed here, I am happy to be offered an opportunity to continue our conversation. Working with Axel for nine months on the theme we had chosen, crisis and critique, and trying to confront diverse intellectual traditions so as to make a collective project emerge, has been a rewarding experience and, to quote Humphrey Bogart's last sentence in *Casablanca*, "the beginning of a beautiful friendship."

BIBLIOGRAPHY

Arnold, David. 2000. "Food Riots Revisited: Popular Protest and Moral Economy in Nineteenth-Century India," in *Moral Economy and Popular Protest: Crowds, Conflict and Authority*, Adrian Randall and Andrew Charlesworth, eds. London: Macmillan, pp. 123–146.

Arnold, Thomas Clay. 2001. "Rethinking Moral Economy." *American Political Science Review*, 95 (1): 85–95.

Atkinson-Grosjean, Janet and Fairley Cory. 2009. "Moral Economies in Science: From Ideal to Pragmatic." *Minerva*, 47 (2): 147–170.

Austen, Ralph. 1993. "The Moral Economy of Witchcraft. An Essay in Comparative History," in *Modernity and its Malcontents*, Jean Comaroff and John Comaroff, eds. Chicago: The University of Chicago Press, pp. 89–110.

Bachelard, Gaston. 2002. *The Formation of the Scientific Mind*. Manchester: Clinamen (1st edition 1938).

Bohstedt, John. 1983. *Riots and Community Politics in England and Wales, 1790–1810*. Cambridge, MA: Harvard University Press.

Boltanski, Luc. 1999. *Distant Suffering. Morality, Media and Politics*. Cambridge: Cambridge University Press.

Booth, William James. 1993. *Households. On the Moral Architecture of the Economy*. Ithaca, NY: Cornell University Press.

Bourdieu, Pierre. 1980. "Le capital social. Notes provisoires." *Actes de la Recherche en Sciences Sociales*, 31: 2–3.

Cheng, Elyssa. 2010. "Moral Economy and the Politics of Food Riots in *Coriolanus*." *Concentric: Literary and Cultural Studies*, 36 (2): 17–31.

Coleman, James. 1988. "Social Capital in the Creation of Human Capital." *American Journal of Sociology*, 94: S95–S120.

Daston, Lorraine. 1995. "The Moral Economy of Science." *Osiris*, 10: 3–24.

Daston, Lorraine and Peter Galison. 2007. *Objectivity*. New York: Zone Books.

Edelman, Marc. 2012. "E.P. Thompson and Moral Economies," in *A Companion to Moral Anthropology*, Didier Fassin, ed. Malden, MA: Wiley-Blackwell, pp. 49–66.

Fassin, Didier. 2003. "Le capital social, de la sociologie à l'épidémiologie. Analyse critique d'une migration transdisciplinaire." *Revue Française d'Épidémiologie et de Santé Publique*, 51: 403–413.

Fassin, Didier. 2009. "Les économies morales revisitées." *Annales. Histoire, Sciences Sociales*, 64 (6): 1237–1266.

Fassin, Didier. 2011. *Humanitarian Reason. A Moral History of the Present*. Berkeley: University of California Press.

Fassin, Didier. 2012. *A Companion to Moral Anthropology*. Malden, MA: Wiley-Blackwell.

Fassin, Didier. 2018. *The Will to Punish*. Oxford: Oxford University Press.

Fassin, Didier and Jean-Sébastien Eideliman, eds. 2012. *Économies morales contemporaines*. Paris: La Découverte.

Foucault, Michel. 2001. *Dits et écrits, 1976–1988*, Volume 2. Paris: Gallimard.

Garland, David. 2001. *The Culture of Control. Crime and Social Order in Contemporary Society.* Chicago: The University of Chicago Press.
Greenhouse, Carol. 2005. "Hegemony and Hidden Transcripts: The Discursive Arts of Neoliberal Legitimation." *American Anthropologist*, 107 (3): 356–368.
Griffith, David. 2009. "The Moral Economy of Tobacco." *American Anthropologist*, 111 (4): 432–442.
Hacking, Ian. 1999. *The Social Construction of What.* Cambridge, MA: Harvard University Press.
Harvey, Alison and Brian Salter. 2012. "Governing the Moral Economy: Animal Engineering, Ethics and the Liberal Government of Science." *Social Science and Medicine*, 75 (1): 193–199.
Hitlin, Steven and Stephen Vaisey. 2010. *Handbook of the Sociology of Morality.* New York: Springer.
Howell, Signe, ed. 1997. *The Ethnography of Moralities.* London: Routledge.
Kohler, Robert. 1999. "Moral Economy, Material Culture, and Community in *Drosophila* Genetics," in *The Science Studies Reader*, Mario Biagiolo, ed. New York: Routledge, pp. 243–257.
Kuah, Khun Eng. 1999. "The Changing Moral Economy of Ancestor Worship in a Chinese Emigrant District." *Culture, Medicine and Psychiatry*, 23: 99–132.
Lalande André. 1993. *Vocabulaire technique et critique de la philosophie*, 2 vol. Paris: Presses universitaires de France (1st edition 1926).
Lloyd, G.E.R. 1983. *Science, Folklore and Ideology.* Cambridge: Cambridge University Press.
Lock, Margaret. 2001. "The Tempering of Medical Anthropology. Troubling Natural Categories." *Medical Anthropology Quarterly*, 15 (4): 478–492.
Lonsdale, John. 1992. "The Moral Economy of the Mau Mau. The Problem," in *Unhappy Valley. Conflict in Kenya and Africa*, Bruce Berman and John Lonsdale, eds. London: James Currey, pp. 265–314.
McCray, Patrick. 2000. "Large Telescopes and the Moral Economy of Recent Astronomy." *Social Studies of Science*, 30 (5): 685–711.
Merton, Robert. 1942. "Science and Technology in a Democratic Order." *Journal of Legal and Political Sociology*, 1: 115–126.
Olivier de Sardan, Jean-Pierre. 1999. "A Moral Economy of Corruption in Africa?" *The Journal of Modern African Studies*, 37 (1): 25–52.
Orlove, Benjamin. 1997. "Meat and Strength. The Moral Economy of a Chilean Food Riot." *Cultural Anthropology*, 12 (2): 234–268.
Parker, Barbara. 1988. "Moral Economy, Political Economy, and the Culture of Entrepreneurship in Highland Nepal." *Ethnology*, 27 (2): 181–194.
Polanyi, Karl. 2001. *The Great Transformation. The Political and Economic Origins of Our Time.* Boston: Beacon Press (1st edition 1944).
Posusney, Marsha Pripstein. 1993. "Irrational Workers. The Moral Economy of Labor Protest in Egypt." *World Politics*, 46 (1): 83–120.
Putnam, Robert, et. al. 1993. *Making Democracy Work. Civic Traditions in Modern Italy.* Princeton: Princeton University Press.

Quintero, Gilbert. 2002. "Nostalgia and Degeneration. The Moral Economy of Drinking in Navajo Society." *Medical Anthropology Quarterly*, 16 (1): 3–21.

Rasmussen, Nicolas. 2004. "The Moral Economy of the Drug Company-Medical Scientist Collaboration in Interwar America." *Social Studies of Science*, 34 (2): 161–185.

Salter, Brian and Charlotte Salter. 2007. "Bioethics and the Global Moral Economy. The Cultural Politics of Human Embryonic Stem Cell Science." *Science, Technology and Human Values*, 32 (5): 554–581.

Saxer, Martin. 2012. "The Moral Economy of Cultural Identity. Tibet, Cultural Survival, and the Safeguarding of Cultural Heritage." *Civilisations*, 61 (1): 65–81.

Say, Jean-Baptiste. 1832. *A Treatise on Political Economy*, Philadelphia: Lippincott, Grambo & Co. http://www.econlib.org/library/Say/sayT0.html#Introduction (1st edition 1803).

Sayer, Andrew. 2007. "Moral Economy as Critique." *New Political Economy*, 12 (2): 261–270.

Scott, James. 1976. *The Moral Economy of the Peasant. Rebellion and Subsistence in Southeast Asia*. New Haven: Yale University Press.

Scott, James. 1987. *The Weapons of the Weak. Everyday Forms of Peasant Resistance*. New Haven: Yale University Press.

Sinnott-Armstrong, Walter, ed. 2008. *Moral Psychology*, 3 vol. Cambridge, MA: MIT Press.

Strasser, Bruno. 2011. "The Experimenter's Museum: GenBank, Natural History, and the Moral Economies of BioMedicine." *Isis*, 102 (1): 60–96.

Thompson, E.P. 1968. *The Making of the English Working Class*. London: Penguin Books (1st edition 1963).

Thompson, E.P. 1971. "The Moral Economy of the English Crowd in the Eighteenth Century." *Past and Present*, 50: 76–136.

Thompson, E.P. 1991. "The Moral Economy Reviewed," in *Customs in Common*. London: The Merlin Press, pp. 259–351.

Tilly, Charles. 2000. "Review: Moral Economy and Popular Protest. Crowds, Conflict, and Authority." *Journal of Interdisciplinary History*, 31 (2): 259–260.

Tresch, John. 2007. "The Daguerreotype's First Frame: François Arago's Moral Economy of Instruments." *Studies in History and Philosophy of Science*, 38: 445–476.

Wise, Norton, ed. 1995. *The Values of Precision*. Princeton: Princeton University Press.

Wolf, Eric. 1969. *Peasant Wars of the Twentieth Century*. New York: Harper and Row.

Young, Allan. 1995. *The Harmony of Illusion. Inventing Post-Traumatic Stress Disorder*. Princeton: Princeton University Press.

Chapter 6

Radical Civility

Social Struggles and the Domestication of Dissent[1]

Robin Celikates

"Civility" has always been an ideological weapon, a stick with which the moral majority beats unruly subjects into conformity, attempts to control opposition by dividing it into good and bad forms of protest, and justifies the repression and silencing of dissent especially by minority groups. Civility discourse thus seems to be an integral part of those "strategies for the maintenance of the cultural hegemony of the socially dominant class" that Axel Honneth has brought to the attention of critical theorists in one of his brilliant early essays (first published in 1981). These strategies operate "by latently narrowing the possibilities of articulating experiences of injustice," thereby "hinder[ing] the manifestation of feelings of social injustice at such an early point that the consensus character of societal dominance is not threatened" (Honneth 2007, 87–88).

Current discussions about the ongoing "incivility crisis" in the time of Trump seem to confirm this claim, as they are triggered not by Trump's cruel and in many senses uncivil policies but by what seem to be rather measured acts of protest against them, such as White House press secretary Sarah Sanders being denied service at a Virginia restaurant, a female cyclist giving Trump the middle finger, or congressional newcomer Rashida Tlaib pledging to "impeach this motherfucker."[2] The sense that civility is in crisis is, of course, not new, and accusations of incivility have usually targeted more vulnerable groups than restaurant owners and members of congress, such as religious and racial minorities, feminists, LGBTQI people, and other historically disadvantaged and marginalized groups engaged in more challenging acts of political contestation.

Drawing the line between the civil and the uncivil is, therefore, never a purely theoretical or conceptual exercise but has to be seen against the background of the essentially power-ridden and political "boundary work" and "boundary struggles" taking place in society at large. How these struggles unfold in concrete cases has eminently practical implications for how dissent and protest are normatively assessed, policed, embraced, co-opted, or repressed – even for whether protest is recognized as protest and thus as political in the first place or whether it is framed as a disturbance of public order, a riot, a security problem to be dealt with by the police rather than politically (see Braunstein 2018; Balibar 2007). As Honneth notes, hegemonic normative frames of interpretation serve to push existing forms of oppositional consciousness as well as social struggles "below the threshold of publically recognized normative conflict" (Honneth 2007, 94). This more insidious and less obvious modus operandi of power places the critical theorist under a special responsibility to question these frames rather than uncritically accept and reinforce them, and to search for practices of critique and contestation also in those social arenas in which a publicly legible social movement has not yet formed, precisely because those struggles might have neither the "right" subjects nor the "right" form to be seen as civil.

The fact that the semantics of civility are so vague and adaptable and can thus be easily enlisted in and weaponized by politically motivated manoeuvres of silencing is also underlined by the astonishing variety of behaviours or attitudes that are taken to constitute its opposite. These run from physical violence via disruptiveness (e.g. blocking an entrance to a building) and rudeness (e.g. "vulgar" language or gestures) to "excessive emotionality" (e.g. angrily shouting slogans). From a naïve point of view, it might appear as if civility and incivility concern the form rather than the content of political claim-making, such that radical or revolutionary claims advanced by marginalized groups could in principle be made in a civil way – and, indeed, this is a suggestion liberals often make to show their sympathy with radical causes while objecting to the form in which they are pursued (lecturing oppressed minorities on how to best struggle against oppression has a long history both in practice and in theory, and in the latter case easily crosses otherwise rigid boundaries between paradigms such as liberalism, Marxism, and feminism). However, attention to how the boundary is drawn in practice reveals that form and content cannot be separated from each other and that, at least in most cases, precisely those claims that fundamentally challenge the status quo are seen as uncivil whereas those that do not threaten it are tolerated or even celebrated as exemplars of civility, both in line with hegemonic and very often class-, race-, and gender-specific social norms. It is precisely this civility-based policing of dissent that led Martin Luther King, Jr. to famously draw "the regrettable conclusion that the Negro's great stumbling block in his stride toward freedom is not the White Citizen's Counciler or the Ku Klux Klanner, but the white moderate, who is more devoted to 'order' than to justice; who prefers a negative peace which is the absence of tension to a positive peace which is the presence of justice; who constantly says: 'I agree with you in the goal you seek, but I cannot agree with your methods of direct action'" (King 2015, 135).

As the history of dissent powerfully underlines, a similar disciplinary dynamic targets the subjects of claim-making. As Linda Zerilli emphasizes in an article with the programmatic title "Against Civility," "throughout American history, disenfranchised minorities such as women and African Americans have been regularly accused of incivility just by virtue of daring to show up in public and press their rights claims" (Zerilli 2014, 112). Invocations of civility thus serve as "calls to order" (Bourdieu) disciplining subjects who behave "out of line," or who are "out of place." Such calls to order also animate critiques of insurrectionary violence that are all too often more than simply one-sided and opportunistic. As Ta-Nehisi Coates (2015) put it in the context of the public reaction to the Baltimore "riots": "When nonviolence is preached by the representatives of the state, while the state doles out heaps of violence to its citizens, it reveals itself to be a con." Correspondingly, movements or individuals that manage to position themselves on the side of the majority population and its hegemonic moral consciousness can engage in forms of action that are unambiguously violent – as long as their violence is targeted at members of minority groups – without therefore being seen as uncivil or having to face repressive consequences. The widespread impunity and indifference in the face of racist state and police violence is a powerful and socially consequential example of the differential distribution of markers of civility and incivility, as is widespread public indifference to the suffering and death of migrants that can be directly attributed to the functioning of the existing border regime.

Against this background, it is understandable that some commentators reject civility discourse in principle as it "enforces a false equation between incivility and violence that works to mask everyday violence as a civic norm" and uses depoliticizing calls for civility as ways to "seek to evade [...] calls for change" (Nyong'o/Tompkins 2018). In the context of these debates, civil disobedience – in virtue of the "civil" it carries in its name – occupies an ambivalent position. To many on the right who see themselves as champions of civility this contestatory practice seems too uncivil and radical, an attempt to procure political power under the mantel of moral principles, a one-sided renunciation of the duty to obey the law and to uphold order that is not to be tolerated.[3] They see it as leading onto a slippery slope descending into violence, vigilantism, and terrorism. Citizens in more or less functioning democracies, they say, must limit themselves to the legally sanctioned possibilities available to them for expressing dissenting views and influencing the political process in line with the "duty of civility" they have as bona fide citizens. From this point of view, "civil" disobedience is little more than political blackmail – and ipso facto uncivil. On the other extreme, many of those on the radical left who seek to debunk the ideology of civility consider civil disobedience too civil, as they see it as nothing more than the impotent expression of a reformist yearning for cosmetic changes within a given system, as a socially permissible and harmless protest of well-intentioned but civility-obsessed citizens, which remains purely symbolic, leaves state violence unquestioned and ultimately only contributes to the stabilization of the status quo (Gelderloos 2007, 2013).

Against both of these widespread views it can be argued that the equivocal and potentially ideological meaning of the "civil" in civil disobedience, and background assumptions about what "civility" is and which limits it imposes on legitimate political protest, are at least partly to blame for the confusion that depoliticizes and thereby distorts how civil disobedience is understood both in public and philosophical discussions. However, insofar as it seems virtually impossible to escape the ideological and disciplining logic of civility discourse that narrows down the field of acceptable forms of contestation to the extent that existing political and social arrangements are essentially shielded from effective questioning, this again raises the problem of whether it is not advisable to just give up the notion of "civility" and the "civil" in civil disobedience. Although there are both strategic and theoretical reasons for favouring this response, I suggest another route is preferable, again for both strategic and theoretical reasons.

Reclaiming the notion of the "civil" and recovering its radical potential from the history and present of political struggle is preferable for at least three reasons that suggest why both the practice and the label of civil disobedience should be at the centre of a critical theory of political and social struggle. First, although political philosophers have often gestured at the legitimacy of other, more militant forms of protest under non-ideal (unjust, undemocratic, etc.) circumstances, there is actually only a very small (albeit slowly growing) body of conceptual and normative work on resistance and other forms of contestation, in contrast with a rich philosophical debate on civil disobedience involving such diverse philosophical figures as Hannah Arendt, John Rawls, Jürgen Habermas, and Etienne Balibar. For pragmatic reasons it seems more fruitful to build on this discussion, and to push it further, rather than to sidestep it.

Secondly, and more importantly, the practice of civil disobedience, from Thoreau, Gandhi, and the Civil Rights movement via the "new social movements" of the 1970s and 1980s to the more recent wave of protest movements in the wake of the "Arab Spring" and Occupy,[4] is much more complex and much more radical than narrow conceptions of the "civil," and of civil disobedience, suggest: Recovering the radical potential of the practice of disobedience can thus serve to develop a more radical understanding of the "civil" that is both more theoretically satisfying and more adequate to the practice philosophical discussions about civil disobedience presumably try to capture. In different variations, a similar consideration can also be found in the work of even the most ardent critics of civility when they refer to the possibility of and the need for developing subaltern and counter-hegemonic forms of "counter-civility" (Nyong'o/Tompkins 2018). Practices of "counter-civility" might provide vantage points for denaturalizing, problematizing, and transforming or dislodging hegemonic forms of civility.

Thirdly, the label "civil disobedience" serves as a political cachet carrying a normative surplus that gives rise to symbolic struggles, first and foremost about the label itself, that also have tangible political and legal consequences. It matters whether protest is successfully framed as "civil disobedience" or not, not just in terms of how the public at large perceives it, but also in terms of who might be mobilized to participate in it, which types of political dynamics it can set in motion, and how the police, prosecutors, and courts approach it. What Homi Bhabha calls "sly civility" has its place in this field of struggle – which often involves agents in settler-colonial or post-colonial contexts – as much as it had its place in the colonial context for which he coined the term (Bhabha 1985). Relatedly, participants in struggles, protests, and movements are not passive bystanders to civility discourse but actively intervene in it and use established notions of both civility and incivility for their own purposes, for example, by trying to catch public attention through the strategic and controlled use of "incivility" or through highlighting state incivility (e.g. in the form of police violence) by contrastive practices of civility. A critical theory of civil disobedience cannot stand apart from these struggles about terminology and framing that are so clearly part of any political struggle, and it seems the wrong move – both theoretically and politically – to give up the label because of its seemingly successful co-optation. As noted, it rather provides an entry point for radical struggles to challenge and destabilize hegemonic forms of moral consciousness and the counter-insurgent conceptions of civility they wield from within.[5]

But how can the "civil" in civil disobedience be understood in a politically radical (and theoretically open-ended) way without falling into the traps of the ideology of civility? The first step consists in problematizing the dominant liberal understanding according to which the civil is primarily conceptualized in terms of reasonable public claim-making by those already recognized as full members of the political community, which also informs influential conceptions of civil disobedience in the work of, for example, Rawls and Habermas. To be sure, Rawls (and contemporary Rawlsians) just as Habermas (and contemporary Habermasians) do not equate the "civil" in civil disobedience with "civility" in the sense of socially contingent, purely conventional norms of courtesy or politeness that primarily serve to delegitimize dissent (although they might, as all norms, also be turned around and used against the powerful – think of Greta Thunberg's "How dare you!" in her speech at the United Nations). Nevertheless, the mainstream understanding of the civil is, both in its presuppositions and its implications, tied to an understanding of civility and of citizenship in terms of reasonable public claim-making that is, ultimately, limiting and domesticating with regard to the actual practices of contestation that claim this label with good reason. In this way, their understanding of the "civil" inherits some of the semantic ballast of the broader discourse on civility. As a result, this conception is drastically under-inclusive as it excludes and invisibilizes a whole range of actually existing forms of civil disobedience that fail to be uncontroversially public, purely symbolic, nonviolent, or enacted by "bona fide" citizens in the required sense.

As I noted, however, it would be the wrong reaction to give up the notion of the "civil" in toto. There is both conceptual and political space for a radical understanding of civil disobedience that does not dispense with the claim to be "civil" (Celikates 2016). The meaning of the "civil," however, is here conceived in contrast to common understandings of the "civil" that echo the bourgeois, the civilized, the well-mannered, the polite, the moderate, or the respectable – that is, markers of civility often attributed to idealized instances of civil disobedience from the past (condensed in mythologized figures such as Gandhi and King) which are then mobilized to discredit and discipline civil disobedience in the present (e.g. Black Lives Matter) (see, for example, Theoharis 2018). Rather, civility is here conceptualized as pertaining to the logic of genuinely political in contrast to military action, rooted in a notion of civil society as a plural space of political self-organization that is neither reducible to interactions between private individuals, nor to the congealing of political relations in state institutions, nor a mythical substantialist vision of the people as a homogeneous actor: civil disobedience is a practice of *political* subjects or agents – citizens, but also those who are governed or subjected but not recognized as citizens – that aims at a reconfiguration of their relations and that can involve a reconfiguration of citizenship and political relations more generally, beyond the confines of the nation-state and those whom we ordinarily consider as citizens. As such, it presupposes some kind of civil bond with the adversary, however strained and contested, and is incompatible with the attempt to destroy or permanently exclude an enemy from the political community (which need not be limited to the nation-state framework). Practices of contestation that aim at excluding individuals or groups on the basis of the – not only anti-democratic but antipolitical and hence "uncivil" – assumption that the political community is grounded in a pre- and extrapolitical culturally, historically, or ethnically specified bond – a bond that is seen as clearly demarcating the community and establishing its boundaries beyond any doubt – therefore do not fall under the label of civil disobedience. This is why, although there may well be conservative, reactionary, and even right-wing civil disobedience, there is no hard-right, fascist, or neo-Nazi civil disobedience despite attempts by such groups to claim the label.[6] In this way, civil disobedience relies on a political acknowledgement of "the open and contestable signification of democracy" and seeks to find ways to "release democracy from containment by any particular form while insisting on its value in connoting political self-rule by the people, whoever the people are" (Brown 2015, 20).

Civility in this sense can be spelt out further in a variety of ways, some of which are more demanding than others, but all of which imply certain forms of self-limitation and self-restraint that are more flexible and less constraining than the liberal emphasis on the nonviolent, purely symbolic, and law-abiding character of civil disobedience suggests. At the minimal end of the spectrum of civility lies the distinction between civil and military forms of interaction; at its maximal end, the idea of prefiguration, that is, the claim that the end has to be present in, or prefigured by, the means (Graeber 2002; also van de Sande 2013; Raekstad 2018). In both cases, those who disobey are seen as managing to resist certain escalations of the friend-enemy logic and to maintain civility in the face of often massive state incivility, but this civility is both a (potentially radical and militant) commitment and an achievement rather than an expression of loyalty or deference to the authority of a state that has often systematically failed them. Accordingly, insofar as the "civil" in civil disobedience is linked to civility, its contrast is not the incivility of confrontational contestation or demands that are deemed too radical and hence unreasonable, but the incivility of organized violence that follows a military logic. And insofar as the "civil" is linked to citizenship, the latter is to be understood not as a formal status assigned by the state, but should be viewed as a practice or in terms of acts of citizenship, that is, the capacity of political agents to act together, as citizens, also outside of and against formal institutions (including those regulating access to citizenship) (Tully 2014; Isin 2008; Ober 2008). Both in its means and in its ends civil disobedience can therefore take much more radical forms than the liberal model allows for. In turn, the proposed democratic understanding suggests that it is not the task of the theorist to clearly delineate the limits of civility as this is itself a matter of dispute in the political contestation in question. In this sense we can speak of "radical civility."

Civility matters for this understanding of civil disobedience because it is the civil bond with one's adversaries that implies certain forms of self-limitation and self-restraint by excluding (quasi-)military action aiming at the destruction of an enemy.[7] The civil bond that this notion of civility invokes and relies on is much more capacious than traditional conceptualizations of the civil bond in terms of the bonds of (formal) citizenship suggest. While being a member of the same political community certainly is one politically powerful (and indeed hegemonic) way of understanding this bond, neither is this the only possible manifestation of this bond nor is such membership reducible to formal citizenship. There are both members of the community who are stuck in the "waiting room" – another disciplinary device propping up hegemonic norms of citizenship – permanently on the way to a citizenship the state might hold out as a promise and at the same time makes increasingly difficult to achieve, and those who are not even in the waiting room but stuck in the darkness of living without any status at all. Furthermore, there are ways to think of the civil bond that go beyond the bounded political community both temporally and spatially. Recent migrant and refugee activism provides plenty of examples that highlight both the temporal and the spatial extension of the civil bond beyond statist imaginaries. Migrants, activists, migrant-activists appeal to a bond that goes beyond the narrowly civil, legally institutionalized, and ideologically dominant bond that exists between citizens of the same polity. The bond their struggles appeal to is civil in a broader and counter-hegemonic sense as it ties the fate of migrants and refugees together with that of the citizens of the wealthier states in ways that are historically deep and politically expansive (especially in the cases in which they are economically and politically entwined, for example, through histories of colonialism and neo-colonialism) (Naples/Mendez 2014; with regard to the "migrant caravan" Viewpoint Magazine 2018; Celikates 2019).

In these struggles, historical contexts and continuities as well as persisting forms of economic and political domination beyond the nation-state are invoked against the amnesia of much of public discourse for which migrants and refugees seem to come from out of nowhere and for reasons that are completely unrelated to one's own political community and its place in the current world order. This public amnesia – a form of motivated ignorance Charles Mills calls global white ignorance (Mills 2015) – is only possible due to ignoring the colonial and imperial histories and present of countries such as the United States, the United Kingdom, Australia, France, the Netherlands, and Germany. Slogans such as "We didn't cross the border, the border crossed us" and "We are here because you were/are there" – which play a prominent role in migrant activism – serve to highlight this historical connection and its political implications, reminding "us" in the West of our own agency and involvement, both past and present, in the production of the conditions under which people are migrating and fleeing – these conditions did not just come into existence ex nihilo, nor are they the outcome of processes to which we have only been passive bystanders. And although the civil bonds that result from these entanglements might be weaker than the links between members of the same institutionalized political community, it is hard to deny that they ground a form of political claim-making that can and should be qualified as civil (Balibar 1996).

In light of these rearticulations of the civil from within social and political struggles of the present, the debate about civility and its ideological discontents provides an exemplary case for how critical theory is bound up with the ways hegemonic normative frames operate. Insofar as critical theory can build on the fact that "groups who experience exclusion or discrimination due to hegemonic interpretations of norms do in fact tend to call these interpretations into question and to rebel against existing social orders," it should take up critiques of civility that show how hegemonic and naturalized interpretations of this norm "lend legitimacy to [...] institutionally entrenched advantages and privileges" members of dominant groups have little interest in questioning (Honneth 2017, 914, 917). At the same time, critical theory can pick up on bottom-up attempts to rearticulate, in a radical and counter-hegemonic key, what civility and the "civil" encompass, which forms of the civil bond they imply, and which practices of citizenship they enable, in an attempt to bring the public face to face with, and thus accept the political force of, "forms of existing social critique not recognized by the political-hegemonical public sphere" (Honneth 2007, 82).

NOTES

1. I have presented longer versions of this chapter at the Institute for Advanced Study in Princeton, the Columbia University Political Theory Workshop, the Fordham Workshop in Social and Political Philosophy, and the Philosophy Department Colloquium at the New School for Social Research, and I thank participants for their helpful feedback. In particular, I am happy that this occasion allows me to thank Axel Honneth, whose work has sparked and shaped my own philosophical interest in social struggles many years ago, when I was still a student, and who has been an inspiring interlocutor ever since, most recently during our common stay at the IAS.

2. See, respectively, https://www.washingtonpost.com/opinions/let-the-trump-team-eat-in-peace/2018/06/24/46882e16-779a-11e8-80be-6d32e182a3bc_story.html?utm_term=.f4bc96b85dba, https://www.politico.com/story/2018/10/10/trump-anger-washington-obscene-gesture-880707, https://www.nytimes.com/2019/01/04/us/politics/tlaib-impeach-trump.html.

3. See, for example, Abe Fortas 1968; while few philosophers hold this position today, it is still popular in legal circles as well as among journalists and politicians.

4. Whether Occupy – and other movements of the "public square" such as those associated with the "Arab Spring" or the Turkish Gezi Park uprising – should be understood in terms of civil disobedience is an interesting question that I will not be able to discuss in this chapter. As will become clear, however, I tend to disagree with the view put forth by Bernard Harcourt in his article "Political Disobedience," which emphasizes the discontinuities but seems to presuppose a narrow liberal understanding of civil disobedience: "Civil disobedience accepted the legitimacy of political institutions, but resisted the moral authority of resulting laws. Political disobedience, by contrast, resists the very way in which we are governed: it resists the structure of partisan politics, the demand for policy reforms, the call for party identification, and the very ideologies that dominated the post-War period. ... Ultimately, what matters to the politically disobedient is the kind of society we live in, not a handful of policy demands" (Harcourt 2012, 33, 55). Arguably, this is also the case for those who subscribe to a more radical understanding of civil disobedience. In addition, it seems useful to make a distinction between movements which use civil disobedience as a core strategy – and are often, but not always, also committed to it ideologically (think of the Civil Rights Movement) – and those, like the more recent ones mentioned above, which employ it as one tactic among many. Even in the latter case, however, where civil disobedience is part of a diversity of tactics, it usually has a special place in that set because of its history and its political position between legal and illegal activism, reform and revolution, violence and nonviolence.

5. At the same time, and in a pluralist spirit, I see this position as in principle compatible with proposals to embrace categories such as "noncivil" or "uncivil" disobedience; see, for example, Mancilla (2013) and Delmas (2018). It is a matter of further debate, however, whether these proposals can escape the twin risk of the close association, in the public's mind, of "non-" or "uncivil" with "unjustifiable (at least in the absence of civil war)," and, more importantly, of subscribing to an overly narrow understanding of civility that excludes not only those activists who want to be excluded from that category (whether they are right to want this is another question) but also movements which often self-describe as civil but engage in protest behaviour that would probably have to be categorized as uncivil on the proposed understanding. A methodological implication of taking this risk seriously is to refuse to take up the task of clearly demarcating the civil from the uncivil as something the philosopher or theorist would be well-equipped to achieve.

6. To give just one example, the German hard-right anti-migrant movement Pegida has called for "civil disobedience" against refugees and asylum seekers.

7. Of course, there are circumstances – for example under colonial conditions or in the face of massive violence by state actors or Nazi groups – that will make such self-restraint very difficult or even impossible and that call for more militant forms of self-defence and resistance. As the example of the African National Congress demonstrates, however, oppressed groups often aim to reconcile armed resistance with some form of self-restraint (and thus civility?) to avoid violence from spiralling out of control. The position is famously set out in Mandela's Rivonia Trial Speech from 1964.

BIBLIOGRAPHY

Balibar, Etienne. 1996. "What We Owe to the Sans-Papiers." http://eipcp.net/transversal/0313/balibar/en.html [last accessed 6 November 2019].
Balibar, Etienne. 2007. "Uprisings in the Banlieues." In: *Constellations*, 14 (2007), 47–71.
Bhabha, Homi K. 1985. "Sly Civility." In: *October*, 34 (1985), 71–80.
Braunstein, Ruth. 2018. "Boundary-work and the Demarcation of Civil from Uncivil Protest in the United States: Control, Legitimacy, and Political Inequality." In: *Theory and Society* 47 (2018), 5, 603–633.
Brown, Wendy. 2015. *Undoing the Demos. Neoliberalism's Stealth Revolution*. Brooklyn: Zone Books.
Celikates, Robin. 2016. "Rethinking Civil Disobedience as a Practice of Contestation – Beyond the Liberal Paradigm." In: *Constellations*, 23 (2016), 1, 37–45.
Celikates, Robin. 2019. "Constituent Power Beyond Exceptionalism: Irregular Migration, Disobedience, and (Re-)Constitution." In: *Journal of International Political Theory*, 15 (2019), 1, 67–81.
Coates, Ta-Nehisi. 2015. "Nonviolence as Compliance." In: *The Atlantic*, April 27, 2015, available at https://www.theatlantic.com/politics/archive/2015/04/nonviolence-as-compliance/391640/ [last accessed 6 November 2019].
Delmas, Candice. 2018. *A Duty to Resist: When Disobedience Should Be Uncivil*. Oxford: Oxford University Press.
Fortas, Abe. 1968. *Concerning Dissent and Civil Disobedience*. New York: New American Library.
Gelderloos, Peter. 2007. *How Nonviolence Protects the State*. Boston: South End Press.
Gelderloos, Peter. 2013. *The Failure of Nonviolence: From the Arab Spring to Occupy*. Seattle: Left Bank Books.
Graeber, David. 2002. "The New Anarchists." In: *New Left Review*, 13 (2002), 61–73.
Harcourt, Bernard. 2012. "Political Disobedience." In: *Critical Inquiry*, 39 (2012), 33–55.
Honneth, Axel. 2007. "Moral Consciousness and Class Domination. Some Problems in the Analysis of Hidden Morality." In: *Disrespect: The Normative Foundations of Critical Theory*. Cambridge: Polity, 80–96.
Honneth, Axel. 2017. "Is There an Emancipatory Interest? An Attempt to Answer Critical Theory's Most Fundamental Question." In: *European Journal of Philosophy* 25 (4) (2017), 908–920.
Isin, Engin. 2008. "Theorizing Acts of Citizenship." In: E. Isin and G. M. Nielsen (eds.), *Acts of Citizenship*. London: Palgrave Macmillan, 15–43.
King, Martin Luther, Jr. 2015. "Letter From Birmingham Jail." In: Cornel West (ed.), *The Radical King*. Boston: Beacon, 127–146.
Mancilla, Alejandra. 2013. "Noncivil Disobedience and the Right of Necessity." In: *Krisis*, 2013/1, 3–16.

Mandela, Nelson. 1964. "I Am Prepared to Die," available at http://law2.umkc.edu/faculty/projects/ftrials/mandela/mandelaspeech.html [last accessed August 10, 2019].

Mills, Charles. 2015. "Global White Ignorance." In: Matthias Gross and Linsey McGoey (eds.), *International Handbook of Ignorance Studies*. London: Routledge, 217–227.

Naples, Nancy A. and Jennifer Bickham Mendez (eds.). 2014. *Border Politics: Social Movements, Collective Identities, and Globalization*. New York: New York University Press.

Nyong'o, Tavia and Kyla Wazana Tompkins. 2018. "Eleven Theses on Civility," https://socialtextjournal.org/eleven-theses-on-civility/ [published July 11, 2018; last accessed August 10, 2019].

Ober, Josiah. 2008. "'The Original Meaning of "Democracy': The Capacity To Do Things, Not Majority Rule." In: *Constellations* 15 (2008), 1, 1–9.

Raekstad, Paul. 2018. "Revolutionary Practice and Prefigurative Politics." In: *Constellations* 25 (2018), 3, 359–372.

Theoharis, Jeanne. 2018. *A More Beautiful and Terrible History: The Uses and Misuses of Civil Rights History*. Boston: Beacon Press.

Tully, James. 2014. "On Global Citizenship." In: David Owen (ed.), *On Global Citizenship: James Tully in Dialogue*. London: Bloomsbury, 3–100.

van de Sande, Mathijs. 2013. "The Prefigurative Politics of Tahrir Square: An Alternative Perspective on the 2011 Revolutions." In: *Res Publica*, 19 (2013), 3, 223–239.

Viewpoint Magazine. 2018. "The Border Crossing Us." https://www.viewpointmag.com/2018/11/07/from-what-shore-does-socialism-arrive/ [last accessed 6 November 2019].

Zerilli, Linda. 2014. "Against Civility: A Feminist Perspective." In: Austin Sarat (ed.), *Civility, Legality and Justice in America*. Cambridge: Cambridge University Press, 107–131.

Section II

RECOGNITION

Chapter 7

Rousseau on the Nature of Social Inequality

Frederick Neuhouser

My aim here is to reconstruct Rousseau's account of the kind of thing social inequality is. His account makes two principal claims: social inequalities are *privileges*, and they are *artificial*, or humanmade. Neither "privilege" nor "artificial" is necessarily a term of critique for Rousseau. In other words, neither of these claims addresses the question of when and why inequalities are unjustified (Neuhouser 2014). Although Rousseau places strict limits on the scope of permissible inequalities, he does not hold that all inequalities are unjust, and – to invoke a concept explained below – he does not believe that only "natural" inequalities are justified. Thus, both of Rousseau's claims – that social inequalities are *privileges* and that they are *artificial* – must be construed such that neither implies the impermissibility of inequalities that possess these characteristics.

Rousseau's account of social inequality is articulated in his *Discourse on the Origin of Inequality* (the Second Discourse) as an answer to the question concerning the "origin" of inequality. His inquiry focuses on whether inequalities have their source in nature – including human nature – with a view to determining whether they are therefore necessary features of human society or whether they have some other, non-natural source that makes them eliminable or alterable by human intervention. As we shall see, he argues for the latter position.

Rousseau's first move in the Second Discourse is to replace talk of inequality in general with terminology that distinguishes two types: "moral" or "political" inequality and "natural" or "physical" inequality. Since natural inequalities lie outside our control and since, as Rousseau believes, they play a negligible role in the most salient inequalities of social life, the Second Discourse concerns itself only with the origin of what Rousseau calls moral inequalities. These differ from natural inequalities in two respects, each of which makes them *social* inequalities. The first concerns their "origin": moral inequalities are not products of nature but depend instead on "convention," which means that they are "established, or at least authorized, by [human] consent" (*DI*, 131/*OC* 3, 131).[1] Moral inequalities are in one sense social, then, because their existence depends on a sort of collective "consent" that "authorizes" them. Second, moral inequalities are social in content because they consist in individuals (or groups) possessing a certain advantage over others. As Rousseau puts it, moral inequalities consist not in "differences in age, health, bodily strength, and qualities of mind or soul" but in "privileges that some enjoy to the prejudice of others, such as being richer, more honored, more powerful than they, or even getting themselves obeyed" (*DI*, 131/*OC* 3, 131).

In explicating these two claims it will be helpful to bear in mind the specific forms of social inequality mentioned in this passage: differences in wealth, honour, (non-physical) power, and the ability to command others and have those commands obeyed. These are the four species of inequality most important to his social critique, and they correspond to the four dimensions of social equality that his vision of a good society will try to promote. In other words, a complete reconstruction of Rousseau's social philosophy must determine the extent to which a good society can tolerate inequalities in *wealth*, *status*, *social power*, and *authority* over others. ("Authority" means not the legitimate right to command others but the actual ability to do so successfully; unjustifiable inequalities in authority constitute *domination*.)

SOCIAL INEQUALITIES AS PRIVILEGES

The BBC once described the former British prime minister David Cameron as follows: "He never made a secret of his privileged background, saying he wanted everyone in Britain to have the kind of advantages in life that he had had" (Wheeler 2016). Rousseau's account of social inequality implies that this statement is both incoherent and (most likely) insincere. The first point is conceptual: it is incoherent to wish that everyone could enjoy the same privileges (advantages) as those oneself enjoys. A privilege is by its nature enjoyed by some but not by all, such that if all had the "privilege" of attending Eton, it would cease to be one. Furthermore, if Rousseau is correct, Cameron's statement is almost certainly insincere. Even if we rephrase the statement to read "I wish everyone could have attended a school as good as mine," it is doubtful that Cameron (or any similarly situated human being) would genuinely wish for such a thing. This is because when genuinely social inequalities are at stake, the benefit of having a certain quality (having attended Eton) decreases when others come to have it too. A good education has benefits even if everyone has one, but when distributed unequally, it confers benefits that would disappear under conditions of equality. Since it is unusual that someone accustomed to such benefits would wish for them to disappear, doubts about the sincerity of Cameron's statement are in order.

What makes such inequalities social is not the mere fact that they consist in *relations* among individuals. This is true of all inequalities, including natural ones: it is impossible for me to be "older" unless my age is situated in relation to the age of someone else. My being older requires that there be others I am older *than*, but this is not a social relation. What makes moral inequalities social in content is their character as privileges, which makes them relational in a more robust sense than natural inequalities, and this in two respects. The first is that the characteristics in terms of which social inequalities are defined are themselves relative, or positional, properties. Health, bodily strength, and wisdom[2] – examples of natural characteristics – are properties individuals possess without regard to whether others possess more or less of the same. The extent of someone's health, physical strength, or wisdom is independent of how healthy, strong, or wise her neighbours might be. Moreover, the (objective) *desirability* of these qualities is non-relative: health, physical strength, and wisdom are desirable independently of whether or to what extent others possess them. Neither point holds, however, for social inequalities. For the *relata* in terms of which these inequalities are defined are positional characteristics that refer to how well others fare along the same dimension. I can possess status, social power, and authority – I consider wealth below – only insofar as others possess amounts of the same that can be compared to mine, which is why Robinson Crusoe can be healthy, strong, and wise but cannot possess status, social power, or authority. Status is always standing compared to the standing of others; social power is always power in relation to another's; and getting one's will obeyed requires another who obeys.

The second respect in which social inequalities are robustly relational is that possessing the characteristics in terms of which those inequalities are defined requires the participation of others. Whereas I can be healthy, strong, and wise all by myself, without being engaged with others, the characteristics that define social inequalities occur within a framework of cooperation or competition in which the persons who possess the relevant advantages and those to whom such persons must relate in order to possess those advantages, actively take part: status requires individuals who bestow a status on others; authority requires that others obey; and social power requires that a plurality of wills be competing for the same things. In all these cases, having one of the characteristics in terms of which inequalities are defined requires engaging with others in a way that having a certain height or age does not. Social inequalities presuppose networks of *interactive agency* in which those subject to such inequalities actively take part.

Yet these two respects in which social inequalities are robustly relational do not fully explain why they are privileges that some enjoy to the disadvantage of others. In order to understand this, we need to note a further consideration: wealth, status, social power, and authority do not track "natural" qualities of those who possess them, by which Rousseau means qualities that are independent of human opinion, especially, opinions about what is desirable or of value. The idea here is that there is a fact, independent of human opinion, regarding the degree to which individuals are healthy, physically strong, and wise, whereas wealth, status, social power, and authority involve opinion-dependent characteristics. This is not to say that there is no objective fact about who in a given society is wealthier or more esteemed than others. The point, rather, is that facts about social inequalities track different kinds of things than facts about natural inequalities. In the latter case, inequalities involve characteristics that humans possess regardless of whether anyone holds an opinion about them; in the former case, there is nothing to be compared – no basis for an inequality to be detected – unless human opinions of some sort enter the picture. This is easiest to see in the case of status, where shared opinions regarding what is valuable are essential to determining one's standing in the social hierarchy, but it is also true of wealth, social power, and authority.

The second consideration that helps us to see why social inequalities are privileges is that the goods tracked by such inequalities are positional in the sense that one person's having them imposes *burdens* or *constraints* on others, even when those goods are equally distributed. Whereas one person's wisdom does not by itself imply burdens or constraints for others; status, social power, and authority always do, even when possessed in equal amounts. This is easiest to see in the case of authority, which a person can have only if someone else obeys. Authority is always authority over someone else who (in some specific respect) lacks authority and is therefore (in that respect) constrained by the will of another. Even if you and I have equal authority, each of our wills constrains the other, though to equal degrees. The same is true of power, as long as we mean by it something more than physical strength. An individual with social power – one who, without issuing a command, is capable of influencing others to carry out her ends or of achieving her ends in a context of competition – is powerful only insofar as her will in some way wins out in relation to others'. And something similar holds of the recognitive relations on which status depends: recognizing another involves accepting a corresponding constraint on the part of the recognizer. Even when we recognize each other as equals, each constrains himself to treat the other in ways appropriate to her recognized status. This implies that when status, social power, and authority are distributed unequally, they become privileges enjoyed by some to the detriment of others.

It might seem that wealth, unlike status, social power, and authority, is not a robustly relational property. Indeed, if wealth is thought of as a relation between humans and things, then there is a sense in which how much I possess is independent of what others have. If wealth is understood in this way, one could say, even of Robinson Crusoe, that he is wealthy (depending on the extent of his ability to use things in order to achieve his ends), and we can understand why he would desire to be so. Wealth in this sense is a non-moral relation between humans and things. Adam Smith articulates such a conception of wealth when he says, of precapitalist societies, "Every man is rich or poor according to the degree in which he can afford to enjoy the necessaries, conveniences, and amusements of human life" (Smith 2000, 33).

This is not, however, the conception of wealth at issue when questions of economic inequality arise. Rather, such questions presuppose a social context in which humans cooperate and where their relations to the things they possess are mediated by moral relations to others. Rousseau's implicit claim is that in such a context wealth is inseparable from relations among persons who bestow on inequalities in wealth the same character that inequalities in status, social power, and authority exhibit, including that of being a privilege. Again, Adam Smith most clearly formulates this conception of wealth. When articulating the "real measure" of wealth "after the division of labor," Smith says that a person "is rich or poor according to the quantity of that labor he can command, or ... afford to purchase" (Smith 2000, 33). On this account, wealth is a robustly relative phenomenon: what it is to have wealth (in commercial society) is to stand in some relation to – as potential "commander" or "purchaser" of – the activity of other humans. Smith seems to have in mind two relations that are constitutive of wealth and that correspond to the distinction Rousseau draws between social power and authority. To possess wealth is to be able to command directly the labour of others (by purchasing and employing their labour power) and to have those commands obeyed, which makes it a form of authority. But to possess wealth is also to be able to command others' labour indirectly by purchasing the products of their labour. In this case no commands are issued, which means there is no relation of obedience, but power ("purchasing power") is exercised nonetheless insofar as one person's wealth determines – indirectly, via market relations – what form others' labour will take. In both cases wealth shares with status, social power, and authority the characteristic of imposing burdens or constraints on others, which implies that inequalities in wealth take the form of privileges for those who have more and disadvantages for those who have less.

Although Rousseau is concerned with all four types of social inequality, economic inequality is the most prominent target of his social critique (*DI*,

161/*OC* 3, 164). Wealth has a special status for him in part because it is intrinsically related to the qualities in terms of which the other three forms of social inequality are defined. Wealth, in its modern form, brings together all the dimensions of sociality highlighted by Rousseau: it *consists in* certain relations of recognition, social power, and authority, even when equally distributed. I have explained how possessing wealth is a form of both social power and authority, but it is also a form of status since ownership is itself a type of recognized standing. For when wealth is a moral phenomenon, rather than merely the physical possession of things, it is a normative relation among persons. Such wealth takes the form of property and consists in a socially recognized right vis-à-vis others to do certain things with the property society recognizes as one's own. For this reason, to own wealth is to be recognized by others as having a certain standing, and being recognized in this way implies socially enforced constraints on the actions of others.

The claim that wealth condenses the three other dimensions of sociality into a single phenomenon is valid only in specific historical conditions, such as those that were coming to prevail in Western Europe as Rousseau wrote the Second Discourse. This issue is complex because the tightness of the connections between wealth and the other dimensions of sociality varies with historical circumstance. The connection between wealth and recognition – that to possess wealth is to enjoy a recognized standing as a bearer of property rights – holds generally, in societies with different forms of economic organization, providing only that wealth takes the form of legally recognized property.

The connection between wealth and social power is less general. The tightness of the relation between wealth and social power that Rousseau emphasizes most – that wealth is relative purchasing power, the ability to win out over others in a market-mediated struggle among competing economic ends – varies in proportion to the extent to which a society's economy involves commodity production: the more market relations structure and determine labour and consumption, the more complete the identity of wealth and social power. Conversely, in societies where the market plays less of a role, inequalities in wealth translate less directly into inequalities in social power.

Finally, the claim that wealth amounts to a form of authority is even less general than the connection between wealth and power. This can be seen by asking under what conditions wealth translates directly into an ability to issue commands and get them obeyed. According to Smith, it is when one person's riches give him the power to purchase and then to direct or command the labour of others. This is not the case in every type of society, not even in every conceivable form of commodity production. To show this, Rousseau offers us the vision of a Golden Age in which independent artisans produce in accordance with a limited division of labour and bring to market the products of their own labour. In such a society, inequalities of wealth might arise, which translate into inequalities in social power but do not necessarily imply inequalities in the ability to have one's commands obeyed. In the Golden Age, inequalities in wealth do not amount to inequalities in authority because in it one particular commodity, labour power, is not for sale. This is why, in explaining the rampant domination of contemporary society, Rousseau places so much weight on the moment when the Golden Age is replaced by conditions in which it appears advantageous for one individual "to have enough provisions for two," with the consequence that "equality disappeared, property was introduced, work became indispensable, and ... slavery and misery were soon seen to germinate and grow" (*DI*, 167/*OC* 3, 171). Thus, it is only in societies where a specific type of inequality – unequal ownership of the means of production – is widespread that the identification of disparities in wealth with domination is complete.

There is a second reason inequalities in wealth occupy a privileged position in Rousseau's critique. It, too, can be traced back to the socio-economic context in which he writes, and it points to a further respect in which such inequalities bring together the other three forms of social inequality. The point here is not that wealth consists in relations of recognition, social power, and authority but that the expansion of commercial society makes it increasingly the case that wealth serves as the primary *means* for attaining status, social power, and authority in its non-economic forms. In commercial societies, possessing large amounts of wealth relative to others' is the principal way of achieving social esteem, as well as of gaining power and authority even in extra-economic domains. Political authority – for example, the ability to command the obedience of others via mechanisms of the state – can be had in most forms of commercial society as a consequence of great wealth.

THE ARTIFICIAL CHARACTER OF SOCIAL INEQUALITY

I turn now to Rousseau's claim that social inequality is artificial – that social inequalities depend on "convention" and are "established, or at least authorized, by [human] consent" (*DI*, 131/*OC* 3, 131). When we ask how this claim is to be understood, we soon discover that "artificial" and "conventional" (like their counterpart "natural") must be carefully defined: "artificial" means humanmade, but in what sense are our social institutions, including the inequalities they generate, made by us? "Conventional" means grounded in human consent, but, again, in what precise sense?

In both English and French "convention" suggests arbitrariness, as in the thought that it is a matter of mere convention whether traffic rules mandate driving on the left or the right. For Rousseau, however, "conventional" does not imply "arbitrary": the laws of a well-governed state, for example, are conventional but not arbitrary. The fundamental meaning of "convention" for Rousseau derives from *con-* and *venire*: a convention is a coming together of different things – in this context, human wills – and this explains why the contract that grounds a legitimate republic counts as a convention (*SC* Book I, ch. 5). At the same time, something close to arbitrariness slips into Rousseau's conception of convention, namely, the idea that if X is conventional, then *it could have been otherwise*, where this means that there is nothing in the basic constitution of nature, including human nature, that necessitates X's existence or its being as it is. Thus, the conventional character of social inequality implies not only that the inequalities we know could have been otherwise but also that nothing in nature requires that there be social inequality at all. The rules governing property in eighteenth-century Geneva are conventional in this sense, whereas the fact that eighteenth-century Genevans are self-interested beings – motivated by what Rousseau calls *amour de soi-même* – is not conventional but due to nature.

For Rousseau, if something exists that is not necessitated by nature, then there is only one other origin it can have: the freedom of human agents. But there is more than one sense in which the existence of social institutions depends on human will for Rousseau. The first is that such institutions *could not have come about* without the intervention of human will at some point in their causal histories. Freedom, then, is implicated in the origin of everything that could have been otherwise. Thus, the property rules of eighteenth-century Geneva could have been otherwise because their coming to be depends, somewhere along the line, on the intervention of free will. That something has its origin in freedom does not imply that a human will consciously created it in the form it eventually comes to have. All it implies is that human freedom intervened at some point in that thing's causal history and that in the absence of such intervention it would not have come about. This point is crucial to the Second Discourse's account of social inequality: institutions that produce social inequality are not consciously chosen or intended; rather, they are the results of complex developments, some of which depend on human choices, but in such a way that the ultimate consequences of those choices are not foreseen, and therefore not intended, by any human agent. Thus, the Second Discourse makes humans causally but not morally responsible for social inequalities.

There are two further senses in which social institutions and inequalities depend on human agency and are therefore artificial. Understanding both requires noting that in the quotation cited earlier Rousseau moves from talking about how inequalities are established to talking about how they are authorized. Putting aside for now what "authorization" means, this is a clear sign that he is less concerned with the historical origins of inequality than with how and why, once inequalities exist, they are maintained over time. His claim is that our freedom in some way sustains inequality-producing institutions, but what does this mean, and why does Rousseau believe it?

One way social institutions depend for their existence on human will – this is the second version of Rousseau's artificiality thesis – is that institutions are our doings because our activity is *constitutive* of them: the continued existence of social inequalities depends on our ongoing participation in the institutions that produce them, and, so, our activity is the (standing) *source* of their being. Here it is helpful to return to my earlier point that a person's being wealthier, of higher status, or more socially powerful depends on the participation of those in comparison to whom that person is wealthier, of higher status, or more powerful. (Recall: status must be bestowed; authority requires that others obey; and social power requires that a plurality of wills be competing for the same goods.) That social inequalities are possible only within networks of agency among human subjects makes them practical phenomena in the sense that they cannot exist apart from the ongoing activities of social members. This makes social inequalities artificial in a sense different from the first one explicated earlier: unlike differences in height or age, social inequalities are *sustained* only through human activity; to be richer or more honoured or more socially powerful is to stand in ongoing practical relations to others. Social inequalities are human practices.

The first two versions of Rousseau's artificiality thesis explain how social inequalities depend on human will, but they do not explain why they are *conventions*, sustained by a collective *consent* that *authorizes* them. Unpacking this claim will lead us to the third and most important sense in which Rousseau holds that social inequalities are artificial.

The claim that social inequality has its source in the consent of the very individuals who stand in relations of inequality is initially puzzling. It can seem perverse to claim that social inequalities exist because the poor, the oppressed, the dominated, and the looked-down-upon have consented to the wealth, power, authority, and status of those above them in the social hierarchy. (On the other hand, this doctrine contains emancipatory potential, too: if the worse off participate in their disadvantages, then they may have the power to withdraw their "consent" and transform the institutions that disadvantage them.) One implication of this claim is that institutions that sustain social inequalities are typically maintained not by brute force but by some (tacit or explicit) acceptance of them on the part of those whose activity sustains them. Rousseau takes it to be a general truth that social institutions that depended primarily on physical force, without any subjective acceptance of them on the part of their participants, would be unstable and inefficient – not to mention, unfree! – in part because a large part of society's resources would have to be spent in maintaining oppressive mechanisms of coercion.

Rousseau's locating the source of social inequalities in authorizing consent signals that, in contrast to the non-moral realm of nature, social institutions are "normatively constituted" phenomena (Jaeggi 2014, 142). What this means is best brought into view by examining his claim that social institutions are "conventional." We have already seen that conventions need not be arbitrary and that they involve some kind of "coming together" of human wills. The idea that must be added to these is that conventions, like the one that grounds the legitimate republic, are normative rules that tell individuals how they *ought* to act and that impose sanctions on behaviour that fails to comply with those rules. To say that the legitimate social contract is conventional is to say that it is the source of a normative principle, the general will that governs citizens' actions. Rousseau's artificiality thesis, in its third version, holds that *we are the source of the rules* that define our social institutions, that we somehow "make the rules" that govern our social life.

In figuring out how we make the rules – or consent to the conventions – that govern our social institutions we must leave behind the potentially misleading example of the legitimate republic, as depicted in the *Social Contract*. It would be wrong, for example, to regard a convention as the result of a contract made when two or more wills expressly agree to be bound by a certain rule. It would be no less wrong to regard our making of the rules of social institutions on the model of positive lawgiving in democracies, where citizens make the rules that govern them in an entirely straightforward sense. Rousseau's artificiality thesis – expounded in the Second Discourse, not the *Social Contract* – is meant to apply to non-political institutions and regardless of their legitimacy. His claim is that we "consent" not only to just political institutions but also to institutions that produce illegitimate inequalities.

Rousseau is best understood as claiming that we "consent" to the rules governing social institutions whenever we *accept*, *apply*, and hence *reproduce* and *reinforce* those rules, even if we inherit them from existing practices. Social inequalities are made by us because they are embedded in institutions whose continued existence depends on our *acceptance* of the rules that define them;[3] social institutions are normatively constituted in that they depend on human agents having a certain normative stance towards their constitutive rules.

John Searle's account of the "construction of social reality" can help us understand what conception of acceptance ("consent") Rousseau's claim depends on (Searle 1995, 39). What we collectively accept when we participate in institutions are *rules* that assign rights and obligations to members of institutions. Searle allows for a wide range of phenomena to count as acceptance, including acceptance of the grammatical rules of a language, implicit conventions governing cocktail parties, and codified laws regulating marriage or property (Searle 2010, 8). To take Searle's paradigm example, the institution of money depends on the collective acceptance of rules that, by defining the rights and obligations of money holders, make what would otherwise be merely a physical thing into a social phenomenon. This is relevant to Rousseau's notion of consent because rule *following* – the *application* of rules – involves an acceptance of the bindingness of rules of which only free agents are capable: expressed in Kantian language, applying rules, as opposed to merely being determined by them externally, involves an exercise of spontaneity that only rational beings can engage in. Speaking a language, for example, requires not that one always speak in conformity with its rules but that one recognize their bindingness such that when I discover my failure to follow a specific rule, I recognize it as an error and take myself to be bound to follow the rule in the future. A well-known passage in the Second Discourse illustrates Rousseau's view:

> The first person who, having enclosed a piece of ground, took it into his head to say, "this is mine," and found people simple enough to believe him, was the true founder of civil society. How many ... horrors would have been spared the human race if someone had pulled up the stakes ... and cried to his fellow beings: "Beware of listening to this impostor; you are lost if you forget that the fruits of the earth belong to us all and the earth to no one!" (*DI*, 161/*OC* 3, 164)

Rousseau's aim here is not to speculate about the historical origin of the private ownership of land but to illustrate the (artificial) nature of that phenomenon. Depicting private ownership of land as entering the world through human fiat reflects his claim that social institutions are not products of nature but contingent results of free human actions. Moreover, the existence of that institution is portrayed as depending not merely on the fiat of a single person but, more fundamentally, on the "consent" of his fellow beings. The pronouncement "this is mine" yields private property only if there are "people simple enough to believe him," where their belief (or "consent") consists simply in *accepting* the pronouncement and its normative implications. The acceptance of rules on which the private ownership of land depends, then, is *collective* (acceptance in general, not by an individual or two), and this makes it conventional, or dependent on a coming together of human wills.

Finally, the "simplicity" invoked to explain the collective acceptance of the rules of land ownership indicates that acceptance of social institutions can fall short of rational consent and that such acceptance "authorizes" institutions only in a weak sense that does not imply actual legitimacy and that may consist in nothing more than unreflective acceptance. Moreover, as the

Second Discourse illustrates, the institutions whose rules we accept are often such that we ourselves are disadvantaged by them. The significance of this point is that it opens up the possibility for a type of ideology critique that Rousseau and his followers made famous and of which the Second Discourse is a paradigm example, namely, genealogies that, in tracing the "origin" of some phenomenon, "de-naturalize the social." If social institutions can be sustained by a collective acceptance of their rules that is unreflective – where individuals are unaware both of their role in sustaining institutions and of the contingent nature of those institutions – then social critique can take the form of *de-naturalizing genealogies* that strip institutions of their apparently immutable character and place them into the "space of reasons," where they then appear as possible objects of critique and transformation. Once the artificial character of institutions is recognized by those whose unreflective acceptance sustains them, it becomes possible for social members to assume responsibility for them and ask: Are the institutions that depend on my acceptance good, or as good as they can be?

THE PERVASIVENESS AND "STUBBORNNESS" OF SOCIAL INEQUALITY

Taken in isolation, Rousseau's artificiality thesis can make it look like his account of social inequality is optimistic: since we create social inequalities, we are free to criticize and transform them. Yet this conclusion is inconsonant with the Second Discourse's pessimistic tone, including its suggestion that our society might be so thoroughly corrupted that no remedy for its ills is within our grasp. This inconsonance indicates that our understanding of Rousseau's account of social inequality is incomplete without an explanation of what makes it so pervasive and so resistant to attempts to eliminate it.

Rousseau's pessimism should caution us not to exaggerate the role that authorizing consent plays in sustaining social inequalities and thereby overestimate the transformative potential of social critique. The Second Discourse is far from claiming that social inequalities depend *only* on the acceptance of them by those whose activities constitute and reproduce them. One reason that acceptance alone does not explain the staying power of social inequalities has to do with the substantial role that need and dependence, both material and psychological, play in human social life: because we are needy and dependent, we can rarely simply opt out of existing institutions that disadvantage us. That inequality-producing institutions are kept in place by more than their members' acceptance of them is easiest to see in the case of economic inequality. Here, of course, the coercive power of the state plays a role, but material need and dependence are more important: even if some of us reject existing property relations, the lack of economic alternatives, together with the fact that our families must eat today, explains why social critique alone seldom suffices for real transformation. If the authorizing consent of social members is necessary for the maintenance of social inequalities, need and dependence also ensure that inequality-producing institutions have ample capacity to absorb, untouched, normative critique from within.

What makes Rousseau's position on the pervasiveness and stubbornness of social inequality interesting is that the need and dependence that explain the inertia of inequality-producing institutions are themselves taken to be largely artificial. This is because they are primarily the consequences of a distinctively human passion, amour propre, whose workings also depend on our freedom in the sense that what our amour propre leads us to seek is the valuing regard of others, where valuing and wanting to be valued depend on "opinions" regarding the good that only rational agents can have and for which they are, at least potentially, responsible. The most important part of Rousseau's account of the pervasiveness and stubbornness of social inequality lies in his answer to the obvious question raised by his artificiality thesis: if inequality is our creation, what explains our nearly irresistible tendency to create it?

Rousseau's answer locates a passion fundamental to human psychology, amour propre, that can furnish humans with a motive to seek inequality for its own sake. The good that amour propre strives for – recognized standing – is an intrinsically social good that directly requires the participation of others, namely, their free valuing of the recognized individual. If, as Rousseau postulates, amour propre is fundamental to human psychology, then the search for recognition will be a pervasive part of social life, and the fact that amour propre's satisfaction requires the participation of others ensures that dependence, too, will be pervasive. At the same time, the "relative" nature of amour propre's objective explains why the quest for recognition can provide us with an incentive to create or maintain inequalities. To desire status is to desire a *comparative* standing in relation to others, which means that the recognition sought by amour propre is a positional and therefore robustly relational good, where doing well for myself (finding the standing I seek) consists in doing well in relation to others (acquiring a standing defined in relation to theirs). This means that the extent to which I am satisfied in my desire for recognition depends on how well or how badly those around me fare with respect to their desire for the same. Once this feature of amour propre is introduced into human psychology, it is not difficult to understand how social inequality can be our creation. For when humans conceive of their good in comparative terms, it is possible for them to seek to do well for themselves by trying to outdo others. The concern for relative standing is susceptible to becoming a desire for *superior* standing, and as soon as one takes the view that confirming one's own worth requires being esteemed as better than others, amour propre requires inequality in order to be satisfied.

It is important, however, that the relative standing sought by amour propre is not necessarily a superior one. If what amour propre leads one to seek is simply the respect one deserves as a human being – a respect one is willing to grant to others in return – then the standing one seeks is comparative but not superior: equal standing is still standing relative to others. Rousseau's thesis concerning the susceptibility of amour propre to being formed and re-formed through contingent conditions of many kinds, including social institutions, implies that the desire for equal standing is one possible configuration of our desire for recognition but not the only or most likely form that desire assumes (Neuhouser 2008, ch. 4).

This helps to explain why humans tend to create social inequalities and why, once they exist, they are so difficult to modify. But there is a further fact that explains inequality's stubbornness: the social institutions we sustain through our own activity exert a formative influence on us. Our desires, values, and self-conceptions, including our desires for recognition, are shaped by the social world we inhabit. Social institutions reproduce themselves by socializing agents to have desires that can be satisfied only by participating in and reproducing those same institutions. Applied to amour propre: many institutions – think of the capitalist economy – reproduce themselves by instilling in their participants various forms of "inflamed" desires to achieve a recognized standing superior to others'. In such instances the need and dependence on which social life feeds become inextricably bound up with the (perceived) need of its participants to achieve superior standing. This results in a self-reproducing social dynamic that accounts for much of the resistance of established inequalities. Even if amour propre is highly malleable in principle, once it has assumed a certain form, the cycle of inflamed amour propre is extremely difficult to break. Because amour propre engages us at the level of our values and self-conceptions, reconfiguring our desires for recognition requires a species of internal transformation that is notoriously difficult to bring about.

Rousseau's account of the intimate relation between amour propre and social inequality implies that effective critique of inequality-producing institutions must find a way of addressing already formed social members whose present values and self-conceptions give them strong incentives to resist the very social changes it aims to bring about. That is, effective social critique must find a way of bringing individuals to cease desiring the conditions of inequality they have been socialized to want to reproduce. Rousseau himself recognized this dilemma, which explains why education plays a central role in his proposed remedies for illegitimate inequality: his account of political institutions in the *Social Contract* reflects on how such institutions form their members' characters, and the domestic education he advocates in *Émile* aims at equipping individuals with the values and self-conceptions they need in order to inhabit and reproduce a well-ordered society. Although Rousseau thought seriously about this problem and tried to solve it, his ultimately pessimistic outlook comes from his recognition of its intractability. In this respect Rousseau's account of the nature of social inequality teaches us an important, and sobering, truth about the challenges faced by attempts at social transformation.

NOTES

1. In citing Rousseau I use the following abbreviations: *DI*: *Discourse on the Origin and Foundations of Inequality*, in Rousseau (1997a); *SC*: *The Social Contract*, in Rousseau (1997b); *OC* 3: Rousseau (1964).
2. The inclusion of wisdom here may seem odd since acquiring it seems to require the wise person's own doings. But this inclusion confirms my account of what natural inequalities are: (i) one's being wise does not depend on human agreement or opinions; and (ii) one can possess, and desire to possess, wisdom independently of the degree of others' wisdom.
3. A full articulation of Rousseau's position requires much more space than I have here; I undertake to provide this in an unpublished book manuscript.

BIBLIOGRAPHY

Jaeggi, Rahel. 2014. *Kritik von Lebensformen*. Berlin: Suhrkamp.
Neuhouser, Frederick. 2008. *Rousseau's Theodicy of Self-Love: Evil, Rationality, and the Drive for Recognition*. Oxford: Oxford University Press.
Neuhouser, Frederick. 2014. *Rousseau's Critique of Inequality: Reconstructing the Second Discourse*. Cambridge: Cambridge University Press.
Rousseau, Jean-Jacques. 1964. *Oeuvres Complètes*, ed. Bernard Gagnebin and Marcel Raymond. Paris: Gallimard, Bibliothèque de la Pléiade, vol. 3.
Rousseau, Jean-Jacques. 1997a. *The Discourses and Other Early Political Writings*, ed. Victor Gourevitch. Cambridge: Cambridge University Press.
Rousseau, Jean-Jacques. 1997b. *The Social Contract*, in *The Social Contract and Other Later Political Writings*, ed. Victor Gourevitch. Cambridge: Cambridge University Press.
Searle, John R. 1995. *The Construction of Social Reality*. New York: The Free Press.
Searle, John R. 2010. *Making the Social World*. Oxford: Oxford University Press.
Smith, Adam. 2000. *The Wealth of Nations*, ed. Edwin Cannan. New York: Modern Library.
Wheeler, Brian. 2016. "The David Cameron Story." *BBC*, September 12, 2016. https ://www.bbc.com/news/uk-politics-eu-referendum-36540101.

Chapter 8

Repressive Empathy?
A Plea for Contextualization
Martin Hartmann

For a while empathy appeared to be the solution to some of the most pressing problems of contemporary society. Public intellectuals proclaimed the age of empathy or praised the empathic civilization; moral philosophers suggested that the capacity to empathize is at the heart of all advanced forms of moral consideration. Seeing the world through the eyes of the other, slipping into her shoes, or feeling what she feels – these were the highly valued qualities of the empathic subject. Empathy appeared to be the psychological force capable of decentring the subject, allowing her to better understand the motives and situational responses of otherwise distant or incomprehensible others. What's more, research on mirror neurons corroborated the impression that some of the wondrous feats of empathy were hard-wired and automated. The biology of humans and of highly developed animals, it appeared, provided the basis for all forms of lower-level empathy and perhaps even for some of the more intricate forms of higher-level empathy requiring the support of our imaginative faculties (see Rifkin 2009; de Waal 2009; Slote 2010; Rizzolatti/Sinigaglia 2008).

Soon enough a countermovement set in and began to collect evidence for empathy's limits. Empathy was kicked off its moral throne and even accused of producing more evil than good. Just listen to these titles: *Against Empathy, Anti-Empathy, Empathy's Blind Spot, The Empathy Trap*, or *The Dark Sides of Empathy* (see Prinz 2011; Bloom 2016; Goldie 2011; Slaby 2013; Singer 2016; Breithaupt 2019). Among the most common criticisms launched against empathy was the claim that the moral reach of empathy was limited and that empathy cannot cover all the morally relevant facts worth our moral reckoning. Furthermore, empathy was seen as essentially biased in a way that alternative moral approaches seemingly were not. Thus, Jesse Prinz claims that "empathy is partial; we feel greater empathy for those who are similar to ourselves" (Prinz 2011, 227). Among the most forceful critiques of empathy was Paul Bloom's *Against Empathy: The Case for Rational Compassion*. Bloom shared many of Prinz's misgivings but added a load of his own to the already impressive catalogue of blame.

How are these criticisms to be assessed? In particular, what does it mean to suggest that empathy is essentially biased or partial? I will begin my discussion of these questions by turning, first, to Bloom's approach.

AGAINST EMPATHY: THE CASE OF PAUL BLOOM

Some critiques of empathy are of a conceptual kind, others accept empathy for what it is taken to be but raise doubts concerning its potential moral achievements. I focus on the latter and treat Paul Bloom's *Against Empathy* as a case study in point. Bloom defines empathy as "feeling what others feel" and adds that "feeling their pain" is of particular relevance for adopting an empathic attitude (Bloom 2016, 35). This notion of empathy is, according to Bloom, the notion first introduced by Adam Smith, though Smith (and Hume) spoke of sympathy instead of empathy. Empathy is a feeling that responds to others' feelings by taking up or adopting these feelings; in a narrower sense, it is a feeling that responds to others' pain and suffering by treating this pain and suffering as if it was one's own. Further, empathy seeks to "make the suffering go away," that is, it has a motivational impetus and is not just contemplative (ibid., 30). Bloom mentions the following example to substantiate his notion of empathy: "I see the bullied teenager and might be tempted initially to join in with his tormenters, out of sadism or boredom or a desire to dominate or be popular, but then I empathize – I feel his pain, I feel what it's like to be bullied – so I don't add to his suffering" (ibid.). According to this example, then, empathy is a form of compassion or fellow-feeling and generates action tendencies in the empathic subject.

Treating empathy as a feeling leads to criticizing it on account of its being a feeling and, in addition, on account of its being a particular feeling closely resembling or being more or less identical to compassion.[1] This leads to one of Bloom's main criticisms, namely to the charge I call the "limitation charge." Empathy is seen as having a narrow focus or spotlight character. We can only empathize with so and so many people and overlook, by psychological necessity, many others worth our (or anybody's) moral consideration. As Bloom puts it: "You cannot empathize with more than one or two people at the same time. Try it" (Bloom 2016, 33). Furthermore, empathy is limited in yet another sense; it preselects those (few) we actually empathize with.

Remember Prinz's similarity condition; this condition suggests that we empathize more with those we consider similar to us than with those dissimilar to us, say, in terms of language, appearance, or cultural habits. Bloom raises the same point by insisting on empathy's inbuilt biases and prejudices. Also, due to the limitation of its reach, empathy focuses on the effects our actions have on the few people we care about and ignores the effects these actions have on people outside this rather narrow circle. Empathy, it appears, literally creates its own narrow-mindedness. What's more, empathy is easily trapped by single events covered in spectacular imagery by the media. A single mass shooting in a school binds more of our empathic attention than the many regular violent deaths occurring elsewhere. As Bloom puts it, empathy is "insensitive to statistical data" (ibid., 31). Lastly, empathy is emotionally quite powerful and binds our moral energies in problematic ways. Empathy causes distress. We can get caught up in the suffering of those we empathize with and, once more, be less attentive to other people's suffering.

I think Bloom's catalogue of criticisms can be reduced to two central problems: problems of moral reach (limitation charge) and problems of moral bias (this I call this the partiality charge); partial empathy is, by definition, limited empathy whereas the limits of empathy's moral reach do not necessarily stem from any inbuilt bias. I stress this distinction, as Bloom is not always clear about it. He begins by claiming that empathy's limits have to do with the difficulty of extending empathy to more than a few individuals, suggesting that my inability to empathize with more than a few individuals isn't necessarily caused by any inherent bias of my empathizing capacities. It just seems to be psychologically impossible to spread my compassion to more than a few suffering others. If I could spread it so, I would certainly do so and no bias would hinder me from extending it to all individuals deemed worthy of my empathy. Unfortunately, as Bloom sees it, empathy does not reach enough individuals worthy of moral consideration. It focuses only on a few (one or two!) and thus neglects the many others in need of help and support. This problem seems to be inherent in empathy *as a feeling* and cannot be avoided. One could call this a conceptual limit of empathy but Bloom's critique of extended empathy is couched in psychological terms and does not insist that these limits could be identified through conceptual analysis alone. Also, as we will see in a second, Bloom himself allows for a more extended understanding of empathy.

Why can we not empathize with more than one or two people at the same time? Because feelings such as empathy (or compassionate empathy) require much motivational energy, aim at individuals with faces and bodies (and stories), depend on concrete visual stimuli, and if they ever evolve into concrete helping acts cannot cover more than a few people. It just seems plausible to say that we cannot feel compassion for, say, ten thousand people *at the same time*. Try it.

At later points in the argument, Bloom suggests that empathy's psychological limits are inextricably linked to the ingrained biases haunting empathy. Thus, when discussing the nationalist, racist, or anti-Semitic biases of empathy, Bloom makes abundantly clear that he doesn't really think that empathy can only be extended to one or two persons; on the contrary, we can be empathically biased about a whole people (see ibid., ch. 5). According to this line of thinking, it is in the nature of empathy to be biased, that is, to favour some groups of people or categories of individuals over others.

The partiality charge is, I think, more severe, which is why it somewhat drowns out the limitation charge. If the limitation charge were the only charge levelled against empathy, one would hardly be justified in calling empathy "morally corrosive" (ibid., 39). After all, doing some moral good is better than doing none, and one cannot imagine Bloom reprimanding a person helping an old lady cross the street out of sheer compassion.[2] Also, the limitation charge depends on identifying empathy with a feeling of compassion and with a tendency to act on that feeling. As to the partiality charge, it raises two questions: first, what is meant by partiality and, second, should we say that empathy is *essentially* partial? As to the first, I have already indicated that the partiality of empathy amounts to favouring some individuals or groups over others. What's more, the favouring of some usually not only implies a disfavouring of others but openly devalues them. In partial empathy, I disfavour others *because* I favour you, and I do not just know this to be true but accept it. In other words, if I could extend my empathy to these others, I would not want to do it. If this were not the case, my empathy with you would not have to be seen as problematic and could be taken as just another instance of a limitation of reach. Of course, often the limitation and the partiality charge overlap. What if I only help white old ladies and refuse to help those who are not white? Clearly, if that is the case my empathy is biased and prejudiced and, in addition, severely limited. The bias preselects those eligible to become targets of my empathic helping behaviour and drives the limitation (again, in contrast to the mere psychological limitation on spreading or extending empathic behaviour). We could call the partiality at stake in the partiality charge *intentionally exclusionary* partiality and differentiate it from other forms of partiality that do factually exclude some but do not intend to do so. Calling empathy morally corrosive, Bloom, I take it, must have exclusionary partiality in mind.

The second question is more difficult to answer. Is empathy *essentially* or *necessarily* biased and partial even if we accept a wider concept of empathy than the one first introduced by Bloom? And if the answer is that empathy really is essentially partial, is the partiality at stake of the exclusionary kind?

So far, the term "essential" might be paraphrased by the term "unavoidable," though the exact sources of unavoidability remain unclear. Empathy, it was said, is not conceptually partial. But this could just be a definitional flaw of (mostly) philosophical accounts of empathy. In fact, as we saw, some philosophers openly admit empathy's partiality but refrain from spelling out the moral implications of this admission.

Let us take the case of racism again. Let's say my empathy is racially structured, that is, it is of the exclusionary kind. Is my empathy (somehow) to take the blame for that fact? Or do racial prejudices infiltrate empathy as much as they infiltrate any other moral approach? Kant, as we now know, is considered by some to be the father of modern racism (see McCarthy 2009; Mills 2017). Classical utilitarianism's record on this count is more complex, it appears, but far from being unequivocal (see Schultz 2007). So even if Bloom is right in stating that we tend to empathize more with those "who are close to us, those who are similar to us, and those we see as more attractive or vulnerable and less scary" (Bloom 2016, 31), it is wrong, I think, to pretend that these biases and partialities strike empathy more than they strike competing accounts of morality. Furthermore, Bloom derives these partialities from the nature of empathy itself and not from other factors that might influence the channels into which our various benevolent impulses flow. But has he really shown that it is something about empathy itself or the nature of empathy that drives it towards moral partiality?

Some statements certainly suggest that he does indeed think himself to have done just that. Empathy, it appears, always seems to favour some over others. Here is an alternative: In his *Ruling Passions*, Simon Blackburn quotes Hume to the effect that what Hume calls sympathy sometimes requires us to take up a common point of view, that is, to abstract from our personal and parochial perspective. In fact, when issuing moral statements such as "this is good" or, in Humean parlance, "vicious or odious or depraved," the one issuing the statements must "depart from his private and particular situation, and must choose a point of view, common to him with others: He must move some universal principle of the human frame, and touch a string, to which all mankind have an accord and symphony" (Hume quoted in Blackburn 1998, 201). For Blackburn, the important lesson to be learned from Hume is that the willingness to take up such a common standpoint would even override given animosities among persons or parties. If my enemy builds a good fortification for a city, there is, in principle, no reason for me not to admire his accomplishment. As Blackburn says, the standards for adjudicating good fortifications are "impersonal" and describe what "anybody who fortifies a city is likely to want" (ibid.). Let's assume for the moment that there really are no differences concerning evaluative standards for buildings and evaluative standards for moral qualities; and let's also assume that what Hume has in mind when talking about an "accord and symphony" among mankind amounts to what we call empathy (and Hume sympathy).

I take it that Bloom's reply to the (musical) image of such a potentially universal concord would be rather straightforward: "This is not how empathy works" (Bloom 2016, 190). More typically, empathy closes the ranks among one's friends or allies and does not extend to our enemies. Bloom's evidence for this is more or less empirical: he cites drastic examples of our seemingly complete inability to empathize across the parochial boundaries set for us by political movements, nations, families, or friendship ties. These social entities define insiders and outsiders and they supply the material (such as images of murdered Palestinians "to generate support for attacks against Israel") necessary to keep empathy within, as it were, and prevent it from crossing the boundaries: "Asking people to feel as much empathy for an enemy as for their own child is like asking them to feel as much hunger for a dog turd as for an apple – it's logically possible, but it doesn't reflect the normal functioning of the human mind" (ibid.).[3]

I assume the drastic character of the comparison is meant to prove just how unusual empathy for one's enemies is. And calling the possibility of eating a dog turd "logical" is to highlight that this possibility may well be entertained in thought but hardly ever materializes – except maybe in harsh circumstances of nutritional deprivation (and in that sense, it is not a "logical" but a real possibility). Be this as it may, the strongest argument Bloom cites to confirm the partiality thesis is not conceptual, but empirical or experiential. What this means, however, is that empathy as such may well extend to people outside one's experiential or group-bound horizon (some forms of deeply committed religious faith seem to attest to that fact). It's just that all forms of empathy are always embedded in social relationships that shape how empathy actually unfolds. Put differently, whatever limits empathy has should not be attributed to empathy as such, but to the social, cultural, economic, and political structures within which empathy (as much as any other moral attitude) exerts its influence. So, yes, empathy does seem to suffer from severe partialities, I fully agree with Bloom. And, yes, empathy can be a powerful psychological tool to exclude certain groups of people from the arc of the moral universe. Again, I agree with Bloom. But much depends on the way in which these partialities are captured and described. We need to get this description right, as it were, to be in a better position to understand what empathy can and what it cannot achieve. After all, even according to Bloom and pace his rhetorical hyperbole we can, in principle, eat dog turds as much as we can, in principle, empathize with our enemies. Or are supporters of, say, *Peace Now* psychologically abnormal? If I am right, some of the problems I have been dealing with up to this point can only be partly attributed to empathy per se and we do not yet know why we should consider empathy to be essentially partial.

HIMPATHY: KATE MANNE'S *DOWN GIRL* AND THE CASE OF EXCESSIVE SYMPATHY

Maybe we just need more arguments. In her book *Down Girl: The Logic of Misogyny* Kate Manne introduces the category of "himpathy" by which she means "the excessive sympathy sometimes shown toward male perpetrators of sexual violence" (Manne 2018, 197). Himpathy, then, clearly is a case of strongly biased empathy, an empathy shown towards a certain group of people and denied to other groups. In Manne's interpretation of himpathy, the himpathic individual is the man *or* woman who cares more about the male perpetrator of sexual violence than about his mostly female victims. To corroborate the phenomenon, Manne cites the case of Stanford University student Brock Turner who brutally assaulted an unconscious woman after a party behind a dumpster and was sentenced to only six months (of which he served three in actual confinement). Manne cites Turner's father who was worried about his son and his "happy-go-lucky-self" and she cites the judge who also worried about "the severe impact" a conviction might have on Turner (ibid., 196–97). Friends of Turner attested to his good character, insisting on the fact that he was not a monster and did not at all fulfil the criteria of being a typical rapist (though it turned out that he had molested women before); many attributed the crime to a college party culture that condoned excessive drinking. These defenders of Turner exhibit what Manne calls "forgiving tendencies," adding that "such tendencies stem largely from capacities and qualities of which we're rarely critical: such as sympathy, empathy, trust in one's friends, devotion to one's children, and having as much faith in someone's good character as is compatible with the evidence." In a footnote, Manne approvingly refers to Bloom's book on empathy remarking, in the spirit of Bloom, that empathy "can make us take sides with the historically dominant, against the less privileged" (ibid., 200). In fact, what the Turner case shows is that himpathy transforms the perpetrator of the crime into the real victim, one who must be defended and empathized with. It is as if he was victim to his own crime, as if he had to be spared the consequences of his deeds which were either not really his own (the alcohol) or were reinterpreted as normal and to be expected in university environments such as the one prevalent in Stanford.

With himpathy we seem to have a variant of empathy that plays an *essential* role in upholding structures of inequality and discrimination. What Manne says about himpathy is straightforward and leaves little doubt about the essential role empathy plays in allowing structures of male domination to persist. At least during legal proceedings, Turner was the object of an empathy withheld from his victim.

At the same time, however, her general line on misogyny suggests a more nuanced view that embeds himpathy in a larger theoretical frame. What is misogyny according to Manne? She rejects a definition of the term (called "naïve") that thoroughly individualizes misogyny and sees it as a property of individual agents (mostly men) prone to feel hatred towards all women because they are women. In contrast, Manne argues that misogyny is an "outgrowth of patriarchal ideology" manifest in a "system that operates within a patriarchal social order to police and enforce women's subordination and to uphold male dominance" (ibid., 32–33). Without going into all the details of her approach, what matters to me at this point is Manne's readiness to treat misogyny as a systemic property of patriarchally ordered cultures and societies that *enforce* and *police* women's subordination. Both terms suggest that some women do not accept their traditional roles as emotional caregivers, domestic workers, or guardians of their men's professional success. It is these women who need to be forced and policed into accepting their traditional role, and it is these women who are the primary targets of misogyny. Misogyny, then, does not amount to hatred of women across the board (as the naive view holds) but to hatred of those women who question the status quo and resist subordination. As Manne says, misogyny tends "to include women entering positions of power and authority over men, and women eschewing or opting out of male-oriented service roles" (ibid., 51). Misogyny is thus a backlash phenomenon: it is reactive, retaliatory, and hateful, and it responds to the female desire for true equality and emancipation (in short: it is Trump). An intact patriarchal order (Manne calls it a "typical patriarchal setting") does not need misogyny; much to the contrary, in an intact patriarchal order men approve of women because and as long as they willingly accept being subordinated to them (ibid., 47).

If these observations are convincing, himpathy as excessive sympathy with male perpetrators of sexual abuse is part and parcel of a larger system of male dominance that it helps to strengthen and stabilize. But is it essential to this system? Given Manne's definition of misogyny, it appears that whatever measures help to enforce and police women's subordination will do. Himpathy certainly helps to do just that, but is it more than just one prop among many other potential props supporting misogynistic structures? Testimonial injustice, for example, seems to be one other prop meant to preserve gendered hierarchies. Also, we should not forget that much of *Down Girl* is about the sheer violence perpetrated by men against women. Misogyny, Manne is adamant about this, kills. In fact, in the United States it kills several women every day.[4] Himpathy thus cannot be identified with misogyny, it just helps to make it easier for misogynistic men to find acceptance for their views or to be exonerated once serious crimes or misdemeanours have occurred.

But even if himpathy is not to be identified with misogyny, could the variant of empathy it represents not still be essential to upholding the system? This is not to say that this is all empathy can be; but it is to say that whenever there is deeply entrenched discrimination against some groups or preferential treatment of others, partial empathy does play a role in it. Recall that Manne's account of himpathy leaves much room for women empathizing with men within highly unequal and gender-biased social structures, thereby helping to uphold these structures. This kind of empathy, then, may be essential to the very definition of what a patriarchal order is and is not just contingently related to it. While this may not be the notion of "essential" partiality that Bloom had in mind, it is a notion of essential partiality nonetheless. Call this partiality *systemic* or *system-related* partiality. Some (maybe even all) systems of repression and discrimination, it could be said, need empathy's partiality. This shows, for example, in the fact that Arlie Hochschild's recommendation to the political left, in *Strangers in Their Own Land*, to slip into the shoes of right-wing Trump supporters in order to "consider the possibility that in their situation, you might end up closer to their perspective" (Hochschild 2016, 234), is misplaced as it leaves intact a culture in which certain misogynistically oriented groups (again, men *and* women) reclaim a form of moral attention that is constitutive of the very social order to be rejected.[5] In a culture like this, the demand for empathy amounts to what one might label, in remembrance of Marcuse's much debated notion of repressive tolerance (see Marcuse 1965), repressive empathy. If the presence of a misogynistic culture is partially defined through established structures of empathy with the oppressor, empathy, in some of its ramifications, essentially stabilizes this culture and is a psychological tool of inclusion and exclusion. As Manne says, "Listening and offering sympathy to those who are prone to ... misogynistic as well as racist outbursts is feeding the very need and sense of entitlement that drives them in the first place" (Manne 2018, 290).

System-related essentiality is difficult to prove in empirical terms and all Manne can do is cite corroborating evidence that will be subject to much interpretational controversy. What is of interest to me is that even the notion of the systemic relevance of empathy's partiality does not seem to show that empathy *as such* is necessarily or essentially partial. It all depends on its role within any given system of social reproduction. Whatever role empathy does play to uphold a repressive or unjust social system, this role is relative to this system and cannot be understood independently of it.

But is this a plausible position? Could there be a social system within which empathy plays a more benign role?

CAN EMPATHY BE RESCUED?

What I have argued so far (following Manne) is that some forms of empathy can be essential to upholding certain repressive forms of inequality. This implies that Bloom's and Prinz's accounts of empathy's partiality are plausible, even though their descriptions of the sources of this partiality are often lacking and even though their suggested moral alternatives may not fare as well as they seem to think (I know that this is a pretty decisive criticism that I cannot elaborate upon within the confines of this chapter). However, it does not follow from this that repressive cultural and social regimes always rely on empathy. In other words, it still does not seem correct to assume that "essential" in "essentially partial empathy" means *conceptually* or, I might now add, *psychologically* necessary. Recall that by "partial" I intend to describe exclusionary partiality, and not just a partiality that could be reconstructed as a variant of the limitation charge. The exclusionary partialities we have found so far are all more or less empirical in nature and that means: they are contingent and depend on contextual and historical constellations. True, Manne goes very far in the direction of essentializing empathy's repressive regime (mostly inflected along the lines of himpathy in her account). If empathy is treated as a specifically feminine moral stance and if it is widely praised as such within social and cultural structures that discriminate against women in various respects, empathy evolves into a psychological tool systematically disadvantaging those whose empathy it simultaneously relies on. The essentially repressive role of empathy is even underlined if one admits, as Manne does, that the goods women secure or give to men are truly important and truly valuable. Consider, she says, that "as well as affection, adoration, indulgence, and so on, ... feminine-coded goods and services include simple respect, love, acceptance, nurturing, safety, security, and safe haven" (ibid., 110). I take it that she might just as well have added empathy to the list. Seen in this more material light, empathy is a good that pretty much all market societies need in order to reproduce themselves as market societies, while at the same time being a free and cheap good that is hardly ever paid for. Adding the economic perspective to the cultural, social, and political perspective, then, deepens the repressive dimension of empathy (and the other feminine-coded values and competencies). Misogyny is not just a cultural battle, it is an economic battle subduing those who desire to receive and not just to give, that is, who desire reciprocal recognitional empathy and not just the historically dominant unequal structures of giving without receiving.[6]

But saying that the goods empathy is able to secure and foster are truly important does introduce a more positive vision of its moral capacities. As difficult as it may be to imagine a more egalitarian structure of gender relations (certainly within Manne's rather bleak frame), the possibility of real empathy with the oppressed cannot be ruled out on conceptual or psychological grounds. Manne's text itself is a case in point. In a way it passionately pleads for a replacement of himpathy with herpathy and is scandalized by the systematic silencing of the (female) victim's voice in the various sexual abuse cases she so vividly captures. She thus tries to make the victim's perspective accessible not to a fully non-partial form of empathy but to a form of empathy we might label more fairly partial or partial in a non-repressive way.

Bloom, in his own way, also admits that empathy might be very valuable. In fact, if I had more space at my disposal, I would try to prove that his alternative to emotional empathy, "rational compassion," clearly contains elements of the very form of empathy he so fiercely rejects. Recall that he usually ridicules the stance of empathy by citing extreme examples. Thus, he suggests that in the context of a suicide bombing in Israel, many notions of empathy would not only require empathy with the victims but also with the perpetrators (Bloom 2016, 190). This rhetorical hyperbole is, of course, meant to completely delegitimize the case for empathy with the enemy. However, if extreme arguments seem to be necessary to devalue an attitude or emotional stance, it might well be that more regular instances of this stance might not be as outlandish. Empathy with suicide bombers may not be very be uncommon indeed, but what about less extreme forms of empathy with, say, economic competitors (see Hartmann 2016) or political opponents? They might be rare but they are certainly not psychologically impossible. It all depends on business cultures or incentive structures, on images of the self and educational focus.

By saying that empathy does not work in the way suggested by those recommending empathy with the enemy, Bloom seems to side with the facts. But are the facts really as univocal as he assumes? Are attempts at understanding the enemy really as rare or untypical as Bloom seems to think? No doubt, certain political pressures or sheer propaganda can incite enemy hatred and a form of empathy reserved for only one's own kin or political allies. But this is a statement about empathy in context and not about empathy per se. Once more, part of the problem of Bloom's approach is that empathy as a psychological phenomenon is isolated and treated in abstraction from social, cultural, political, and economic contexts. Smith, in his *Theory of Moral Sentiments*, says that acts of sympathy contain mostly implicit judgements about the suitability of the other's emotional response to the situation at hand (the question is whether these responses are "suitable to their objects"?) (see Smith 1976, 16). In other words, as suicide bombing never appears to be suitable to whatever situation, acts of empathy are not exactly called for and may therefore also be difficult if not impossible to generate. We certainly would not expect it in normative terms. Defining empathy as feeling what the other feels or as feeling *for* her as in compassion leaves out all of these complexities and tends towards an unduly psychological isolation of the phenomenon. But even apart from Bloom's reductionism, think of how much attention even brutal killers sometimes get (certainly as compared to the attention the victims receive). If it's not just pure sensationalism, we want to understand how one gets that way in order to develop more sensitivity to, say, derailed biographies or violence-prone careers. Would it really make sense to refrain from calling this empathy? It is by no means easily achieved and some of us, true enough, recoil from the attempt to enter these dark avenues. But we seem to be able to do it. True, Bloom might reply that this is not the kind of empathy he has in mind. Maybe it is what he labels "cognitive" empathy and lacks the emotional component of feeling what others feel, in particular, of feeling their pain (Bloom 2016, 36). The serial killer may just enjoy his brutal sprees, so empathy (along Bloom's lines) may not even be possible as there is no pain to empathize with.

What this shows, however, is that it may not be very helpful to strongly associate empathy with a feeling and even go further in aligning it with some form of pain-oriented compassion. Hume and Smith, for that matter, do not treat sympathy as a feeling at all, rather, they take it to be a psychological mechanism *communicating* feelings (see Taylor 2015, 189; Raphael 2007, ch. 2). In Smith, sympathy amounts to an awareness of *concurring* feelings and should not be identified with any of these respective feelings. Why is this important? It is important because it helps us to better understand and analyse the various factors shaping and influencing our concrete emotional responses to others (be this love, hate, compassion, envy, jealousy, contempt, or other feelings). In other words, instead of identifying empathy with a phenomenologically distinct feeling as such, we should better understand the factors influencing how likely it is that we will feel what the other feels, how likely it is, for example, that we take the life of the other to be grievable at all (Butler 2009). Empathy, in short, is governed through distance or proximity, similarity or dissimilarity, prejudice or fairness, wealth or poverty, through gender, race or class – and in that sense it is frequently biased, it allows for degrees and can sometimes be taken to aim, ideally, at all human beings. But this is empathy in context, and if contexts can change, so can empathy. Hume thought that we are more naturally sympathetic to our relatives and acquaintances. However, as indicated in the quote earlier, he thought that our more narrowly moral judgements try to touch a string to which "all mankind have an accord." This may be more of a normative expectation than a concrete feeling reaching out to all others. But as an expectation, it clearly aims at an enlargement of our sympathetic circles that should not be ruled out on grounds of conceptually narrowing down our other-oriented attitudes.

NOTES

1. Bloom openly distinguishes his notion of empathy from compassion (see Bloom 2016, 39–40), but I simply cannot see why; in fact, at one point he says this: "If

you feel bad for someone in pain, that's sympathy, but if you feel their pain, that's empathy" (Ibid., 40). I would say that's compassion or, if you like, compassionate empathy (literally compassion means "suffer together"). The fact that Bloom calls his alternative to empathy "rational compassion" complicates matters even further. Later in the book, Bloom distinguishes "sentimental compassion" from "great compassion" and suggests that great compassion is "more distanced and reserved, and can be sustained indefinitely" (ibid., 138). However, in quoting Tania Singer and Olga Klimecki (ibid.), Bloom then goes on to argue that compassion of the "great" kind is "characterized by feelings of warmth, concern and care for the other" (but does not imply sharing the suffering). How can warmth, concern, and care be shared indefinitely? And why should they not very often be based on some form of empathy (or sharing of feelings or, to use a more complicated phrasing, awareness of shareability of feelings)?

2. Though one should not be too sure about this. Listen to the following statement: "If you are struggling with a moral decision and find yourself trying to feel someone else's pain or pleasure, you should stop" (ibid., 39). Let's assume you are not struggling, you are actually feeling the pain of the other and you immediately turn to help her. Should you still stop? And what would be morally corrosive about the helping act? The fact that you could help many other suffering individuals (Bloom's alternative to empathy, rational compassion, clearly has a Singerite utilitarian ring to it)? Well, could you? Right then and there? What if you chose to do nothing? Would that also be morally corrosive? I assume that Bloom's main criterion for calling acts morally corrosive is quantitative: doing *more* moral good versus doing less (or none). However, applying this criterion has some awkward implications. Thus, a single act of moral good seems to be able to turn bad or less good if doing it prevents me from doing more good somewhere else. In fact, if the option of doing more good is on the table, the single act would not even be considered wholeheartedly good or moral. The utilitarian logic feeding Bloom's account is this: helping the old lady cross the street turns bad or less good if it happens while next to you a bus you could somehow stop runs over fifty children. Calling an act less good is, of course, not the same thing as calling it morally corrosive. The latter charge leads, I think, to the partiality problem.

3. One may ask, of course, who really wants us to feel more empathy for our enemy than for our child. That demand in itself sounds morally obtuse.

4. "On an average day in the United States, there are between two and three intimate partner homicides" (ibid., 109, fn. 3).

5. Ibid., 290. In defence, Hochschild might argue that her plea for empathy is only meant to overcome the empathy wall separating the American left and right and establish some understanding of the right-wing perspective. However, by adding that xenophobia might be the natural response to its situation, Hochschild's understanding of the right seems to turn into a form of acceptance or forgiving (as in *tout comprendre c'est tout pardonner*).

6. Honneth (2018) emphasizes the reciprocal nature of recognition in his reconstruction of Hume and Smith. His account is, however, an interpretive reconstruction of Hume's and Smith's respective accounts and only barely attempts to extend the analysis to the historically material conditions of recognition (or non-recognition).

BIBLIOGRAPHY

Blackburn, Simon. 1998. *Ruling Passions*. Oxford: Oxford University Press.
Bloom, Paul. 2016. *Against Empathy: The Case for Rational Compassion*. London: The Bodley Head.
Breithaupt, Fritz. 2019. *The Dark Sides of Empathy*. Translated by Andrew B. B. Hamilton. Ithaca: Cornell University Press.
Butler, Judith. 2009. *Frames of War: When is Life Grievable?* London: Verso.
Goldie, Peter. 2011. "Anti-Empathy." In *Empathy: Philosophical and Psychological Perspectives*, edited by Amy Coplan and Peter Goldie, 302–17. Oxford: Oxford University Press.
Hartmann, Martin. 2016. "Invisible Hand and Impartial Spectator: The Adam Smith Problem Reconsidered." In *The Philosophy of the Market*, edited by Hans-Christoph Schmidt am Busch, 49–69. Hamburg: Meiner Verlag.
Hochschild, Arlie R. 2016. *Strangers in Their Own Land: Anger and Mourning On the American Right*. New York: The New Press.
Honneth, Axel. 2018. *Anerkennung: Eine europäische Ideengeschichte*. Berlin: Suhrkamp.
Manne, Kate. 2018. *Down Girl: The Logic of Misogyny*. Oxford: Oxford University Press.
Marcuse, Herbert. 1965. "Repressive Tolerance." In *A Critique of Pure Tolerance*, edited by Robert Paul Wolff, Barrington Moore Jr., and Herbert Marcuse, 81–117. Boston: Beacon Press.
McCarthy, Thomas. 2009. *Race, Empire, and the Idea of Human Development*. Cambridge: Cambridge University Press.
Mills, Charles W. 2017. "Kant's Untermenschen." In *Black Rights/White Wrongs: The Critique of Racial Liberalism*, 91–112. Oxford: Oxford University Press.
Prinz, Jesse. 2011. "Against Empathy." *The Southern Journal of Philosophy* 49 (2011): 214–33.
Raphael, D. D. 2007. *The Impartial Spectator: Adam Smith's Moral Philosophy*. Oxford: Oxford University Press.
Rifkin, Jeremy. 2009. *The Empathic Civilization: The Race to Global Consciousness in a World in Crisis*. London: Polity Press.
Rizzolatti, Giacomo and Corrado Sinigaglia. 2008. *Mirrors in the Brain: How Our Minds Share Actions and Emotions*. Translated by Frances Anderson. Oxford: Oxford University Press.
Schultz, Bart. 2007. "Mill and Sidgwick, Imperialism and Racism." *Utilitas* 19, no. 1 (2007): 104–30.
Singer, Peter. 2016. "The Empathy Trap." *Project Syndicate*, https://www.project-syndicate.org/commentary/danger-of-empathy-versus-reason-by-peter-singer-20 16- 12?barrier=accesspaylog, December 12, 2016.
Slaby, Jan. 2013. "Empathy's Blind Sport." *Medicine, Health Care and Philosophy* 17, no. 2 (2013): 249–58.
Slote, Michael. 2010. *Moral Sentimentalism*. Oxford: Oxford University Press.
Smith, Adam. 1976. *The Theory or Moral Sentiments*. Indianapolis: Liberty Fund.

Taylor, Jacqueline. 2015. "Sympathy, Self, and Others." In *The Cambridge Companion to Hume's Treatise*, edited by Donald C. Ainslie and Annemarie Butler, 188–205. Cambridge: Cambridge University Press.

Waal, Frans de. 2009. *The Age of Empathy: Nature's Lessons for a Kinder Society*. New York: Harmony Books.

Chapter 9

On Human Sociability

Joel Whitebook

THE FREUDIAN DIVIDE

Taking my cue from Jan Assmann's study of Moses, I will begin by introducing the notion of the Freudian Divide (Assmann 1998). My claim is that Freud's intervention created a substantial rupture in the history of Western rationality, and that, after it, things can never be the same. What this means theoretically is this: as a result of the discovery of psychic reality and demonstration that the ego is not master in its own house, "the objectivity of the object and the subjectivity of the" subject, as Hans Loewald observed, can no longer be taken for granted and our ideas about rationality must be substantially revised (Loewald 2000, 399).[1] And anthropologically, the consequence of Freud's findings regarding narcissism – with its reality-denying conatus – and aggression is that the essential sociability of the human animal must be called into question. Just as sophisticated contemporary philosophers insist that any admissible philosophical position cannot regress behind Kant's Copernican Revolution, I would maintain that any psychoanalytic social theory, if it is not to suffer from unacceptable naiveté, must be located on this side of the Freudian Divide.

Having said this, I must immediately make one thing clear. By introducing the Freudian Divide, I am not arguing for the sort of anthropological pessimism that has a well-known history among conservative psychoanalysts, beginning with Freud himself. I am only maintaining that the negative features of our anthropological inheritance must be granted their rightful place in psychoanalytic social theory. As we will see, I subscribe to a dualistic position *that seeks to assign the correct weight to both the prosocial and the antisocial forces in human nature.*

Furthermore, although I believe that we must continue to theorize the notion of instinct, understood as the "demand made upon the mind for work in consequence of its connection with the body," in one way or another, my position does not tie me to a defence of Freudian instinct theory in its classical form (Freud (1915) 1975, 122). Given where the field is at today, that would be a fool's errand. For the purposes of my argument I am only asking that I be granted that narcissism, aggression, and sexuality – which means conflict, broadly conceived – are ubiquitous and systemic forces in human life, and that, with the exception of Winnicott, I am not required to delve into the details of the contemporary theories that underlie this claim. Indeed, it seems to me that anyone who glances at the morning newspapers can hardly deny my request.

Having introduced the notion of the Freudian Divide, I want to examine a problematic that appears in psychoanalysis and reappears in critical theory, partly as a result of its appropriation of its psychoanalysis. Like many great thinkers, Freud can often be cited on both sides of major questions. Nevertheless, it is safe to say that the central thrust of Freud's position tends to hypostatize the antisocial "Hobbesian" forces in psychic life and that his anthropological pessimism and scepticism about progressive politics is a result of that fact. This is especially true in his later writings. Not only does he declare that "every individual is virtually an enemy of civilization" in *The Future of an Illusion*, but three years later, in *Civilization and Its Discontents*, he ontologizes a *pre-established disharmony* between the instinctually embodied individual and the collectivity – between biology and society (Freud (1927) 1975, 6). In what may be his magnum opus, Freud observes,

> What decides the purpose of life is simply the programme of the pleasure principle. This principle dominates the operation of the mental apparatus from the start. There can be no doubt about its efficacy, and yet its programme is at loggerheads with the whole world, with the macrocosm as much as with the microcosm. There is no possibility at all of its being carried through; all the regulations of the universe run counter to it.

And as a result of this observation, Freud concludes "the intention that man should be 'happy' is not included in the plan of 'Creation'" (Freud (1930) 1975, 76). Since the earliest days of the field analysts have challenged Freud's hypostatization of the antisocial forces in mental life in various ways. Two of the most important challenges were made by Heinz Hartmann and John Bowlby. I do not want to minimize the criticisms that the Lacanians and the Frankfurt School levelled against American Ego Psychology. It is true that in practice notions such as "adaptation" and "an average expectable environment" often resulted in a strong conformist streak in the American analysts that blunted the radical edge of Freud's contribution. Nevertheless, the shortcomings of actually existing Ego Psychology notwithstanding, Hartmann made several theoretical points that constituted necessary corrections of the Freudian perspective. For our purposes, the most important one is this. Hartmann granted that there are obviously numerous areas in which the demands that biology imposes and the demands that society imposes on the individual conflict, as Freud had stressed. But the postulation of a nearly absolute opposition between biology and society – as Freud and, following him, the members of the first generation of the Frankfurt School tended to do – is a mistake, which, in fact, borders on incoherence (Hartmann 1939). Hartmann rightfully insists that, if there had not been sufficient prosocial potentialities within our biological make-up that made adaptation possible, the species would not have survived.

Where Hartmann made this point theoretically, Bowlby substantiated it empirically with his theory of attachment (Bolwby 1983). And for this, the orthodox Freudians of his day duly excoriated him. Bowlby argued, for example, that if infants had not been sufficiently attached to their mothers on the African savannahs, wild animals would have picked them off and the species wouldn't have survived. It is striking that although Freud considered himself an ardent Darwinian, his theory did not contain sufficient conceptual resources for explaining adaptation.[2]

Since the 1970s, a number of schools – including, object relations theorists, intersubjectivists, attachment theorists, self-psychologists, and social constructionists – whom I will collectively refer to as the Relational Left, have moved in the opposite direction. In an effort to correct the orthodox Freudians' hypostatization of the antisocial forces in psychic life and to refute the anthropological pessimism and scepticism about progressive politics that follow from it, they have emphasized the prosocial aspects of mental life: for example, relatedness, mutuality, recognition, empathy, reality-attunement, the competent infant, and so on. But, I would maintain, there is a difficulty with their strategy. In their attempt to counteract the one-sidedness of the orthodox Freudians, the members of the Relational Left are often guilty of one-sidedness in the opposite direction. That is to say, *they often tend to hypostatize the prosocial qualities of the human animal and thereby regress behind the Freudian Divide*. Whereas Freud's position appears to result in a *pre-established disharmony* between the individual and society, theirs tends to postulate a *pre-established harmony* between the two domains. *Both positions fail to correctly elucidate the relation of sociability and anti-sociability, which, I am arguing, is the proper desideratum for psychoanalytic social theory.*

The position of the Relational Left often rests on a misguided assumption that is widespread among well-intentioned progressively oriented thinkers in general, inside and outside of the field. They assume that to acknowledge the significant role that biological factors play in determining human life necessarily condemns one to a reactionary position, which excludes the possibility of progressive social change. To be biological, in other words, is to be immutable; and to be immutable is to preclude the possibility of the amelioration of social wrongs. In short, because "biology is destiny," it must be eschewed in toto.

Moreover, it is not only the representatives of the Relational Left that adhere to this assumption; it is also widespread among progressively oriented social scientists in general. Indeed, I would maintain that anti-biologism is one of the most widely shared prejudices among social scientists on the Left, and it often leads them to embrace a "sociologism" that is just as much in error as the biologism they reject. Both forms of one-sidedness must be avoided (see Laplanche 1989, 17ff.).

Their anti-biologism often compels thinkers on the Left to defend the thesis that it is language, which they believe means society, all the way down. Their presupposition is this: while biology is immutable, language is plastic. Therefore, if the self is constituted by language, it can be (indefinitely) moulded and reshaped by social practice in a desirable fashion. To cite an example that is close to my concerns, Habermas claims, "The self ... is socially constituted through and through" (Habermas 1992, 183). This is one of the reasons that led Habermas to declare *ex cathedra*, that is, without adequate argumentation, that the notion of a prelinguistic unconscious is "unacceptable" (Habermas 1972, 237; see also Whitebook 1997, Whitebook 2019, 38–43). It must be stressed that this is not simply a claim about a scholastic point in psychoanalytic exegesis. Rather, it is symptomatic of the linguistic monism that characterizes Habermas's project as a whole. The existence of such a "thicket of nonlinguisticality" at the centre of the self would constitute a limit to how far the reach of language, and therefore of society and sociability could extend (Whitebook 1997).

Motivated by the same sociologizing assumptions, Michel Foucault carries this line of reasoning to its absurd conclusions in the first volume of *The History of Sexuality*. In that confused text, he rejects the idea that human sexual identity rests on a biological substratum of any sort, however minimal (Whitebook 2005, 331–338). He argues instead that it is altogether a product of social construction. And Foucault doesn't stop there. He also maintains that the idea of a biological substratum is merely "an imaginary point," which was "posited" by the modern *Scientia Sexualis*, so that the "deployment of sexuality" could manipulate and control the population (Foucault 1978, 155).

Given the reactionary uses for which biology has often been employed with regard to racism and sexism, one can understand the scepticism towards it on the Left. Nevertheless, political motivations, however laudable, shouldn't lead us to theoretical conclusions that sometimes border on the absurd and deny the critical role that biological factors play in determining social life. What's more, Melvin Konner – an anthropologist who has made it his task to oppose the anti-biologism in the human sciences – has observed that today's biological research often support progressive political positions. For example, with regard to the idea that "biology is destiny," he argues that "despite limits to plasticity, cultural influence on human development is strong because its power is biologically assured" (Konner 2010, 16).[3] In short, not only does biology only limit the mutability of human identity, it also makes it possible. And more recently, Konner has attempted to demonstrate that, contrary to the received opinion, there are compelling biological arguments supporting a strong feminist position (Konner 2016). Indeed, given the destructiveness of the patriarchal heritage, he argues that its continued dominance threatens the survival of the species

HABERMAS' SOCIOLOGISM

When the first generation of the Frankfurt School appropriated psychoanalysis it inherited the deep structure of Freud's theory that absolutized the conflict between the biology and culture or the individual and civilization. For example, in his essay "On Hedonism," Marcuse more or less recasts the basic argument of *Civilization and Its Discontents* in philosophical terms. Marcuse contended that "the idealist philosophy of the bourgeois era" absolutized the conflict between the universal and the particular, where he understood the universal as representing the demands of the collective for rationality and civilized social life, and the particular as representing the demands of the biologically embodied individual, with his or her "empirical manifold of needs, wants and capacities," for happiness. Marcuse claimed that this state of affairs necessarily entailed "the sacrifice of the individual," whose demand for happiness is seen as merely "arbitrary and subjective" (Marcuse 1968, 159–200). In order to counter this idealist configuration, Marcuse claimed that the truth content of hedonism consists in its assertion of the embodied individual's right to concrete material happiness against the demands of the universal thus conceived.

In contrast to the Relational Left, the first generation of the Frankfurt School tenaciously stuck to the Freudian opposition of biology and society – of the individual and the collective. They did so for two reasons. First, empirically and diagnostically, they believed that it in fact accurately described the dynamic of civilization. This can be seen, for example, in Horkheimer and Adorno's claim that Odysseus's "sacrifice" of his inner nature constituted "the core of all civilizing rationality" and provided "the germ cell of proliferating mythical irrationality" from which the dialectic of enlightenment inexorably unfolded (Horkheimer/Adorno 2002, 42).

And the first generation also subscribed to the opposition between the two realms for a political reason. In this case, their motivation was the exact opposite of Habermas's – who, as we have seen, maintains that it is "language all the way down" in order to remove any limits to the socializability of the human subject. What Habermas fails to recognize, however, is the possible Orwellian consequences of his claim: if individuals are socializable through and through, they are also manipulable through and through.[4] Given the first generations' thesis of a totally administered world and their fear of "the direct socialization of the superego," they believed that an ultimate limit and point of resistance to the totalizing dynamics of instrumental reason was not only desirable, but that the biological dimension of individual identity could provide it. As opposed to other theorists on the Freudian Left, who were concerned about the supposedly reactionary implications of Freudian instinct theory, the first generation of critical theorists sought to construe it as a source of resistance thereby attempting to give it a progressive twist.

At the beginning of his career, Habermas, as a young German, who was committed to the construction of a liberal and democratic polity out of the ashes of the Nazi catastrophe, could not accept Horkheimer and Adorno's political resignation and quietism. And he believed that, theoretically, their political disposition was tied to the theoretical impasse of *Dialectic of Enlightenment*. As a result, the wish to circumvent the dialect of enlightenment became a primary motive for his revision of critical theory.

As I have argued elsewhere, one aspect of this revision consisted in rejecting the Freudian theory of socialization and replacing it with George Herbert Mead's account of identity formation (Whitebook 1997, 2008, 382–389). Mead opposed the Freudian claim that socialization involves an essential conflict between biology and society and requires, in an important sense, the repression of the individual. On the contrary, rather than entailing the sacrifice of the individual, Mead argued that socialization is in fact the medium in which individuation occurs. Habermas sought to encapsulate Mead's position with the slogan "individuation through socialization" (Habermas 1992, 149–204). But this slogan constitutes an attempted solution of the problem by fiat. It amounts to an a priori harmonization of the individual and the collective that radically minimizes the dimension of opposition and conflict between them. *The consequence is in an overly socialized conception of the self.* Paraphrasing Adorno, the individual does not go into the collective without a remainder, which can be a source of resistance and creativity as well as of anomie, psychopathology, and suffering. And this remainder, if it is not absent, is at least sorely undertheorized in the Habermasian approach.

I do not mean to deny that a significant component of the individuation process takes place through identification with the viewpoint of the other – the internalization of the object to put it in psychoanalytic terms – as Mead maintains. Both Mead and Habermas, however, lack a sufficiently elaborated conception of the "I" – of "the constitutional factor," as Freud called it, which the child brings to the table – and without it, two serious problems arise.

First, the theory is threatened with incoherence. Because it lacks the notion of a pre-reflective self-precursor that can pick itself out in mirroring phenomena and internalize the viewpoint of the other, the theory cannot explain how the process of self-formation gets going in the first place. Second, and more disturbingly, the spectre of conformism haunts the theory. As Ernst Tugendhat argues, without a sufficiently robust conception of the "I" that can resist and challenge the internalized demands of the collective – of the superego – it is difficult to see how conformism can be avoided. Tugendhat observes that without the countervailing force of a sufficiently robust "I," Mead's "generalized Other" is in danger of shading into Heidegger's "the they" (Tugendhat 1986, 251).

There is something odd about Habermas's adoption of the Meadian position. At the same time as he maintains that the self develops through the interaction of the "I" and the "me," he denies a dualistic conception of the self, which means, he also denies the existence of a divided and conflicted self. One place where this denial can be observed is in Habermas's rejection of Durkheim's definition of man as "*homo duplex*" (Durkheim 2005, 37). The French sociologist and anthropologist's description of our anthropological situation is exceedingly close to the one that Freud presents in *Civilization and Its Discontents*:

> Precisely because society has its own specific nature that is different from our nature as individuals, it pursues ends that are also specifically its own. ... Society requires us to make ourselves servants, forgetful of our own interests. And it subjects us to all sorts of restraints, privations, and sacrifices without which social life would be impossible. And so, at every instant, we must submit to rules of action and thought that we have neither made nor wanted and that sometimes are contrary to our inclinations and to our basic instinct. (Durkheim 1995, 219)

Just as earlier Habermas declared the unacceptability of the notion of a pre-linguistic unconscious *ex cathedra*, now he summarily dismisses Durkheim for his "unsatisfactorily dualism," without explaining what is unsatisfactory about it (Habermas 1985, 57). And as we would expect, he maintains that the Frenchman's error results from his adherence to the philosophy of consciousness, arguing that Durkheim had moved to a position similar to Mead's and embraced the philosophy of language, he would have avoided this problem. In other words, if he had accepted the proposition that "it is language all the way down," this annoying dualism wouldn't have appeared in the first place.

Habermas makes similar dismissive criticisms of Castoriadis's dualistic position. Castoriadis, who was obviously influenced by Durkheim, recasts the Greek distinction between a private *kosmos idios* and a public *kosmos koinonia* into his distinctive psychoanalytic distinction between the psychic imaginary and the social imaginary, arguing that, as divided beings, we are citizens of two realms. Habermas raises the objection that, for Castoriadis,

> the socialized individual is produced and, as in Durkheim, remains divided into monad and member of society. ... Intrapsychic conflicts are not internally linked with social ones instead, psyche and society stand in a kind of metaphysical opposition to one another. (Habermas 1987, 334)

In the first place, it is simply false to assert that "intrapsychic conflicts are not internally linked with social ones" in Castoriadis's position. One of the central *desiderata* of Castoriadis's theory is to elucidate the interaction between the psychic imaginary and the social imaginary, which is often highly conflicted. But more significantly, now that we are all post-metaphysical philosophers, Habermas believes that by labelling the opposition between psyche and society as "metaphysical," he has thereby invalidated it. But this philosophical *leger de main* doesn't work. While the opposition may not be metaphysical, I would maintain that it is anthropological, in other words, it is a fact of human nature. And the only thing that is objectionable about it – at least for Habermas – is that it interferes with the attempt to present an overly socialized, which is to say, an overly harmonistic account of the human subject.

OUR DUAL INHERITANCE

To illustrate the type of theoretical approach I am advocating, I will examine *Mixed Messages: Cultural and Genetic Inheritance in the Constitution of Human Society*, a text by the psychoanalyst and anthropologist Robert Paul (Paul 2015). Paul sets himself the precise task of elucidating the relation between the prosocial and antisocial forces in human nature. What's more, *Mixed Messages* has the advantage of eschewing psychoanalytic jargon and presenting its arguments in terms of evolutionary theory. It therefore avoids the polemical overtones that can be attached to the jargon, while presenting the logic of the problem in a perspicuous fashion.

The way that the perennial conflict between the positivists and the hermeneutists that characterizes the human sciences in general manifests itself in anthropology is in the opposition between the biological and the sociocultural schools. Paul turns to dual inheritance theory in an attempt not only to affect a rapprochement between the two research traditions but to also do justice to the truth content of each. He articulates the problem in the following way. The success of the so-called modern synthesis in biology in the 1970s resulted in a triumphalism among the evolutionary biologists. It led them to claim that they now possessed the theoretical resources to produce an exhaustive account of human evolution, which included social evolution, in terms of neo-Darwinian theory alone. But like the hermeneutists, late Wittgensteinians, phenomenologists, and others who contested the hegemonic claims of the positivists in philosophy during the same period, the cultural anthropologists challenged the monolithic assertions of the neo-Darwinians.

Paul maintains that the opposition between the two schools was problematic. At the same time that each camp possessed valid truth claims to which justice had to be done, they tended to dismissively ignore each other's positions, and a standoff occurred as a result. Paul therefore adopted a program to develop a comprehensive theory that integrates both positions, making sure to incorporate the truth content of each.[5] His thesis is this: the information contained in two distinct channels, which are "in principle, to a large degree independent and capable of operating on the basis of different agendas and values," provides the instructions for the development of the individual, and that both must be adequately realized if a mature individual of the species *homo sapiens* is to be achieved (Paul 2005, 91).

The genetic information contained in DNA comprises the code of the first channel. It is transmitted privately, that is to say, through sexual intercourse where the gametes of each parent, containing their DNA, are combined to provide the genetic instructions for the autopoiesis of the phenotype. Insofar as it seeks solely to maximize reproductive success, the development that occurs according to the instructions of the genetic channel is Darwinian. One might say, moreover, that the Darwinian perspective is basically "Hobbesian" in that "the agenda and values" of the genetic channel of information transmission is a primary source of the antisocial tendencies in human life. This idea was popularized with the notion of "the selfish gene" (Dawkins 1996). The evolutionists, who are often armed with sophisticated mathematical techniques, can be compared to positivists in other fields insofar as they hold that culture is an epiphenomenal realm that could be and should be explained away by hard science.

As a philosophical position, however, "Hobbesianism," contains a fatal flaw. On the basis of its assumptions about human nature, it cannot account for the possibility of society: its methodological individualism and egoistic anthropology make it impossible to explain how the prosocial attitudes and behaviour, which are the condition sine qua non for society – that is to say, cooperation, broadly conceived – is possible. And, according to Paul, the same problem arises with Darwinian version "Hobbesianism." As the anthropologist Walter Goldschmidt argues, only a theory of culture, in one form or another, can explain how the "Hobbesianism" of the genetic channel can be sufficiently "trumped" so that a distinctively human form of society becomes possible (Goldschmidt 2006).

With this observation, we arrive at the cultural channel of information transmission that provides a second set of instructions for human development. The cultural channel comprises the already existing symbolic complexes – what Habermas refers to as the "lifeworld" – into which the human infant is born. It is a well-established anthropological doctrine that, because the human neonate enters the world in relatively premature and helpless state, its maturation requires a period of socialization, acculturation, and education – of social learning – in a kinship unit of one sort or another that is exceptionally long compared to that of other species (Freud [1926] 1975, 154–155). The fact that the infant is equipped with an unspecialized and flexible human brain makes this socialization *qua* learning possible. According to Goldschmidt, the extended period of *paidea* transforms "the neonate into a responsible and competent member of his or her society" (Goldschmidt 2006, 37, 61). Or, as Castoriadis puts it more vividly, it transforms the little animal into a citizen of the *polis*. The members of the parental generation transmit the information encoded in the cultural channel to the members of the younger generation who internalize the information – especially the *nomoi* – contained in the symbols inscribed in the group's institutions in a variety of modalities, for example, in the decorated artefacts of everyday life, shrines, temples, architecture, and town planning, as well as in rituals, prayers, songs, and dance.

Where the genetic code provides the instructions for the autopoiesis of the phenotype, according to Paul, the symbolic code instructs social individuals how they "should construct themselves" and informs them of "what they need to do to survive, flourish, and reproduce" (Paul 2015, 74). And, as opposed to genetic information, which is transmitted privately, that is, by means of copulation, cultural information is, as we have seen, transmitted in the "'public' interpersonal world" (ibid., 68).

The strong culturalist position in anthropology is the correlate of the constructivist position in philosophy and social theory. Although the strong culturalists may pay lip service to the importance of the genetic channel in determining human evolution, they tend to emphasize the constitutive power of the symbolic and the greater efficiency of symbolic learning over genetic learning to such a degree that the cultural channel becomes overwhelmingly preponderant in their theories.

But, as Paul observes, despite the massive importance of the emergence of the cultural-symbolic channel in the course of evolution, "the genetic program did not simply go away" as a result (ibid., 93). On the contrary, it continued and continues to exert powerful influence in determining individual and collective development. To deny this is to succumb to a progressivist illusion.

I will consider another related question that can be formulated in the following way. If we assume, as we must, that until the point in the history of nature where the symbolic channel emerged, evolution operated only in accordance with the code of the genetic channel, and if we also assume that creation *ex nihilo* is impossible, then we must conclude that elements must have existed within the original Darwinian stratum that "gave rise to" and "supported" the emergence of symbolic culture and the possibility of human sociability (Castoriadis 1987, 229–230). In other words, emergence is a bootstrapping operation, which means that the resources for that bootstrapping must have been present in "first nature" if "second nature" was to emerge. Let me be clear, there was nothing teleological or inevitable about the process; it unfolded in strict accordance with the laws of "first nature," that is to say, natural selection.

Different evolutionary theorists propose different candidates for that antecedent element. Goldschmidt's candidate is "affect hunger." He argues that it was not only "inherent in mammalian procreation," but also that it is the ingredient of our biological inheritance that helps to trump the selfish gene and make a specifically human form of learning and sociability possible (Goldschmidt 2006, 19). "Affect hunger" is, as he puts it, the conative force that "does for sociality what sex does for reproduction" (ibid., 74). According to Goldschmidt, "both child and mother are programmed to seek and give expression of affection," and, in the early phases of evolution, that program "began" as an attachment "device" which assured "the care and feeding of the neonate among [the] social animals" that were our precursors. Then, with the appearance of early hominoids, it was "built upon to motivate the neonate to learn from adults [and] to undergo the lengthy curriculum" – the *paidea* or *Bildung* – "necessary to become an adult" who would conform to the expectations of the group (ibid., 37).

Regarding parents, "affect hunger" assumes the form of "nurturant love." As parents have known for millennia, the extended period of dependency, development, and enculturation required to raise a human child to maturity involves considerable "difficulties and unpleasantness." Consequently, the fact that parents manage to transcend their "selfishness" and accept the attendant hardships – which is to say, their "generosity" – must be explained. Goldschmidt claims that pleasure-in-nurturance appears in the course of evolution in conjunction with the emergence of mammals. While nurturant love may have been "foreshadowed" in some earlier species, strictly speaking, it "is a more recent animal attribute, coming with live births that are the hallmark of the mammal class of animals." And while it first appears with mammals, nurturant love reaches its fully developed form with *Homo sapiens*. "To nurture is to respond to a call to give one's time, energy, and resources to the welfare of another," and, Goldschmidt argues, not only do humans "regularly tend to their own infants," but they "are programmed to enjoy it despite its many difficulties and unpleasantness" (ibid., 35–36).

Where affect hunger, in the form of nurturant love, motivates the parent to tolerate the unpleasure that is necessary for raising a child, affect hunger, in the form of the desire for parental and especially maternal love, motivates the child to relinquish the biological pleasure principle and to progressively come to terms with the reality principle. Culture, Goldschmidt observes, "builds" on the infant's hunger for maternal love "to motivate the neonate to learn from adults and thus conform to the expectations of the troop, pride, or band [and] to undergo the lengthy curriculum necessary to become a human adult" (ibid., 37). In other words, learning involves delayed gratification as well as considerable unpleasure, and children are willing to accept the pleasure of maternal affection as compensation for relinquishing the more immediate id-pleasures that is necessary for development and acculturation.

As we have seen, with all their tough-minded science, the neo-Darwinians cannot explain how cooperation is possible. And as we have also seen, the cultural anthropologists can only account for sociability by disregarding the domain of evolution. In contrast to both these approaches, Goldschmidt, with his notion of "affect hunger," offers us a plausible theory that explains human sociability in terms affect hunger, one of the most fundamental facts of our evolutionary history.

THE MISUSE OF WINNICOTT

Generally speaking, the members of the Relational Left believed that, in order to counter Freud's hypostatization of the antisocial forces in psychic life and thereby vitiate his anthropological pessimism as well as his scepticism concerning progressive politics, it was necessary to fulfil two theoretical objectives. In addition to refuting Freud's instinct theory, the move from a "one-person" to a "two-person" psychology also had to be made. And they regularly invoked D. W. Winnicott as the psychoanalytic theorist *per excellence* who had fulfilled both of these objectives. While the claim that is not entirely without merit, following Noëlle McAfee, I argue that the Relational Left's appropriation of the British psychoanalyst is highly selective, and that they only make use of the aspects of his work that suit their theoretical and political program, while ignoring the darker, antisocial, and what one might call more "Kleinian" dimension of this theory. It should not be forgotten that, although Winnicott belonged to the independent group in British psychoanalysis, he acknowledged the profound influence that Klein had on his thinking (Winnicott (1962) 1974; McAfee 2019).

Like his writing, Winnicott's psychoanalytic persona is far more subtle and complex than it is often taken to be. Because he was a paediatrician as well as an analyst, who tends to be associated with teddy bears, bits of string, and security blankets, Winnicott is regularly viewed as benevolent, jovial, and reassuring – as an avuncular and helpful figure, standing in stark contrast to the dark, demanding, and severe Dr. Freud. This is one of the reasons why so many people, inside and outside of the field, are attracted to him.

But this is only part of the story. Winnicott didn't only develop his revolutionary theory of early development out of his work with infants and young children. It also grew out of his intensive clinical experience with deeply regressed borderline and psychotic patients. Indeed, he tells us that the later experience *played an even more important role* than his work with young children and their mothers in formulating his position:

> My experiences have led me to recognize that dependent or deeply regressed patient *can teach the analyst more* about early infancy than can be learned from direct observation of infants, and more than can be learned from contact with mothers who are involved with infants. (Winnicott (1960a) 1974, 141, emphasis added)[6]

Where Winnicott learned the essential features of "good enough," that is to say, "normal" development from his work as a paediatrician and child analyst – and thereby provided a positive conception of "health" that was sorely missing from Freud's theory – his experience with borderline patients taught him about the "primitive agonies" and severe pathologies that can result when development isn't "good enough" and the journey from dependence to independence, from omnipotence to reality acceptance, and from destructiveness to concern is disrupted by early trauma. Through his work with severely regressed individuals, he acquired first-hand knowledge of the antisocial forces in psychic life – of archaic aggression, hatred, and destructiveness, and of the primitive defences (identified by Melanie Klein) that are associated with them.

Because of their desire to construe early childhood as a realm of sociability, relatedness, and recognition, and to view Winnicott as the theorist of that realm, members of the Relational Left tend to focus on the first half of his psychoanalytic persona that I have attempted to describe and to disregard to gloss over "all the destructiveness that is bound up with living," as he refers to it (Winnicott (1962) 1974, 174). In other words, they tend to focus on what we might call "the developmental Winnicott,' who constructed a theory of ideal or normal development, and to minimize "the clinical Winnicott," who was a pioneer in the exploration of borderline and psychotic psychopathology. As a result, they believe they have found an appealing alternative to Freud's anthropological pessimism. But they have done so at the cost of splitting-off and denying the darker and less sociable aspects of Winnicott's perspective.

While there are a number of ways to describe the developmental journey, described by Winnicott, which culminates in maturity, creativity, and healthy living, I will attempt to elucidate it in terms of the concept of "reality acceptance" – or the acceptance of the "not-me." If things are "good enough" and the "facilitating environment" fulfils its task during the earliest stage of development, infants remain in a state of "going-on-being" – that is, plenum-like state of "totalitarian inclusion," as Castoriadis refers to it – in which they have no inkling of the "not-me" (Castoriadis 1987, 103; McAfee 2019, 48–49). As Winnicott observes, during this stage, "the infant ... with the mother operating as an auxiliary ego ... has not yet separated out the 'not-me' from the 'me,'" which "cannot happen apart from the establishment of the 'me'" (Winnicott 1974, 104).[7]

Remaining in a state of "going-on-being" is possible, he argues, because in normal development mothers enter into a state of "primary maternal preoccupation" after the birth of their infants, and, as a result, they are so finely attuned to their babies' needs that they can fulfil them as if by "magic," which is to say, almost instantaneously (Winnicott 1956, 300–306). Consequently, their infants continue in their state of "going-on-being" without interruption, and the "not-me," in the form of privation, never intrudes into the plenum. Moreover, by "magically" fulfilling their infants' needs, mothers provide them with an experience in which, Winnicott observes, "omnipotence is nearly a fact of existence" (Winnicott (1953) 1986, 11).

But "the clinical Winnicott" is all-to-familiar with the fact that "environments can fail," as McAfee notes. "Sometimes," she writes, "the holding environment fractures before the infant is capable of tolerating it, that is, before it has become integrated enough to tolerate the impingement" (McAfee 2019, 49). This can happen owing to a variety of internal and external factors, including war and migration, maternal depression, or the death of a sibling. Because the consequences of the failures that occur at this early stage are generally so catastrophic, Winnicott uses the term "annihilation" to describe them. Because a "unit self" or the "me" has not yet been differentiated from the "not-me," the severest forms of psychopathology, in which a person's relation to reality as such is impaired, can be the consequence.

It is during the next developmental stage that the distinction between subject and object and "reality acceptance" begins to emerge (Winnicott (1963) 1974, 87). In a "good enough" situation, the mother's "de-adaptation" to her infant's needs begins naturally when her "primary maternal preoccupation" gradually recedes as she returns to her life outside the micro-cosmos of the infant-mother dyad. Obviously, her "magical" adaptation to her infant's needs cannot continue, which means that the "not-me," in the form frustration and need, begins to intrude into the baby's circle of omnipotent control. The primary task that mothers must perform during this phase is to titrate the introduction of frustration and *eo ipso* of reality into their babies' worlds at a manageable pace so that their "infant[s] can gradually abrogate omnipotence." In so doing, "good enough" mothers make the acceptance of the "not-me" tolerable. Winnicott's theory of transitional phenomena, which may be his most famous contribution, is meant to explain how this graduated mitigation of omnipotence and acceptance of reality can occur.

Paradoxical as it may seem, "the developmental Winnicott" tells us that, in normal development, "destructiveness" plays a role not only in accepting the object but also in loving it. When it begins to dawn on young children that they are almost completely dependent on their mothers for the fulfilment of their needs – who, they simultaneously beginning to realize, are independent persons operating beyond their omnipotent control – the wish to destroy them typically results. It must be stressed that Winnicott is not using the term "destruction" metaphorically, but is using it in a concrete and elemental sense, that is, as the "actual impulse to destroy the breast," which manifests itself in "biting" and "hurting" (Winnicott (1969) 1986, 92). As he puts it, "the baby gets a kick out of kicking" (ibid.).

In this situation, Winnicott argues, the mother's task is to "survive," where "survival" doesn't only mean actual physical survival, but also "survival" in the sense of remaining constant and not suffering "change in quantity, in attitude" (ibid., 93). Most importantly, she must not "retaliate" in the face of her infant's attempts to destroy her. If things go well and mothers survive the repeated attempts to destroy them without retaliation, two propitious development achievements typically follow.

First, the mother's survival results in the mollification of infantile omnipotence and the acceptance of reality. Her indestructibility is the cipher for the hardness and recalcitrance of reality – for what Freud refers to as *Atropos* (the "inexorable") (Freud (1913) 1975, 296). Therefore, as infants eventually recognize that they cannot destroy their mothers, they concomitantly come to realize that reality as such is beyond their control, which means that their omnipotence is limited. In other words, they learn to accept the "not-me."

Secondly, although unconscious destructiveness will remain a ubiquitous feature of unconscious life, the mother's survival is expected to modulate the infants' overt destructiveness to the degree that they can assume their place as functioning members of conventional society. Furthermore, infants can in fact come to love and have concern for their mothers in virtue of the fact that they have survived their destructiveness. "From now on," Winnicott writes, "the subject says: 'Hello object!' 'I destroyed you.' 'I love you.' 'You have value for me because of your survival of my destruction of you'" (Winnicott (1969) 1986, 90).

But, as McAfee observed, "environments can fail." And when this happens, "the clinical Winnicott" becomes relevant. When infants aren't provided with a workable means for dealing with separation and loss or for taming their destructiveness serious pathologies can result. If reality isn't introduced to them in a graduated fashion that they can tolerate, their omnipotence won't be mollified. On the contrary, when reality intrudes into their plenum in a traumatic way, children may resort to the type of omnipotent defences, described by Klein, that are meant to deny the independence of mother, the experience of loss, and the existence of the object. That is to say, they may attempt to maintain their position of "totalitarian exclusion" and omnipotently deny the existence of the "not-me." Similarly, if mothers fail to survive the attacks that are made against them, their infants' destructiveness will not be modulated and transmuted into love and concern. When this happens, children can become consumed by destructive rage and hatred of the mother and thereby of the "not-me" in general, which can become as fierce and truly terrible" as the original need for the mother (Winnicott (1963) 1974, 88). As we know, these are the types of symptoms that are associated with the borderline syndrome.

THE POLITICAL CALCULUS

In this chapter I have argued for the following *theoretical* point. Against the conservative Freudians, on the one side, and the Relational Left, on the other side, I have maintained that an acceptable psychoanalytic theory must provide a balanced account of the antisocial and the prosocial forces that are both essential features of our species' anthropological inheritance. However, with respect to the *political* application of that theory – that is, with respect to diagnosing the social pathologies that characterize the contemporary historical constellation – the situation is different. In this case, one must make an empirical assessment of how the relative strength of those forces are aligned in what Freud called "the battle of the giants" (Freud (1930) 1975, 122).

While the post-war world order was in its ascendance, many progressives were confident that the forces of liberal democracy – representing the prosocial dimension of human nature – would ultimately triumph on a global scale. But with the developments that have accompanied the unravelling of the post-war world order in recent decades, which have ranged from the illiberal to the barbaric, that confidence proved to be unfounded. Today, the other combatant in the battle of the giants, namely, destructiveness, seems to be gaining the upper hand.

Given this state of affairs, I would suggest that Winnicott's clinical doctrines – specifically, the "hatred of the not-me" – are particularly well suited for addressing a world that is awash in racism, tribalism, religious hatred, nationalism, misogyny, and xenophobia.[8] "Misrecognition of the other" is too weak a concept to describe these phenomena. In too many of the "hot spots" around the world, we are not simply witnessing the refusal to recognize the other. With ethnic cleansing, genocide, mass beheadings, rape as a weapon of war, intentional starvation, and indiscriminate aerial bombing, we are witnessing the attempt to destroy the "not-me" (Castoriadis 1997b, 19–31). If it is to be effective, psychoanalytic social theory must be guided by political realism rather than wishful thinking.

NOTES

1. See also Castoriadis: "Psychoanalysis obliges us to see that the human being is not a *zoon logon ekhon* [an animal possessing reason], but essentially an imagining being, one endowed radical, unmotivated, defunctionalized imagination" (Castoriadis 1997, 351).

2. There is one place where Freud broaches the question of the adaptedness of the human mind to the world. But by providing a more or less tautological, which means, a relatively empty answer to it, he in effect dismisses the question: "[A]n attempt has been made to discredit scientific endeavour in a radical way, on the ground that, being bound to the conditions of our own organization, it can yield nothing else than subjective results, while the real nature of things outside ourselves remains inaccessible. But this is to disregard several factors, which are of decisive importance for the understanding of scientific work. In the first place, our organization – that is, our mental apparatus – has been developed precisely in the attempt to explore the external world, and it must therefore have realized in its structure some degree of expediency" (Freud (1927) 1975, 56).

3. For a general defence of the role of biology in the human sciences see Konner 2002.

4. This is what the first generation referred to as "the direct socialization of the superego."

5. Paul's dualist program in *Mixed Messages* invites comparison with the one that Habermas pursued in *The Logic of the Social Sciences* (Habermas 1990).

6. This observation runs counter to the claim of the infant researchers – whose work the Relational Left often marshals in support of its position – and is therefore is important for our purposes. Where the "baby watchers" claim that infant research

provides us with a more accurate account of early development than the reconstructions arrived at through the analysis of adults, Winnicott is maintaining that just the opposite is the case. See also McAfee 2019, 42.

7. The received wisdom, which is shared by the Relational Left, is that when Winnicott declared that "there is no baby without a mother," definitively refuted Freud's doctrine of primary narcissism. But this is inaccurate. Winnicott unequivocally states that, when infants are in the plenum-like stage of complete dependence, "primary narcissism" is a "living realit[y]" for them. Rather than refuting Freud's theory of primary narcissism, Winnicott's canonical intervention supplemented it. In other words, Winnicott accepted Freud's claim that, in the earliest phase of development, the infant is in a state of primary narcissism, but he added that an infant in such a state – which is self-enclosed and operates according to the pleasure principle – could not survive on its own but requires a mother acting as an auxiliary ego. This is a correction that has important implications for the entire theory of omnipotence (Winnicott [1960b] 1974, 44).

8. This is the strategy that McAfee pursues to great advantage in McAfee (2019).

BIBLIOGRAPHY

Assmann, Jan. 1998. *Moses the Egyptian*. Cambridge, MA: Harvard University Press.
Bowlby, John. 1983. *Attachment and Loss*. New York: Basic Books.
Castoriadis, Cornelius. 1987. *The Imaginary Institution of Society*. Trans. Kathleen Blamey. Cambridge, MA: The MIT Press.
Castoriadis, Cornelius. 1997a. "Psychoanalysis and Philosophy." In *The Castoriadis Reader*. Trans. David Ames Curtis. New York: Wiley-Blackwell, 348–360.
Castoriadis, Cornelius. 1997b. "Reflections on Racism." In *The World in Fragments: Writings on Politics, Society, Psychoanalysis, and the Imagination*. Trans. David Ames Curtis. Stanford, CA: Stanford University Press, 19–32.
Dawkins, Richard. 1996. *The Selfish Gene*. New York: Oxford University Press.
Durkheim. Émile. 1995. *Elementary Forms of Religious Life*. Trans. Karen E. Fields. New York: Free Press.
Foucault, Michel. 1978. *The History of Sexuality, Vol. 1: An Introduction*. Trans. Robert Hurley. New York: Pantheon Books.
Freud, Sigmund. 1913. "The Theme of the Three Caskets." In *The Standard Edition of the Complete Psychological Works of Sigmund Freud, Volume. XII*. Trans. James Strachey et al. London: The Hogarth Press, 289–302.
Freud, Sigmund. 1975 (1915). "Instincts and their Vicissitudes." In *The Standard Edition of the Complete Psychological Works of Sigmund Freud, Volume XIV*. Trans. James Strachey et al. London: The Hogarth Press, 109–140.
Freud, Sigmund. 1975 (1926). *Inhibitions, Symptoms and Anxiety. The Standard Edition of the Complete Psychological Works of Sigmund Freud, Volume XX*. Trans. James Strachey et al. London: The Hogarth Press, 75–176.
Freud, Sigmund. 1975 (1927). "The Future of an Illusion." In *The Standard Edition of the Complete Psychological Works of Sigmund Freud, Volume XXI*. Trans. James Strachey et al. London: The Hogarth Press, 1–56.

Freud, Sigmund. 1975 (1930). *Civilization and its Discontents, The Standard Edition*, Vol. XXI. Trans. James Strachey et al. London: The Hogarth Press, 3–148.
Goldschmidt, Walter. 2006. *The Bridge to Humanity: How Affect Hunger Trumps the Selfish Gene*. New York: Oxford University Press.
Habermas, Jürgen. 1972. *Knowledge and Human Interests*. Trans. Jeremy J. Shapiro. Boston: Beacon Press.
Habermas, Jürgen. 1985. *The Theory of Communicative Action, Vol. 2: Lifeworld and System: A Critique of Functionalist Reason*. Trans. Thomas McCarthy. Boston: Beacon Press.
Habermas, Jürgen. 1987. *The Philosophical Discourse of Modernity: Twelve Lectures*. Trans. Frederick Lawrence. Cambridge, MA: The MIT Press.
Habermas, Jürgen. 1990. *On the Logic of the Social Sciences*. Trans. Sherry Weber Nicholson and Jerry A. Stark. Cambridge, MA: The MIT Press.
Habermas, Jürgen. 1992. "Individuation through Socialization: On Mead's Theory of Subjectivity." In *Postmetaphysical Thinking*. Trans. William Mark Hohengarten. Cambridge, MA: The MIT Press, 149–204.
Hartmann, Heinz. 1939. *Ego Psychology and the Problem of Adaptation*. Trans. David Rappaport. New York: International Universities Press.
Horkheimer, Max and Theodor W. Adorno. 2002. *Dialectic of Enlightenment: Philosophical Fragments*. Trans. Edmund Jephcott. Stanford, CA: Stanford University Press.
Konner, Melvin. 2002. *The Tangled Wing: Biological Constraints on the Human Spirit*, revised edition. New York: Henry Holt and Co.
Konner, Melvin. 2010. *The Evolution of Childhood*. Cambridge, MA: Harvard University Press.
Konner, Melvin. 2016. *Women After All: Sex, Evolution, and the End of Male Supremacy*. New York: W.W. Norton & Co.
Laplanche, Jean. 1989. *New Foundations of Psychoanalysis*. Oxford: Blackwell.
Loewald, Hans. 2000. "The Waning of the Oedipus Complex." In *The Essential Loewald: Collected Papers on Monographs*. Hagerstown, Maryland: University Publishing Group, 384–404.
Marcuse, Herbert. 1968. "On Hedonism." In *Negations: Essays in Critical Theory*. Trans. Jeremy J. Shapiro. Boston: Beacon Press.
McAfee, Noëlle. 2019. *Fear of Breakdown: Psychoanalysis and Politics*. New York: Columbia University Press.
Paul, Robert A. 2015. *Mixed Messages: Cultural and Genetic Inheritance in the Constitution of Human Society*. Chicago: The University of Chicago Press.
Tugendhat, Ernst. 1986. *Self-Consciousness and Self-Determination*. Trans. Paul Stern. Cambridge, MA: The MIT Press, 1986.
Whitebook, Joel. 1997. *Perversion and Utopia: A Study in Psychoanalysis and Social Theory*. Cambridge, MA: The MIT Press.
Whitebook, Joel. 2005. "Against Interiority: Foucault's Struggle with Psychoanalysis." In *The Cambridge Companion to Foucault, Second Edition*. New York: Cambridge University Press, 312–347.
Whitebook, Joel. 2008. "First Nature and Second Nature in Hegel and Psychoanalysis." *Constellations* 15, no. 3 (2008): 382–389.

Whitebook, Joel. 2019. "Psychoanalysis and Critical Theory." In *The Routledge Companion to the Frankfurt School*. New York: Routledge, 32–47.

Winnicott, Donald W. 1974 (1960a). "Ego Distortions in terms of True and False Self." In *The Maturational Process and the Facilitating Environment: Studies in the Theory of Emotional Development*. New York: International Universities Press, 140–157.

Winnicott, Donald W. 1974 (1960b). "The Theory of the Parent-Infant Relationship." In *The Maturational Process and the Facilitating Environment: Studies in the Theory of Emotional Development*. New York: International Universities Press, 37–55.

Winnicott, Donald W. 1974 (1962). "A Personal View of the Kleinian Contribution." In *The Maturational Process and the Facilitating Environment: Studies in the Theory of Emotional Development*. New York: International Universities Press, 171–178.

Winnicott, Donald W. 1974 (1963). "From Dependence Towards Independence in the Development of the Individual." In *The Maturational Process and the Facilitating Environment: Studies in the Theory of Emotional Development*. New York: International Universities Press, 83–92.

Winnicott, Donald W. 1974. "The Fear of Breakdown." *International Review of Psychanalyses* (1974) I, 103–107.

Winnicott, Donald W. 1978 (1956). "Primary Maternal Preoccupation." In *Through Paediatrics to Psycho-Analysis*. London: The Hogarth Press, 300–306.

Winnicott, Donald W. 1986 (1953). "Transitional Objects and Transitional Phenomena." In *Playing and Reality*. New York: Tavistock Publications.

Winnicott, Donald W. 1986 (1969). "The Use of an Object." In *Playing and Reality*. New York: Tavistock Publications.

Section III

SOCIAL FREEDOM

Chapter 10

Ethical Life and Anomie
From Social Philosophy to Sociology of the State

Bruno Karsenti

INTRODUCTION: FREEDOM AND THE STATE

It can be argued that social theory rather than political theory is capable of solving the difficulties that the democratic rule of law is currently confronted with in winning general approval and establishing itself as a legitimate form, in a context of ever more pronounced internationalization of political problems. This view is one that the Frankfurt School's recent work reflects quite well. Axel Honneth's writings represent one of the major positions in this debate. But the particular path he has taken makes his work stand out, particularly in view of the prevalence of references to Habermas's version of the debate. For in *Freedom's Right* (Honneth 2014) Honneth has resolutely situated himself not in the line of Kant and Rawls but rather of Hegel and Durkheim, especially Hegel, whose thought is portrayed as a model for forging a new idea of freedom. For Honneth this is the concept that should guide the efforts that modern societies must make in conceiving and acting upon themselves. Hegel, then, assumes the identity of a social thinker or a philosopher primarily interested in social phenomena – not at all an obvious role to ascribe to him, and an identity that requires setting aside the more metaphysical elements of his doctrine (ibid., 59). A driving force behind this undertaking is a critique of modern political philosophy; specifically, its contractualism, and some recent liberal theories of justice that rely on contractualism. But Honneth also has a unique way of using the *Elements of the Philosophy of Right*, which is to steer it in the direction of a philosophy of the social that, as such, may in fact be used to change our view of the state's function in modern societies and of individuals' attitude towards and ways of relating to the state.

Honneth, then, does not so much interpret Hegel's *Elements* as employ it as a means to gain impetus. He defines his task as a "normative reconstruction" of modernity: that is, not a construction that follows transcendental principles of the sort that a purely philosophical method might establish and to which reality must then conform. Rather Honneth offers a means of apprehending reality as it exists, in accordance with its internal structuration and the norms that orient it in the direction of its essential aim in the modern age: achieving freedom through the rights societies have endowed themselves with, and on the basis of the achievement known as the state. "The system of right is the realm of actualized freedom," Hegel announces at the outset of *Elements* (Hegel 1991, §4). What this means, Honneth explains, is that it is not the modern state's aim to guarantee freedom as if it were a given in the subject's possession, but rather to create the "realm" in which freedom will be actualized, apprehended and discovered through the experience of individuals within the instituted reality in which they live (Honneth 2012, 19–31.).

Within that experience – to the extent that it is defined as *democratic*, a term that Honneth wants to be flexible enough to encompass both the constitution of our political regime and the immanent norm of our social relations – lies our relationship to the state, a relationship that is necessarily ambivalent. Indeed, the state may well be the most enigmatic element, the most difficult crux-of-the-matter to analyse. That relationship manifests itself in different ways along a spectrum that ranges from appealing to the state to guarantee rights all the way through to harsh critiques of the same state for violating rights, of which it is always suspect. The strength of Honneth's expression "freedom's right" lies in the fact that it concentrates that ambivalence: in one and the same movement, the state constitutes our freedom as a right but implies that freedom can turn against the very same state: if the right is truly the right to freedom, if the right is a matter of freedom or proceeds from it, then the right must allow criticism of the state. This in turn means that the right must justify itself on new bases, entirely different from those used by superseded forms of the state, wherein freedom was not the cardinal value of all legitimate policies as it has become for us. Hegel was the first thinker to enunciate this so clearly – to claim, in short, that what makes us modern is first and foremost the fact that we have conferred this role on freedom, and that the justification of our institutions – institutions synthesized and epitomized, as it were, by the modern state – has to respect that role. Any critique of the state conscious of being rooted in modernity must therefore assume the stance expressed in Honneth's critique: not frontal opposition, but a call for inflecting and reorienting public policy in response to social mobilizations and the demands for and expectations of justice that such mobilizations continually uphold and express. What is radical in this critique is not its rejection of the state but indeed the rigour and acuity of its institutionalism. This is why Honneth quite naturally views his thinking as being in line with Hegel.

It is clear, at any rate, that his "social" approach cannot proceed by describing political and legal institutions. Its point of entry must be different, located at the level of the experience that subjects have of their socialization within a democratic, law-governed state – an experience, therefore, that is bound up with manifestations of freedom. Bearing this in mind, we should be able to begin to untangle the afore-cited ambivalence and attain a more coherent view of ourselves, despite our paradoxes. The danger is a deficit of self-understanding. Freedom in the specific form it has assumed in the course of the development of our modern societies has been misunderstood, and it has therefore brought with it a misrepresentation of the state. In other words, it is because we do not properly understand what freedom means *in its modern sense* that we have lent credibility to a representation of the state that works to the advantage of falsely critical attitudes. We represent the state as a concentration of powers elevated to the level of sovereign power, as the ultimate source of rules, and as an acting subject detached from the society it acts upon. We must learn to overcome this vision in the debate on the state as it currently stands, which is focused either on the state's role in political societies or on its intervention in an international context where it is, at the very least, in competition with other sources of norms and where, on the strongest interpretation, it it has already been superseded by them.

At any rate, it is important to note that despite the fact that Honneth's critique refers to the particular substance of the "social," he does not develop it along strictly sociological lines but rather in connection with a strand of political philosophy that he considers has not been sufficiently explored. There are two aspects to that strand: the critique of an idea of freedom that reduces it to absolute individual subjective rights, and the critique of the state as a normative and material power whose role is to guarantee such rights. When, early in the nineteenth century, Hegel founded the philosophy of right on principles other than those identified by the science of natural right, he opened up a perspective that has never ceased to be of concern to us. His position, linked as it was to a historical form of constitutional monarchy, was understandably infused with a certain emphasis on the state: what could be defined as a sort of ineliminable statism that Marx was either the first or one of the first readers to critique as an obstacle to conceiving genuine emancipation (Marx 1977; Abensour 2011). But beneath this veneer lies an idea of *political society* of which we should endeavour to take advantage, Honneth suggests, as it inclines us towards an entirely different image of the state than the one targeted and attacked by Marxism and post-Marxism. In sum, thanks to Hegel it is possible to rise beyond Hegel. Again, this is because Hegel conceptualized freedom in a new way, as the touchstone of a vision of the state in turn substantiated by an analysis of the structures of modern society and the way they are instituted.

At this point, let me clarify what I mean by "political society": a society that has been politicized *by way of* social relations; that is, a society whose constitutive groups – groups within which individuals relate to each other according to differentiated, interconnected norms – are themselves politicized. In this sense, political society cannot be conceived without reference to a definition of civil society, a concept Hegel uses and redefines based on the English-Scottish philosophical tradition and classical political economy (Hegel 1991, 259–313; Kervégan 2007, 177–211). However, in contrast to this earlier tradition, Hegel argues that society cannot be seen as the affirmation of a plurality of individuals endowed with what comes down to an essentialized attribute of freedom that qualifies each of them in isolation. Rather, society is nothing but the reality of social relations, relations that, in a modern context, ultimately determine the form taken by individuality in that society. In sum, such a society is broken down into distinct spheres within which the meaning of freedom varies considerably.

Therefore, for Hegel, the social and political varieties of freedom prevail over individual freedom. They are not an outer shell that guarantees for each individual the ability to assert his or her freedom, but rather the fundamental plane on which subjective freedom is constructed in the first place and evolves. That is why it is also necessary to redefine the state. For without the state, social and political freedom would lose all support and be in danger of collapsing.

However, there are two increasingly distinct visions of how we ought to reconceptualize the state. If that is indeed our objective, should we not, first of all, turn to forms of knowledge whose particular task is to analyse social relations – namely, the social sciences, in their disciplinary plurality—for the empirical knowledge they produce? The social sciences represent a typically modern epistemic form that is radically different from political philosophy (Karsenti 2013; Callegaro 2015). And it is not immediately apparent why Hegelianism, the acme of speculative thought, would not be affected by the divergence that sociology introduces in political concepts. At a more general level, on what grounds should philosophy remain the compulsory path for reconceiving freedom and the state, given that sociology set itself free from the philosophical framework and produced its own scientific method – which seems much more appropriate for investigating the state?

Let me stress that this is not a mere matter of cross-disciplinarity or disciplinary boundaries. We are confronted here with a dilemma that concerns the very possibility of diagnosing the present in such a way as to break free from the confusions it foments and, consequently, provide critical tools to contribute effectively to its transformation. Moreover, as we shall see, the problem itself leads us to the question of what the sociology of the state means. The very fact that sociology finds it so difficult to objectify the state (Bourdieu 2014, 106), without reducing it to a matter of public law or an object of administrative science, is evidence that we cannot take for granted the aforementioned autonomization of the sociological perspective. After the emancipation of sociology from modern political philosophy, is sociology still dependent on philosophy for expounding norms, or is sociology in fact capable – as a form of knowledge in its own right – of identifying and explaining those norms? For if we want to bring the discussion to a point where the above-specified alternatives become clear, there is no choice but to examine whether a sociological concept of the state is possible.

That is my aim in this article. I draw on Honneth's *Freedom's Right* to try to determine the conditions under which Hegelian social philosophy may account for the normativity specific to modern societies, normativity deciphered with the help of a concept of freedom in which relations between the individual and the state have been redefined. Ultimately, the question tackled is whether the Hegelian perspective suffices to construct a representation of individuals' attitudes towards or relations with the state that matches the real development of those societies, or whether, instead, the Hegelian perspective needs to be relayed by a properly sociological one that would not just illustrate Hegel's view but in fact realize or fulfil it.

ETHICAL LIFE AND ANOMIE

At the core of his book, Honneth makes an important conceptual distinction that may be seen as the keystone of his demonstration. He does so after reviewing the three levels at which freedom had previously been defined and which Hegel was able to interrelate; namely, right, morality, and ethicality or ethical life (*Sittlichkeit*). This last term should be understood as all forms of relations in which freedom is apprehended objectively and practised relationally – in other words, freedom understood at the level of the social institution of individual relations: family, market, and, ultimately, the state. It is at this point that Honneth analytically separates what he calls "pathologies" from what he names, adopting an equally Durkheimian term, "forms of anomie"[1] (Honneth 2014, 129). What is at stake in this distinction, exactly, and why is it inescapable?

It can be argued that Hegel's real invention, or reinvention, is the concept of *Sittlichkeit*. That concept, though first developed by Aristotle, has a specific meaning for moderns, who have been able to construct and implement social structures whose aim is the institution of individual freedom, structures in which such freedom is recognizable and by means of which it can be objectively fostered. The decisive point, however, is that this dimension, the ethicality of social life – ethical life – cannot be perceived as long as we remain captive to instantiations of the legal person or entity and of the moral subject. Honneth's entire reading revolves around this point: ethical life only becomes perceivable when the *social* subject is taken into account – that is, when we accept that relations and relational modes are implicated in the construction of individuality, that relations and relational modes are what construct us as individual subjects in the cases of friendship, love, family, the market, and, lastly, as citizens of the state.

That sequence should not be comprehended as a list in which each term displaces and relativizes the previous one while subsuming it at the same time. The Hegelian idea does not amount to a progressive outlook whereby one moves from the legal person and moral subject to the ethical sphere. Instead, it amounts to saying that, in reality, ethical life is the foundation of all relations in each sphere of activity, and therefore the very condition of the aforementioned freedoms, which only seem to precede it and only seem self-sufficient due to an optical effect engendered by our experience and the theoretical discourse that has come to coincide with it. That illusion was nurtured by modern political philosophy itself, Honneth claims, in that it continued to be dominated by the science of natural right, the instantiation of subjective individual rights by the science of natural right, and that science's acme, which was nothing other than the separation of civil society and the state. Moreover, that illusion is likewise maintained – and to the same degree – by individualistic classical political economy, particularly by the weight it grants and the form it gives to the modern idea of civil society. Hegel's thought ran counter these conceptualizations, Honneth argues, while exposing the unperceived truth of them. Hegel's thought affirms that ethical life is not the highest point of a rising movement but rather what, in the final analysis, is the foundation for that movement (Duso 2013, 132). Right, morality, and the economy are not without any substance; there is nothing illusory in thinking of them in terms of their relative autonomy. But in the final analysis, it should be understood that they are conditioned by ethical life. Similarly, it can be said that modern political philosophy until Hegel – that is, the philosophy Hegel overturned – is congruent with a common sense meaning of freedom that is itself truncated. When we think of ourselves as legal persons, moral agents, and even economic agents with our own interests, and when we correlate our freedom with that individualized thinking, we are analysing ourselves incorrectly, for we are severing that freedom from its effective reality. This reality reappears the moment ethical life is restored to its rightful place.

This is why the entire philosophy of subjective freedom is summed up in the concept that Honneth highlights in the book's subtitle: "*Grundriss einer demokratischen Sittlichkeit*": elements of a *democratic ethical life*.

The reference to democracy here must be explained. The word "democratic" defines the ethicality specific to modernity; it is the foundation not only of moral but also of legal freedom, even though this is not immediately apparent when we first consider freedom. For what turns out to be specifically modern is a form of diplopia, or double vision, and the obligation we have, in order to live socially, to adjust that vision in such a way that neither of the two levels prevails over the other. From the perspective of democratic ethical life, we are individuals *and* socialized – those dimensions are correlated and inseparable; neither can be trammelled in favour of the other. What links the two can be formulated as follows: *We are individuals in that we are socialized.* As paradoxical as that may sound, socialization that defines us operates through our individuality, the way that individuality is constructed and comes to be asserted as free. It is because democratic ethical life affirms individuals' freedom and equality that it can be said to comprise conjointly the two above-cited levels, internally connected, yet not to be conflated.

This only highlights more starkly the distinctive feature of democratic ethical life. Pre-modern ethical life was not constrained to articulate the individual and social levels. It had not produced the legal and moral individuation that we moderns experience; nor had it produced an economic vision of civil society as a system of agents maximizing their own interests on a market. Therefore, it did not encounter the same difficulty of making socialization fully intelligible to the socialized. By contrast, being modern requires a more ambivalent and therefore more vigorous conceptual effort than pre-modern social life. This was decisive for epistemology as well, for it was based on this requirement that a new type of procedure for acquiring knowledge was necessarily triggered – that is, procedure of the social sciences.

One could say that, unlike no other modern philosopher, Hegel helps us in this endeavour of achieving clear vision and thinking. But that is also (and perhaps first and foremost) true of sociology as a modern form of knowledge, at least if we focus on its political aim, which has always been to suggest and foster the production of norms adequate to a society composed of socialized individuals, or rather human beings socialized as individuals – that is, legal persons and moral subjects. Our reasoning must therefore rely on those two pillars: the legal person and the moral subject. And Honneth is entirely right to claim that a genuine theory of justice cannot be merely deductive but must be founded on the analysis of society and, consequently, on empirical investigation (Honneth 2014, 5). Moreover, when it comes to re-establishing political philosophy, we cannot grant the status of privileged concept-maker to formal law and classical individualist political economy. To be consistent, Hegelian and Hegel-inspired social philosophy ought to recognize that the legitimate, appropriate sources of the concepts we must use to conceive ourselves are not law and economics but the social sciences.

We must of course still reflect upon how to make use of these two pillars. The question is how *sociology* and *philosophy* are articulated. A sociology that is conscious of its political nature, and a philosophy that is conscious, thanks to Hegel, of how modern it must be, but *differently* modern than philosophy, trapped in the vice of theories of natural right. Therefore, what the "analysis of society" means emerges as a crucial question. On what basis could such analysis provide a theory of substantive justice; that is, a concrete conception of what a social order would be in which individuals' and groups' longings, hopes, and demands for justice could find ways of being met or resolved here and now? Clearly, a strict opposition between the theoritical and the empirical can only lead us astray. For once the philosophical approach has overcome deductivism and formalism, we see that it *is* anchored to some degree in the experience of social relations and cannot do without describing them. Symmetrically, sociology, in its descriptive approach, aims to explain the principles of judgement involved in these same relations that it studies empirically and therefore to uncover the normativity underlying them. Moderating the debate between sociology and philosophy on this Hegelian ground, therefore, requires proceeding quite differently than by accrediting the simplistic image of a fully external clash between the two. It seems to me that the correct method is to follow the lines of convergence between the two disciplines as far as possible, precisely by focusing on the development of the concept of ethical life once it has been restored to its dual position as foundation and end point of a full elucidation of the freedom of we moderns.

PATHOLOGIES OF FREEDOM

Let us return to Honneth's distinction regarding these Hegelian foundations. He argues, at the first two levels of the edifice – law and morality – that the systems of action operate as unconscious socialization. However, those levels are beset with internal difficulties that necessarily induce deviations and thus pathologies in the strict sense of the term – that is, ailments engendered by the system of action itself. This does not happen at the third level, ethical life. At that level there is no pathology, if the term refers to a deviation inherent in the system and produced only by its own internal unfolding. However, this does not mean any form of dysfunction should be excluded a priori. In a way, the opposite is true. The distinction between pathology and anomie serves primarily to highlight a crucial difference in the degree of room for manoeuvre available in the two cases. Law and morality allow both diagnosis and remedy. But the third level, ethical life, allows neither of them. And this is a serious problem since, as explained, in reality this level constitutes the foundation of the other two.

What exactly does Honneth mean by "pathology?" A pathology becomes manifest as soon as a misinterpretation of freedom causes the system of action to deviate. The tendency to misinterpret freedom is in fact inevitable. At the levels of law and morality alike – but let us not forget economy – it is impossible for the actors not to lose sight of normality; in other words, on these levels individualization is necessarily followed by its counterpart: de-socialization. Therefore, freedom is necessarily conceived as the realization of a self-centred self, detached from the relational supports that in truth are what enable it to assert itself. Therein resides the main force activating the pathologies of freedom. Should we use the terms scrupulously, pathologies of freedom cover, in the final analysis, *the pathologies of legal freedom and moral freedom*. And they define a general modern condition that there is no good reason to believe will disappear. Indeed, we moderns are condemned to experience these types of ailments unceasingly, since they are the direct effect of our double vision, that is, of the difficulty we have keeping simultaneously in sight the person-subject – the modern individual as defined by right and morality – and the socialization that enables individuals to come into being and assert themselves.

Honneth makes sure to distinguish pathologies from feelings of injustice (Honneth 2014, 87). Obviously, there is injustice in our societies. This fact must not be minimized, but we must also grasp its real meaning. The question is how to address the existence and manifestation of injustice, how to adjust our critical perspective so as to apprehend injustice properly as an objective fact; namely, to reach a perspective that can identify and utter the *norm* that makes what is experienced as unjust objectively unjust. The approach in terms of pathologies, which is a conceptual innovation inherited from the social sciences (Durkheim 1964) not the legal or moral lexicon, is precisely the one we need in order to avoid critique talking to itself. This happens when we engage in denouncing injustice as lived experience because the very concept of experience is fettered to the particularity and the variety of its forms. Moreover that obstacle to critique is favoured by another aspect of the pathologies of freedom, once again endogenous to the modern system: the pathology affecting morality. For morality, too, with its tendency to absolutize and de-socialize norms, necessarily individualizes us, thereby turning norms into abstract judgemental principles that activate external criticism of reality. Hegel portrayed quite impressively this abstract moral posture at work in the social and political field. Honneth is no less severe than Hegel regarding the resources that the spontaneous critique draws from a moral sense of injustice projected onto a reality from which the individual has withdrawn herself – a reality that is then neither analysed nor even simply observed (Honneth 2015, 180). This pathology is also inescapable because directly related to the fact that in our societies we assert ourselves as moral subjects whose limited – if not diminished – vision of the world is correlative to the specific mode of subjectivation that produced it. This enables Honneth to elucidate, in counterpoint, what he considers satisfactory conditions for genuine critique: its aim must be derived from reality, constructed on the basis of reality's particular normative supports, and for the purpose of genuinely transforming that reality. In this respect, the necessary condition for producing a true critique is the critique of critique – in the form of a critique of the pathologies of freedom.

Such lucidity is possible, however, only if we take into account democratic ethical life. It is indeed democratic ethical life that defines modernity's *normality* in relation to which it is legitimate to speak of pathologies at all. Still, if reality is to become the object of internal (rather than external), normatively founded critique, philosophy must analyse ethical life itself. The meaning and scope of our main distinction are concentrated in this point: *There is no pathology of ethical life, since there is only pathology from the point of view of ethical life*. What prevails at the level of ethical life is the "therapeutic" virtue we can draw from it (Honneth 2010, 67). In this sense, ethical life is itself the condition for social critique. In order for critique to be genuinely *social* – that is, *guided by the idea of a more just society* – it must present itself as the critique of pathologies. However, ethical life is not an abstract idea. It is a structure of actual, historically deployed relations, animated by a movement producing its own meaning, which is that of continually constructing and deepening social freedom (Honneth 2014, 42–43; Neuhouser 2000, 5–6). In this respect it is absurd to pretend that actors fail to understand that meaning. On the contrary, they fully grasp it precisely when they come to see what is pathological about legal rights and claims and moral judgements that destroy the social relations that condition the very existence of those rights, claims, and judgements.

Furthermore, Honneth argues, actors always comprehend that meaning in the same manner: by drawing on their "lifeworld," by returning to the level of social practices – a reality that can, of course, be understood by reference to Husserl's phenomenological lexicon; but for the sake of staying close to Hegel's vocabulary, itself rooted in classical political philosophy – Montesquieu's, in this case – we should designate it by the classical term "mores." Actors play mores off against positive law, or against the rigidity of certain situations of moral conformism. In sum, they perceive the pathological by returning to an infra-institutional level that engenders aspirations for justice of a sort not expressed in instituted law or fossilized moral precepts, rigidified into meaningless models for action. What they discover at that level is a stratum that, nonetheless, is related to institutions, just not those of law or morality. It is the stratum of *relational institutions*: family, civil society, and the state.

Those institutions certainly exist in Honneth's diagnosis of the pathologies afflicting legal and moral freedom, but they do not intervene directly. Here again what is at stake is the highly specific aspect of the modern experience, understood as a unique kind of social and political experience; namely, the individualistic expansion we face because we think of ourselves as legal persons and moral subjects – and therefore, first and foremost, as individuals. We would be terribly mistaken to view that individualistic expansion as a distortion or rip in the social texture. It does stretch our ethical life to an extreme degree, but ethical life does not disappear (see Kervégan 2007, 213–241). On the contrary, the misleading path consists in affirming that the social fabric is torn. That illusion stems from the failure to see the social freedom that underlies our moral and legal freedom. The social form of freedom cannot disappear as long as the beings identifying and thinking of themselves as legal and moral persons are social beings, acting and thinking within a society. But in that case, we also have to admit that the most fitting level from which to apprehend ethical life cannot be individual experience, even if it is highly reflexive. It can only be practices, specifically those practices forming the background to our acting and thinking of ourselves as free subjects. Those practices represent permanent resources for restoring the unconscious ethical life from which law and morality must be nourished if they are to become actual law (rather than arbitrary force) and actual morality (rather than hypocrisy or explosive, primitive drive-related pronouncements or actions dressed up as moral indignation and righteousness).

THE MARKET AND THE STATE

In *Freedom's Right*, Honneth inflects modern societies' self-analytical movement in a remarkable way. Drawing on Hegel, he develops a diagnosis of our entire social and political present, ranging from love relationships and family relations to forms of political representation and government, by way of a reconstruction of the capitalist economy and relations between private and public actors in both national and global markets. What enables such a wide-ranging diagnosis is not just the scope of Hegel's own construction, upon which Honneth's relies, but more fundamentally, the thread that firmly draws and holds together all these relational strata; namely, democratic ethical life – the ethicality that innervates the modern's lifeworld.

Now the aforementioned and crucial distinction comes into play: *at the level of relational institutions* – couple, family, market, the state, perhaps even supranational entities – *there can be no pathology*. Indeed, it would make no sense to speak of pathology in reference to these relational systems because their particular structures cannot generate endogenous deviations; each is in itself correctly and necessarily regulated to produce social freedom. This also means that none of these systems individualizes its members by producing forms of individuality that would erase its own relational substance. But can we really think of the state as a relational institution in the way we think of the family and civil society? What tools are needed to conceive it that way?

It is hard to produce a definition of the state as a relational institution if we stick to legal-political theories of the modern state – that is, if we fail to approach the state sociologically. But before examining this question, it is important to note the general category Honneth uses to formulate it. To designate what disrupts modern ethical life – and consequently the economic and political level – and what threatens to counteract efforts to correct their pathological double vision at the moral and legal levels, Honneth uses the word "*Fehlentwicklung*" ("misdevelopment") which he immediately specifies in terms of the Durkheimian concept of "anomie": "the misdevelopment that we will encounter in our discussion of relational institutions does not consist in systemically induced deviations; they are not 'pathologies' in the true sense but rather anomies whose sources must be sought elsewhere, not in the constitutive rules of the respective system of action" (Honneth 2014, 128–129; translation revised[2]).

So if not constitutive rules, what is the locus of anomie? Constitutive rules are rules without which there can be no social room for manoeuver in the systems concerned. Such rules impose themselves upon individual members of families, civil society, and the state, not physically but in terms of meaning: within those spheres, individuals can only behave meaningfully – in their own eyes and those of others – with respect to the obligations governing their mutual relations. There can be no misunderstanding of the game actors are playing. That is why there is no risk of double vision either. The only way ethical life can be perceived – and is necessarily perceived – is through the relational structuring it entails.

But from another perspective there is an even greater risk; namely, that relational spheres will be attacked from without, destroyed by external forces, forces whose very externality makes them structurally non-ethical. For this phenomenon, the accurate word – though not the only word – is "anomie" in the sense that, unlike rule-breaking, it designates the dissolution of those spheres by corrosive powers originating at an entirely different level than social life with its proven normative dynamic at the level of practices. Those forces may properly be called external to modern ethical life in that, by nature, they cannot be captured in the language of freedom's right. We can even designate them as material forces, to emphasize the fact of their "indifference to" or "recalcitrance to" being integrated into any ethical – or, to remain with an openly assumed Durkheimian vocabulary – "moral" configuration.

Those exogenous factors produce anomies rather than pathologies. But anomies have the same effects as pathologies: they de-socialize freedom, hinder its assertion, atomize individuals and confine them to themselves in each and every sphere of action. They impede freedom precisely *as social freedom*, that freedom which is an integral part of systems wherein individuals freely engage in actions *together*, where they can only experience their own freedom as proceeding from a freedom to act that belongs not only to some others but to *all and everyone*. That is how one can fathom the difference between anomie and pathology. Anomie is the sign of a much more serious ailment in modern societies than the fact that their normative structure has been made invisible to its actors. Indeed, what is removed from the actors is the use of a social normality based on the ethical order, common practices, or mores. Other practices, in this case, take precedence, which are neither moral nor legal. The question that arises then for the Hegelian–inspired social philosophy, pushed to the point of drawing a strictly sociological distinction, not simply between the normal and the pathological but between the pathological and the anomic, is how to grasp this exogeneity of unethical practices capable of harming ethical life as such.

In Honneth's analysis, those forces culminate in the competitive logic of the market, a logic that operates at the levels of both production and consumption, and corrupts even the ethical structure of personal relationships, family, and – eventually – the political formation of the democratic will in the state. Once this is comprehended, it becomes clear that the appropriate therapy for anomie must, likewise, be implemented at the level of economy. Formally, the difficulty of designing and implementing this therapy is considerable. It does not suffice to settle matters by citing the systemic normality from which pathology, by definition, deviates, but we must instead reconstruct the concept of the market against its own tendency to individualize and flexibilize – that is, against the de-socializing power it has acquired from the moment it was taken up into the dynamics of capitalism. That exogenous and therefore properly anomic force resides in capitalism, understood in an *institutional* sense: its epicentre is in the institution of competitive market society. It is hardly surprising that Honneth's main reference in his critique of the misdevelopments affecting freedom – the dissolution of social freedom rather than the pathologies of legal and moral freedom – is Karl Polanyi, author of *The Great Transformation*, whose major contribution was to inflect Marxist analysis by integrating it into the framework of a history of the market (Honneth 2014, 185–187). In this understanding, the triumph of capitalism is subordinated to the penetration and infusion of the liberal creed, a process that began with and then exceeded mercantilism. The idea came to be accepted of a *market society* – a contradiction in terms – where the institution of the market alone would suffice to organize and bring order into the global society. In and of itself, the market does not necessarily de-socialize; on the contrary, it can work to create social freedom – but only if and only as long as it remains entangled in a set of social relations where norms other than those founded exclusively on the market can also, and simultaneously, come into play. The market remains a social institution to the degree that it exceeds the logic of acting to yield a profit; it remains a social institution for as long as the "chrematistics" it encompasses is not elevated to the rank of a social action norm. Polanyi showed, however, especially by way of nineteenth-century English history, how and why the aberration of an asocial market could be produced. And it is this aberration that we continue to confront in attempting to deal with the anomies of social freedom, all of which involve the destruction of the structures of ethical life.

Thus, in shifting focus from pathologies to anomies, *Freedom's Right* becomes a critique of capitalism grounded in Polanyi's thought and culminating in recommendations for moralizing the market. It is of great interest that Honneth reveals the foundations of a different concept of the market, which can be found in both the past and the present: a concept of the market that could be practised as an institution of freedom. In doing so, he recovers the early twentieth-century socialists' notion of a consumers' market, in order to reactivate the market's inherent property of constructing ways to satisfy needs freely feeding into a structure of reciprocity. However, as Honneth is well aware, attending to this other side of the market does not suffice to combat the destructive forces at work and is likely to amount to wishful thinking (Honneth 2014, 220). The problem is that the political armoury needed for such an undertaking is deficient and that, as suggested earlier, the misdevelopments or anomies of social freedom have a second, non-economic source. The main obstacle lies at the political level, in view of the authority of the state – or rather what remains of the state in a world dominated by the logic of the market, which seeps deeply into the relational practices of the actors, and recruits the political entities themselves by bringing them into the same type of arrangement or role.

Wolfgang Streeck has shown that when critique of capitalism became, in the late 1960s, a critique of "late" or "advanced" capitalism, it advocated and indeed predicted a scission between economy and politics, a scission that we struggle to repair today, even though the current situation is in sore need of it (Christ and Salmon 2018). In the "crisis theories" developed by the Frankfurt School, that scission amounted to claiming that the major issue capitalism would face in the near future was democratic legitimacy and its own consolidation of domination – meaning that the entire critique should bear down on just this weak link. It can be said that Honneth remains faithful to this view, far from Streeck's approach, which instead seeks to rectify the situation and restore the Marxian foundations of a critical political economy. Crisis theories more or less tacitly accepted that capitalism as a mode of production would be enduring, and it is true that they have tended to subordinate the analysis of exploitation to other, presumably more strategic processes. Honneth's emphasis on democratic ethical life goes in the same direction. However, Honneth's Hegelian position, in the social or sociologizing form that Honneth confers to it, produces a significant divergence. Precisely because he distinguishes between pathology and anomie, he forces us to reformulate the problem of relations between the state and the market. For, in the final analysis, it is those relations that are responsible for the anomic situation now afflicting modern law-governed states, traversed as they are with capitalist-type logic. In his critique of crisis theory, Streeck (2014, 6ff.) makes the very same point, in a different manner. The error, he explains, was to fail to ascribe real social-actor intention to capital, to have treated it as an inert power, and not to have seen that states were gradually bending to intentions that were not and could not be their own as democratically constituted authorities. That awakening should lead us to assert the opposite possibility; namely, that by re-connecting the state with its democratic structure and deploying that structure on the basis of relational institutions all founded on ethical life, we will again be able to infuse the state with the capability to thwart those intentions. In this respect, Honneth's highly original extension of crisis theory, with its Hegelian guiding argument, may offer an unprecedented possibility for getting out of the rut of those very theories.

But for this to happen, we need to be clear on the category of "state" being evoked. What type of state are we referring to exactly, once it has been reintegrated into the order of ethical life? That Hegelian question relates to our frequent experience of internal misalignments that impair state action, preventing the state from looking and acting like the state when it is enmeshed with the market. In sum, what is being tested is the *idea of the state* as a sphere of action favouring social freedom and endowed with its own specific resources for producing ethical life, that life which, due to the internal recursiveness of the state's particular order, underpins all other relational institutions down to the minutest interactions of social life.

In sum, the task is to reconnect the state, as reformulated by Hegel, to a truly substantive concept of social freedom. In Hegel's understanding of the use of social freedom and the foundation that such freedom provides for moral and legal freedom, we face contradictory inclinations. The logic of Hegel's conception required him to appeal to the state and bring his system to completion through that final synthesis. But as Honneth explains, if he were to do the same, Hegelian statism would re-emerge too strongly, as a kind of "over-institutionalization" of ethical life (Honneth 2010, 63ff) and the state would appear a superseded figure both in light of the forms that the contemporary democratic state has come to assume and the supranational institutions to which it must now adjust. When one reads those sections of *Elements of the Philosophy of Right* that discuss the state today, it is clear that democratic ethical life must flourish beyond the tendencies of the state today to capture – in the corporate structure that Hegel had assigned it, as well as in its ability to embody the universal – all the tendencies towards socialization, in order to give them a legal foundation and to determine their forms (ibid., 75–77). It seems unlikely, in any case, that Hegel's thought can really guide us in analysing the present on this crucial point, even if we attempted, paradoxically, to use it to decipher the ever-incomplete transformation of our "culture of freedom" (Honneth 2014, 62). Specifically, the question arises whether the state's political culture – that is to say, the political culture of those states that have proved capable of integrating freedom in the relational sense as a guiding principle in norm production – can really favour the aim of integrating more subjects called upon to contribute to the common project of all being free together, *because they are free* and *to the extent that they are free* together.

Honneth is clearly doubtful that it might. Why? By necessity, the state selects those whom it makes free by integrating them into a closed community (ibid., 318). Moreover, it is partial in the power it exerts over the categories of citizens it integrates, and, likewise, it cannot avoid being permeable to class interests (ibid., 319). And in a way that inflicts even greater damage on the entire logic of the system, state procedures for institutionalizing freedom act as a limitation to the extension of social freedom. In sum, there seem to be an ever increasing number of objections to the notion that the state could be adequate to its idea in a way that would truly make it the locus of the modern ethical life it is meant to represent. It seems then that we need to think with Hegel, but without the state. That is, without *his* state, the Prussian-style corporate state, more suitable to a constitutional monarchy than a modern democracy of the sort we know today. And more to the point, without *our* state: the nation-states that have risen up over the last two centuries and are still standing, if unsteadily, in a normative globalized space or simply a Europeanized one. The end of *Freedom's Right* clearly reveals the author's desire to overcome those versions of the state.

THE STATE AS IDEAL STRATUM OF PRACTICE

Yet, there is no doubt that the state must be integrated into ethical life. As I indicated from the outset, this is the particular modern contradiction, the contradiction that has become ever more acute over the twentieth century, especially after the crisis of nation-states represented by the experience of the two world wars, the exit from colonialism, and our modern reflexive analysis of this crisis. The contradiction consists in calling upon the state to intervene while in the same breath engaging in radical critique of it. In the end, we must therefore recommence from this necessity of integrating the state into ethical life.

If it is indeed necessary, that is because only the state-as-form, and when comprehended in a certain way, enables modernity to realize itself as a culture of freedom, a culture in which social freedom, once filtered through the sieve of ethical life, grows deeper. Despite – and surely thanks to – the critique of the state focused on nation-states over the last two centuries, this question ought to be raised if we are to confront not only the pathologies but also the anomies of modern societies. The concept of the state that we have inherited, together with our concept of freedom, turns out to be infused with our modern philosophical presuppositions, those very illusions we may finally be able to relinquish by delving into Hegel's works. For Hegel's state is not the state accredited either by our common sense or the spontaneous political philosophy that consolidates that common sense notion. If we want to restore the Hegelian concept of freedom in its concreteness, and therefore fully appreciate and make use of its fundamental break with the idea of liberal-individualist freedom used and promoted by modern political philosophy, we also have to restore the literally unparalleled aspect of his concept of the state – an imperceptible concept or nearly so – and learn how to identify it as the culmination of ethical life as a whole (Duso 2013, 206–213). As a matter of fact, what renders the concept hardly detectable? And in what way is that concept a resource for social criticism of the anomies of modern societies, namely, in Honneth's final analysis, for critiquing the hindrances and obstacles to social freedom that capitalism has erected at all levels of ethical life, including those that constitute the invisible supports of the moral and legal spheres?

To represent how Hegel's thinking departs from the dominant conception of the modern state I would make the following proposition: The state is an idea, and essentially so, for it is by being an idea that it has true practical reality, real substance at the level of practice and practices. A very special idea, therefore: the state as practical thought, capable of producing ethical life, and even of fructifying the ethical life that modern society can induce, precisely because modern society *is* society in the strict sense of the word and not an aggregate of conflicting interests or individuals obsessed with their subjective rights and personal evaluations, however heavily veiled in morality they might be.

But making this claim leads back to the core of the problem: What kind of analytical work will make the state socially perceptible as *the ideal stratum of practice*, a layer of society capable of engendering and bestowing ethical life – that is, producing ever-deepening social freedom, a freedom in which all are free only because all are free together? This definition of the state enables to understand what is truly democratic in modern ethical life. But we would find it difficult to achieve the aforementioned objective if we stuck to the line of argument found in philosophical thinking on the state, even though this thinking has developed into social philosophy by way of its critique of the legalism that currently dominates political philosophy. Because, in order for the state to be reconstructed along the lines identified by Hegel, we ought to scrutinize the various *ideas of the state* – as long as they represent ideas of practical enfranchisement of individuals – both revealed and produced by social practices. These practices integrate their own social spheres of relational action with a political sphere that encapsulates them and confers upon them that "logic of practice" (Bourdieu) where social freedom comes into play – or, more to the point, wherein social freedom is experienced, and constituted by being experienced.

It is here that Durkheimian sociology – at least if interpreted as a sociology of the reflexive practices through which the mode of solidarity specific to modern societies is realized and fulfilled (Lemieux 2013) – may take over from Hegelian philosophy. Or rather, it can be argued that Durkheimian sociology embodies the sociological relay needed to take on not just the pathologies but also the misdevelopments or anomies that weigh on the existence of modern societies.

However, Durkheimian sociology is exposed to the same risk of rejection as Hegel's philosophy of the state. In some respects, the reservations it elicits are even stronger. Entirely shaped in conjunction not with a constitutional monarchy but the civil-servant-based state of France's Third Republic, it does not even have the speculative energy that would allow it to counter the impression of being an ideological discourse. In his 1992 lectures on the state, Pierre Bourdieu endorsed that accusation. He also pointed out its limitations. Durkheim, he explained, could not speak of the state without formulating an eulogy of the type of state that he himself fully upheld due to his functions within it – "like a duck in water," Bourdieu claimed (2014, 214 transl. rev.). But far from relativizing or discrediting Durkheim's discourse, it in fact empowered it. For in order to be adequate to a reality like the state, the sociological idea of the state must return to what Bourdieu called "state thinking," ("*pensées d'État*") – that is, thinking simultaneously produced by the state and by the fact that the thinker belongs to the state. While we need to manage an objectifying distance between ourselves and a mental reality of this sort, whose source is always dual, we can only do so by fully appreciating the resonance of that reality, and therefore the way it lives inside the person – including the sociologist – who thinks it. This is what Durkheim enables us to understand, if we make the effort to relate his explicit writings on the state – in *Leçons de sociologie*, where his eulogy of the state reaches its acme – to his thinking on the co-constitution of social and mental structures in his most fully accomplished works, *The Elementary Forms of Religious Life* and *Primitive Classification*.

Significantly, it is precisely those last texts of Durkheim's – rather than texts by Elias or Weber – that Bourdieu relied on as an ultimate resource to indicate how to produce an authentic sociology of the state. That they correspond more closely to religious sociology and sociology of knowledge than political sociology should not mislead us. Their relevance and value lie in the fact that they reach that level of experience where the idea of the state proves constitutive of social reality for subjects experiencing that reality. They also show that this reality takes on consistency for socialized individuals through their belonging to the state, since that membership cannot be reduced to belonging to just any collective but rather to the collective that de-particularizes all others and enables the individual, understood as a universal, to become distinct within those other collectives.

Hegel set us on the path that would lead to the *sociologist*'s state, an object of study that the sociology of the state was able to reach by filtering out what was not yet *sociology's state* but only the state as other disciplines required it to be seen, disciplines themselves incapable of grasping what is properly social in the state: how it is itself – strictly speaking – a social phenomenon. Only an empirical study of the social experience of the state – that is, of the thinking immanent in the practices that social experience consists in – can really enable us to put our finger on it. This in turn means that the state in question is not the one described in existing definitions shaped by the dominant framework of modern political philosophy, definitions that are in fact versions of the concentration/monopolization-of-social-forces model. When sociology confines itself to this vision, it remains captive to a concept that is in fact imported from an approach whose realism is only apparent. That the state is objectified in an apparatus of power – or constraint – does not mean that its truth is condensed therein. On the contrary, this enables us to see a distinction concealed by modern political philosophy: that of the thinking that brings the state into existence as a certain mode of being for the society of which it is the state, an entity that cannot be reduced to its bureaucratic structure or the fact that it is a matter of positive law. What is revealed then is the state as a structure of thought whose core of mental and perceptual stabilization should be distinguished from the structures of power that emanate from it. In Durkheim's language, the state condensed in the *government* is what a political society establishes at its centre (Durkheim 2012), the idea being that government is essentially a reflexive social function, a pole engendered and strengthened by modern social differentiation, understood as the necessary condition for its own development and for the regulated life of societies that conceive and produce their norms themselves (Karsenti 2014).

For sociologists, the state is therefore necessarily a two-sided entity. The sides are not symmetrical, as one is a legitimating authority and the other is a resource for an equally legitimate critique of that authority. This explains why government, in Durkheim's sense, has priority over administration, which is not the state in its essence, he explains, but only its executive arm, the apparatus its "deliberating consciousness" has endowed itself with to put into practice its ideas and deliberations, given that in the modern context, thinking and deliberating have increasingly come to represent the nature of its activities

CONCLUSION

At the outset of this chapter, I asked whether sociology had its own, in-house concept of the state. We see that it does, if we take our analysis of modern political society far enough to discover that individuals' practical experience of their freedom is an effect of their socialization. Here lies the elective affinity between Durkheim-inspired political sociology and neo-Hegelianism translated into social philosophy. The whole of Honneth's normative reconstruction leans in this direction. At least that is what becomes apparent in this attempt fully to reproduce the move through which it shifts from a theory of the pathologies of freedom to a theory of the anomies of ethical life. At this point, however, because that reconstruction remains faithful to Hegel's topos, Honneth's own definitions of the state suffer from an excess of institutionalism that democratic ethical life can only resolve by enfranchising itself. This is because before being a philosophical problem, the state is a sociological problem. It is not the crowning achievement or self-contained and disconnected summit of the institutional system that modernity had the privilege of erecting, but rather the ever-reopened possibility of social life. Such social life can be said both to presuppose and to constantly reconstitute the state *as a certain state*, or rather a certain condition of political societies that have reached the point where social freedom appears as the defining principle of their mode of solidarity. In this respect, the state is really nothing more than a determinate layer of the existence of individuals, a layer actualized in and through social practices that always concern the question of freedom, as long as freedom is understood as and functions as a driver of socialization. In order for it to do so – and this is the most demanding effort we moderns must make at the theoretical level – it must be acknowledged that individuals are not defined by some abstract attribute of freedom, of which they are the depositaries and the source, but rather that they are obliged, bound by freedom, that they are called upon to confer on freedom an ever-determinate reality, with the aim of forming a society that seems just to them. This means, in fact, collectively to produce themselves as free individuals.

NOTES

1. The German text clearly says "*Anomien*" (Honneth 2011, 231). Indeed, both the French and the English translators chose curiously to erase the reference to Durkheim and to translate by "anomalies."
2. As said in footnote 1, the English translator choses to translate the German word "*Anomie*" by anomaly, although the traditional translation of this Durkheimian concept in English is "anomie."

BIBLIOGRAPHY

Abensour, Miguel. 2011. *Democracy Against the State: Marx and the Machiavellian Moment*. Cambridge: Polity.

Bourdieu, Pierre. 2014. *On the State: Lectures at the Collège de France, 1989–1992*. Cambridge: Polity.

Callegaro, Francesco. 2015. *La science politique des modernes. Durkheim, la sociologie et le projet d'autonomie*. Paris: Economica.

Christ, Julia & Gildas Salmon (eds.). 2018. *La dette souveraine. Économie politique et État*. Paris: Éditions de l'EHESS.

Durkheim, Émile. 1964. *The Rules of Sociological Method*. New York: The Free Press.

Durkheim, Émile. 2012. *Leçons de sociologie*. Paris: PUF.

Duso, Giuseppe. 2013. *Libertà e costituzione in Hegel*. Milan: Franco Angeli.

Hegel, Georg Wilhelm Friedrich. 1991. *Elements of the Philosophy of Right*. Cambridge: Cambridge University Press.

Honneth, Axel. 2010. *The Pathologies of Individual Freedom: Hegel's Social Theory*. Princeton University Press.

Honneth, Axel. 2011. *Das Recht der Freiheit*. Berlin: Suhrkamp.

Honneth, Axel. 2012. *The I in We*. Cambridge: Polity.

Honneth, Axel. 2014. *Freedom's Right: The Social Foundations of Democratic Life*. Cambridge: Polity.

Karsenti, Bruno. 2013. *D'une philosophie à l'autre. Les sciences sociales et la politique des modernes*. Paris: Gallimard.

Karsenti, Bruno. 2014. "Politique de Durkheim. Société, humanité, État." In: *Scienza & Politica. Per una storia delle dottrine*, 26 (51), 41–62.

Kervégan, Jean-François. 2007. *L'effectif et le rationnel. Hegel et l'esprit objectif*. Paris: Vrin.

Lemieux, Cyril. 2013. "L'ambition de la sociologie." In: *Archives de philosophie*, 76 (4), 591–608.

Marx, Karl. 1977. *Critique of Hegel's Philosophy of Right*. Cambridge: Cambridge University Press.

Neuhouser, Frederick. 2000. *Foundations of Hegel's Social Theory: Actualizing Freedom*. Cambridge, MA and London: Harvard University Press.

Streeck, Wolfgang. 2014. *Buying Time: The Delayed Crisis of Democratic Capitalism*. London and New York: Verso.

Chapter 11

Socialism and the Nation-State

David Miller

Socialism appears to have crept back on to the mainstream agenda in that most unlikely of places, the United States, in the person of Bernie Sanders and the young radicals he has inspired. Whether it has really done so is another question: the policies that Sanders advocates are ones that in European political discourse would be described as social-democratic, not socialist. But along with political realignments in other countries, including the United Kingdom, this development suggests that it may be a good moment to reassess the socialist project, as Axel Honneth has done in his book *The Idea of Socialism* (2017). Honneth believes that the renewal of socialism as a realistic utopia, to borrow John Rawls' phrase, depends on jettisoning certain quite fundamental aspects of the socialist tradition, including its narrow focus on the working class as the agent of socialist transformation, and embracing what he calls "historical experimentalism." His thought here is that we do not yet know what form of economic organization will in any given context best realize the underlying goal of social freedom, so we should be open-minded and aim to create the space in which different models can be tried out. This of course immediately raises the question of how that space is to be delimited. In particular we need to think again about the relationship between socialism and the nation-state, which to date has been the container within which socialist transformation on a large scale has been attempted. But many now think that this form of political organization is fast becoming obsolete in the face of global capitalism. So does socialism need the nation-state, and if so, can it any longer rely on it?

Honneth's brief discussion of this question in the closing pages of *The Idea of Socialism* is characteristically nuanced. He begins by formulating the problem explicitly:

Must socialism be understood as a national or as an international project? The answer to this question is much more difficult than might appear at first sight, given the contemporary blurring of national borders. (Honneth 2017, 99)

He next rehearses the reasons for thinking that the development of capitalism as an international system calls for normative regulation that can only be achieved through a "transnationalized" democratic public sphere. But then he addresses the difficulties with this proposal: the fact that in other spheres of social life, such as personal and sexual relationships, regulation remains local; the fact that constitutions guaranteeing basic rights are still enacted by sovereign states; and the fact that the political authorities that democratic citizens want to hold to account are those that are "visible" and connected to them. He concludes, therefore, that socialism has to operate at two levels at once:

Socialism can only represent social freedom globally by means of a political doctrine, whereas it can only mobilize concrete and local publics by means of an ethically compact theory adapted to the cultural features of a certain region. (Honneth 2017, 103–4)

In this chapter I wish to explore in greater depth the reasons why socialism as a realistic utopia depends on the nation-state as its vehicle. I shall suggest that both "nation" and "state" are important here: socialism requires both the bonds of solidarity that national identities provide, and the formal apparatus of the state, with its capacity to regulate the economy and to deliver egalitarian social policies. I assume that the socialism we are interested in is democratic socialism – a socialist project capable of being freely endorsed by those who are involved in taking it forward. Historically, of course, we have had the experience of externally imposed socialism, but I assume that any version of socialism that would need to be coercively imposed on unwilling subjects, or introduced through manipulation of their preferences, is today both morally and politically unacceptable.

THE COMMUNIST MODEL OF SOCIALISM

There is no single "idea of socialism." In theory, and to some extent in practice, it has taken a variety of forms, so we can speak of different models of socialism. These models reflect different understandings of what is empirically feasible – how socialism can be made to work in practice – but also different combinations of underlying values. For present purposes, it will be helpful to arrange these models along two dimensions. The first dimension captures the extent to which a socialist society should be organized in a "top-down" or "bottom-up" way. In bottom-up versions, people are understood first to self-organize in small groups, normally on a local level, and then these small cells will establish relations of cooperation, perhaps federating voluntarily for certain purposes. In top-down versions, a central political authority is given the task of creating the institutions that are appropriate to a socialist society, for purposes of economic production and so forth. Democratic control of social life, which as noted above I assume to be an essential element in any normatively plausible version of socialism, is here indirect. People exercise control over the central authority, for example by electing representatives, but the authority then creates the institutional framework within which they carry on their daily lives. In contrast, bottom-up models give a large role to direct democracy at local level (e.g. in workers' co-operatives).

The second dimension captures the extent to which the economic market is used to coordinate the production and consumption of goods and services. At one extreme, the market is abolished entirely; at the other it is used to supply everything. One might wonder whether a model at the latter end of the spectrum could really count as a model of *socialism*. I do not see why not, if the market was organized in an egalitarian way, for example, without reliance on material incentives.[1] At mid-points on this dimension, there will be models that use markets for some purposes but not others.

These two dimensions are, to a significant extent, independent of one another. For example, there can be predominantly bottom-up versions of socialism that make little or no use of market mechanisms, and other bottom-up versions that use them extensively. So now we have a two-dimensional space in which we can place the many different alternatives to capitalism that socialists have proposed. The question is, which of these models seem on reflection to be both feasible and normatively appealing – in Honneth's terms, to be ways of achieving the social freedom that capitalism fails to achieve?

Let's start with the philosophically influential model of socialism that sits at the bottom-left corner of this space, by virtue of being both bottom-up and non-market: this is, "communism" as envisaged by Marx, Kropotkin, William Morris, and others in the late nineteenth century, and recently revived in a provocative essay by G. A. Cohen (2009). The central theme of this model is that in a socialist society people should cooperate voluntarily to meet the needs of others without requiring material incentives to induce them to do so. They will develop their own cooperative practices from below – for example, ways of signalling to each other which goods and services need to be produced and who should go about delivering them. Although people are expected to exercise self-restraint in only drawing what they really need from the common stock, this model assumes the overcoming of scarcity: it comes into its own only when, as Marx famously put it, "the springs of co-operative wealth flow more abundantly" (Marx 2000, 615).

It would be wrong to dismiss this model of socialism as wholly unfeasible. There are historical examples that come close to exemplifying it: the Israeli kibbutzim are among the more recent of these. But notice that these examples have always been small scale, and there are obvious reasons why this is so. On a small-scale, people can coordinate through face-to-face discussion, assigning tasks and agreeing on how to divide what they produce between immediate consumption and storage for future needs or investment. They can also monitor one another's behaviour informally, thereby discouraging free-riding. Although defenders of the model will argue that small communes can voluntarily federate for purposes that require coordination on a larger scale (e.g. creating a transport system to allow people to move around between local communities), it is hard to see how this can be achieved in practice without moving either upwards in my two-dimensional space – towards more top-down organization – or rightwards – towards more use of the market as a means of regulating relationships between communes. So it is questionable whether a large, complex, and technologically advanced society could be organized entirely on communist principles.

Beyond issues of feasibility lies the question of whether communism as described by Marx et al. would succeed in realizing social freedom if it were implemented.[2] I want to propose two reasons for thinking otherwise. The first is that it is too restrictive of individual autonomy. At first glance this may not be obvious. Proponents of the model are keen to emphasize that it is a model of *voluntary* cooperation. In a much cited passage, from *The German Ideology*, Marx speaks of hunting in the morning, fishing in the afternoon, and so forth, "just as I have a mind," which seems to suggest that each person has a completely free choice about how to occupy their time (Marx 1978, 160). But this does not consort well with the feature that appears to make the communist model workable on a small scale at least, namely that each person should be willing to carry out the tasks that they have been assigned, following whatever process of deliberation is used to coordinate production. If the task assigned to me today is fishing, and my comrades can therefore legitimately anticipate fish for their dinner, then conscientious fishing is what is required, and if I fail to perform I can expect the after-dinner criticism to be directed at me. Of course, if I am well-socialized in the egalitarian ethos that communism demands, I will fish without complaint. The point is, under this system, I am not encouraged to think creatively about alternative possible uses of my talents, or about talents I do not yet possess but might try to acquire. My existing talents are at the disposal of community, to be used to satisfy needs according to the familiar formula, "From each according to their ability, to each according to their needs." So whereas in market economies a person may choose to work part-time and live cheaply in order to pursue some ambition that produces nothing that others might want or need, such an option is unlikely to be available under non-market versions of socialism.

The second reason why such a form of socialism may fall short of realizing social freedom is that it does not grant adequate recognition to individuals' productive contributions. This claim may appear paradoxical at first sight. Marx in particular argued that because of the direct relationship between production and need-satisfaction, unmediated by market exchange, that prevails under communism, people would grant one another mutual recognition – I produce for you and you produce for me, and so each of us recognizes the other as having made a valuable contribution. The problem, however, is that these contributions are valued only in terms of the use-value they create for particular others, and they are therefore incommensurable. From a social perspective, I may be recognized as engaging in production of a specific kind – as a fisherman, say – but I am not recognized as a better or worse than average contributor because there is no medium through which such judgements can be made. In contrast, markets register the interpersonal value of what people produce, through the price mechanism, and reward people accordingly. Of course in practice they do so very imperfectly, and under capitalism there will be systematic divergences between productive contribution and reward, so this is not intended as a defence of existing market economies. Instead it is intended as a reminder that market exchange may be important not just as an efficient device for aligning production and consumption but also as a way of providing what Honneth calls "social esteem" (and tangible reward) to those who produce goods and services.

A defender of non-market socialism might at this point reply *either* that the need for this particular form of recognition is itself a product of market-based societies and so would disappear under socialism *or* that social esteem can be granted in ways that do not involve the formal valuing of achievement and corresponding material reward. Consider the second defence first. It is of course possible to honour people and recognize their achievements in ways that do not confer material advantages – by laudatory speeches, gold stars, and awards of the Order of Lenin. But local comparisons apart, we would still need some way of comparing different contributions if the granting of recognition is not to be arbitrary. In other words, we might praise fisherman A because he regularly brings home a larger catch than the other fishermen, but it is less easy to say whether he deserves more or less recognition than computer programmer B in the absence of a price mechanism to commensurate their contributions. This brings us back to the first defence: would such a form of individual recognition become redundant under socialism?

Here we enter deep waters, because what is really at stake is whether a transition to socialism should be seen as involving the creation of a wholly new order of society, or instead as the making good of unfulfilled promises implicit in the order we already inhabit, especially the promise of social justice. If following Honneth we take the second view, then the model of socialism we adopt must provide each of the three forms of recognition he spells out, including "social esteem." This, I have argued, rules out the Marx/Kropotkin/Morris/Cohen model and it rules it out not merely on practical grounds – the problem of showing how it could actually work on a scale beyond the local commune – but on grounds of principle. Whether or not it is hard-wired into human nature, the need to be recognized, praised, and rewarded for valuable accomplishments is deeply embedded in contemporary culture and it is hard to imagine that we could rid ourselves of it. It is important to underline that the objections to communism I have been presenting are principled objections, and not merely feasibility constraints. In this way we can avoid casting a pall over other models of socialism as merely second-best versions of the social order we would ideally like to create but are prevented from doing so for practical reasons.[3] That would be politically demotivating: why exert yourself to struggle for a social order that is only a pale imitation of what you really value?

HISTORICAL EXPERIMENTALISM AND ITS LIMITS

The aim of the previous section was to show that proposals for socialist transformation should not be aiming at the bottom-left corner of my imaginary diagram. Besides community, they need to incorporate some combination of elements of both market and state. For it seems unlikely that moving directly from the origin along either of these two axes will create a plausible model. If we simply add in market elements – that is, continue to think of production as being organized entirely from the bottom up, but now envisage producers' co-operatives interacting with one another on a market basis – the outcome is likely to be steadily increasing inequality, as some thrive and others fail. To keep inequality within acceptable limits, political regulation of the market is needed. On the other hand, if coordination between producer groups were to be attempted using only administrative means – that is, some kind of planning – we know from historical experience that the outcome is likely to be very inefficient; the signalling function of the market is essential if a multitude of producers is to coordinate effectively. So if a feasible and normatively attractive model of socialism can be found, it will be located some distance away from both axes in two-dimensional space.

But should we in any case be looking for a single preferred model? This is the challenge thrown down by Honneth's defence of "historical experimentalism." He begins by observing, contra Marx, that capitalism should not be regarded as a monolith, such that the only alternative to living under it is total social transformation. Rather we should see any historically given variety of capitalism as an assemblage of different parts – rules that define forms of ownership such as the joint stock company, other rules defining labour contracts and conferring rights on workers, investment institutions and practices, and so forth. This means that it is possible to experiment with changing some parts of the current economic order, but not others, and then to evaluate the effects of the changes by appeal, in Honneth's case, to the criterion of expanding social freedom. It also means that it is possible to learn from the successes and failures of past experiments, and Honneth recommends assembling "an internal archive of past attempts at economic collectivization as a kind of memory bank detailing the advantages and disadvantages of specific measures" (Honneth 2017, 70). The net should be cast widely:

> When it comes to experimenting with institutional models, we must welcome all proposals that are somehow committed to freeing producers from constraints and dependencies, thus enabling them to see themselves as free contributors to the task of equally satisfying the needs of all members of society, a task that can only be fulfilled in reciprocity. (Honneth 2017, 69)

One specific feature of capitalism that Honneth does *not* envisage replacing wholesale is the market itself as a coordinating device. Instead "one of socialists' most urgent tasks therefore consists in cleansing the concept of the market from all subsequent capitalist additives in order to examine its own moral sustainability" (Honneth 2017, 67). This is of course consistent with saying that a market economy is only morally sustainable if counter-balanced by non-market institutions that serve to limit the scope of market transactions and/or partially redistribute monetary rewards earned in the market in the name of social justice. Nonetheless, "we cannot categorically exclude the possibility that the economic form anticipated by the socialist concept of social freedom might lead to relations that could only be termed 'market socialist'" (Honneth 2017, 74).

In the light of the sometimes catastrophic failures of socialist experiments in the past, Honneth's open-mindedness about possible new directions of travel must be warmly welcomed. But there are also some problems and ambiguities that need to be addressed. One result of the experimental approach is that it gives us no clear-cut way of saying where capitalism ends and socialism begins. We may be able to say that a particular reform has had the effect of moving our (capitalist) society in a socialist direction – let us say a reform that requires companies to distribute some percentage of their shares to their employees. We might then propose a further reform that safeguards workers from being arbitrarily dismissed, and so forth. But could we say, following a series of such reforms, that socialism has now been achieved? Honneth's approach does not provide guidance here. Perhaps he would say that the question being asked is the wrong one. We should cease thinking of socialism as the definite end point of a process of social change. Instead, we should see it as a guiding ideal in the light of which we can interrogate any particular set of economic institutions to see how far they are able to realize social freedom. But in that case the normative work is being done by the idea of social freedom itself, and socialism just becomes the name of whatever arrangements turn out, in particular circumstances, to realize it most fully.

Another ambiguity concerns the scale on which the experimental approach is to be applied: should it be national or sub-national? On the one hand, we might think of models of socialism that have been put into practice at the macro-level: the Cuban model, the Swedish model, the Yugoslav model, and so on. On the other hand, we might think of socialist experimentation carried on at local level within nation-states. In Britain, we used to speak about "municipal socialism," where towns and cities would take the initiative of supplying a range of public services that previously had been privately provided (or not provided at all). In the Basque region of Spain, we can point to the Mondragon group of co-operatives funded by a local credit union, the Caja Laboral. Elsewhere there have been small-scale experiments in providing workers with unconditional basic incomes that give them greater freedom of choice over whether and for whom to work. Many other such initiatives could be entered into the archive that Honneth envisages. But when he calls for "experimenting with institutional models" is it these or is it national-level models that he has in mind?

Small-scale socialist-inspired initiatives face two main challenges. One is the possibility of adverse selection: the experiment is tried in circumstances or by people who represent failures of capitalism. For example, if the workers in a firm that is failing and due to close decide to buy it out to save their jobs, this may not tell us much about the general effectiveness of worker-managed firms. Or if a local authority announces that it is about to implement a generous income support scheme, this may have the effect of attracting a disproportionate number of people with little prospect of secure employment. Perhaps more serious is the possibility that the experiment uses institutional forms that are liable to succumb in a capitalist environment but would be successful if they themselves became socially dominant. I have argued elsewhere that this applies in the case of worker co-operatives: faced with competition from capitalist firms they are liable either to fail through lack of investment or to be incentivized to become capitalist firms themselves, taking on additional workers as wage labour; whereas an economy made up of co-operatives, with supporting financial institutions, might be stable and efficient (Miller 1981).

If so, observing actual experiments will yield far too pessimistic a prognosis as concerns the feasibility of socialism on a larger scale.

So although there is no reason to ban small-scale experiments, it seems that the most revealing attempts to move capitalism in a socialist direction will be those that have taken place at the national level. An institution with the organizational and financial power of the state is required to counter the systemic power of capitalism, which otherwise tends to shape all sub-components of the system in its own image. It might be argued at this point that the problems I have identified with small-scale experiments are going to recur even if we move up to this level. A socialist Sweden, say, might be perfectly viable if it were isolated from the global economy, but once immersed in it will come under severe pressure to revert to capitalist institutions and practices in order to remain competitive. Socialism in one country is no longer an option, if it ever was. However, I believe this underestimates the extent to which states can create for themselves the breathing space in which to try out new economic forms, if necessary by controlling international flows of capital. At the same time, the breathing space is not so great that any single state will be able to conduct a wide range of different experiments at the same time. Citizens wanting to move in a socialist direction will need to decide what to prioritize. This of course leads us directly to the question of how political mobilization in favour of socialism is going to be possible in the first place.

SOLIDARITY, NATIONAL IDENTITY, AND EUROPE

Honneth is I believe correct to insist that socialist transformation of capitalist societies can only take place through "democratic will-formation," whereby citizens deliberate in public over changes to the present order that would better realize "social freedom." As he puts it, "Citizens assembled in the democratic public sphere are the only ones who can be convinced to tear down existing limitations and blockages cautiously in order to enable free cooperation in all major social spheres" (Honneth 2017, 97). However, he does not say very much about how to bridge the gulf between the current state of democratic politics and this demanding ideal. Citizens would need first of all to be motivated to engage in democratic deliberation and then to familiarize themselves with the quite complex issues surrounding proposed institutional changes. Moreover, the incentives to engage and become informed aren't equally distributed. Groups with a great deal to lose from shifts in the direction of socialism – big business, the financial sector, and so forth – have a large incentive to gather information and attempt to influence the course of public debate. Nor is it possible to rely on group-specific complaints against the status quo launched by ethnic, religious, and other minorities. Although achieving social justice will require addressing these complaints (if they are well-founded), the institutional changes that any version of socialism will demand must rely on bringing about a broad cross-group consensus, based to some extent on shared interests in improving the conditions of working life but also on shared norms of justice. People must be able to look beyond their specific concerns and be willing to support long-term changes from which they themselves may not gain much materially (if they are already among the better off).

The fundamental issue here is one of solidarity: how, in a large, anonymous society, can people become sufficiently committed to advancing one another's interests that they are willing to set aside some of their own individual or group-specific concerns.[4] Solidarity emerges most easily through direct face-to-face interaction, and this is clearly an impossibility at the level of even the smallest contemporary state. Instead people have to learn to feel solidarity with those who they will never meet, and about whom they lack specific information. In my view the solution is to cultivate a shared identity. To support this, I rely on the simple psychological claim that we are disposed to sympathize with, help, trust, and take responsibility for those that we perceive to be like ourselves, and a sense of shared identity creates this feeling of likeness even towards people with whom we have no direct contact. There is ample evidence to bear this claim out, for example, evidence from psychological experiments in which some participants, but not others, are told that they are interacting with people with whom they share some common attribute: those who are given this information prove to be more willing to engage in various forms of helping behaviour.

The problem with identity as a source of solidarity, however, is that it is liable to exclude as well as to include: where there is an in-group, there is also an out-group. So the debate about identity has revolved around the question of whether it is possible to have a society-wide identity that is strong enough to generate solidarity but accessible enough to different subgroups that all are able to adopt it. More specifically, the debate has been between those who believe that a thinner "citizen identity" is sufficient to the task, and those who think that a thicker "national identity" is required – though it can also be recast as a debate about national identity itself, and the extent to which this needs to include cultural alongside more narrowly political elements. As one might expect, the evidence suggests that those who adhere to a richer, and therefore more exclusive, understanding of what it means to belong to a particular nation are also likely to identify more strongly with their fellow nationals – and therefore are more willing to display solidarity with them, so long as they are regarded as members in good standing. The corresponding problem, therefore, is how to ensure that those who are regarded at best as "marginal" members by those who place themselves in the core are included in the collective "we" when questions of public policy are at stake.

Honneth is fully aware of the historically problematic relationship between nationalism and the democratic state.[5] On the one hand, it seems that the state must be "ethically neutral" in order to gain the allegiance of all of its citizens, not just the historically dominant group. On the other hand, it seems that national identity is what binds people to the state and motivates them to take responsibility for its actions. So a democratic state that wishes to safeguard its own future has reason to ensure that national identity is reproduced over time, albeit with input from different groups in civil society. Such an exercise cannot be culturally neutral: it involves choices over which language is to be used in the national media, which cultural symbols are to be supported, how national history is to be taught in schools, and so forth. It does not seem that the emotional bond that such identities create can be substituted by a purely rational allegiance to the founding political principles of the state, as is proposed by advocates of "constitutional patriotism" such as Habermas.[6] As Honneth puts it:

> The idea of constitutional patriotism ... continues to have too little attractiveness to count as a sound alternative to national solidarity among citizens. It lacks historical concretion, a narrative of collective triumphs and defeats in the light of which citizens can view themselves as sharing a common destiny and commit to mutual support. (Honneth 2014, 328)

Besides the dilemma of how to create a political identity that allows citizens to see themselves as continuing an historical narrative replete with "collective triumphs and defeats" while at the same time remaining open to minority groups, especially newcomers whose ancestors were far away when those events were happening, there is the further dilemma created by the nation-state's limited capacity for autonomy in the face of globalization. Does this mean that "democratic will-formation" must now also take place at a level above the nation-state? This of course connects to Honneth's question with which I began, about whether socialism must now be understood as a national or as an international project. The problem is that although it may be possible to create the formal institutions that would allow supranational democracy to exist, it may be impossible to create sufficient solidarity between citizens across national borders, so long as national identities remain strong. This, of course, is the lesson we have learned from the experience of the European Union. Although most citizens of member-states also feel that they are Europeans, their strongest ties are still with their own compatriots, and their political choices, in elections to the European parliament, are made mainly on national grounds. One would be hard-pressed to say that decisions made in that parliament qualify as a form of democratic will-formation on the part of European citizens generally. Such political deliberation as occurs at European level takes place among elites, with input from ordinary citizens occurring only in the form of sectional lobbying activity in Brussels.

European experience also has a lesson to teach about the prospects for socialism understood as "historical experimentalism." I argued in the previous section that experimenting with new models of socialism was most likely to succeed at the national level, since anti-capitalist forms of organization would need the support of the state if they were not to be driven out by the inherent logic of capitalism itself. The problem, then, with transnational forms of political organization, even if they are democratically controlled from below, is that they will want to promote economic integration, and therefore to impose a common model of economic organization on each of their constituent parts. The effects can be seen most clearly when a common currency is created, as in the case of the Euro. Participating countries that attempt to depart from neoliberal orthodoxy in financial matters have to be brought back into line if the currency is to remain stable.

Commenting a century and a half ago on why European countries had been progressive while China had remained "stationary," John Stuart Mill pointed to the "remarkable diversity of character and culture" that existed within the European family of nations. Each had attempted at various points to compel the others to follow its self-chosen path, but because these attempts had always failed, European countries had been able to learn from one another's successes and failures (Mill 1972, 129–30). Adapting Mill's insight, we might think of Europe as the laboratory within which different socialist models might one day be tried out. But in order for that to happen, it is essential that the nations of Europe retain the freedom to experiment in economic and social policy. The role of a European Union could only be to provide some level of insurance in case an experiment should fail, not to try to guide its individual members along the same economic path.

CONCLUSION

Among people who like to think of themselves as "progressive," there is an understandable tendency to believe that the various goals they are bent on pursuing are all at least compatible with each other, if not mutually reinforcing. Two such objectives, in the present day, are new forms of economic organization that can deliver social justice, and cosmopolitan political institutions that can supersede the nation-state. Drawing inspiration from Honneth's idea of socialism as historical experimentalism, I have argued that these two goals may not in fact be compatible. Having eliminated models of socialism that are clearly utopian (and may not anyway on closer inspection deliver "social freedom"), we should warmly embrace nation-states as the spaces within which other, more feasible, models can be tried and assessed.

NOTES

1. See, for example, the model proposed by Joseph Carens in *Equality, Moral Incentives and the Market* (1981) and more recently defended in qualified form in his "The Egalitarian Ethos as a Social Mechanism" (2015).
2. I draw here on my longer discussion in "Marx, Communism and Markets" (Miller 1987). In that article, I suggest that, despite his well-known (though somewhat cryptic) avowals of communism as the ideal of the future, Marx himself recognized that markets had liberating as well as constraining properties.
3. I have explored this point at greater length with reference to Cohen's version of socialism in "Our Unfinished Debate about Market Socialism" (Miller 2014).
4. In this paragraph and the one following, I draw upon my longer discussion of solidarity in "Solidarity and Its Sources" (2017).
5. See his discussion in *Freedom's Right* (2017, section 6.3.2).
6. See Habermas (1996, 1999, 2001). For a sustained discussion of the necessary role of emotions in political life, and in support of justice, see Martha Nussbaum's *Political Emotions: Why Love Matters for Justice* (2013, esp. Part III).

BIBLIOGRAPHY

Carens, Joseph. 1981. *Equality, Moral Incentives and the Market*. Chicago: University of Chicago Press.

Carens, Joseph. 2015. "The Egalitarian Ethos as a Social Mechanism." In *Distributive Justice and Access to Advantage: G. A. Cohen's Egalitarianism*, edited by Alexander Kaufman, 50–78. Cambridge: Cambridge University Press, 2015.

Cohen, Gerald A. 2009. *Why not Socialism?* Princeton, NJ: Princeton University Press.

Habermas, Jürgen. 1996. "Citizenship and National Identity: Some Reflections on the Future of Europe." In *Between Facts and Norms: Contributions to a Discourse Theory of Law and Democracy*. Trans. Willliam Rehg, 491–515. Cambridge: Polity Press.

Habermas, Jürgen. 1999. *The Inclusion of the Other: Studies in Political Theory*, edited by Ciaran Cronin and Pablo De Greiff. Cambridge: Polity Press.

Habermas, Jürgen. 2001. *The Postnational Constellation*. Cambridge: Polity Press.

Honneth, Axel. 2014. *Freedom's Right: The Social Foundations of Democratic Life*. Cambridge: Polity Press.

Honneth, Axel. 2017. *The Idea of Socialism*. Translated by Joseph Ganahl. Cambridge: Polity Press.

Marx, Karl. 1978. "The German Ideology." In *The Marx-Engels Reader*, edited by Robert C. Tucker, 146–200. New York: W.W. Norton and Co.

Marx, Karl. 2000. "The Critique of the Gotha Programme." In *Karl Marx: Selected Writings*, edited by David McLellan. Second Edition, 610–616. Oxford: Oxford University Press.

Mill, John Stuart. 1972. "On Liberty." In *Utilitarianism, On Liberty, and Considerations on Representative Government*, edited by Harry B. Acton, 65–170. London: J.M. Dent, 1972.

Miller, David. 1981. "Market Neutrality and the Failure of Co-operatives." *British Journal of Political Science* 11: 309–29.

Miller, David. 1987. "Marx, Communism and Markets." *Political Theory* 15: 182–204.

Miller, David. 2014. "Our Unfinished Debate about Market Socialism." *Politics, Philosophy and Economics* 13: 119–39.

Miller, David. 2017. "Solidarity and its Sources." In *The Strains of Commitment*, edited by Keith Banting and Will Kymlicka, 61–79. Oxford: Oxford University Press.

Nussbaum, Martha. 2013. *Political Emotions: Why Love Matters for Justice*. Cambridge, MA: Harvard University Press.

Chapter 12

Hegel's Concept of the Person and International Human Rights

Seyla Benhabib

The seventieth anniversary of the Universal Declaration of Human Rights in 2018 received a muted and lacklustre reaction worldwide.[1] Like a person who has reached the mature age of seventy, and who looks back at her choices and their consequences, idealism has waned and a certain mature wisdom – maybe even, melancholy – has set in. In an important article called "Ist die Zeit der Menschenrechte vorbei?" [Is the Time of Human Rights Over?], the historian Stefan-Ludwig Hoffmann argued in *Die Zeit*:

> Already before the authoritarian revolts of our time, a feeling of exhaustion and disappointment had set in, and in particular among those born after 1968 and before 1989. ... Is the time of human rights over? Yes and No. Yes, in the sense that the human rights idealism of the late 20th century has itself become historical. ... No, one can argue opposing this view, that past experiences can serve as a repertory of possible futures. (Hoffmann 2018, my translation)

Three types of criticism have contributed to the sense of intellectual exhaustion and disillusionment with the politics of human rights: the charge of humanitarian interventionism; that humanitarianism has generated a politics of victimhood; and that international human rights have an aporetic relation to state sovereignty.

Humanitarian Interventionism: This is the claim that the defence of human rights has served as a "fig leaf" for humanitarian interventions and the imperialist ventures of Western powers in Kosovo, Afghanistan, and Iraq from the 1990s onward. Such imperialist ventures undertook overt military interventions that destabilized the entire Middle East, and eventually led to the Syrian civil war. Even parallel to the unauthorized NATO intervention in Kosovo, under the Clinton administration measures of neoliberal globalization in Latin

America and Africa extended financial capital markets into these continents, weakened the power of the state and led to extensive privatizations. Shared by Perry Anderson (2015) as well as Jacques Rancière (2004) and Slavoj Žižek (2000, 2011), this line of critique confuses doctrine and ideology, intention and consequence, and conflates the strategic manipulation of human rights with the theoretical critique of the philosophical underpinning of these rights. It exercises what Paul Ricoeur (1970) had once called "a hermeneutics of suspicion" and has little to say about the doctrinal and institutional development of human rights as a global phenomenon in the post–World War II period.

The Critique of Humanitarian Reason. According to Didier Fassin (2012), to whom we owe this phrase, the rise of human rights and of the humanitarian politics of rescue has led to a privileging of victimhood and injury. Focusing on the logic of refugee protection, Fassin and others have shown how contemporary bureaucratic and administrative procedures have medicalized the requirement of the 1951 *Refugee Convention* that refugees and asylum seekers show "well-founded fear of persecution" (Fassin 2012, 246ff.). Through reliance on the testimony of doctors and psychologists, the proof of persecution has been reduced to the presence of wounds and signs of torture on the refugees' and asylum seekers' body. Unlike in the aftermath of World War II and the Cold War years, the refugee is no longer viewed prototypically as a political dissident and resister against authoritarianism, but as a victim of torture, abuse, and persecution. Humanitarianism thus robs the refugee of his or her agency and risks reducing her to an object of pity.

What distinguishes this critique of humanitarianism from that of humanitarian interventionism is the close attention paid to the practice of international human rights. Instead of vague generalizations about the misuse of human rights doctrine as political propaganda to serve strategic ends, this second critique emphasizes both doctrine and institutionalization. As regards international human rights doctrine, it is asked: why is the proof of "well-founded fear of persecution," required by the 1951 *Refugee Convention* translated into proof that bodily torture and abuse have taken place?[2] Institutionally, why are the medical and psychological professions thus privileged? This approach, which follows a Foucauldian methodology of the critique of administrative power, is indispensable for evaluating the current ironies of refugee protection in general.

SOVEREIGNTISM AND THE APORIAS OF HUMAN RIGHTS

In his well-known book *The Last Utopia: Human Rights in History*, Samuel Moyn has argued that "the history of human rights reveals the persistence of the nation-state as the aspirational forum for humanity" (Moyn 2010, 212).

Sharply dismissive of Kantian cosmopolitanism for pursuing misplaced utopian dreams, in his later work, *Not Enough. Human Rights in an Unequal World* (2018), Moyn criticizes the human rights movement not primarily for its dismissal of the nation-state but for its neglect of socio-economic justice on a global scale.

Despite its frequently polemical edge, Moyn's insistence on the relationship between human rights and the state raises one of the most important problems for human rights doctrine and practice of the last seventy years. Since 1948, human rights have been legally and politically institutionalized and professionalized via a complex network of conventions, treaties, monitoring and compliance bodies, giving rise to a set of interlocking jurisdictions as well as considerable legal doctrine and commentary. These developments have been mostly neglected in the critical philosophical literature.[3]

The *aporia* of sovereignty and international human rights consists of the following: although international human rights are rights (in the legal and to some extent also in the moral sense) that human beings as such are entitled to, states alone are the signatories of the international conventions that codify such rights as international law. Yet states are also the principal, even if not exclusive, agents that commit abuse of such rights but also paradoxically which have the obligation to uphold and to realize them.

The *Universal Declaration of Human Rights* was not a legally binding document but an aspirational one urging the peoples of the world to protect the inherent dignity and equal and inalienable rights of all members of the human family. This promise was given *justiciable* form first with two major human rights conventions:[4] the *International Covenant on Civil and Political Rights* (ICCPR) (1966), signed in 1966 and entered into force in 1976, with 172 state parties as of 2018, and the *International Covenant on Economic, Social and Cultural Rights* (ICESCR) (1966), entered into force the same year with 169 state parties as of 2018. These documents and the institutions of compliance and monitoring they have created have altered the legal landscape for the entitlement to and exercise of international human rights. Known as the *International Bill of Human Rights*, these two major treaties have been followed by other major conventions such as:

- The *International Convention on the Elimination of All Forms of Racial Discrimination* (1966), adopted 21 December 1965, entered into force 4 January 1969; with 182 state parties;
- The *Convention on the Elimination of All Forms of Discrimination against Women* (1979), adopted 18 December 1979, entered into force 3 September 1981, with 189 state parties;
- The *Convention on the Rights of the Child* (1989), adopted 20 November 1989, entered into force 2 September 1990, with 196 state parties;

- The *Convention on the Rights of Persons with Disabilities* (2006), entered into force 3 May 2008, with 181 state parties.

These are some of the best-known conventions of international law, which oblige signatory states to uphold and to implement such rights through institutional and other measures.

If states remain the principal addressees of these conventions – that is, in the sense that they are the ones whose signature binds them to certain behaviour and to take certain measures such as to realize these rights, are human beings capable of exercising these rights only insofar as they are members of states – either as citizens, residents, or guests?

It is this aporia of the relationship between state sovereignty and international human rights that I want to analyse in greater detail in this chapter by focusing on Hegel's discussion of "abstract right" in the opening sections of *The Philosophy of Right* (Hegel [1952] 1971). On the one hand, Hegel makes the recognition of the individual as a "person," that is, an individual entitled to the exercise of certain rights, the cornerstone of the legitimacy of the modern state as a *Rechtstaat*. On the other hand, he limits such rights to the private enjoyment by subjects of certain economic, moral, and personal liberties in a well-organized state, thereby blunting any critical potential that may result from the critical exercise of citizenship rights. But, as I will argue, the right of personality has a subversive and expansionist dynamic which even Hegel's well-known pronouncements on the inequality of the sexes and the backwardness of African peoples cannot contain (Hegel 1975a, 195; 1970, 413). Precisely because freedom must realize itself as Idea, that is, as concept and actuality, Hegel cannot limit its manifestations to the institutions of the early nineteenth-century Prussian state (Hegel [1952] 1971, 20–21, par. 4).[5] The left-Hegelians were right after all that freedom transcends these historical boundaries.

I will then focus on the surprising convergence between the Hegelian concept of the person and Hannah Arendt's concept of "the right to have rights." The international human rights regime emerged after 1948 precisely because the European nation-state system and the institutional regime of sovereignty of the interwar years had collapsed. Hegel's *Philosophy or Right* and Hannah Arendt's *The Origins of Totalitarianism* (1979) can be read as bookmarks of this epoch of European history.

In attempting to retrieve from Hegel's discussion of abstract right a concept of the person such as may help illuminate some of the aporias of the present, I am not denying the significance of Hegel's theory of ethical life – *Sittlichkeit*. Unlike the early communitarian interpretations of Hegel in the past decades, I believe that Hegel is also a theorist of a differentiated modern state structure in which individual rights and modern law; morality and ethical life complement rather than exclude one another. Axel Honneth is correct that Hegel's concern is with "Das Recht der Freiheit."[6] Today the right of freedom has a transnational dimension in our world which Hegel could not have anticipated and may be even would not have endorsed.

PERSONS, PROPERTY, AND CONTRACT

In an early work entitled, *Über die wissenschaftlichen Behandlungsarten des Naturrrechts, seine Stelle in der praktischen Philosophie und sein Verhältnis zu den positiven Rechtswissenschaften*, dated 1802–03 (Hegel [1802–1803] 1970, translated as Hegel 1975b), Hegel criticizes "empiricist" and "formalist" natural right and social contract theories. Although in this text Hegel defends an Aristotelian conception of *Sittlichkeit*, according to which, the polis, which he mistakenly identifies with "das Volk," is prior to the individual, his methodological critique of these theories[7] is crucial for understanding the opening arguments of the *Philosophy of Right* of 1821.

By "empiricist natural right theories" Hegel has in mind Hobbes, Locke, Rousseau, but also Grotius and Pufendorf (Hegel 1975b, 63–64); by "formalist natural right theories" he refers principally to those of Kant and Fichte (Hegel 1975b, 75–86). All these theories contain two elements: first they prescribe a *system of rights,* conceptualized under the metaphor of the "state of nature" (*Naturzustand*), and second, they specify a *public institutional procedure* – which they call the "social contract" – through which individuals can enjoy these rights as publicly guaranteed liberties. From Hobbes to Fichte natural or basic rights are defined as those inalienable claims of human nature and rationality the respect for which is a necessary condition of legitimate political obligation. Hobbes names this the "right to self-preservation"; Locke calls them "the right to life, liberty, and property"; for Rousseau it is the right to natural and equal liberty of the human person. Kant in his *Metaphysik der Sitten* names state of nature metaphors a "Gedankenexperiment" and dismisses their anthropological and historical assumptions.[8]

Yet, like other social contract theories, Kant too shares the assumption that the unlimited exercise of such rights would lead to a state of conflict which is incompatible with the peaceful and prosperous coexistence of all. The thought experiment of the social contract of civil government asks: "Under what conditions would autonomous individuals agree to a system of public political authority that would limit the exercise of their rights?" The answer to this question provides a model of ideal legitimacy the first aspect of which is the "rule of law" or the *Rechtsstaat*. The social contract, or "covenant" as Hobbes ([1651] 1980, 195) also calls it, upholds the *equality* of subjects, the *generality* of the law, and *uniformity* of treatment of individuals under the law. Whether such visions of politics are liberal or authoritarian depends upon the degree to which sovereign authority established through such a procedure respects a sphere of individual rights, and in particular the right to private property, and refrains from intervening in the free flow of early commodity exchange relations and capital accumulation. Particularly for Locke, the most bourgeois of the social contract theorists, the state is like a "fiduciary" trust that administers the affairs of those who confide in it, but the people retain the right of revolution when and if such trust is violated (Locke [1690] 1988, 366–367, par. 149).

Though no comparable methodological fiction of a state of nature or of the social contract is to be found in the *Philosophy of Right,* Hegel also begins his discussion of persons, property, and contract with a conceptual abstraction. Proceeding from the single basic norm that each individual is a person, that is, to say, a being entitled to rights, he seeks to define the content and relations among individuals consistent with this norm.[9] Hegel begins with the right of personality precisely because the universal and inalienable right of every individual to be recognized as a person is the foundational norm of the modern legal system. We read: "Personality essentially involves the capacity for rights and constitutes the concept and the basis (itself abstract) of the system of abstract and therefore formal right" (Hegel [1952] 1971, 37, par. 36). Hegel further explicates the relationship between the norm of personality and the system of modern law in paragraph 211: "The principle of rightness becomes law (Gesetz) when, in its objective existence, it is posited (gesetzt), i.e. when thinking makes it determinate for consciousness and makes it known as what is right and valid; and in acquiring this determinate character, the right becomes positive law in general" (Hegel [1952] 1971, 134–135, par. 211). With the formation of a positive legal system, normatively binding rules of conduct assume their most adequate form and specification as laws. What is right, argues Hegel, must have objective existence. It must be publicly known and posited (*gesetzt*). The public character and positedness of law upholds the formal right of persons as rational agents to be obliged only by those rules whose cognitive significance they grasp. Hegel concludes that "it is only because of this identity between its implicit and its posited character that positive law has obligatory force in virtue of its rightness" (Hegel [1952] 1971, 136, par. 212).

But why is abstract right restricted to the rights of property and contract? In paragraph 40 of the *Philosophy of Right*, Hegel writes:

> Right is in the first place the immediate embodiment which freedom gives itself in an immediate way, i.e. (a) possession, which is *property*-ownership. Freedom is here the freedom of the abstract will in general or, *eo ipso*, the freedom of a single person related only to himself. (b) A person by distinguishing himself

from himself relates himself to another person, and it is only as owners that these two persons really exist for each other. Their implicit identity is realized through the transference of property from one to the other in conformity with a common will and without detriment to the rights of either. This is *contract*. (Hegel [1952] 1971, 38, par. 40. Emphasis in the text)

This passage reveals the materialist anthropological premises of Hegel's concept of the person. In the edition of Hegel's lectures on the *Rechtsphilosophie* prepared by Dieter Henrich (Hegel 1983), based on a manuscript found in the Indiana University Library, this is made more explicit: "Freedom must first be determined as a Person and must give itself existence. I am not only a person but also an individual. As such, we are also particular and have needs, drives, and inclinations" (Hegel 1983, 68, my translation). Hegel is not proceeding from a fictive state of nature where an isolated individual appropriates the external world facing it; rather, as the discussion of abstract right proceeds from possession (*Besitznahme*) to property (*Eigentum*) and to contract (*Vertrag*), we realize that the person is situated in a context of social relations with other persons wherein the principal mode of property appropriation is contractual transfer. In the years succeeding the early essay of *Naturrecht*, Hegel had immersed himself in a reading of British political economy and had discovered the structure of modern exchange relations.[10] He will name this system of modern exchange among individual commodity owners "System der Bedürfnisse" (Hegel [1952] 1971, 126–134, par. 189–209).

It is precisely because he has uncovered the structure of commodity exchange relations in the capitalist marketplace that Hegel rejects the appropriateness of the contract metaphor to describe the founding of political authority in the modern state. In exchange, two distinct individuals engage in a monetary transaction to transfer their property rights over certain goods. Exchange relations are formal. As long as they do not violate the rights of ownership of the parties, the content and substance of such exchange is determined by the will of the parties involved. Property rights are transferred in return for the equivalent payment of the value of the property in monetary form.

Precisely because Hegel understands contract as the modern exchange of equivalents through a monetary transaction, he considers the social contract metaphor to be wholly inappropriate to define the legitimation basis of modern relations of authority.

> The intrusion of this contractual relation, and relationships concerning private property generally, into the relation between the individuals and the state has been productive of the greatest confusion in both constitutional law and public

life. Just as at one time political rights and duties were considered and maintained to be an unqualified private property of particular individuals, something contrasted with the right of the monarch and the state, so also in more recent times the rights of the monarch and the state have been regarded as the subjects of a contract and as grounded in contract, as something embodying merely a common will and resulting from the arbitrariness of parties united into a state. However different these two points of view may be, they have this in common, that they have transferred the characteristics of private property into a sphere of a quite different and higher nature. (Hegel [1952] 1971, 59, par. 75 Remark)

Whereas in the pre-French Revolutionary tradition of the *ancien régime*, the right to collect taxes, to conduct trial, or to own other human beings as property (*Leibeigen*) were considered the special privileges of feudal lords, the modern contract tradition, although it rejects the ancient regime, still falsely uses the paradigm of contract to describe relations of political obligation. *But the specificity of the modern state is precisely that the right of personality is not a property right*. No one can own another as his property either as a slave or as an indentured servant. "The object about which a contract is made is a single external thing, since it is only things of that kind which the parties' purely arbitrary will has the power to alienate" (Hegel [1952] 1971, 58, par. 75). Slavery then cannot be based on a contractual exchange of one's life for service, as even Locke and sometimes Grotius consider it to be, but as already discussed in the *Phänomenologie*, the relationship between "Herr und Knecht" is a relationship of domination where the mutual right of personality of each individual has not yet been recognized (Hegel 1977, 111, chap. IV A; see also Honneth 1995). Under such circumstances there is no right, but only conflict and war.

Furthermore, *jus realiter personale,* which Kant adopts from Roman law to describe the rights of the male head of household over his children, his spouse, and his servants is a category mistake (Kant 1975, 57, par. 10). There are no "personal rights" over others; there may be rights to the performance of certain services on the part of others but no rights to the personality of the other (Hegel [1952] 1971, 58–59, par. 75 Remark).

Hegel's next step is to limit the threat that the universalization of exchange relations poses to the human right of personality by prescribing the extent to which the human capacity, not only to labour but to the performance of one's mental aptitudes, erudition, artistic skills, and even sermons, masses, and prayers, must be set (Hegel [1952] 1971, 40, par. 43 Remark). What is the point at which alienability through contract (*Veräußerlichung*) becomes commodification (*Verdinglichung*)? Hegel differentiates between these two processes in a manner totally compatible with a bourgeois commodity economy in which labour power itself has become a *Ware*, a commodity.

Single produces of my particular physical and mental skill and of my power to act, I can alienate to someone else and I can give him the use of my abilities for a *restricted* period, because, on the strength of this restriction, my abilities acquire an external relation to the totality and universality of my being. (Hegel [1952] 1971, 54, par. 67, my emphasis)

Yet some aspects of my activities are inalienable:

Therefore those goods, or rather substantive characteristics, which constitute my own private personality and the universal essence of my self-consciousness are inalienable and my right to them is imprescriptible. Such characteristics are my personality as such, my universal freedom of will, my ethical life, my religion. (Hegel [1952] 1971, 52–53 par. 66)

Precisely because the right to personality, one's ethical life and religion, are inalienable, Hegel recommends to the Prussian state to respect the freedom of conscience of the Quakers, Anabaptists, and others in resisting military service. "To sects of this kind, the state's attitude is toleration in the strict sense of the word, because since they decline to recognize their duty to the state, they may not claim the rights of citizenship" (Hegel [1952] 1971, 168n, note to par. 270).

Hegel qualifies this rather harsh condition with the condition that members of these sects may "fulfill their direct duties to the state passively, for instance by such means as commutation or the performance of a different service" (Hegel [1952] 1971, 168n, note to par. 270, my translation).

A footnote of the same passage of the *Rechtsphilosophie* also discusses Jewish emancipation, that is, the granting of civil rights to those of Jewish faith. Hegel rejects the view that Jews cannot be granted civil rights because they are supposedly not merely "a religious sect but" belong "to a foreign race" altogether, and he writes: "That they are above all, men; and manhood, so far from being a mere superficial abstract quality ... is, on the contrary itself the basis of the fact that what civil rights rouse in their possessors is the feeling of oneself counting in civil society as a person with rights, and this feeling of self-hood, infinite and free from all restrictions, is the root from which the desired similarity in disposition and ways of thinking comes into being" (Hegel [1952] 1971, 169n, note to par. 270).[11] The state, by excluding the Jews from civil rights, "would have misunderstood its own basic principle, its nature as an objective and powerful institution" (ibid.). Besides which, to exclude them is not prudent but is the "silliest folly." The mighty state can benefit from the efforts, intelligence, and services of its Jewish subjects, as Hegel himself, who had many Prussian Jewish students visiting his courses, well knew.

THE UNIVERSALITY OF PERSONHOOD

What light, if any, does this long excursus into Hegel's abstract right throw on the contemporary aporia of human rights with which I started? Is not Hegel's position simply one of legal positivism according to which individual rights are justiciable (*anklagbar*) only insofar as they are upheld by the law of the state? Maybe Hegel agrees with Jeremy Bentham who quipped that natural rights are but "nonsense on stilts" (Bentham 1943, 501). This is not Hegel's position. Although critical of the natural rights tradition, he incorporates the main insights of this tradition into his *Rechtsphilosophie* and defends that the recognition of the individual as a Person, a subject entitled to and capable of the exercise of rights, is fundamental to the legitimacy of the modern state.

However, how plausible is the universalist interpretation I am giving Hegel's concept of the person in view of his metaphysical justification of gender difference as grounded in Spirit dirempting itself into two: the element of subjective will and knowledge represented by the male and the element of substantial unity embodied in the female (Hegel [1952] 1971, 114–115, pars. 165–166)?[12] Likewise, don't Hegel's comments about Africa in his *Vorlesungen zur Philosophie der Geschichte* reveal the racism of his ontology of spirit?[13] Since my purpose in this chapter is not to vindicate all aspects of Hegel's political philosophy but simply to call attention to the importance of his concept of the person in thinking about human rights, I will only say that Hegel's understanding of freedom vacillates between an essentialist and a performative element.[14] Since Freedom as Idea must embody itself in actuality, Hegel cannot deny the subjectivity of those who seek to realize freedom through their own struggles and actions. This is how I understand that peculiar phrase: "Be a person and respect others as persons" (Hegel [1952] 1971, 37, par. 36). To be a person involves a certain attitude towards oneself that recognizes one's own self-worth as well as extending such recognition and respect to others. But this must not be understood in the meritocratic sense that only certain human beings are capable of becoming persons. Hegel himself at times obviously thought so. That is how we can interpret some of his comments about women and black people who did not show themselves to be capable of personhood in this Hegelian sense. But the other side of the coin in Hegel's philosophy is that these individuals prove that they are persons and worthy of freedom through their actions and struggles. There is nothing in Hegel's philosophy that can preclude this possibility categorically; hence the project of freedom remains open to future struggles for the recognition of freedom.

At this point a surprising convergence between Hegel and Hannah Arendt shows itself. In an article written for the journal *Die Wandlung* in 1949, edited by Karl Jaspers, and in part later reproduced in *The Origins of*

Totalitarianism, Arendt argued that there was only one *human* right, and that was "the right to have rights," to be recognized as a member of an organized political community.[15] The right to have rights is the right to be recognized as a *person* in the Hegelian sense. Arendt never analysed Hegel's political philosophy in great depth and always dismissed Hegel as a speculative philosopher of history. Nonetheless, their convergence on insisting that the recognition of the individual as a person, entitled to the right to have rights is striking. Also striking are Arendt's own inconclusive reflections on the realization of human rights in the state, as when she discusses the establishment of the State of Israel in *The Origins of Totalitarianism,* for having made concrete the human rights of the Jewish people (Arendt 1979, 299).

Separated by nearly a century and a half, Hegel's *Philosophy of Right* of 1821 and Hannah Arendt's *The Origins of Totalitarianism* of 1951 stand as bookmarks for the rise and decline of the European nation-state system. It was precisely the unchecked sovereignty of the modern state to grant or remove the status of legal personhood by denationalizing certain groups of people that Arendt criticized.

In Arendt's famous words:

> We become aware of the existence of a right to have rights (and that means to live in a framework where one is judged by one's actions and opinions) and a right to belong to some kind of organized community, only when millions of people emerge who had lost and could not regain these rights because of the new global political situation. ... The right that corresponds to this loss and that was never even mentioned among the human rights cannot be expressed in the categories of the eighteenth-century because they presume that rights spring immediately from the "nature" of man ... the right to have rights, or the right of every individual to belong to humanity, should be guaranteed by humanity itself. *It is by no means certain whether this is possible.* (Arendt 1979, 196–197, my emphases)

Since then the "right to have rights" has become the well-known phrase through which to characterize the plight of the stateless, the refugee, the asylum seeker, and the displaced person, that is, the plight of those who have been cast out of a framework where they are recognized as persons.[16]

The destruction of the European nation-state system through two world wars, and the emergence of millions of stateless, the *apatrides,* would have been inconceivable for Hegel. Although he was well aware of the contingent historical conditions that made the modern *Rechtstaat* possible through revolution, reform, the spread of market commodity relations, and of reformed Christianity (Hegel [1952] 1971, 51, par. 62 Remark), he also believed that precisely because the modern state respected the freedom of the individual, it rested on a principle which could not just be swallowed by the stream of history, but which possessed a certain stabilizing force because it was also philosophically correct: Freedom is the principle of the modern world for Hegel.

By contrast, turning her melancholy eyes upon the debris of the devastation caused by two world wars, what Arendt saw was not stability through the recognition of freedom but a project of state sovereignty that was bound to end in disaster. This is the historical point at which the Universal Declaration of Human Rights, which recognizes all human beings as persons, as beings equally entitled to dignity and to the protection of their rights, was adopted. Article 15 of the UDHR prohibits denaturalization and rendering human beings stateless. The obverse side of denaturalization is "naturalization" or gaining access to citizenship or to some kind of permanent membership and residency in a polity. Article 15(1) declares that "everyone has a right to a nationality," and this is reiterated in the *International Covenant of Civil and Political Rights* and in Article 34 of the 1951 Refugee Convention.[17] Nonetheless, granting some form of political membership and/or citizenship as well as the conditions under which this is done remain sovereign state privileges, as the 10 million stateless in our current world still attest to.

The "right to personality" and "the right to have rights" have both been transformed as a consequence of developments set into motion after 1948. The right to personality is no longer restricted to the rights to property and contract but entails a whole set of civil, political, social, economic, and cultural rights which signatory states have committed themselves to upholding. And it is not only as citizens or nationals that one is entitled to the "right to have rights." The protection of human rights such as the rights to life, liberty, property, due process of law, non-discrimination, freedom of religion and conscience, among others, are guaranteed to all humans regardless of their status upon the territory of the state.[18] The concretization of certain social, political, economic, and cultural rights, such as the right to health insurance, old age pensions, child subsidy, and so on are dependent upon the relationship to the territory formed by the non-citizens through various forms of civil connections. Increasingly, political membership and the entitlement to rights are conceptualized not as jus sanguinis or *jus soli* but as a form of *jus nexi*.[19]

The content of such rights as well as who is or who is not entitled to exercise and enjoy them are objects of political struggle within states as well as at the boundaries of the state. The aporia of sovereignty and human rights continues to define the tension within domestic as well as international law. But precisely because, despite all cynicism and scepticism, we live in an age when the consciousness and knowledge of such international human rights is widespread, these conventions and the institutions that monitor them have become the political battleground of our time. The desiderata of all authoritarian regimes of our time (from Erdoğan to Putin, from Orbán to Bolsonaro and to Trump) is to free the state from the binding force of these conventions and international agreements.

Despite all his belief in raison d'état, *Staatsräson*, I don't think that the old Hegel would have been on the side of the autocrats of our time. Rather, he would have seen the development of the international human rights regime as an inevitable evolution of the principle of modernity, that is, of human freedom and the recognition of the individual as a person.

NOTES

1. This chapter is based on the Hegel lecture delivered upon the invitation of the Freie Universität Berlin on 5 June 2019. It is a pleasure for it to be published in revised form for the first time in a *Festschrift* for Axel Honneth, with whom I share not only an interest in the work of the Frankfurt School and Jürgen Habermas that dates back thirty years but also an immersion in Hegel's practical philosophy.

2. For a detailed analysis of the text of the 1951 Refugee Convention and some of the difficulties of establishing what constitutes "well-founded fear of persecution," such as to enable the refugee to be granted asylum, see Hathaway and Foster (2012, 91–174).

3. This is changing and more philosophers are paying attention to the institutionalization of international human rights. See the important volume *The Philosophy of International Law* (Besson and Tasioulas 2010).

4. For an important overview of these developments, see Steiner and Alston (1996).

5. Reconstructing crucial features of Hegel's concept of freedom such as to show its continuing relevance for the project of a critical theory of society in our times has been one of Axel Honneth's principal achievements. Beginning with his analysis of Hegel's "struggle for recognition" and culminating in *Freedom's Right*, Honneth has shown how Hegel's philosophy can illuminate the struggles of our times. Particularly important is Honneth's rational reconstruction of the conceptual as distinct from the institutional dimensions of Hegel's *Philosophy of Right*. Likewise, I am attempting to show in this chapter how Hegel's concept of the person can be further developed and situated in the context of international human rights theory today. See Honneth (1995, 2000, 2014).

6. For a comparative analysis of Honneth's and my perspectives on freedom and justice, see Schmalz (2019).

7. For an extensive discussion of Hegel's methodological critique of natural right theories, see Benhabib, (1986, 22–32).

8. Cf. Kant (1965, 80): "The act by means of which the people constitute themselves a state is the original contract. More properly, it is the Idea of that act that alone enables us to conceive of the legitimacy of the state."

9. See my discussion, "Obligation, Contract, and Exchange: The Opening Arguments of Hegel's Philosophy of Right" (Benhabib 1984). Parts of the discussion which follow are adopted from this article.

10. For well-known early accounts of Hegel's evolution, see Habermas (1973), Plant (1973), Riedel (1970), and Wood (1990).

11. For a more extensive critical discussion of Hegel's attitude towards the Jewish religion, see Yovel (1998) and Markell (2003, 123–152).

12. On the complex question of Hegel's views of gender, see my essay "On Hegel, Women and Irony" (Benhabib 1991).

13. Hegel's famous words in his *Philosophy of History* (Hegel 1975a, 190) about World Spirit leaving Africa behind, need to be contrasted with his persistent rejection of slavery (Hegel [1951] 1971, 241, par. 66 Addition). In an original study, Susan Buck-Morss (2009) shows how avidly Hegel followed the news of the Haitian revolution and how his discussion in the *Phenomenology of Spirit* of lordship and Bondage, was most likely influenced by these developments.

14. See Charles Taylor (1979, 1989) on the centrality of the experience of freedom for modern individuality.

15. "Die Nachkriegsbezeichnung 'displaced persons' ist ausdrücklich erfunden worden, um diese störende 'Staatenlosigkeit' ein für allemal einfach durch ignorieren aus der Welt zu schaffen" (Arendt 1949, 755, my translation).

16. For further discussion of Arendt and the contemporary refugee condition, see Benhabib (2018, 101–125).

17. *Universal Declaration of Human Rights* 1948, article 15, *Convention relating to the Status of Refugees 1951*, article 34 ("The Contracting States shall as far as possible facilitate the assimilation and naturalization of refugees. They shall in particular make every effort to expedite naturalization proceeding and to reduce as far as possible the charges and costs of such proceedings."). *The International Covenant on Civil and Political Rights* (1966, article 24.3) enjoins that "every child has the right to acquire a nationality."

18. One disagreement I have with Honneth concerns what he calls "the pathologies of legal freedom" (Honneth 2014, 86–94). Undoubtedly, legal freedom, insofar as we conceive of individuals as litigants who are in an antagonistic relationship to one another (as in the breakdown of a marriage or civil union which result in divorce proceedings), has its limits. Law structures enmity and social animosity such as to lead to peaceful, even if not always just solutions, when reciprocally recognized norms and values have deteriorated. Even in such moments, however parties must accord a certain respect to one another. And when the content of such respect is not limited to individual relationships alone but concerns an individual facing institutions such as a workplace or state agencies, to be able to say to those in authority "you have violated my rights" is, in my view, not a moment of social pathology but of just social conflict. Consider here the case of the elderly before the development of social security and retirement rights: as opposed to being dependent upon the moral good will and generosity of children and relatives, that person can now say: "I have worked all these years, and I am entitled to a decent old age or I have served my country, and I am entitled to be taken care of, etc." We may wish for a moral universe in which all ethical obligations, such as financial support for dependent others, may be fulfilled without conflict, but the function of the development of rights claims is to free individuals of the inevitable conflicts that such demanding moral obligations may entail. In that sense, rights claims can also help hinder pathologies by introducing

into ethical relations a moment of reciprocal respect and recognition that respect for personality demands. Likewise, for the refugee to be able to claim a human right to being granted asylum is radically different than the refugee being dependent upon the moral good will and charity of those offering hospitality. I have discussed the significance of Kant's formulation of cosmopolitan right in terms of the right to hospitality in Benhabib (2004, 26–43).

19. On Jus Nexi, see Shachar (2009).

BIBLIOGRAPHY

Anderson, Perry. 2015. "Arms and Rights. Rawls, Habermas and Bobbio in an Age of War." *New Left Review* 31 (January–February): 5–40.

Arendt, Hannah. 1949. "Es gibt nur ein einziges Menschenrecht." *Die Wandlung* 4 (December), 754–770.

Arendt, Hannah. 1979. *The Origins of Totalitarianism*. New York: Harcourt Brace Jovanovich.

Benhabib, Seyla. 1984. "Obligation, Contract, and Exchange. The Opening Arguments of Hegel's *Philosophy of Right*." In *The State and Civil Society. Studies in Hegel's Political Philosophy*, edited by Z. A. Pelczynski, 159–78. Cambridge: Cambridge University Press.

Benhabib, Seyla. 1986. *Critique, Norm, and Utopia: A Study of the Foundations of Critical Theory*. New York: Columbia University Press.

Benhabib, Seyla. 1991. "On Hegel, Women and Irony." In *Feminist Interpretations and Political Theory*, edited by Molly Shanley and Carole Pateman, 129–146. Oxford: Polity Press.

Benhabib, Seyla. 2004. *The Rights of Others: Aliens, Residents, and Citizens*. Cambridge: Cambridge University Press.

Benhabib, Seyla. 2018. *Exile, Statelessness and Migration. Playing Chess with History from Hannah Arendt to Isaiah Berlin*. Princeton: Princeton University Press.

Bentham, Jeremy. 1943. *The Works of Jeremy Bentham, Vol. 2*. Edinburgh: Simpkin, Marshall, and Co.

Besson, Samantha and John Tasioulas, eds. 2010. *The Philosophy of International Law*. Oxford: Oxford University Press.

Buck-Morss, Susan. 2009. *Hegel, Haiti and Universal History*. Pittsburgh: University of Pittsburgh Press.

Convention on the Elimination of All Forms of Discrimination against Women. New York, 18 December 1979. Entry into force 3 September 1981, *United Nations Treaty Series*, vol. 1249, p. 13. Available from https://treaties.un.org/Pages/ViewDetails.aspx?src=TREATY&mtdsg_no=IV-8&chapter=4&clang=_en.

Convention on the Rights of the Child. New York, 20 November 1989. Entry into force 2 September 1990, *United Nations Treaty Series*, vol. 1577, p. 3. Available from https://treaties.un.org/Pages/ViewDetails.aspx?src=TREATY&mtdsg_no=IV-11&chapter=4&clang=_en.

Convention on the Rights of Persons with Disabilities. New York, 13 December 2006. Entry into force 3 May 2008, *United Nations Treaty Series*, vol. 2515, p. 3. Available from https://treaties.un.org/pages/ViewDetails.aspx?src=TREATY&mtdsg_no=IV-15&chapter=4.

Convention Relating to the Status of Refugees. Geneva, 28 July 1951. *United Nations Treaty Series*, vol. 189, p. 137. Available from https://treaties.un.org/Pages/ViewDetailsII.aspx?src=TREATY&mtdsg_no=V-2&chapter=5&Temp=mtdsg2&clang=_en.

Fassin, Didier. 2011. *Humanitarian Reason: A Moral History of the Present.* Berkeley: University of California Press.

Habermas, Jürgen. 1973. "Labor and Interaction: Remarks on Hegel's Jena Philosophy of Mind." In *Theory and Practice*, translated by John Viertel, 142–69. Boston: Beacon Press.

Hathaway, James C. and Michelle Foster. 2014. *The Law of Refugee Status.* Second edition. Cambridge: Cambridge University Press.

Hegel, Georg Wilhelm Friedrich. 1970. *Philosophy of Nature: Being Part Two of the Encyclopaedia of the Philosophical Sciences.* Translated by Arnold Vincent Miller. Oxford: Clarendon Press.

Hegel, Georg Wilhelm Friedrich. (1802–1803) 1970. "Über die wissenschaftlichen Behandlungsarten des Naturrrechts, seine Stelle in der praktischen Philosophie und sein Verhältnis zu den positiven Rechtswissenschaften." In *Jenaer Schriften 1801–1807*, edited by Eva Moldenhauer and Karl Markus Michel, 434–533. Werke 2. Frankfurt a. M.: Suhrkamp.

Hegel, Georg Wilhelm Friedrich. (1952) 1971. *The Philosophy of Right.* Translated with notes by T. M Knox. Oxford: Clarendon Press.

Hegel, Georg Wilhelm Friedrich. 1975a. *Lectures on the Philosophy of World History.* Translated by Hugh Barr Nisbet. Cambridge: Cambridge University Press.

Hegel, Georg Wilhelm Friedrich. 1975b. *Natural Law: The Scientific Ways of Treating Natural Law, Its Place in Moral Philosophy, and Its Relation to the Positive Sciences of Law.* Translated by T. M Knox. Philadelphia: University of Pennsylvania Press.

Hegel, Georg Wilhelm Friedrich. 1977. *Phenomenology of Spirit.* Translated by A.V. Miller. Oxford: Clarendon Press.

Hegel, Georg Wilhelm Friedrich. 1983. *Philosophie des Rechts. Die Vorlesung von 1819/20 in einer Nachschrift.* Edited by Dieter Henrich. Frankfurt a. M.: Suhrkamp.

Hobbes, Thomas. (1651) 1980. *Leviathan.* Edited by Crawford B Macpherson. Harmondsworth: Penguin Books.

Hoffmann, Stefan-Ludwig. 2018. "Ist die Zeit der Menschenrechte vorbei?" *Die Zeit*, 13 December 2018, https://www.zeit.de/2018/52/menschenrechte-allgemeine-erklaerung-jahrestag-veraenderung.

Honneth, Axel. 1995. *The Struggle for Recognition.* Translated by Joel Anderson. Cambridge, UK: Polity.

Honneth, Axel. 2000. *Suffering from Indeterminacy.* Translated by Jack Ben-Levi. Spinoza Lectures. Amsterdam: Van Gorcum.

Honneth, Axel. 2014. *Freedom's Right. The Social Foundations of Democratic Life*. Translated by Joseph Ganahl. Cambridge: Polity Press.
International Covenant on Civil and Political Rights. New York, 16 December 1966. *United Nations Treaty Series*, vol. 999, p. 171 and vol. 1057, p. 407. Available from https://treaties.un.org/Pages/ViewDetails.aspx?chapter=4&clang=_en&mtdsg_no=IV-4&src=IND.
International Covenant on Economic, Social and Cultural Rights. New York, 16 December 1966. *United Nations Treaty Series*, vol. 993, p. 3. Available from https://treaties.un.org/Pages/ViewDetails.aspx?src=TREATY&mtdsg_no=IV-3&chapter=4&clang=_en.
International Convention on the Elimination of All Forms of Racial Discrimination. New York, 7 March 1966. Entry into force 4 January 1969, *United Nations Treaty Series*, vol. 660, p. 195. Available from https://treaties.un.org/Pages/ViewDetails.aspx?src=TREATY&mtdsg_no=IV-2&chapter=4&clang=_en.
Kant, Immanuel. 1965. *The Metaphysical Elements of Justice. Part I of the Metaphysics of Morals*. Translated by John Ladd. The Library of Liberal Arts 72. Indianapolis: Bobbs-Merrill.
Locke, John. (1690) 1988. *Two Treatises of Government*. Edited by Peter Laslett. Cambridge: Cambridge University Press.
Markell, Patchen. 2003. *Bound by Recognition*. Princeton: Princeton University Press.
Moyn, Samuel. 2010. *The Last Utopia: Human Rights in History*. Cambridge, MA: Belknap Press.
Moyn, Samuel. 2018. *Not Enough: Human Rights in an Unequal World*. Cambridge, MA: Belknap Press.
Plant, Raymond. 1973. *Hegel*. Bloomington: Indiana University Press.
Rancière, Jacques. 2004. "Who Is the Subject of the Rights of Man?" *South Atlantic Quarterly* 103 (2–3): 297–310. https://doi.org/10.1215/00382876-103-2-3-297.
Ricoeur, Paul. 1970. *Freud and Philosophy: An Essay on Interpretation (The Terry Lectures)*. Translated by Denis Savage. New Haven: Yale University Press.
Riedel, Manfred. 1970. *Studien zu Hegels Rechtsphilosophie*. Frankfurt am Main: Suhrkamp.
Schmalz, Dana. 2019. "Social Freedom in a Global World: Axel Honneth's and Seyla Benhabib's Reconsiderations of a Hegelian Perspective on Justice." *Constellations* 26 (2): 301–17. https://doi.org/10.1111/1467-8675.12391.
Shachar, Ayelet. 2009. *The Birthright Lottery: Citizenship and Global Inequality*. Cambridge (MA): Harvard University Press.
Steiner, Henry J. and Philip Alston. 1996. *International Human Rights Law in Context: Law, Politics, Morals*. Oxford: Clarendon Press.
Taylor, Charles. 1989. *Sources of the Self. The Making of the Modern Identity*. Cambridge: Harvard University Press.
Taylor, Charles. 1979. *Hegel and Modern Society*. Cambridge: Cambridge University Press.
Universal Declaration of Human Rights. 1948. United Nations General Assembly Resolution. A/RES/217(III). https://www.un.org/en/ga/search/view_doc.asp?symbol=A/RES/217(III). Accessed 25 October 2019.

Wood, Allen. 1990. *Hegel's Ethical Thought*. Cambridge: Cambridge University Press.
Yovel, Yirmiyahu. 1998. *Dark Riddle. Hegel, Nietzsche, and the Jews*. Philadelphia: Pennsylvania State University Press.
Žižek, Slavoj. 2000. *NATO As the Left Hand of God?* Ljubljana: Arkzin.
Žižek, Slavoj. 2011. *Did Somebody Say Totalitarianism?: Four Interventions in the (mis)use of a notion*. London : Verso Books.

Chapter 13

Fashioning Our Selves?

On Understanding and Criticizing the Digitized Society

Beate Roessler

New information and communication technologies are radically transforming our personal, social, and political lives. Living in an information society means that almost everything we do is tracked and no one seems to be surprised any longer to realize this. For instance, the information we spread about ourselves on social platforms, the purchases we make online, and so on reveal a great deal about what interests us and, more generally, about who we are. The same holds for the information we provide to the big tech firms simply by using the internet – which websites do we visit? How long do we stay on these websites? Which ones do we visit next (see Susser, Roessler, and Nissenbaum 2019; Mayer-Schoenberger and Cukier 2013; Harcourt 2015)?

For the last decade or so, it was the topic of privacy that formed the centre of both the public debate and the scholarly literature on digitization. Big Data and the near-comprehensive surveillance of our daily lives as *consumers* by the tech giants (the *Big Five*: Amazon, Facebook, Microsoft, Google, Apple), as well as the surveillance of *citizens*, raised the question: how can we safeguard and protect our privacy? What does the loss of privacy entail for our freedom and for our autonomous lives? These debates – together with the rapid technological developments of the last years and a number of legal challenges – led in Europe to the adoption of the General Data Protection Regulation (GDPR) and thus also to an increased awareness of the relevance of the protection of privacy (see Hoofnagle, van der Sloot, and Zuiderveen Borgesius 2018 for an overview). By now, it has become clear, though – both in research contexts and in the public debate – that the threat to and loss of private life constitute only one particular aspect of the comprehensive development that is called, somewhat euphemistically, the digitization of society. For this digitization permeates every fibre of our everyday lives, our relationships, our self-understanding, and influences, impacts, and changes us.

Even in the context of the debate about privacy, the right or adequate question was not, or at least not only: what do we lose when we lose privacy and a sense for its significance? Instead, the right question was: how do we *change*, and *how does society change* when we lose privacy? This possible transformation of individuals and society as a consequence of structural surveillance has been pointed out by Jeff Reiman already more than twenty years ago. He called it "the risk of psycho-political metamorphosis" and wrote: the danger of structural surveillance "is not that we shall lose something we now enjoy [viz., privacy] but that we shall become something different than we currently are, something less noble, less interesting, less worthy of respect" (Reiman 2004, 206).

Thus, going beyond privacy in the following, I suggest that the quintessential question vis-à-vis the digital society is: how do we – as individuals and as a society – change when the fundamental conditions of our societies change under the influence of digital technologies? The problem of surveillance that confronts us now is obviously much more dramatic than it was for Reiman twenty years ago: due to the incredible acceleration of technological developments, data have become Big Data, and on the basis of extremely powerful algorithms, these data are being collected, processed, reused in some sense against us, or at least not in our own interests. We are no longer dealing with voyeurs who like to watch us, but with voyeurs who can co-determine what they want to see.

TWO QUESTIONS

What interests me in this chapter is, first, the question of how the digitization of society influences us, again, as individuals and as a society, and to what extent and in what respects this influence might affect our fundamental notions of autonomy, agency, and freedom. Secondly, and at the same time, I'm interested in the question of what might be the best philosophical way to discuss these problems, since different philosophical traditions have approached the general problem of the relation between persons and technology (or humans and technique) in very different ways. To be able to answer the first, rather general question, I shall point out examples, use illustrations, describe practices, which demonstrate ways in which it might make sense to speak about persons "changing" under digital influences. Answering the question, I shall argue that digital technologies embody forms of manipulation and power structures which are prone to put in danger the social and political conditions which we need to become autonomous subjects and to enjoy successful relationships.

The second question is concerned with the most adequate philosophical approach to discuss these problems. Phenomenology and critical theory as well as Foucauldian authors and analytically oriented political and social philosophy all analyse aspects of the digital society, each in different ways. And although the different philosophical traditions seem prima facie to be asking different questions, it is promising to combine them: asking phenomenologically how to understand the specific relations between subjects and technologies, and interpreting them within a normative and historical framework. So, in order to be able to understand and criticize the digital society and its challenges to human beings, and to answer the critical question of what it means to change in the first place, it is helpful to refer to different philosophical traditions and approaches. What will turn out to be central, though, is that the consequences of the digital technologies for our social lives are not analysable without reference to normative concepts; this makes some philosophical approaches less convincing than others. Yet only this way will it be possible to demonstrate more precisely what it might mean that the digital society turns us into, as Reiman put it, "something less noble, less worthy of respect" (Reiman 2004, 206).

I will start – after raising some terminological questions – by illustrating the digital life with a few examples, in order to give some idea of what kind of change we are talking about. In the next step, I'll briefly discuss the *post-phenomenological* approach to the relation between human beings and (digital) technologies. Subsequently, I will go deeper into some of the consequences of the new technologies, and into the question of how exactly they interfere with or are embedded in our daily lives and activities, taking up other philosophical perspectives, namely *Foucauldian analysis* and *critical theory* and *analytic* social philosophy. By discussing digital surveillance, commodification, and manipulation, I aim at pointing out the consequences digital technologies have for our daily lives. Finally, I shall return to the question of what it means to say that we change under the influence of the digital society and what would be the best philosophical way to analyse this.

Note that what I am interested in are not the ethical questions surrounding robots or autonomous cars and, for example, the responsibilities of their designers, that is, not the "human side of the machines." What I am interested in is the side and perspective of the ordinary, unexceptional human being living in the digital society. As Brett Frischmann puts it: "Alan Turing wondered if machines could be human-like, and recently that topic's been getting a lot of attention. But perhaps a more important question is a reverse Turing test: can humans become machine-like and pervasively programmable?" (Frischmann, *The Guardian*, 9 August 2015).[1]

SOME EXAMPLES FROM THE DIGITAL LIFE

"Digitization," "datafication," or "algorithmification" – mostly used interchangeably – of society means that increasingly many (some would say: all) aspects of our daily lives are turned into data and thus into easily shareable information. Think of social platforms like Instagram, turning experiences into photos, or Snapchat, Twitter, and social platforms in general, but also search engines, internet shopping, and so on. In fact, this development encompasses all aspects of the consumerist society. However, this "digitization" means not only that our behaviour generally is turned into data or represented as data but also that these data can be used in turn to predict our behaviour in ever more precise ways depending on the mass of data the respective technology is being fed with.[2] The following sketches provide us with some illustrations of lives changing, and all of them have something decidedly worrying about them.

(1) *"Self-knowledge through numbers"* is the advertising motto of the quantified-self (QS) movement. On its website (quantifiedself.com) you find everything that has to do with self-tracking: with measuring, noting, and registering all of your activities 24/7. The apps and wearables used for this purpose are mostly free of charge because the data you collect – for instance, through Fitbit ("The Fitbit family motivates you to stay active, live better and reach your goals," as they advertise on their fitbit.com) – are shared not only with the friends in your quantified-self group but also with companies and data brokers. Fitbit alone (only one of hundreds of health apps) has tens of millions of users (see Lupton 2016).

The aim of proponents of the QS is to measure their own behaviour as comprehensively as possible, to be able to record in principle every detail that can be quantified. Through apps like Fitbit, one is able to improve one's *self-management* by tracking the behaviour and by receiving personalized feedback on one's performances. At the same time, the idea of *self-knowledge* of the QS is modelled on the observation of the self from the perspective of the third person: Dormehl describes the case of "Angela," who "was working in what she considered to be her dream job, when she downloaded an app that 'pinged' her multiple times each day, asking her to rate her mood each time. As patterns started to emerge in the data, Angela realized that her 'mood score' showed she wasn't very happy at work, after all. When she discovered this, she handed in her notice and quit" (Dormehl 2014, 15; see Lupton 2016).

(2) John Danaher has done research on the quantification of romantic relations, analysing apps which track one's own and one's partners intimate behaviour. He differentiates between three ways in which these apps

are used: *First*, there is "intimate tracking," for instance the tracking of sexual behaviour (of "sexual encounters; duration; heart rate reached during sexual encounters; decibel level, etc.") or of "romantic behaviours" ("number of gifts purchased, household chores done, messages/cards sent, conversations had"). *Second*, there are "intimate gamification" apps which try to change your behaviour with the help of little games (if you do these-and-these household chores, you are entitled to this-and-this number of gift cards or benefits from your partner). The *third set* of apps are what Danaher calls "intimate surveillance" apps which monitor your partner in everything she does (where is she, what is she doing, what is she saying, who is she with?). All these apps have hilarious names, such as "Flexispy," "Sex Keeper," "Sex Tracker," "Nipple," and "Glow" – a fertility tracker (see Danaher 2018; see also Dormehl 2014, Frischmann and Selinger 2018, 147ff, esp 156).

Another example of the quantification of intimate relations can be found in a recently published piece in *The Guardian* about apps managing the relationship between baby and parent: the app tells the mother when to nurse, how much the baby should drink, and so on, while she tracks and registers – and shares – every movement of her baby. Mothers are encouraged to continuously search for registrable signs and facts about their baby in order to share them with the app and get (seemingly free) advice in response (Godwin 2019).

(3) In the US 2016 election campaign as well as in the 2016 Brexit campaign, the company Cambridge Analytica collected the data of millions of voters from many sources – demographic information, consumers' internet behaviour, data from social platforms and other public and private sources. These data were then processed and used for political advertisements, targeting voters whose profiles were based on hugely specific personal data. It is difficult to prove but very likely that these campaigns heavily influenced the results (see *The Guardian*).

(4) The almost addictive desire to have as many likes on Instagram or Facebook as possible, or re-tweets on Twitter, has been increasingly deplored over the last years. To use an example Bruce Feiler describes: "Few have learned that lesson better recently than Rameet Chawla, the founder of the mobile app company *Fueled*. Mr. Chawla was so busy last year that he didn't have time to like his friends' photos on Instagram. As a result, he felt ostracized. 'To my friends, their feed was their life,' he said. So, he designed a program to automatically like every photo. Suddenly, his popularity soared. Friends gave him high fives on the street; his follower count surged; the number of likes that appeared on his photos doubled. One friend he had alienated texted: 'Ah, it's fine, you've been giving my photo lots of life. I forgive you'" (Feiler 2014).[3]

UNDERSTANDING HUMANS-AND-TECHNOLOGIES

For a start, we can pose the question concerning the consequences of the digital society in terms of the more general question of the relation between human beings and technology: and it is helpful to turn to the phenomenological tradition since it is here that this relation between humans and technology has been given a central place, albeit in very different ways. The members of the latest generation of phenomenological philosophers call themselves post-phenomenologists, and one of the influential contemporary thinkers in this tradition is Don Ihde.[4] He connects to phenomenology's fundamental critique – in the tradition of Heidegger and Merleau-Ponty – of the Cartesian and Kantian dichotomies between subject and object and thus their epistemological primacy or precedence over what Ihde calls the "praxical orientations for philosophy" (Ihde 1990, 31). This very dichotomy obscures the fact, according to Ihde, that our perceptions and experiences are always already mediated by technology.[5] This mediation co-shapes our concepts as well as our experiences of subjectivity and objectivity. Furthermore, we must assume that we get used to technologies to such a degree that they become unnoticeable and grow to be part of us, and yet at the same time mediate our relation to the world. Ihde paints the image of technologies functioning like spectacles: when we use such technologies, they recede from view. We attend not to the spectacles themselves, but to what we can see *through* them (see Ihde 1990, 33ff; also Verbeek 2005, 36f.). Verbeek, one of Ihde's students, argues in a similar vein that information technology in particular, as represented by personal computers, "shapes specific aspects of its user's subjectivity and the objectivity of that user's world. It is more than a functional instrument and far more than a mere product of 'calculative thinking.' It mediates the relation between humans and world, and thus *co-shapes their experience and existence*" (Verbeek 2005, 198–99; my italics BR.). Post-phenomenologists "do not approach technologies as merely functional and instrumental objects, but as mediators of human experiences and practices" (Rosenberger and Verbeek 2015, 9).[6] This idea is given more content by Frischmann and Selinger (2018): they analyse a vast array of aspects of the digital technologies which influence, affect, and impact our behaviour. From analysing health apps used for school children, to the quantification of relationships, GPS, and extended-mind technologies, they picture the digital life as being dangerously manipulative: "Techno-social engineering is occurring everywhere and (has) a common theme running throughout: We are being conditioned to obey. More precisely, we're being conditioned to want to obey" (Frischmann and Selinger 2018, 6).

In one sense, it certainly must be right that we shape and form technologies and *thereby* shape our world, whereas at the same time we are being formed and shaped by these technologies and their "affordances." However, in order to be able to take up a critical standpoint, it might be more helpful to focus on the concrete consequences of technological interferences. We should, therefore, engage in a more detailed discussion of *how* we use these technologies in daily life and of *who* has the power to develop and control them, with a focus on restriction and curtailments of agency and autonomy in the digital society – and on the worrying character of the examples above.

TECHNOLOGIES: INFLUENCING DAILY LIFE

How are we to conceptualize the digital structures which we can discern in the examples of digital daily life? In this section, I make an attempt to analyse them in more detail by explaining the practices of *surveillance and commodification* and, most importantly, of *manipulation*. The idea is that, this way, we better understand the workings of the digital structures and find a way to criticize them: therefore, I shall attempt to critically reconstruct the practices first with the help of Foucauldian surveillance studies; second, for the analysis of commodification, it is helpful to turn to critical theory. The problem of digital manipulation, finally, has been analysed by different theories, a prominent one being analytic social and political philosophy. Let me discuss the problems in turn.

Surveillance and the Commodification of Personal Data

Everything we do – certainly online – is being tracked and observed in our surveillance society; we all assume this. No one is surprised when we talk about the merciless collection of data, and different opinions are expressed only with respect to the question of how dangerous this practice is. The philosophical tradition that has analysed the surveillance of modern society and its history programmatically and extensively is the Foucauldian tradition that studies the "discipline" exercised by institutions that monitor and punish us, such as in Bentham's Panopticon, which for many years was the pre-eminent symbol of the surveillance society. The Foucauldian interpretation is still extremely important, although surveillance studies have moved beyond the panopticon long ago. It is no longer (mostly) the state that monitors us: surveillance has been multiplied, pluralized, and quantified. Everybody does it, and the big tech companies in particular monitor their customers on a scale that is unimaginably larger than that of the panopticon (see Galič, Timan, and Koops 2016; Haggerty and Ericson 2000; on Foucault see Behrent 2013).

For this reason, analyses of the surveillance society started to draw on Gilles Deleuze's societies of control and the notion of assemblage (for instance in Haggerty and Ericson 2000) in order to scrutinize the multiplication of surveillance. Assemblage theory analyses the way "entities" are connected with one another in enormously complex ways, thereby demonstrating their exchangeability and varied functionalities. Interesting for surveillance theory is that these "assemblages" are component parts of a general whole (in this case: the surveillance society) and that the relationships between these parts are not stable and fixed but can be displaced and replaced within and among other bodies. Thus, different companies, state institutions, and also people who monitor us in very different ways can be added up and put together in order to magnify the surveillance, although they do not stand in institutionalized (let alone transparent) relations to one another (see Lyon 2018, 57ff.).

The last step in these surveillance analyses is taken by Shoshana Zuboff's project of surveillance capitalism in her monumental *The Age of Surveillance Capitalism* (Zuboff 2019). She argues that since tech firms constantly harvest our data from every possible different online source, they create a "behavioural surplus" – the key concept of surveillance capitalism – which is used to gather data even more efficiently, thereby creating an ever more precise and predictable individual pattern of consumption that is turned on the user through microtargeting adverts and through ever more personalized communications.[7] However, this form of surveillance – and this is one of Zuboff's central assumptions – can only work when all our data (personal, intimate, relational) are turned into commodities. They *have* to be turned into commodities in order to be collected, sorted, sold, and processed into extremely detailed personal profiles. The personalized advertisements we constantly receive when using social media or browsing the internet illustrate this process. Following this logic, not only companies but also individual persons learn to treat data about what others do as potentially digitized products, as reducible to exchange value: this is how the digital economy is trying to take hold of every area of our life (see Susskind 2018, for example, 61ff.). Going one step further, we can see that the digital economy also tends to shape our perspective on ourselves: the digital self increasingly takes it for granted that everything she does can be translated into commodified data, even – or indeed especially – personal and intimate messages. The consequences of the commodification of our private lives can be analysed in terms of Michael Sandel's (2013) moral criticisms of the marketization of everything or, more comprehensively and within a social theory, in terms of Jürgen Habermas's (1984) criticism based on the necessary distinction between "system" and "lifeworld": both present conclusive arguments against this form of commodification, for limiting the sphere of market exchange and for protecting the private sphere (see also Roessler

2015). When Sandel argues that "as markets reach into spheres of life traditionally governed by nonmarket norms, the notion that markets don't touch or taint the goods they exchange becomes increasingly implausible" (Sandel 2013, 144), we can certainly apply this to the norms which govern information about (intimate) relationships, friendships, or the self-relation of subjects. In these areas, the digitization of social relations has led to the development of norms increasingly blurring the difference between markets and the private realm. Let me also remind you here of the example of parental relations being governed by and through an app, quantifying as well as commodifying the relation (the data the mother shares is how she pays for the advice she gets since all the data she sends through the app are contributing to the company's profit).

Note, though, that I'm focusing here exclusively on *commodified digitization*: the turning of behaviour into data and *thereby* turning it into a commodity. If the collected data were not being used by the company for further purposes, if they were collected by and for the users themselves, staying as it were solely on their own devices and shared only with people of their own choice, we would face different problems. We can imagine, of course, a form of digitization which is not bound up with commodification: we could still be critical of this form of digitizing behaviour but would need to focus on different aspects.[8]

The (commodified) digital reinterpretation of our relations reifies our self-understanding and our relations to others – we comport ourselves towards ourselves and others as we comport ourselves towards things. Axel Honneth characterizes reified social relations in his theory of reification as violating ethical principles, since these relations do not respect other persons in their individuality. Instead, the others are seen "as 'things' or 'commodities'" (Honneth 2005, 19). He also applies this idea to the relation of the subject to herself, that is, to self-reification (*Selbstverdinglichung*), which the subject cannot escape if and because the social relations in which she finds herself are commodified (Honneth 2005, 78ff).[9] Therefore, it seems helpful to frame these transformations of social life as representing restrictions of *social freedom*: with Honneth, we can then analyse these *effects* of economic or technological developments as forms of social pathologies since they impede in specific, not necessarily legally regulatable ways our possibilities to live an autonomous, ethically flourishing life.[10] I will return to this idea of a normative framework later in this chapter.

Manipulation

Let me turn to the third perspective, considering surveillance and commodification as conditions for the possibility of subtle and not so subtle forms of *manipulation*. Foucault and Honneth put us on the track of this notion, but it is debates in analytic philosophy which reveal its precise meaning (Coons and Weber 2014; Yeung 2017; Susskind 2018; Susser, Roessler, and Nissenbaum 2019). The collection and processing of data by the tech firms allows them to understand what motivates their targets, what their weaknesses and vulnerabilities are, when they are most susceptible to influence, and how pitches and appeals can be most effectively framed (see Boerman, Kruikemeier, and Zuiderveen Borgesius 2017 for a wide-ranging review of the literature on targeted advertising). Because information technology makes generating, collecting, analysing, and leveraging such data about us cheap and easy, and allows for it to be done at a scarcely comprehensible scale, the worry is that such technologies render us deeply vulnerable to the whims of those who build and control these systems. What makes manipulation so treacherous is the fact that it constitutes a covert influence on our decision procedures. Manipulation, I want to suggest, is stronger than nudging, the paternalistic jostling of someone into the right sort of behaviour. But it is weaker than coercion, which is to force someone without any alternative. However, manipulation is also scarier, because it takes place behind our backs. Manipulation, I suggest, undermines a person's capacity for reasoning and decision-making to achieve the manipulator's ends, by invisibly steering the deliberation, emotions, desires in a certain manner and by exploiting cognitive or other vulnerabilities (see Susser, Roessler, and Nissenbaum 2019 for a more detailed argument).

A particularly pressing example for this kind of manipulation are personalized advertisements of which we usually don't know how it is that they fit our interests quite so precisely – and in the future also our moods (see Bell 2019). Equally or maybe even more dangerous than this consumerist form of manipulation is political manipulation via advertisements as we saw in the example of the Trump and Brexit campaigns, where advertisements were created and distributed by Cambridge Analytica – which in the meantime has been bankrupted not only in the moral sense (see again Susser, Roessler, and Nissenbaum 2019 for a more precise analysis of the issues around Cambridge Analytica).

In this context, data from all possible devices are relentlessly (and sometimes illegally) collected in order to establish a perfectly precise profile of the target, the person – for example, the data of 87 million Facebook users were used by Cambridge Analytica. The data were used not only to influence considerations, convictions, and feelings but also – and this is particularly upsetting – to exploit cognitive and emotional vulnerabilities. The possibility of this form of exploitation has been shown, for instance, in a Facebook study, where advertisers were allowed to target teenagers with advertisements for beauty products at moments when they felt especially "worthless" and "insecure." In this way, manipulative intentions can easily succeed. Manipulative practices aim at changing our decisions and decision procedures by changing the choice architecture – what we are presented with on the websites, and how the adverts are formulated, placed, and so on – of our decisions and thus by evading and avoiding our rational capacities. The person (the target) cannot reflect and act in anything like an autonomous manner any longer – knowing what the options are, reflecting on them, acting for her own good reasons – since the options she can usually at least roughly oversee have been covertly changed. It is precisely this that undermines the conditions for the possibility of autonomous agency. Therefore, manipulation has to be hidden: if persons knew about the set-up, they would or at least could act differently. Thus, personalized advertisements and communications use the collections of data provided by the tech companies not only to understand or to predict but to heavily influence our behaviour, to "make us dance," as Zuboff writes (2019, 293).

Again, it is helpful to briefly put the harms of manipulation in a framework which enables us to understand them as restrictions of social freedom, or of autonomy. Since manipulation intentionally prevents us from deliberating and reflecting freely on options and choices we have to make, it is reasonable to claim that manipulative digital technologies not only limit but *distort* our autonomy in fundamental ways (for a more detailed analysis, see again Susser, Roessler, and Nissenbaum 2019).

A CRITIQUE OF TECHNOLOGIES

What have we seen so far? The discussion of surveillance, commodification and manipulation as well as the reference to the different philosophical traditions pointed out the different and differently harmful effects of digital technologies on our social life. We also saw that, in contrast with the postphenomenologists, not only critical theories but also the more analytically oriented tradition of ethics and political philosophy insist that it is helpful to analyse these harms as restricting us in our exercise of social freedom, our social relations and relations to ourselves, and as thereby precluding possibilities to live a flourishing life.[11] Therefore, the consequences of the digital technologies for our social lives can only be understood with explicit reference to normative concepts.

Let me explain and recapitulate: philosophers like Selinger, Frischmann, Verbeek, and Ihde understand themselves as working in the (post-)phenomenologist tradition and as being interested in *understanding* what it means to be human vis-à-vis developing technologies. They helpfully stress the meaning of the deep, almost intimate relation that we always already have with the technologies we live with, and thus the meaning of our experiences as technologized or digitized people. However, this post-phenomenological analysis leaves us without a standard for critique: criticizing the new technologies or simply taking them in stride, for them, seem equally good options. Both perspectives are clearly presented in an observation by the digital anthropologist Daniel Miller. He writes that the consequences of the digital society can be perceived very differently for different populations: for some, "There is [...] a *sense of dehumanization* where people come to see themselves more as visualizations of data, rather than simply as persons" (Miller 2018, 10). This critical perspective is taken up philosophically by, for instance, Dormehl, when he refers to the activities of "Angela" (described in one of the illustrations above) as "having the potential to transform our very understanding of what it means to be human" where "algorithmic ideology is challenging the Enlightenment conception, that, at bottom, we're autonomous individuals" (Dormehl 2014, 38).

In contrast with this first group, Miller delineates "populations that either do not particularly embrace or refuse digital technologies, but rather simply accept them rapidly as normative within their daily life. Most people in this group engage with the latest digital technologies such as smartphone apps. For them, Artificial Intelligence and algorithms are experienced as, for example, more effective instant foreign language translation services, more effective GPS navigation, or more accurate voice dictation. Far from dehumanizing, they see their phone as increasingly aligned with their particular personality and tend to feel bereft if by chance they have accidentally left their digital companion at home" (Miller 2018, 11).

Sheila Jasanoff in her *Ethics of Inventions* suggests the same from a philosophical perspective when she pictures the "subjective changes that come about through our interactions with technologies (viz. the smart phone or laptop) that have become, in some sense, our most intimate companions, extensions of our minds and of our potential selves, *as we fashion those selves now and in the future*" (Jasanoff 2016, 152; see also Rey and Boesel 2014, 173).

Both Miller's second group and Jasanoff imply that we should take these technological developments in our stride and make sense of the new relationships we have with them: we should try to understand what it means to be human, or a subject, under these new technological circumstances. However, this does not seem to be sufficient: it seems difficult to even *understand* the practices and structures of the digital society without interpreting them at the same time within a normative framework. Not only critical theories, but also analytical philosophers of ethics and political philosophy for this reason claim a different set of basic concepts – concepts like loss of agency and autonomy, power, manipulation, alienation. Again, we have to realize that the complex effects of the digital technologies on our social lives are not analysable without reference to normative concepts.

We should be careful, though, not to make the double mistake of idealizing pre-digital relationships – in the tradition of the Luddites – and pretending there was a moment in time when they changed into digitized ones (see Rey and Boesel 2014; Verbeek 2005, 42ff.). The concepts of digital and of pre-digital relations arise and are developed, obviously, at the same time, and one shouldn't be naïve when analyzing their historical dimensions. Regarding the concept of privacy, we can see how a traditional idea of privacy blurred into a more digitally convenient one, where for many people privacy is at least of very different, although not necessarily lesser value (see, for example, Harcourt 2015). The loss of privacy and the transformations caused by it have often been interpreted as a "conventionalization" of users' behaviour. Being extensively surveilled, they do not seem to dare any longer to make unconventional, dangerous choices (the "chilling effect") – as, for instance, Zuboff argues (see also Penney 2016, and for a recent example of such critique Valentino-DeVries 2019). If we go beyond privacy, as I have done throughout this chapter, and take the digital world more generally in view we can see that the same interpretation can be applied to the digitization of daily life. Let me briefly revisit three digital practices – thereby also coming back to the examples given earlier – which could be an indication of what it means to turn into, as Reiman put it, "something less noble, less worthy of respect."[12]

To like and to rate: An essential feature of the digital world is the constant and unabashed liking and rating which is demanded from users of the internet: "likeability" on social media, but also the various forms of evaluating and rating everything which is rateable – teachers, doctors, services, friends, companies – make it easy (or even necessary, as we saw in the fourth example, describing the program to automatically "like" other people's pictures in order to be "liked back") to give a quick, unambivalent "yes or no" reaction to whatever is to be rated. This is made even clearer if we analyse the phenomenon of "influencers" and the marketization of "likes": a marketplace for influencers has developed over the last years, whose sole aim and task is to influence, steer, and manipulate consumer behaviour. This way, the lines between sharing experiences of wonderful holidays and recommending the hotel one stayed in not only blur but vanish: there is no longer any difference between being a friend and being a marketeer.[13] The next logical step would evidently be the holistic rating of persons, based on scores given by friends, by colleagues, or by businesses they use and visit. One version of this overall rating system has arguably started in China.[14]

To quantify and to commodify: Another typical form of interaction which seems to be worrying is the digital practice of quantifying relationships and the commodification of personal data. A huge number of apps are, as we saw above, exclusively meant to quantify our behaviour; and quantification assumes – or goes along with – commodification, as we saw as well. Following critical theories of commodification, these practices are an indication of reified – or alienated – interaction, which, again, shifts our practices towards less respectful forms of interaction.[15]

To buy and to vote: Given the pervasive practices of tech firms trying to manipulate us not only into buying things but also into voting, the idea of "fashioning our selves" on the basis of, or with the help of, our digital companions seems at best naïve and at worst dangerous. Rey and Boesel write that "because we use digital technologies both to communicate and to represent ourselves across time and across space, we express our agency through those technologies; at times, we may even experience our Facebook profiles or our smartphones as parts of ourselves" (Ray and Boesel 2014, 173). Frischmann and Selinger point to the risk of "turning humans into simple machines under the control or influence of those in control of the technologies" (Frischmann and Selinger 2018, 9), making meaningful autonomous choices virtually impossible, since the technologies are not being controlled democratically, but are simply under the control of the tech companies (see also Susskind 2018).

Again, so far, only particular dimensions of our lives in the digital society are affected and permeated by these practices. Still, I suggest that the most important philosophical contribution to understanding and criticizing the digital world lies in a broad philosophical analysis of how it affects the conditions we still take for granted, the social, political, and democratic conditions under which agency, freedom, autonomy, and flourishing intersubjectivity can be developed and preserved, or perhaps we ought to say: regained. Of course, one could argue that these conditions have always changed in response to new technological developments, and this is evidently true (regarding privacy and technologies, see, for example, Igo 2018). If, however, we continue to accept manipulative or alienating practices in ever more dimensions of our lives, thereby tampering with or undermining those conditions, then we should expect the idea of what it means to be human to change in a far more fundamental way. Why is this problematic or worrying? It is worrying – indeed, only a problem at all – if or because we object to the idea of living in a society where the principles of freedom, equality, mutual respect, or autonomy are no longer valued; and we do have quite a number of dystopic novels showing us what such a society would look like.[16]

NOTES

1. See also: Frischmann and Selinger (2018, 17) "How we engineer ourselves and are engineered by others is one of the most important questions of the twenty-first century;" and the indeed rather scary Google vision of the future human being in the leaked Google promotion film *The Selfish Ledger* (Google).

2. One could distinguish between "digitization," turning physical behaviour into data and "digitalization," referring to how the different digitizations influence our behaviour (see Cukier and Mayer-Schoenberger 2013); this is not necessary in my context. The term "algorithm" is defined in surprisingly many ways (see, for example, Mittelstadt, Allo, Taddeo, Wachter, and Floridi 2016; Matzner 2019). "Learning algorithms" function autonomously and what they "do" is not predictable, since they interpret data in different ways and thus "learn" by defining rules to determine how new inputs will be classified.

3. See also Susskind (2018, 290) who radicalizes the interpretation that we are getting dependent on the "likes" of others: "Services like reputation.com already exist to help you get better scores. I've suggested the possibility that our access to goods and services in the digital lifeworld might eventually be determined by what others think of us."

4. See Rosenberger and Verbeek (2015, 1): "All of these studies label themselves as 'post-phenomenological,' in order to express their ambivalent relation to the phenomenological tradition. On the one hand, they are heavily inspired by the phenomenological emphasis on experience and concreteness, while on the other hand they distance themselves from the classical-phenomenological romanticism regarding technology and find a starting point in empirical analyses of actual technologies." Frischmann and Selinger (2018, pp. 225f, 246, 247ff) describe a vast array of phenomena, which they collectively term "techno-social engineering" – that is, "processes where technologies and social forces align and impact how we think, perceive, and act" (2018, 4).

5. This is also a recurrent example in Sheila Jasanoff's philosophy of technology, see Jasanoff (2016).

6. However, I cannot even start to enter the debate on the "neutrality" of technology, on the question whether technologies are the frame, the *Gestell* which alienates us from the world, and so on. Borgmann, Idhe and Verbeek are very helpful here (Borgmann 1984; Idhe 1990; Verbeek 2005).

7. See Zuboff (2019, 42ff) and also her earlier articles on surveillance capitalism and what it means for social relations; it is surprising that recent critical theory's reflections on capitalism do not mention the big internet companies (more powerful than any pre-digital industry) or their specific form of exploitation, see Fraser and Jaeggi (2018).

8. Edward Snowden, for one, still has the vision of the internet "as it used to be": "The internet was mostly made of, by, and for the people. Its purpose was to enlighten, not to monetize, and it was administered more by a provisional cluster of perpetually shifting collective norms than by exploitative, globally enforceable terms of service agreements" (Snowden 2019, 44); see also the Netflix series *Black Mirror* and the film *Anon* (by Andrew Nicoll, also produced by Netflix) which picture the loss of privacy and anonymity without focusing on the commodification of data.

9. Bernard Harcourt calls this form of exposure and quantification a *moral transformation*: "In our digital world [...] when subjects voluntarily [...] expose their intimate lives, *moral transformation happens* when they no longer resist the virtual transparency of the digital life" (Harcourt 2015, 227); see Franzen, criticizing the "neutral" analysis of digital communication structures by Sherry Turkle: "Our

digital technologies aren't politically neutral. ... Digital technology is capitalism in hyperdrive, injecting its logic of consumption and promotion, of monetization and efficiency, into every waking minute" (Franzen 2018, 73).

10. See Honneth (2014, 127ff.); also Honneth (2005, 84ff) on social pathologies.

11. It is contested whether or to what extent Foucault or Adorno and Horkheimer can be seen as providing us with a normative critique of societies; see for instance Honneth (1993).

12. This should not be interpreted as an elitist thesis: "they" change into something less noble whereas "we" stay worthy of respect. On the contrary, Reiman argues regarding the loss of privacy and the transformation of people in a society with no or significantly less privacy that we all change without realizing it. Therefore I think that Harcourt is not completely convincing when he argues for making a difference between people ("them") who fall into the trap of the new forms of digital communication and "us who defy control and are critical, even disobedient," see Harcourt (2015, 260ff); see again Zuboff (2019) and Susskind (2018) for a more thorough analysis.

13. See, for example, the influencer platform FameBit (https://famebit.com); on the analogies between the increasingly important system of scoring the "reputation" of users and the Chinese social credit system see Sitigh and Siems (2019).

14. See Sitigh and Sims (2019); see also the rather predictive episode of the Netflix series *Black Mirror, Nose-Dive* (season 3, 1st episode) which dramatizes this easy, omnipresent scoring of people and the dire consequences for their social and personal lives.

15. See again Frischmann and Selinger (2018, ch 9) on the optimization of relationships; Habermas' approach (1984) gives us, as far as I can see, the only theory which, in criticizing the colonization of the lifeworld, presents a quasi-transcendental argument against these practices, since they destroy or undermine the very interactions they claim to be optimizing; see also Roessler (2015).

16. See, for example, Eggers (2014); Orwell (1949); Huxley (2007); most recently and from an interestingly different perspective: McEwan (2019).

BIBLIOGRAPHY

Behrent, Michael C. 2013. "Foucault and Technology." *History and Technology* 29 (1): 54–104.

Bell, Emily. 2019. "How Ethical is it For Advertisers to Target Your Mood?" *The Guardian*. 5 May 2019. https://www.theguardian.com/media/commentisfree/2019/may/05/how-ethical-is-it-for-advertisers-to-target-your-mood.

Boerman, Sophie C., Sanne Kruikemeier, and Frederik J. Zuiderveen Borgesius. 2017. "Online Behavioral Advertising: A Literature Review and Research Agenda." *Journal of Advertising* 46 (3): 363–76. https://doi.org/10.1080/00913367.2017.1339368.

Borgmann, Albert. 1984. *Technology and the Character of Contemporary Life. A Philosophical Inquiry*. Chicago: University of Chicago Press.

Coons, Christian and Michael Weber. 2014. *Manipulation: Theory And Practice*. Oxford; New York: Oxford University Press.

Cuckier, Kenneth and Viktor Mayer-Schönberger. 2013. *Big Data: A Revolution That Will Transform How We Live*. Harcourt: Houghton Mifflin.

Danaher, John, Sven Nyholm, and Brian D. Earp. 2018. "The Quantified Relationship." *The American Journal of Bioethics* 18 (2): 3–19.

Dormehl, Luke. 2014. *The Formula: How Algorithms Solve All Our Problems ... and Create More*. New York: Perigree.

Eggers, David. 2014. *The Circle*. London: Penguin Publishing Ltd.

Feiler, Bruce. 2014. "For the Love of Being 'Liked.'" *The New York Times*, 9 May 2014, sec. Fashion. https://www.nytimes.com/2014/05/11/fashion/for-some-social-media-users-an-anxiety-from-approval-seeking.html.

Foucault, Michel. (1977) 1991. *Discipline and Punish: The Birth of the Prison*. Translated by Alan Sheridan. Toronto: Penguin Random House.

Franzen, Jonathan. 2018. *The End of the End of the Earth*. New York: Harper Collins.

Fraser, Nancy and Rahel Jaeggi. 2018. *Capitalism: A Conversation in Critical Theory*. Cambridge: Polity.

Frischmann, Brett. 2015. "Will the Internet of Things Result in Predictable People?" *The Guardian*, 10 August 2015.

Frischmann, Brett and Evan Selinger. 2018. *Re-Engineering Humanity*. Cambridge: Cambridge University Press.

Galič, Maša, Tjerk Timan, and Bert-Jaap Koops. 2016. "Bentham, Deleuze and Beyond: An Overview of Surveillance Theories from the Panopticon to Participation." *Philosophy and Technology* 30 (1): 9–37.

Godwin, Richard. 2019. "'You Can Track Everything': The Parents Who Digitise their Babies' Lives." *The Guardian*, 2 March 2019. https://www.theguardian.com/lifeandstyle/2019/mar/02/apps-that-track-babies-and-give-data-to-tech-firms-parents.

Google. n.d. "The Selfish Ledger (Video)." *YouTube*. Accessed 17 May 2018. https://www.youtube.com/watch?v=QDVVo14A_fo.

Habermas, Jürgen. 1984. *The Theory of Communicative Action: Lifeworld and Systems, a Critique of Functionalist Reason*. Translated by Thomas McCarthy. New York: Beacon Press.

Haggerty, K. D. and R. V. Ericson. 2000. "The Surveillant Assemblage." *British Journal of Sociology* 51 (4): 605–22.

Harcourt, Bernard E. 2015. *Exposed: Desire and Disobedience in the Digital Age*. Harvard: Harvard University Press.

Honneth, Axel. 1993. *Critique of Power: Reflective Stages in a Critical Social Theory*. Translated by Kenneth Baynes. Cambridge: MIT Press.

Honneth, Axel. 2005. *Reification. A New Look at an Old Idea*. The Berkeley Tanner Lectures, edited by M. Jay. Oxford: Oxford University Press.

Honneth, Axel. 2014. *Freedom's Right. The Social Foundations of Democratic Life*. Translated by Joseph Ganahl. Cambridge: Polity Press.

Hoofnagle, Chris, Bart van der Sloot, and Frederik Borgesius. 2019. "The European Union General Data Protection Regulation: What It Is and What It Means." *Information & Communications Technology Law* 28 (1): 65–98.

Huxley, Aldous. 2007. *Brave New World*. New York: HarperCollins Publishing Inc.
Igo, Sarah. 2018. *The Known Citizen: A History of Privacy in Modern America*. Princeton: Princeton University Press.
Ihde, Don. 1990. *Technology and the Lifeworld. From Garden to Earth*. Bloomington: Indiana UP.
Ihde, Don. 2004. "Has the Philosophy of Technology Arrived? A State-of-the-Art Review." *Philosophy of Science* 71 (January): 117–31.
Jasanoff, Sheila. 2016. *The Ethics of Invention: Technology and the Human Future*. New York: Norton.
Lupton, Deborah. 2016. *The Quantified Self. A Sociology of Self-Tracking*. Cambridge: Polity.
Matzner, Tobias. 2019. "The Human is Dead- Long Live the Algorithm! Human-algorithmic Ensembles and Liberal Subjectivity." *Theory, Culture & Society* 36 (2): 123–44.
McEwan, Ian. 2019. *Machines Like Me*. London: Vintage Publishing.
Miller, Daniel. 2018. "Digital Anthropology." In *The Cambridge Encyclopedia of Anthropology*, edited by Felix Stein e.a. http://www.anthroencyclopedia.com/entry/digital-anthropology.
Mittelstadt, Brent Daniel, Patrick Allo, Mariarosaria Taddeo, Sandra Wachter, and Luciano Floridi. 2016. "The Ethics of Algorithms: Mapping the Debate." *Big Data & Society* 3 (2): 1–21.
Orwell, George. 1991. *1984*. New York: Penguin Books Ltd.
Penney, Jonathon W. 2016. "Chilling Effects: Online Surveillance and Wikipedia Use." *Berkeley Technology Law Journal* 31 (1): 117–82.
Reiman, Jeffrey H. 2004. "Driving to the Panopticon: A Philosophical Exploration of the Risks to Privacy Posed by the Highway Technology of the Future." In *Privacies: Philosophical Evaluations*, edited by Beate Roessler, 194–214. Stanford: Stanford University Press.
Rey, P. J. and Erin Boesel. 2014. "The Web, Digital Prosthesis, and Augmented Subjectivity." In *Routledge Handbook of Science, Technology and Society*, edited by Daniel Lee Kleinman and Kelly Moore, 173–88. London: Taylor and Francis.
Roessler, Beate. 2015. "Should Personal Data be a Tradable Good? On the Moral Limits of Markets in Privacy." In *Social Dimensions of Privacy: Interdisciplinary Perspectives*, edited by Beate Roessler and Dorota Mokrosinska, 141–61. Cambridge: Cambridge University Press.
Rosenberger, Robert and Peter-Paul Verbeek (eds.). 2015. *Postphenomenological Investigations: Essays on Human-Technology Relations*. Lexington: Rowman and Littlefield.
Sandel, Michael J. 2013. *What Money Can't Buy: The Moral Limits of Markets*. New York: Farrar, Straus and Giroux.
Sitigh, Mac Daithi and Mathias Siems. 2019. "The Chinese Social Credit System: A Model for Other Countries?" *EUI Working Paper Law* 2019/01.
Snowden, Edward. 2019. *Permanent Record*. London: Macmillan.
Susser, Daniel, Beate Roessler, and Helen F. Nissenbaum. Forthcoming. "Online Manipulation: Hidden Influences in a Digital World." In *Georgetown Technology Law Review*, December 2019.

Susskind, Jamie. 2018. *Future Politics*. Oxford: Oxford University Press.
The Guardian. n.d. "The Cambridge Analytica Files." Accessed 20 August 2019. https://www.theguardian.com/news/series/cambridge-analytica-files.
Valentino-DeVries, Jennifer. 2019. "How E-Commerce Sites Manipulate You Into Buying Things You May Not Want." *The New York Times*, 24 June 2019, sec. Technology. https://www.nytimes.com/2019/06/24/technology/e-commerce-dark-patterns-psychology.html.
Verbeek, Peter-Paul. 2005. *What Things Do. Philosophical Reflections on Technology, Agency, and Design*. Philadelphia: Pennsylvania University Press.
Yeung, Karen. 2017. "'Hypernudge': Big Data as a Mode of Regulation by Design." *Information, Communication & Society* 20 (1): 118–36. https://doi.org/10.1080/1369118X.2016.1186713.
Zuboff, Shoshana. 2019. *The Age of Surveillance Capitalism: The Fight for a Human Future at the New Frontier of Power*. London: Profile Books.

Chapter 14

The Crisis of Liberalism
The Dialectic of Politics and Police
Christoph Menke

Liberalism is a theory and practice of the public order that establishes an entirely new normative basis for the community, differing from all orders that historically preceded it (and also differing from all that have sought to break its dominance). This basis is individual freedom. Liberalism proceeds from the claim that the individual *is* free, that each person *has* the capacity for freedom. For Hobbes (the first liberal), freedom is a "natural" property (Hobbes 1996, ch. 14). According to Kant, the right to freedom is therefore "innate" (Kant 1991, 63). As John Rawls puts it, the persons with whom the liberal order deals "possess" the "capacity" to guide themselves (Rawls 2001, 18). Liberalism's basis is therefore not an end or a good that could only be realized by politics, but a fact that it presupposes and wishes to preserve. Securing and safeguarding the freedom that everyone – supposedly – already has is the liberal order's point.

In the following I would like to show that liberalism, precisely through this – theoretical as well as practical – presupposition of the fact of freedom, engenders a non-liberal, even anti-liberal practice. The fact that liberalism turns into its opposite, indeed, produces this opposite itself (as we now see again everywhere), is neither coincidence nor a sign of merely insufficient realization of its – allegedly good – basic idea, but the very law of its operation: the dialectic of liberalism. The reason for this lies in the fact that the freedom which the liberal order presupposes as a fact is actually a practical accomplishment. What is assumed by the liberal order to be given of its own accord must, in reality, be *done*. The political dialectics of liberalism, its turn into its anti-liberal opposite, follows from its ontological inversion (of practice into fact: its "positivism" [Adorno] or "naturalism" [Foucault]). Since both the liberal order and the non-liberal practice are forms of governing – in the broad Foucauldian sense – we can also say that the liberal mode of government engenders non-liberal modes of government by which the – social and psychic – conditions which the liberal order presupposes as a given are fabricated.

The manifestation of this inner logic of opposition is the crisis of liberalism: the crisis is the moment in which the dependency of the liberal order on its opposite emerges and the anti-liberal forces of government assert themselves. This can happen in very different ways, and it is an open question (which I will not even try to answer here) how to interpret the current forms of "authoritarian liberalism" in the light of the oppositional logic outlined here.[1] But it is important to see that the authoritarian understanding of the anti-liberal is only *one* possibility. For the crisis is not only the time when the inner contradiction of an existing order reveals itself, but also the moment of decision – in the original medical sense of "crisis": the decision on the outcome of a disease. The critical manifestation of liberalism's inner hidden opposite has accordingly a double, contradictory significance which defines the dialectic of liberalism: that the liberal order turns into its non-liberal opposite has a bad and a good meaning. This turnover can be carried out in a reactionary or in an emancipatory sense. The crisis of liberalism is fundamentally ambiguous, even contradictory. It reveals both the structural link between liberalism and authoritarianism, even fascism, as well as the point of resistance to liberal rule. If "critique" means to grasp the crisis in thought then its task is also to lead to the point where this ambiguity comes into view.

My reflections are divided into two parts. The first part will outline the thesis in general terms: first by explaining the liberal logic of "presupposition," then by sketching the "paradox" of liberal government. In the second part I will discuss in more detail the consequences of the liberal politics of presupposition for the processes of subject-formation. The paradox of liberal government will show here in the way it is internally connected with forms of authoritarian subjectivation. This will finally lead back to the twofold significance of the critique and thus of the crisis of liberalism ("Coda: Where Does the Critique of Liberalism Lead?").

THE PARADOX OF LIBERAL GOVERNMENT

(i) The presupposition of freedom is liberalism's self-evident starting point. According to the traditional liberal self-understanding, individual liberty exists first and by itself and, on this ground, a political order is established, with no other task than to secure it. To the liberal presupposition of freedom corresponds the liberal reduction of politics to the sole goal of security. One could tell the history of liberalism as the back and forth between a merely negative, restricting and preserving, and a positive, enabling interpretation of what the securing of freedom demands. The latest round in this debate are the ideological confrontations between the so-called "neoliberal" policy of de-regulation, on the one hand, and "social-liberal" attempts at regaining a minimal degree of state control of the various markets on the other hand.

But beneath the dependence of freedom on the state for the security of its existence and reality operates another, in fact opposite logic of dependence which alone can explain to what extent – and above all, in what precise sense – freedom becomes in liberalism the presupposition of the political (i.e. what "presupposition" means here[2]). It is true that individual freedom depends for its security on the state order. But this implies that the liberal state has made itself dependent on individual freedom as that which is pre-given to it. And that has a double meaning. On the one side, it means that the dependency of the liberal state on individual freedom is its own act, through which it first emerges (or through which the state first becomes "liberal"). But if the dependency of the political on the pre-political fact of freedom is itself political, then this also, secondly, means that individual freedom thus does owe not only its security but its very existence to the liberal state. Even more, it owes its existence as pre-political to the political order. The pre-political nature of freedom is a political effect.

The liberal state is thereby defined by its paradoxical subject-position. The liberal state is the subject of its subjection – of the subjection of politics to the presupposition of freedom, to the goal of the security of freedom. The liberal state *makes itself* dependent. Its presupposition of freedom thus contains an irresolvable ambiguity: individual freedom is simultaneously posited by the state *and* precedes it; it is posited by the state *as* that which precedes it (and hence is not posited). On the one hand, individual freedom is a pre-*supposition* of the state, it is instituted by the state: it does not exist of its own accord or by nature; individual freedom is a political effect. At the same time, however, the state (which thereby becomes liberal) *pre*-supposes individual freedom as that which it is *not* able to produce or regulate. This defines the liberal state's specific, paradoxical form of activity: its power is its powerlessness, or liberal state power is the power *of*, indeed the power *towards* its own dis-empowerment. The liberal state is the free carrying out of the downfall of the state.

(ii) The thesis to be outlined in the following is that, due to the dialectics of presupposition, liberal government is defined by a logic of self-contradiction. The operation of liberal government splits itself in itself, it turns against itself. This is the paradox of liberal government: liberal government results – necessarily – in non-liberal government.

To understand this paradox, we first need a better understanding of the liberal form of government. The basic definition of the liberal activity of government consists in the presupposition of freedom. A more precise formulation of this logic of presupposition (i.e. of presupposing givenness) consists in saying that individual freedom exists for and through the liberal state in being recognized or deemed "valid." The givenness of freedom is a category of validity. It is therefore a legal category. The state's presupposition of individual freedom is the recognition of its entitlement. This occurs in the (new, specifically modern) form of individual or subjective rights. The liberal state presupposes freedom by declaring, adopting, and enforcing rights. Liberal government is government in the form – in other words, by means or through the medium – of individual or subjective rights. This definition of the liberal form of government is brought about by the liberal constitution. The liberal constitution imposes on government the form of rights.[3]

On the one hand, this determination of its form means that liberal government is normatively defined. The formal definition of rights established by the liberal constitution has a normative content. "Rights" mean equal rights to freedom. The fact that the governing activity of the liberal state results in the form of rights therefore signifies that its aim is to realize the equality of each person's freedom. The basis of the liberal state's governing activity is the equality of freedom. In the state created by the liberal constitution, no political objectives or ends are valid independently of their normative determination by the equality of individual freedom (and thus no objectives or ends could be deemed valid contrary to this normative determination). But the concept of liberal government does not only bind state power to a specific normative content. It also thereby defines state power *as* normative (or "noumenal" [Forst 2017, ch. 2]) power. The power exerted by the liberal state is nothing but the power of its normativity.

At the same time, however, the definition of liberal government by the form of rights limits its normativity. This follows from the fact that this form of government expresses the presupposition of individual freedom. The normativity of liberal power consists in protecting, promoting, and enabling freedom, which, to it, is given in advance (or which it has pre-given to itself through the declaration of rights). The legal definition of liberal government therefore excludes – it does not permit – the judgement, criticism, creation and (re- or trans-)formation of the freedom of the individual.[4] For trying to do this would, according to liberalism, lead us back to a pre-modern, traditional policy that tries to educate individuals and thus necessarily becomes un-free and repressive; this is how liberalism, from Humboldt and Constant through Mill to Rawls, understands the paternalism, authoritarianism, or even totalitarianism of modern revolutions. According to liberalism, a policy that does not take individual freedom as a given but as politically produced undoes the "divisions" (Joachim Ritter) or "separations" (Michael Walzer) – between the collective and the individual, the public and the private, politics and ethics – that constitute modernity, in other words, make it liberal. Liberal government is normative power, through and through, and it is at the same, due to its constitutive legal form, the power of denormativization (or of naturalization).

With this clarification, the paradox of liberal government can be more precisely defined. According to the thesis stated before, this paradox consists in the fact that liberal government necessarily has to proceed in a non-liberal manner. As we have just seen, the liberal mode of government is committed to the form of equal individual rights. The establishment of this commitment is the role of the liberal constitution. The claim that the implementation of liberal government must necessarily proceed in a non-liberal manner thus signifies that it is always already implementing an entirely different government that does *not* adhere to this form. This different or other government divests itself of the form of equal rights, it takes place outside of and against this form – and is therefore an exercise of power that is non-liberal, indeed that is anti-liberal. Since, however, in the liberal model of government it is only its commitment to rights which constitutes the normativity of political power (which makes political power normative), government without rights is at the same time necessarily non-normative. It is an after-effect and a counter-effect of liberal government in the name of equal individual rights, but it is not based on its normativity. It is a government without normativity: a government that does not adhere to the form of rights and that is therefore not committed to the norm of equal freedom.

But why does the naturalized freedom that the liberal state presupposes as a mere fact require a form of government at all that does more than delimit the individual spheres of freedom against each other? This is the conclusion drawn viz. (but not only) by German ordoliberalism after the Second World War from the experience of fascism. The insight is that freedom cannot merely be secured from the outside, but that it requires "inner regulatory forces" (Böckenförde 1991, 112). According to this diagnosis, liberal government, by setting individuals free in the form of rights, also produces irregular effects by the enactment of freedom which threaten its very existence. Since these effects are but the side-effect of the presupposition of freedom through individual rights, they cannot be in turn remedied by creating new, further rights, but are only reproduced by such rights in another way. In order to bring about the inner regulatory forces of individual freedom, liberal government thus must turn against itself. It must create a different form of government that governs freedom *internally* and not through its legal entitlement. It must become a government in non-liberal form.

It is only in this way that the liberal state can give an answer to the question that the ordo-liberal tradition has put at the centre of its thinking. The question is: "How will this state sustain itself on the day of crisis?" (Böckenförde 1991) And the answer is that what will then sustain the state can only be non-liberal forms of government. "Non-liberal" here means government that does not proceed in the form of rights. Since, however, rights are the only way, on the liberal paradigm, of linking governmental power to the force of normativity, non-liberal government, which is produced by liberal government, is a government without normativity: without commitment to equality and freedom. It is carried out in the shadow of liberal normativity.

This dialectic can also be stated with reference to the liberal concept of security. In liberal politics, freedom means security (Arendt 1961, 147–149). And security means the external coexistence of self-contained – hence: "individual" – spheres of freedom. Freedom means security, because security means equality of freedom. In the liberal concept of security, therefore, the normative power of politics is bound to the condition of externality vis-à-vis the individual. If now it turns out that this boundary of externality must be abandoned – namely, in the name of the security of freedom – then this means that the liberal politics of security thus at the same time suspends its bond by the norm of equal freedom. This is, in another formulation, the paradox of the liberal government. Either the government operates in the name of the norm of equal freedom, but then it remains external in form. Or the government regulates freedom internally – as turns out to be necessary at the moment of crisis – but then this government is necessarily a-normative. It is a-normative in content and in form: it is not defined by the norm of equality of freedom and hence not defined by any norm; it is power beyond normativity or power exempt from normativity. In the face of crisis, which requires the inner regulation of freedom, liberal government thus becomes a politics of exception – of the suspension of liberal normativity itself.

The thesis outlined to this point states that the liberal order is defined by a logic of presupposition and that this logic of presupposition produces two effects which together form the paradox of liberal government: (1) the liberal order naturalizes individual freedom; it treats it as a given, that is, it releases freedom, by *pre*-supposing it to the political order, from its normative grip. But because the freedom so naturalized actually requires inner regulation, the liberal constitution (2) produces a non-normative form of government, which we can call with Hegel "police-"government. The "police" in Hegel's definition is the state, or the government, "of necessity" and hence operated merely by the "understanding" (*Verstand*) (Hegel 1969, § 183), that is, not by reason. It is not "the will which thinks and knows itself, and carries out what it knows, and in so far as it knows," as Hegel defines the truly political state (ibid., § 257). The first effect of the liberal logic of presupposition is the naturalization of freedom, the second effect is the "policization," the becoming-police (*Verpolizeilichung*) of politics. Both effects are strictly correlative. The liberal presupposition of the natural givenness of freedom directly leads to the de-politization of politics, its reduction to a government in the form of police. The concept of "police" here means, that the liberal government in the form of rights produces as its counter-effect the need for a regulation of freedom which can in turn not operate in the form of rights and is hence released from any normativity (for in the liberal order there is no normativity but by rights). This form of government is subject to other imperatives. The liberal presupposition of freedom thus empowers governmental mechanisms whose mode of operation turns against the liberal order of freedom itself.

LIBERAL DISCIPLINE: THE FABRICATION OF THE AUTHORITARIAN PERSONALITY

The dialectical turn of liberal government into non-liberal government, the becoming-police of politics, is grounded in the need for an "inner regulation" of freedom. This need takes different shapes. One is the establishment and preservation of "order" in the field of bourgeois society (to which Hegel's concept of police refers); for individual freedom only exists socially. In the following, I want to explore the sketched paradox of liberal government in a different dimension. This is the dimension of subjectivation. For the liberal order does (and can) not only presuppose individual freedom. It must also presuppose that its recognition of the fact of individual freedom is also shared by individuals themselves: they must make the same presupposition as the order of which they are members. The liberal presupposition of freedom must be the individuals' own or the individuals must be liberals. But the being- or becoming-liberal of the members of the liberal order cannot be brought about by liberal means, that is, by government in the legal form of rights. It necessitates a non-liberal politics of subject-formation.

(i) The need for a non-liberal regulation of freedom has its roots in the gap that opens in the foundation of the liberal state.[5] As we have seen, the liberal presupposition of freedom has a legal form: it consists in acknowledging the subjective *right* to freedom. This legal form shapes its content; that is, it defines what freedom can only mean in the liberal state. Legal freedom – the freedom that is legally acknowledged or freedom as security – is but the freedom of choice. To be sure, the liberal declaration of rights *aims* to open up opportunities or chances for a self-determined, responsible, successful (and maybe even good, accomplished) life. The impetus for the declaration of rights stems from ethical or moral conceptions of freedom. Due to their form, however, subjective or individual rights only ever *comprise* the freedom to realize one's "interests" according to one's own arbitrary "choice." "Interests" and "choice" are the two correlative determinations of the content of rights; there can be no other individual, subjective rights than rights to the realization of interests according to my arbitrary choice.

The problem is that this form of freedom that the liberal order secures and creates cannot itself ground the liberal order, for individual interests and choices do not ground any normative order. Only a form of freedom which is morally or ethically self-regulated is able to do this: the ground of the liberal order can only be autonomy, not interest and choice. Because, however, it governs in the form of individual rights (which can only refer to interests and choice), the liberal order is unable to safeguard its own normative ground; its ground is beyond its reach. The liberal form of rights produces a gap in grounding that – under liberal conditions – can never be closed or filled up. At the moment of crisis, this gap becomes a chasm, a chasm of groundlessness, which threatens to topple the liberal order.

This brings about the need for the inner regulation of individual freedom. Such regulation would have to transform freedom. "Regulation" means here: the transformation of freedom from a capacity for realizing one's interests according to one's arbitrary choice (which the liberal order of rights creates by permitting and safeguarding it) into the freedom of normative self-determination (which is the ground of the liberal order but cannot be brought about by it). Willing at one's own discretion, according to one's preferences and in one's interests, must become willing the normative order of equality and freedom itself. Only such transformation of freedom (or of the will) can create the subjects on which the liberal order can be based; only by means of this transformation, the subjects of the liberal order convert from legally entitled members of bourgeois society into active citizens of the state. It needs a regulatory intervention into the freedom of self-interest and arbitrariness which the liberal order legally entitles (and thus creates) in order to produce the normative subjects which support the liberal order itself. But where – and above all *how* – does this subjectivation, the transformation of freedom, take place? How does the self-interested bourgeois become a "support" (Böckenförde) of the liberal state?

Liberalism's familiar response to this question is that this takes place through culture. "Culture" is the umbrella term employed by the liberal state for the sites, media, and authorities of normative subjectivation. The liberal state relies on liberal culture to secure its foundations. There are very different, indeed opposed ways to define these cultural potentials of subjectivation: Kantian liberals identify them with the education to morality and responsibility (John Rawls); communitarians refer to the "habits of the heart" (Robert N. Bellah) and meaningful "narratives" (Robert Cover) that gather communities around shared values and meanings; postmodern bourgeois ironists rely on the capacity for distance from oneself and empathy with others which are to be acquired by means of aesthetic education (Richard Rorty). Yet however liberal culture's potential is defined, it therein functions as the pre-political presupposition of liberal politics. And however much culture might be conceived as processual and performative, for the liberal state it remains passively presupposed and merely taken up as independently, that is, pre-politically, achieved and realized. For the liberal state, liberal culture is thus like nature, which operates (or does not operate) of its own accord. By relegating it to the field of culture, the liberal government treats the acts of normative subjectivation, that is, of the fabrication of its normative ground, as a quasi-natural, evolutionary process. The field of culture and its forms of subjectivation, however, is marked by struggles and practices that the liberal order is thus unable to grasp and also powerless to control. This can be shown by a brief look at the category of the authoritarian personality.

(ii) The studies on *The Authoritarian Personality*, which Theodor W. Adorno, Else Frenkel-Brunswik, Daniel J Levinson, and R. Nevitt Sanford conducted in the late 1940s seek to determine the "structure" that renders an individual "particularly susceptible to anti-democratic propaganda" (Adorno et al. 1950, 1). The authors call such an individual "potentially fascistic" and its "personality" (in German: *Charakter*) "authoritarian." The basic assumption of the studies is that this personality can be analysed by an investigation of its morality. "Conventionalism, authoritarian submission, and authoritarian aggression all have to do with the moral aspect of life – with standards of conduct, with the authorities who enforce these standards, with offenders against them who deserve to be punished" (ibid., 233 f.). This assumption, the focus on the "moral aspect," is of course not without problems. One should note though that the study is not concerned with the content of morality but with its form. It is not a matter of identifying authoritarian convictions and recording their distribution and frequency in a population. The concept of the "authoritarian" rather refers to the *way* someone has a moral conviction – to the kind of subject she is in having that morality. Using Foucault's distinctions (Foucault 1990, 25), we can say that the study of the authoritarian personality is the study not of a "moral code" but of "moral behaviour," and within such behaviour more specifically of that dimension which Foucault calls the "mode of subjection": of the "way in which the individual establishes his relation to the rule and recognizes himself as obliged to put it into practice" (ibid., 27). The basic methodological claim of the study on the authoritarian personality is that *what* this "type" or "character" believes – that is, its authoritarian convictions – can be explained by *how* it has (normative) convictions at all.

The decisive factor here is the "weakness in the ego" that *The Authoritarian Personality* defines as "a lack of integration between the moral agencies by which the subject lives and the rest of his personality" (Adorno et al. 1950, 234). The ego is thus not just a further psychological agency alongside others, but that particular agency which is at the same time responsible for the "relations" between the agencies and to the outside world. The ego (which is only weakly developed in the authoritarian personality) is a relationship; the ego is the relation between the ego and its other. Thus understood, "It is a function of the ego to make peace with conscience, to create a larger synthesis within which conscience, emotional impulses, and self operate in relative harmony" (ibid.). In his own contributions to these studies Adorno calls the character who succeeds in this – not least for strategic reasons – the "construct of the *Genuine Liberal*." This type, he says, "may be conceived in terms of that balance between superego, ego, and id which Freud deemed ideal" (ibid., 771, cf. 781–3). In the authoritarian personality, on the other hand, that is, "[when] this synthesis is not achieved, the superego has somewhat the role of a foreign body within the personality, and it exhibits those rigid, automatic, and unstable aspects discussed above" (ibid., 234). The authoritarian personality is therefore unable to establish a "consistent and enduring set of moral values" that operates independently of "outside agencies." Conscience remains "externalized" (ibid.).

This unretainable externality of the normative explains a trait of the authoritarian personality that became central to the Frankfurt analysis of fascism: namely the fact that it is as authoritarian as it is rebellious or "pseudorevolutionary" (Adorno et al. 1950, 763) – that it is authoritarian *by* being rebellious (and the other way around). Because there remains in every normative claim to which "the authoritarians" (as Horkheimer says) submit a merely external, overwhelming power, their "whole life [...] is an ongoing effort to suppress and humiliate nature, inwardly or outwardly" (Horkheimer 2004, ch. 3). Therefore "their own natural impulses, antagonistic to the various demands of civilization, [...] lead a deformed, underground life." Their "unconscious [is] fixed at the level of oppressed rebellion" (ibid.), which occasionally erupts. It erupts in "fury" (ibid., 68) against all and everything that does not seem to submit to this effort of drive suppression. In the authoritarian personality, the "rebellion of nature" (Horkheimer) thus serves domination. Or the other way around: "Typical of our present era is the manipulation of this revolt by the prevailing forces of civilization itself, the use of the revolt as a means of perpetuating the very conditions by which it is stirred up and against which it is directed" (ibid., 64 f.). The authoritarians, Adorno writes, are "rebels in whose impatient punch on the table the worship of the Lord was already booming."[6]

The analysis of the potentially fascist personality allows for a first definition of what the liberal order does when it relegates subject-formation to the field of culture: it thereby makes the forces and processes which operate in this formation politically invisible. The displacement of subject-formation into the field of culture, the conceptualization of subject-formation as culture, *is* its invisibilization. Culture is a black hole; to speak of "culture" means to invisibilize. By being described as "culture," it necessarily remains politically unthematic, indeed unthematizable, how subject-formation in fact takes place. As the studies by Adorno and his companions show, the field of cultural subject-formation is stretched between the authoritarian and the "genuinely liberal" type (between which there are various intermediate types which are to be captured inter alia by the famous F-scale – "F" for fascism). This difference is obviously utterly fundamental; it decides on the persistence or dissolution of the democratic order. At the same time, the liberal order by relegating subject-formation to the sphere of culture removes this difference from political access and control. And necessarily so. For without abandoning the liberal form of government, that is, without abandoning liberalism, there can be no politics that actively refers to – that is, *makes*: produces and reproduces – this normative distinction: a politics that does not merely accept as its destiny how this difference is played out in the field of culture, which side retains the supremacy, but that intervenes itself in this game (in which the question of the life and death of democratic politics is at stake). In a liberal order the authoritarian personality is – normatively speaking – just as possible as the "genuinely liberal" one. For the liberal order it is a matter of chance or fate whether one or the other type of personality prevails.

In this sense the liberal order, precisely by invisibilizing it, makes the authoritarian personality possible (in strict analogy to the way the liberal order makes capitalist exploitation possible). It makes it possible because it allows it – because it cannot fight it with its means. Stronger and more precisely: because by tying politics to the legal form of individual rights, the liberal order deprives itself of the means to fight the cultural practices of authoritarian subjectivation. This is what the liberal invisibilization of the cultural processes of subject-formation means: it means their depoliticization and therefore the facilitation (by permissiveness) of the authoritarian personality by the liberal order. Invisibilization as depoliticization as facilitation is one of the mechanisms that links liberalism and fascism (or authoritarianism).

*

The logic of facilitation (by invisibilization) is a first way of grasping the connection between the liberal order and authoritarian modes of subject-formation. But now liberalism itself describes exactly this same process as "privatization." Liberalism thus defends the political invisibilization of subject-formation as a necessary requirement of freedom. In the liberal order, the private sphere is the sphere of things which have to remain – politically – latent: which are not to be publicly addressed and governed (because they are about the individual's freedom). To shield culture as the field of subject-formation from political intervention is a central liberal demand. Anything else would be authoritarian (or even totalitarian).

The first way of describing the fatal consequences of liberal privatization is to say that the liberal order is thereby committed to neutrality towards the difference between the authoritarian and the genuine liberal personality. In fact, however, liberal neutrality is itself not neutral. This is not because the liberal order is actually taking sides. The liberal order may *prefer* the "genuine liberal" character to the authoritarian one. But that remains just a question of taste and cannot become a matter of political decision. Rather, liberal neutrality is not neutral because, in being privatized, subject-formation is understood and performed in a way that distorts its essence: liberal privatization (or "culturalization") is a distortion of normative subject-formation. The analysis of this distortion leads to a better understanding of how liberal order and authoritarian personality are connected. For "distortion" means that the liberal order does not only facilitate in a negative sense the formation of authoritarian subjects, by invisibilizing it and thus shielding it from political intervention, but rather contributes to it.

(iii) We must therefore go beyond the liberal self-description of the relationship between politics and subject-formation in merely negative terms, as privatization (and hence invisibilization). For this it is helpful to look at Adorno's attempt at clarifying what the collaborative research in *The Authoritarian Personality* has achieved – and what its limits are, that is, what necessarily remains excluded from its perspective.[7] The reason why such critical self-reflection is urgent for Adorno lies in the tendency, indeed the danger, that this research methodologically reproduces the exact same abstract perspective that defines liberal neutralization. This refers to the "subjective focus" of *The Authoritarian Personality*: "Our probing into prejudice is devoted to subjective aspects. We are not analyzing objective social forces" (Adorno 1948, 1). This restriction is due to the methodology of the investigation. At the same time, it is in itself political: "The relative negligence with which this task [i.e. the 'analysis of objective social forces,' which Adorno just in the sentence before had declared 'the most pressing issue in contemporary research into anti-minority bias'] is treated throughout American research is due to its 'democratic bias'" (Ibid., 2). Adorno explains this bias as the focus of the investigation on the "opinions and attitudes" of a "vast number of people" (ibid.). But more important is the limitation – and, if ignored, the distortion that follows from it – of the "subjective" focus on the individual, be whether in great or small numbers, as such. For, as Adorno writes with reference to the "Freudian school" (with which according to Adorno the study "is in full harmony"; ibid., 7), such a focus "tend[s] to reduce anti-semitism to psychological events": it "treat[s] phenomena of objective spirit as well as those of social reality as if they were neuroses and could be understood in terms of some primary experience" (ibid., 27). *The Authoritarian Personality* itself thus "tended to reify the psychological as the antecedent condition" (Gordon 2018, 52).

This corresponds to the claim of the fundamental "inadequacy" of psychology in general to grasp contemporary forms of subjectivity that Adorno had already formulated in 1941 in his "Notizen zur neueren Anthropologie": "Psychoanalysis [as the most advanced form of psychology] is entirely liberal and individualistic" (Adorno 2004, 453).[8] To study types of personality, whether the authoritarian or the genuinely liberal one, psychologically in their inner structure means to partake in the perspective of the liberal order on them. For it means to look at these types as if their production and reproduction were a private, that is, an individual matter: a matter for the individual, which is constituted in one way or the other. The thesis to which for methodological reasons any psychological approach has to subscribe is that "all [our experiences] are within a self-contained context, defined by the unity of the person by which they are constituted" and hence "makes each individual a small autarky, a kind of competing firm" (ibid.). What the psychological perspective thereby necessarily ignores, however, is the "objective" fact, that is, the fact of social objectivity: that, and how, the personality and its psyche are an effect of "social power" (ibid., 454). Psychology is structurally blind to power. It operates on the assumption that the specific "type" of personality can be understood by grasping its inner mechanisms; psychology cannot understand the psyche as the effect of power: the way and place in which social power operates. Furthermore, it is precisely this individualistic invisibilization of power which makes the psychological approach "completely liberal" (or constitutes its "democratic bias"). For it is exactly the same blindness that is inscribed in the liberal concept of culture – the blindness that the (theory and practice of) liberal culture *is*: blindness to the efficiency and forms of power.

This is true in a double sense. The blindness of liberal culture to the power that is effective in the processes of subjectivation has the result, on the one hand, that the hierarchies and hegemonies that already exist anyway are reproduced in it without question (a). And on the other hand, it has the result that the power effective in subjectivation takes on a specific form that can be called "discipline"; this form can explain why the dominant mode of subjectivation in liberal culture is not liberal but authoritarian (b).

(a) If the cultural processes of subjectivation are effects of power, then they are also inscribed in a field of struggle between social powers. Power only exists in the plural. But the plurality of powers does not follow the logic of difference. Culture is not a field of "differences" – different styles, traditions, religions, and so on – but rather of conflicts. The most fundamental of these conflicts is the conflict between the authoritarian and the "genuine liberal," that is, the free or liberated personality. Now, if *every* form of personality must be understood as the effect of social power, then this is at the same time the conflict between an authoritarian and a liberating working of power (or the working of an authoritarian and a liberating power). This is what the politics which is immanent to the cultural field is all about; it is about the struggles between authoritarian and liberating forms of subjectivation. The liberal order invisibilizes these struggles, although they are concerned with nothing other than the liberal order's own normativity, which is the idea of equal freedom. Or more precisely: The liberal order privatizes the struggles between authoritarian and liberating forms of subjectivation and neutralizes them to mere cultural differences. In this way, however, the liberal order fails to recognize not only what is happening in the thus privatized field of culture. The political neutrality that the liberal order claims towards these disputes also actually means that it facilitates (or even aims at) the maintaining and reinforcing of the ruling asymmetries of power between the parties involved: by not actively intervening in these struggles in favour of liberating forms of subjectivation, the political order de facto allows for the perpetuation of the socially existing hegemony of the authoritarian forms (for that hegemony is the natural order of things in a society defined by relations of domination).

(b) The second sense in which the liberal depoliticization of culture is in itself political goes one step further. For liberal privatization does not only allow for the unhindered effectiveness of existing power relations; what's more, it also *generates* the very form in which power operates in the liberal culture. That the exercise of power in subjectivation is "private" means that it is shielded from normative political intervention. The exercise of power, or governing, in liberal culture is thus denormativized (or "naturalized"). Liberal normativity thus has a paradoxical effect: through its legal form, liberal normativity produces the denormativization of the politics of subject formation. This is how liberal normativity is productive: by its own (legal) form, it produces a new (denormativized) form of politics. This corresponds to the logic of "presupposition" that we have briefly analysed, following Marx, at the beginning (see (i) in "The Paradox of Liberal Government" above). The liberal order not only permits and thus makes possible the performance of processes that in themselves already exist before it, but, by allowing it, it posits these processes as its precedent; the precedent is posited (or the natural is a political effect: the effect of de-politization). If the liberally produced denormativized forms of politics make up the broad field which Hegel called the "police," we can call – taking up (and modifying[9]) Foucault's term – the micro-politics of subject-formation which takes place in that field, the politics of "disciplines." Like the police in general, discipline is a mode of power which is excluded *from* liberal normativity and produced *by* liberal normativity. It is one form of the liberal order's inner state of exception.

It is therefore this transformation, that is, the shaping of the form of subjectivation as discipline, that explains the connection between the liberal order and the authoritarian personality. By carrying out the subject-formation in a state of exception, the liberal order makes the authoritarian personality the "normal case." That liberal culture produces the authoritarian personality is no coincidence or accident, but – paradoxically or ironically – a structural feature of its being "liberal" (for culture being liberal means to be private, shielded from the normativity of the political).

(iv) We have thus arrived at the following thesis: The liberal order and the authoritarian personality are internally connected. This connection consists in the politics of depoliticization. Liberal politics depoliticizes the exercise of power in subjectivation. Depoliticization means the denormativization of power. The denormativized power of subjectivation is the power of (or as) discipline. But the effects of discipline can only be disciplinary: disciplines can only have an authoritarian, not a liberating effect, they can only produce an authoritarian, not a free personality. The concept of discipline is thus the link that connects the liberal order and the authoritarian personality. The liberal denormativization of power is not neutral, but authoritarian in its effect. This has to be explained now in more detail. I will do this by returning once more to Adorno's critical remarks against psychology.

In the account given before, I have reduced Adorno's critique of the psychological investigation of the authoritarian personality to one basic and simple point. According to this reading, Adorno claims that psychology must miss the working of social power in the fabrication of subjectivity. However, in his attempt at understanding "the new type of human being formed under the conditions of monopoly- and state-capitalism" (Adorno 2004, 453), Adorno has a more specific, but also further reaching point in view. This "new type" is not merely an effect of social power as such, but of "immediate social power" (ibid., 454); in the production of this new type, social power is *immediately* effective.[10] If we understand the "new type of human being" of which Adorno speaks here as the authoritarian personality, then this leads to a crucial difference in its understanding. In my reconstruction before I have treated the authoritarian personality as yet another repressive form of normative subjectivity – the most recent specimen in a long list on which figure prominently, among others, the characters of repressive protestant ethics, as analysed by the early Hegel, Weber, and Freud. Adorno's understanding of the authoritarian personality is different though. For in the light of his concept of the new "type of human being" that is produced by contemporary, monopolistic, or state capitalism, the authoritarian personality must be understood as a kind of subjectivity that is not normative at all anymore. The authoritarian personality is not an effect or instance of repressive normativity, but rather of the repression – the "annihilation" (Adorno) – of normativity as such.

That this is what Adorno means when he speaks of the "immediacy" with which social power forms subjects in contemporary capitalism is shown by his further descriptions. The (still traditionally psychological) view that the authoritarian and the free personality are two – although opposite – types of normative subjectivity further implies the view that they are two – also opposite – ways of dissolving the Oedipus complex; that is, they are two ways of dealing with the normative entities of father and mother and the repression that they normatively impose. In contrast, Adorno claims the "invalidity of the Oedipus complex for the new anthropology" (Adorno 2004, 460). Here, "The concept of repression is no longer valid" (ibid., 454). The "new type" is the extreme case in which the psychological vocabulary that describes the character or type of personality as an internalization of normative forces and distinguishes within this field between more repressive and more liberal forms loses its validity. Thus to understand the authoritarian personality merely as the (more or most) repressive variant of normative subjectivation proves to be just as "bound to liberal preconditions" (ibid.) as psychological investigation in general: precisely the merely repressive account of the authoritarian personality is still too liberal. For it assumes that normative subjectivation always already (and somehow) occurs in the – thereby – "cultural" field. The "new type of human being," however, shows that the authoritarian personality is not a normative subject anymore; the psychological concept of repression cannot account for it.[11]

This sheds a new light on the diagnosis (quoted above) of the weakness, or even dissolution, of the ego in the authoritarian personality. This diagnosis refers to the foreignness and externality of the demands to which the authoritarian personality submits (or, put the other way around, the authoritarian personality renders those demands foreign by externally submitting to them). This external submission describes the weakness of the ego. For, as we have seen, the ego in Adorno's conception is not, or not primarily, the locus of self-control but, rather, of self-mediation: for Adorno, the ego is the entity which has the power to appropriate the external demand and thus to create a "synthesis" (or "to make peace" within the subject). Ego-weakness thus means that the demand remains external and unappropriated. In the repressive account of the authoritarian personality this unappropriated externality is traced back to an overwhelming normative power: a repressive superego. According to Adorno, however, in the contemporary condition and in its "new type of human being," "the taboos occupied until now by the superego were transferred to the overt social power" (Adorno 2004, 458). That the demand is external now holds in the most literal sense of the term; as Adorno quotes Sartre, the anti-Semite's inner reactions and attitudes are "all outside" (Adorno 1948, 22). Literally taken, a merely external demand is not normative anymore. For any normative demand is – somehow – appropriated. For a demand to be normative means that it is a reason for its addressee. If, on the other hand, a demand to which the subject submits is but "overt" power which works "immediately," that demand loses its normative character. The merely external power is not normative but natural: the "overt," unmediated social power is like a force of nature; it is the power of society as second nature. Ego-weakness in its extreme forms means the dissolution of the difference between norm and nature and hence the regression to nature (which, as regression, means second, not first nature).[12]

Read in this way, the authoritarian personality is not defined by its submission to the overwhelming power of a normative entity (the "father"), as the "repressive" interpretation would claim. Rather, the authoritarian personality as the "new type of human being" in contemporary capitalism is a subject whose relation to any power is "immediate." This immediacy can take different forms: it can be a relation of mere "imitation," the blind repetition of a pre-given social pattern, or of strategic calculation, that is, the clever, even cunning exploitation of social opportunities for one's own advantage. But in all its forms it is a "regression of the social into nature" (Honneth 2009, 57). The subject behaves as if the social were natural: not a normative claim that can be acknowledged, internalized, or contested, but rather a given to which it has to adapt or which it can utilize. Precisely this denormativization of the subject is the effect of discipline. Disciplines are not repressive – not because they are liberating but because they do not operate in the normative register (to which "repression" belongs). Disciplines produce disciplinary subjects, and disciplinary subjects are subjects for whom the socially given patterns or opportunities are quasi-naturally given. Disciplines are thus mechanisms of regression; they produce re-naturalized subjects.

From Adorno's analysis of the new type of human being thus follows a new understanding of how the liberal order and the authoritarian personality are internally connected. They are connected by the operation of denormativization or naturalization. Liberalism is the politics of denormativization, and the denormativization of subject-formation produces a new, post-repressive type of authoritarian personality. But what does the concept of the normative mean here? The concept of the normative is the concept of infinite difference or negativity. The basic definition of the normative is not the (positive) fulfilment of a standard, but the (negative) confrontation with a claim, a call, or an appeal that pulls the addressee out of its natural, that is, social existence, that is, subjectivizes it. Normativity is thus the condition, the scene, of liberation. In actively contributing to the dissolution of the normative (by its specific legal form), the liberal order thus has authoritarian effects by systematically blocking the possibility of liberation.

CODA: WHERE DOES THE CRITIQUE OF LIBERALISM LEAD?

These critical observations lead to the decisive political question. That *cannot* be the question as to whether we should negate or affirm liberalism. For, if liberalism is its own negation, then the affirmation of liberalism is the (affirmation of the) negation of liberalism, and a negation of liberalism which is up to the task is its affirmation – the affirmation of its self-negation. The question is therefore not whether, but *how* the negation of liberalism is carried out. The political question that results from the critique of liberalism is the question concerning the right manner of, and the adequate form for, the negation of the liberal order.

The critique of the liberal order aims at bringing the non-liberal practices of governing that are presupposed by that order from out of their latency and turn them into the matter of a political decision. For just as the normativity of liberalism combines two specifications, so too does its negation hold two contradictory forms. Liberalism is an order that connects the idea of the equality of freedom to the form of individual rights. For liberalism, they are the same. The critique of liberalism shows, however, that the form of individual rights effects the suspension and undermining of the idea of equal freedom. Therefore, the negation of liberalism can be directed either against the idea of equal freedom or against the form of individual rights. In the first case, the negation of liberalism leads to forms of government which are un-free and unequal. This is the effect of the inner or self-negation of liberalism: it turns into authoritarian forms of politics and subjectivity. The second strategy of the negation of liberalism on the other hand is directed against its basic form of individual rights and operates in the name of a different politics of equality and freedom. This is where the criticism of liberalism leads: it leads to the struggle between two opposing forms of non-liberal politics that is fought out in the shadow of the liberal constitution. While the existence of the liberal order depends on the outcome of this struggle, it cannot at the same time contribute anything to it.

NOTES

1. See Brown/Gordon/Pensky (2018). Brown puts the question as follows: "How and why have freedom and illiberalism, freedom and authoritarianism, freedom and legitimized social exclusion and social violence, become fused in our time?" (Brown 2018, 11) The answer to these questions would have to analyse how "authoritarianism in freedom's name" (ibid., 23) works.

2. On the following, see Marx's analysis in "On the Jewish Question," which unfolds the immanent dialectic of the logic of presupposition (*Voraussetzung*) (Marx 2010).

3. For some more details, see my *Critique of Rights* (Menke 2020).

4. The liberal state does not *form*, or transform, individual freedom, but interprets or defines it. For a right to freedom does not exist "in general." All rights are specific rights to this or that freedom – of opinion, of conscience, of choice, of contract, and so forth. These categorizations, however, are not normative decisions. They are determinations of the facts of social life.

5. On the following, see Habermas (1992, ch. 3).

6. Adorno (2003, no. 123). For an illuminating contextualization and interpretation, see Thomä (2016, 452). In *Dialectic of Enlightenment*, Horkheimer and Adorno write: "Fascism is also totalitarian in seeking to place oppressed nature's rebellion against domination directly in the service of domination" (2002, 152).

7. See Adorno's "Remarks on '*The Authoritarian Personality*'" which, understandably, were not included in the published volume. For a detailed analysis and contextualization, see Gordon (2018). I thank Thomas Assheuer for drawing my attention to this important text.

8. The "Notizen" anticipate in many respects the argument in the *Dialectic of Enlightenment*, especially in the section on "Elements of Antisemitism." The same argument is also more or less directly reproduced in the final section of Adorno's "Remarks" in which he formulates his conception of total social integration (which wipes out the autonomous individual and hence dissolves the very object of psychological investigation). I will therefore mainly refer to Adorno's early "Notizen" in the following.

9. The modification refers to the sequence or typology of forms of power in Foucault. I use "discipline" here in reference to the – historically unprecedented – modern practice of a non-normative pedagogy.

10. In a later article on the relation between sociology and psychology, Adorno speaks of an "annihilation of mediating instances." For an illuminating, although critical, reconstruction of this argument, see Honneth (1985, 100).

11. This does of course not mean that there is no (self-)repression in the "new type of human being." But it does say that this repression is not normative anymore (and in this sense rather than discipline a form of "control"; cf. Deleuze 1992). So, it is economic or instrumental: It arises because (or when) "people transfer the mode of production to their lives," it shows "how relations of production finally replace psychology" (Adorno 2004, 459). This allows also for a new understanding of the "rage" which defines the authoritarian personality: it is the rage ("Wut") of "devastation" ("Verwüstung") which according to Hegel is the manifestation of a freedom devoid of any normativity; see Hegel (2002, 43) and the illuminating interpretation of this passage by Jean-Luc Nancy (1993, § 12).

12. Axel Honneth has claimed that there is a tension, even contradiction between Adorno's claims of the "destructuring of the superego" and of the "regression of the ego"; see Honneth (1985, 102 f.). In my reading they are but two sides of the same process of a denormativization of the social. For a later reading that puts this motive at the centre, see Honneth (2009).

BIBLIOGRAPHY

Adorno, Theodor W. 1948. "Remarks on '*The Authoritarian Personality*'" (1948). In: Max Horkheimer Archiv VI. 1 D. 71-100.

Adorno, Theodor W. 2003. *Minima Moralia*. Frankfurt am Main: Suhrkamp.

Adorno, Theodor W. 2004. "Notizen zur neuen Anthropologie." In: Theodor W. Adorno/Max Horkheimer. *Briefwechsel*, vol. II. Frankfurt am Main: Suhrkamp, 453–471.

Adorno, Theodor W., Else Frenkel-Brunswik, Daniel J. Levinson, and R. Nevitt Sanford. 1950. *The Authoritarian Personality*. New York: Harper & Brothers.

Adorno, Theodor W. and Max Horkheimer. 2002. *Dialectic of Enlightenment: Philosophical Fragments*. Stanford: Stanford University Press.

Arendt, Hannah. 1961. "What is Freedom?" In: *Between Past and Future. Six Exercises in Political Thought*. New York: Meridian Books, 142–169.

Böckenförde, Ernst-Wolfgang. 1991. "Die Entstehung des Staates als Vorgang der Säkularisation." In: Ernst-Wolfgang Böckenförde. *Recht, Staat, Freiheit*. Frankfurt am Main: Suhrkamp. 92–114.

Brown, Wendy. 2018. "Neoliberalism's Frankenstein. Authoritarian Freedom in Twenty-First Century 'Democracies'." In: Wendy Brown, Peter E. Gordon, and Max Pensky. *Authoritarianism. Three Inquiries in Critical Theory*. Chicago/London: The University of Chicago Press, 7–44.

Deleuze, Gilles. 1992. "Postscripts on the Societies of Control." In *October*, vol. 59, Winter 1992, 3–7.

Forst, Rainer. 2017. *Normativity and Power: Analyzing Social Orders of Justification*. Oxford: Oxford University Press.

Foucault, Michel. 1990. *The History of Sexuality*. New York: Vintage Books.

Gordon, Peter E. 2018. "The Authoritarian Personality Revisited. Reading Adorno in the Age of Trump." In: Wendy Brown, Peter E. Gordon, and Max Pensky. *Authoritarianism. Three Inquiries in Critical Theory*. Chicago/London: The University of Chicago Press, 45–84.

Habermas, Jürgen. 1992. *Faktizität und Geltung. Beiträge zur Diskurstheorie des Rechts und des demokratischen Rechtsstaats*. Frankfurt am Main: Suhrkamp.

Hegel, Georg Wilhelm Friedrich. 1979. *Grundlinien der Philosophie des Rechts*. Frankfurt am Main: Suhrkamp.

Hegel, Georg Wilhelm Friedrich. 2002. *System der Sittlichkeit*. Hamburg: Meiner.

Hobbes, Thomas. 1996. *Leviathan*. Cambridge: Cambridge University Press.

Honneth, Axel. 1985. *Kritik der Macht. Reflexionsstufen einer kritischen Gesellschaftstheorie*. Frankfurt am Main: Suhrkamp.

Honneth, Axel. 2009. "A Physiognomy of the Capitalist Form of Life. A Sketch of Adorno's Social Theory." In: *Pathologies of Reason. On the Legacy of Critical Theory*. New York: Columbia University Press, 54–70.

Horkheimer, Max. 2004. *Eclipse of Reason*. London/New York: Continuum.

Kant, Immanuel. 1991. *Metaphysics of Morals*. Cambridge: Cambridge University Press.

Marx, Karl. 2010. "On the Jewish Question." In: *Marx & Engels Collected Works*, vol. 3. London: Lawrence & Wishart, 146–174.

Menke, Christoph. 2020. *Critique of Rights*. London: Polity Press.

Nancy, Jean-Luc. 1993. *The Experience of Freedom*. Stanford: Stanford University Press.

Rawls, John. 2001. *Justice as Fairness. A Restatement*. Cambridge/London: The Belknap Press of Harvard University Press.

Thomä, Dieter. 2016. *Puer robustus. Eine Philosophie des Störenfrieds*. Berlin: Suhrkamp.

Section IV

PROGRESS

Chapter 15

John Dewey Goes to Frankfurt

Pragmatism, Critical Theory, and the Invisibility of Moral/Social Problems[1]

Philip Kitcher

Several years ago, Manuel Kaeppler, then a talented Columbia senior, came to me with an unusual request. He started by explaining that, as well as being enrolled in my course on naturalistic ethics, he was simultaneously taking Axel Honneth's seminar in social and political philosophy. He had been struck by the fact that we seemed to be addressing versions of the same problem, and wondered if, instead of writing separate final essays for the two classes, he might compose a single longer paper, exploring the parallels. He made the same proposal to Axel, and the two of us acceded enthusiastically. In due course, we recognized the insight that had moved Manuel. So we became aware of the interesting relations between my version of Deweyan pragmatism[1] and Axel's development of critical theory.

My aim in what follows is to elaborate what our common student had glimpsed. I shall try to offer an account of a difficulty that arises for the approach to moral and social issues I favour, and to connect it with recent articulations of Frankfurt School social critique. Beside the parallel, there are also differences of emphasis, and appreciating those differences might, I think, be useful to both projects.

*

---

[1] It is an honour and a pleasure to offer this chapter to Axel on the occasion of his seventieth birthday. It has benefited from discussions with Rahel Jaeggi, although she should not be held responsible for my errors. I'm grateful to her and to Fred Neuhouser for helpful comments on an earlier version.

From the outside, the history of critical theory, from Horkheimer and Adorno to Axel Honneth and Rahel Jaeggi, looks like a process in which the transcendental framework, derived from Kant and his nineteenth-century successors, plays an ever diminishing role.[2] The idea of some set of a priori conditions governing the inevitable unfolding of human events gives way to sophisticated appreciation of the contingencies of history.[3] Teleology is abandoned, but a conviction of the possibility of progress remains.

Many intelligent people do not see how this can be. They are beguiled by the thought that progress is invariably towards some fixed goal. To make progress, they suppose, is to diminish the distance between your actual condition and the state at which you aim. Plainly for some examples of progress, that is so: journeys sometimes end in lovers' meetings, pregnancies move towards birth. Other cases are different. Aspiring artists do not make progress by approximating some ideal form of their chosen genre, computer technology does not progress by bringing us closer to the perfect PC, medical research is not bent on realizing some state of complete human health (just how long would the healthy individual live, and how fast could she run?). In all such instances, progress modifies a current state, a state that is unsatisfactory in some respects, and progress is made through solving problems and overcoming limitations.

Besides teleological progress there is also pragmatic progress – there is progress *from* as well as progress *to*.[4] Critical theory can happily give up a grand vision of history marching towards some end state, without sacrificing its concern with human progress. It can share in pragmatism's hopes for amelioration, without invoking utopia.

To recognize that bare possibility is not, however, sufficient. For to talk of states as unsatisfactory, or to refer to problems and limitations, might well disguise a residual teleology. Indeed, if progress is to make sense when we are discussing morality or forms of social life – the domains of principal interest to critical theorists and Deweyan pragmatists alike – it might seem that teleology inevitably lurks in the background. Understanding advances in these domains as instances of pragmatic progress reformulates the image Martin Luther King, Jr. borrowed from Theodore Parker: the arc of history is seen as bending *away* from *in*justice. Yet if our only purchase on the notion of injustice is as a lapse from justice, the ideal apparently returns as a goal, towards which progress is directed.

Neither pragmatists nor critical theorists need deny that human beings and human societies have ideals. They can nevertheless reject thinking of them as attempts to characterize an ultimate state towards which we aim. Rather, they serve us as diagnostic tools, local devices for identifying the problems of the current condition, likely to be refined, amended, or even discarded, as our practices evolve. Often the total collection of ideals harboured by members of a social group is inconsistent, and yet the evolution proceeds better than it would have done if the group had venerated the "hobgoblin" of consistency. Clashing ideals can be used opportunistically, to disclose places at which changes would be welcome.

So far a brief response to an important challenge. Too brief, however. Critical theorists and Deweyan pragmatists share a picture, holding that particular problems are intrinsic features of particular social arrangements and particular moral practices. In doing so, they provoke an obvious challenge: What exactly is a problem – or, perhaps more fundamentally, what is it for a state to be problematic?[5] This question, the *ontological* question, arises for both traditions. It lies at the heart of the shared predicament Manuel Kaeppler had detected.

If you find yourself in that predicament, the obvious strategy is to provide a direct answer. The two most important recent works in critical theory – Honneth's *Freedom's Right* (Honneth 2014) and Jaeggi's *Critique of Forms of Life* (Jaeggi 2019) – seem to me to take significant steps in realizing that strategy.[6] They offer theoretical characterizations of structural features within societies that embody limitations, thus serving as sites for pragmatic progress. By contrast, pragmatist efforts to answer the ontological question appear unimpressive.

In fact, pragmatists are well advised to deploy a familiar pragmatist tactic: Change the subject. The most famous paragraph in pragmatist writings consists of three sentences in Lecture II of James's *Pragmatism*, sentences he had used almost a decade earlier in the Berkeley lecture in which pragmatism was announced to the world (James 1975, 30).[7] James enjoined philosophers to concentrate on questions that make a difference, a concrete difference to "somebody, somehow, somewhere, and somewhen." Following this injunction, the pragmatist might ask whether the ontological question is really the one we need to answer. Wouldn't it be enough if we had a method for identifying social arrangements and moral practices as problematic? What do we want an answer to the ontological question for, if it isn't for this diagnostic work?[8]

So the Deweyan pragmatist – well, this Deweyan pragmatist – poses a different question, the *methodological* question. At first sight, the manoeuvre might seem unprofitable. How can anyone expect to elaborate a method for detecting X's without a prior characterization of the X's? Ontology, it might be supposed, must precede methodology. The simple answer is that the history of inquiry, particularly in the natural sciences, demonstrates how fashioning methods of detection often precedes any ability to describe the entities detected. Classical genetics began without even the vaguest understanding of the apparently particulate factors involved in inheritance, and the full characterization of genes only came after 1953, in the flowering of molecular biology.

Contemplation of examples like this one might prompt a leap to the opposite pole: ontological questions can be addressed (if there is any need to address them) only when the important work of methodology has been completed. That would be to overreact. This chapter will not continue with a celebration of the pragmatist methodological cavalry, as they ride to the rescue of forlorn critical theorists. As we shall see, approaching the methodological question is possible and useful. But, *as in the case of genetics*, there comes a stage at which thinking about the ontological question is valuable for the *further* advance of methodology. The pragmatist program doesn't supersede critical theory. John Dewey needs to go to Frankfurt. He has things to learn there.

*

Dewey's copious writings are pervaded by expressions of the need for "intelligence" in addressing the problems of life. Surveying the history of human societies and of human practices, he is struck by the chanciness of what progress our species has made. The episodes we count as advances depended on events that might easily have gone differently. The abolition of slavery in the Americas during the nineteenth century surely counts as an instance of moral and social progress. Yet historical contingency is all over the process as it played out in the United States: in the early resistance to owning slaves, in the development of conditions in which the voices of slaves and ex-slaves could finally be heard, in the reluctant measures to limit the expansion of slavery, in the outbreak of war in reaction to that legislation, in the course of the war itself, and the bumpy road to the Emancipation Proclamation. Moreover, as the subsequent history shows, many important problems have endured, and are still in urgent need of being addressed.

With respect to this and kindred examples of moral or social progress – the expansion of opportunities for women, the recognition of same-sex love as valuable – people who grow up after the advance has occurred frequently fail to understand how their predecessors could have failed to see the hideous defects in their practices. Yet the lessons from history are unambiguous. People whose conduct and attitudes were otherwise admirable, people apparently as morally and socially sensitive as those who are perplexed at their blindness, overlooked glaring problems. Kindly and godly slave owners thought of other human beings as property. Moral and social problems are often *invisible*. As a result, cruel arrangements persist, and are only repudiated through long and tortuous processes that can easily be derailed. Once the permanent danger posed by invisibility becomes evident, it is entirely natural to demand, as Dewey does, a method for making our moral and social progress more systematic and sure-footed than it has historically been.[9]

Even without answering the ontological question, it is possible to begin the search for method. The history of moral and social change, including not only the progressive episodes but also the attempts that failed, can inform and educate. Studying the historical examples, it is possible to discern common features. Symptoms can be noted, and courses of treatment assessed. My own reflections on the three examples I have cited lead me to identify two general indicators of troublesome conditions.

In his exploration of moral life, William James makes an optimistic, but helpful, claim. Moral philosophers, he thinks, often err. Yet, if they go astray, he suggests, "the cries of the wounded" will alert them to that fact (James 1979, 158). Probably not. As the historical examples show, even the most renowned philosophers can share the general moral deafness of their contemporaries – we need only read Enlightenment discussions of race to recognize James's unwarranted confidence. On the other hand, his judgement hints at how people might do better. We can take steps to listen for attempts to express human suffering. Or, to switch sensory modes, we can be on the lookout for groups of people who complain about the *status quo*, attempting to discern what was previously invisible.

One general class of symptoms, prominent in the historical examples, consists in the *exclusion* of perspectives. Sometimes that comes about because those who participate powerfully and comfortably within society never listen to a particular class of people. If those people voice complaints, the protests are simply dismissed, treated as mere noise. Until the nineteenth century, very few people heard the cries of the suffering slaves. On other occasions, the individual *people* are often heard, but only if they avoid discussing particular areas of their lives. In post-Enlightenment societies, women have frequently managed to exchange thoughts with husbands, fathers, sons, and male acquaintances, so long as they stopped short of expressing their desires for an expanded public role. Gays and lesbians have had wide-ranging conversations with their straight friends, aware always of the need to hold back important aspects of their selves and of their lives.

All three examples show how exclusion is entangled with a second class of symptoms, indicators of a species of *false consciousness*. The intertwining is most evident in debates about the roles to which women can aspire. Female voices calling for entry to this or that sphere of activity, currently off-limits to women, have routinely been dismissed on the grounds that they exhibit a deviant, "unnatural" character. The conservative points to the many women – the "true" women – who are reconciled to the supposed restrictions, women who are satisfied, often delighted, with their social roles. Here, the false consciousness consists in acquiescing in practices of restricting an ideal of the self: a way of living, or of finding an identity, held to be appropriate for some groups is denied to others, and many members of the debarred groups assent in and even celebrate the social practice. In this form of false consciousness, people take on the social identity prescribed for them, perhaps never contemplating the possibility of different ways of living or, when alternatives are presented, rejecting them immediately. Those who suffer false consciousness of this type are willing allies for the conservatives who dismiss the cries of other members of the excluded group – and, we should note, none of those involved need be insincere, exploitative, or anything other than well intentioned and kind. Moral and social problems are invisible – or, better, inaudible – in part because many of the wounded do not even cry.

It would be folly to suppose that two general forms of invisibility, drawn from a very small sample of historical instances, exhaust the ways in which moral and social problems can disappear from view. Yet they offer an entering wedge to the project of fashioning a methodology, of crafting ways of making moral and social progress more reliably than our predecessors have managed. Deweyan "intelligence" is not an all or nothing affair. It can be developed gradually, by discerning ways of coping with recurrent scenarios. The comparison with natural science (of which Dewey was so fond!) proves helpful here. The great advances in physical science, achieved in the seventeenth and eighteenth centuries, were intertwined with and facilitated by methodological reflections that, from a later perspective, appear vague, ambiguous, underdeveloped, and (almost) trivial. Contemporary natural science, divided into many branches, some of them unimaginable to the early pioneers, subsumes a wide diversity of well-articulated methods under a bland overarching methodology derived from early modern proposals. Classes in "method" for the aspiring particle physicist, the apprentice geneticist, the budding climate scientist, and the fledgling experimental psychologist are necessarily sharply differentiated. Each group needs a special set of precise guidelines. The lore passed on has been amassed in gradual steps, through the application of prior, less refined, methodological canons to particular problems. Early ventures in method, laughably crude by later standards, inspire specific lines of research, and the successes and failures contribute to methodological refinement. As we have learned more about nature, we have learned more about how to learn about nature. So too I suggest with attempts to identify problematic features of moral practices and social arrangements. A small handful of historical examples can prompt some first suggestions about how to deal with two recurrent situations. Following those suggestions may (*may!*) help to disclose many further kinds of symptoms and more sophisticated techniques for responding to them. Hence the pragmatist approach I am outlining here is only the first step in a methodological venture I take to be potentially progressive (potentially capable of making *pragmatic* progress).

As we shall see, a pragmatist who goes to Frankfurt might be helped to take further steps.

*

Attentive readers will surely have noted that, while I have pointed to some symptoms that *might* enable the identification of moral or social problems, I have not explained how to pick out the genuine problems or how to respond to them. It is time to remedy that. So I shall sketch the (crude) methodology I favour, preparing the way for a discussion of its promise and of its limitations.

Despite his emphasis on the importance of method, Dewey's conception of method in moral and social inquiry is remarkably elusive. Indeed, the important essay he wrote on the influence of Darwin on philosophy can be read as postponing the enterprise of working out methodology in these domains. Dewey sees Darwin as building on the achievements of Copernicus, Kepler, and Galileo, and opening "the gates of the garden of life" to the generic method pioneered in the early seventeenth century. He continues:

> Only through this garden was there access to mind and politics. The influence of Darwin upon philosophy resides in his having conquered the phenomena of life for the principle of transition, and thereby freed the new logic for application to mind and morals and life. (MW 4, 7–8)

Plainly, Dewey doesn't think of a *single* "scientific method" susceptible of automatic application to all domains. Rather, a major scientific achievement – the work culminating in Darwin's *Origin* – was required to show how to pursue inquiry in the organic domain. If that provides a *basis* for continuing to the human, social, and moral sciences, it is also a reminder of the scale of work needed to develop methodology in these areas.

It is, I believe, a common mistake in interpreting Dewey to see the *Logic* as providing all the canons necessary for pursuing inquiry in any domain whatsoever. Better to understand that synthetic work as offering a general framework within which the great figures of the past – the seventeenth-century giants who explored the physics of motion, Lavoisier in the eighteenth century, and Darwin in the nineteenth century – worked out fruitful methods for particular fields. Extending their achievements is plainly central to Dewey's philosophical program. How he, or anyone else, can build on their work, emulating their accomplishments with respect to moral and social inquiry, is left as an open problem.[10] Important though the project is, attempts to carry it out in the twentieth-(or twenty-first) century context may be premature.

Dewey's writings contain some hints about the first steps. The middle section of the jointly authored *Ethics* (in the second edition of 1932) concludes by proclaiming ethical life as something that grows naturally out of the human condition: "*Moral conceptions and processes grow out of the very conditions of human life*" (LW 7, 308. Italics are Dewey's.). In particular, Dewey emphasizes our social character, and the "demands, claims, expectations" expressed in our social relations (ibid.).[11] That provides a clue to how one might develop a Deweyan method for moral inquiry, even if it falls short of a full-fledged methodology.

His most explicit proposals come in *Human Nature and Conduct*, where the concluding chapter – "Morality Is Social" – prefigures the thought of moral life as growing out of the human social predicament. At first sight, Dewey's account of the responsible moral inquirer looks strikingly *a*social. In combating the popular model of deliberation as a kind of calculation, the weighing up of expected costs and benefits, he appears to isolate the moral agent from any broader community.

> What, then, is choice? Simply hitting in imagination upon an object which furnishes an adequate stimulus to the recovery of overt action. Choice is made as soon as some habit, or some combination of habits and impulse, finds a way fully open. Then energy is released. The mind is made up, composed, unified. (MW 14, 134)

At first sight, this looks like egoism: I choose by following *my* habits and impulses. It is all too easy to forget Dewey's commitment to the social character of the self – that endures long after Darwin has replaced Hegel as his preferred historicist.[12] The dangers of solipsism and egoism vanish once we appreciate that the ambient society is *already present* in the healthy operation of habits and impulses. The closing chapter of *Human Nature and Conduct* makes this apparent.

> In language and imagination we rehearse the responses of others just as we dramatically enact other consequences. We foreknow how others will act, and the foreknowledge is the beginning of judgment passed on action. We know *with* them; there is conscience. An assembly is formed within our breast which discusses and appraises proposed and performed acts. The community without becomes a forum and tribunal within, a judgment-seat of charges, assessments and exculpations. Our thoughts of our own actions are saturated with the ideas that others entertain about them, ideas which have been expressed to us not only in explicit instruction but still more effectively in reaction to our acts. (MW 14, 216)[13]

The picture of decision-making thus embodies how our fellows are *currently disposed* to react. It doesn't yet show, however, how we might aim for moral progress.

To take the further step of beginning to craft methods of moral and social change, it helps to return to passages in Dewey's earlier work where the social character of the self is emphasized. *Democracy and Education* characterizes the idea of the isolated self as "the very antipodes of the truth" (MW 9, 304).[14] To see our intercourse with others, the joint projects in which we engage with them, as fundamental to our individual being is to begin to understand the importance of democracy. For, in Dewey's distinctive conception, democracy is about far more than elections and voting, constitutional checks on power, free speech and open discussion.

> A democracy is more than a form of government; it is primarily a mode of associated living, of conjoint communicated experience. The extension in space of the number of individuals who participate in an interest so that each has to refer his own action to that of others, and to consider the action of others to give point and direction to his own, is equivalent to the breaking down of those barriers of class, race, and national territory which kept men from perceiving the full import of their activity. (MW 9, 93)

The educative function of our interaction with others is, Dewey thinks, a form of liberation.

The moral deliberator responds to the ways in which habits and impulses, tuned by imagining the reactions of others, find "the way fully open." If the deliberator imagines only the reactions of those who have so far shaped the self, the responses are likely to reflect the current views of the local community. Dewey's invitation to *extend* the class of interlocutors suggests that the rehearsal in imagination might proceed more widely. It leads naturally to a proposal for method in moral and social inquiry directed towards one of the general troubles discerned in my three historical examples: the problem of exclusion.

*

I've been trying to assemble clues from Dewey. Following them up will go beyond anything I have found in his writings.[15] Let's start by recognizing that moral progress can occur in the lives of individual people and in the historical careers of societies. So we might ask how a particular moral agent might engage in moral inquiry, or how a society might pursue collective moral inquiry. If we envisage individual agents trying to *imagine* reactions to their conduct, there is an obvious possibility of mistakes: they may err in predicting what others would say. That possibility can be circumvented by bringing people into conversation with one another. Collective inquiry would proceed by enabling people to express their own perspectives, or, when this is impossible (when the pertinent subjects are too young, disabled, demented, or belong to future generations), by appointing representatives (people best qualified to understand their points of view) to speak on their behalf. Collective moral inquiry is fundamental; when individual inquirers have to make up their minds without benefit of exchanges with others (as will often be the case, since an assembly can't be convened for every difficult moral or social situation), they will try to simulate the course a collective inquiry would follow.

When should moral or social inquiry begin? How should it be conducted? When should it end? James's reference to the "cries of the wounded," echoed in Dewey's talk of "demands, claims, expectations," suggests an inclusive attitude: any complaint has a prima facie right to be heard. Since human resources (time, energy, etc.) are finite, we should expend them on the most important cases. Thus, the first issue concerns whether a complaint is important enough to investigate thoroughly; the second concerns how the investigation should be conducted.

Dewey's conception of democracy is central to both questions. To decide whether a complaint should initiate moral inquiry, whether it is weighty enough to demand thorough investigation, requires the collective to engage with the perspectives of all its members. Because exclusion is a general form of moral and social problem, deliberation must be inclusive. There must be representatives of each of the perspectives affected by the class of situations giving rise to the complaint. At the first stage, deliberators assume that the complaint is warranted, focusing on whether the amount of harm or suffering from which relief is sought is significant. Equipped with the best available information, they endeavour to understand what motivates the plaintiffs and what improvements they might expect if their pleas were heard.

If the complaint passes the significance test, deliberation turns to consider whether it is warranted, and, if it is, what should be done to remedy the situation. Here, too, the conditions central to Deweyan democracy prevail. The perspectives of all potentially affected parties must be represented. Participants must be given, and must employ, the best available information. Most crucially, they must attempt to understand the sources of the viewpoints of their fellow deliberators. As they proceed, they should try to share others' visions of how the matters under discussion are: "Each has to refer his own action to that of others, and to consider the action of others to give point and direction to his own." (MW 9, 93)

The method I commend can be summarized as suggesting that the critical questions are addressed by instituting conversations of a particular type:

representative, informed, and mutually engaged. The following are three questions to be resolved.

1. Do these complaints merit a full inquiry?
2. Are they justified?
3. What changes, if any, should be made?

Plainly, the issues occur in sequence. The second only arises if the first receives an affirmative answer; the third is only posed when the complaints have been endorsed as justified.

The idea of approaching moral and social issues through deliberations of this sort has obvious connections to the historical examples. In effect, the abolition of slavery, the emancipation of women, and the acceptance of same-sex love were achieved through seriously compromised versions of public discussions of the sort I envisage. Inequalities of power, lack of representation, refusal to listen, factual mistakes, relentless selfishness, and callous indifference all played their parts in slowing down, disrupting, and blocking conversations that would have led to moral and social progress. The Deweyan method takes the rather obvious step of advocating public deliberations whose form increases the chances of suppressing or eliminating these contrary factors. If you hope to learn how to make moral and social progress by studying the successes and failures of human history, identifying the positive and the negative forces looks like a good way to fashion your method.

However, there are complications. First, the representation condition may need to be applied differently at different stages of inquiry. The class of those affected by potential *solutions* to complaints endorsed as justified may include people who were not involved at earlier stages of deliberation. Consider any persecuted minority within a particular society. Once the justice of the minority's complaints has been recognized, concerns about lingering prejudice may incline deliberators to explore providing them with a homeland in some other place. If the potential homeland is already populated, that will properly require consulting representatives of its current inhabitants.[16]

More generally, there are worries about the idealizing conditions. For almost all of the moral and social issues weighty enough to prompt moral inquiry, deliberations conforming to the ideal conditions would be hard, if not impossible, to bring about. Can one seriously expect to have a *fully representative* discussion? To have deliberators who always understand and employ the *best information*? For them to *explore sympathetically* the viewpoints of people whose ideas are completely different from their own? To reach *consensus* on some verdict?

That last word offers the core of an answer. Although we cannot expect *perfect* (or even approximate) realizations of the three conditions, we *do* expect rough-and-ready versions to promote important social goals. Juries are composed of ordinary citizens, not all of them unbiased, not all of them good at assimilating new information, not all of them empathetic. They rarely represent a cross-section of their society. Yet we take them to work better in settling cases than other methods we might use, and theorists ponder whether particular rules might enhance their functioning.

Ideals, I said earlier, are diagnostic tools. My three conditions point us in a direction, indicating ways of making progress with respect to methods for making moral and social progress. Dewey and I concur in thinking that human societies are capable of making moral and social progress, and that history shows how chancy our moral and social progress is. For both of us, the question is not "How can we institute a perfect method for making systematic moral and social progress?" Instead, it is "How can we do better than we now do?" History shows how particular deficiencies endangered actual episodes of progress. Conclusion: try to set up conditions under which those deficiencies would be removed, or, if present, would be less powerful.

These general remarks can be supplemented with more specific proposals. Representation can be more or less fine-grained. In a society with a wide diversity of perspectives on the focal questions, complete differentiation would indeed be impossible. Nevertheless, each perspective can be represented – coarsely, perhaps – by lumping. Certain kinds of differences can be ignored. One requirement on grouping viewpoints together to form some genus should be that the principle guiding the lumping should be applied uniformly. If species with some kinds of differences are grouped together for one collection of perspectives, then those kinds of differences should be overlooked across the board.

The history of moral and social debates offers clear evidence of differences in human capacities for assimilating new knowledge. Some people are remarkably resistant to well-established facts that bear on important questions. If the deliberators include some who show themselves to be incorrigibly stubborn, they would better be replaced by people who share the same perspective but who are more amenable to evidence. As with jury selection, that would best be achieved by an advance process, in which potential representatives were assessed for their capacities to learn, and to use the knowledge they had acquired. Similarly, efforts might be made to pick people who are able to appreciate the psychological attitudes of others – to understand and sympathize with their anxieties, uncertainties, aspirations, and disappointments.

Finally, consensus can come in a number of forms. The strongest type of agreement is reached when a group endorses a single proposal as the best way of going forward. Where that fails, they may nonetheless manage to find an option acceptable to each member. (Imagine that each deliberator has an acceptable set of possible outcomes; within the sets, the rankings are different; yet the sets have a non-empty intersection, and an option from that intersection is chosen.) Even weaker is a historically patterned consensus. Here, over a sequence of deliberations, it is always the case some groups are disappointed, finding themselves in a minority and disliking the outcome endorsed by the majority. But in different decisions, different groups find themselves in the minority. Indeed, as deliberation proceeds, efforts are made to ensure that those who were disappointed in the past will not always be marginalized. So, contemplating the entire sequence, each group finds it (taken as a whole) acceptable. The last and weakest form of consensus occurs when different outcomes are endorsed, and conditions are set up to separate the groups, so that each may live in a way so that the effects of the decision it dislikes are lessened.

My sketch of a methodology is directed towards problems of exclusion. As I already remarked, the historical examples show how such problems typically involve false consciousness. Slaves in the New World sometimes accepted their masters' assessment of their status. Self-loathing has afflicted some homosexuals, who have acquiesced in judgements that their inclinations are deviant, perverted, and sinful. Perhaps most common has been the easy acceptance by women of men's conceptions of ideal femininity; when defenders of the *status quo* can confidently declare that a large majority of women do not clamour for opportunities currently denied to them, it becomes easy for them to marginalize those who do. Hence, deliberations must always be framed by a prior review of any ideals of the self-presumed to be inapplicable to those who call for change.

Recognizing the importance of overcoming false consciousness sets limits on the speed with which the methods I have proposed can be expected to act. Unless the excluded group is largely united on the need for moral or social change, those opposed to its demands will reasonably see those of its members who accept current orthodoxy as needing representation in the pertinent deliberations, and they will have powerful weapons to deploy against those who fail to conform to the approved social role. Even if some ideal of the self is unequally applied, the differential treatment can be rationalized by declaring that members of groups to which it is denied would not flourish if they were to use it in planning their lives. The Victorian patriarchs who predicted misery and social disruption if women's opportunities were expanded were frequently sincerely concerned for their wives, sisters, and daughters. To rebut such declarations, as Mill and Taylor saw, required "experiments of living" – women needed to be able to try out the roles for which some of them (but only a few of them) clamoured (Mill – and, surely, Harriet Taylor –, 2008, 493–5). Moreover, those experiments might fail, particularly if they were to be conducted in an atmosphere of scepticism and opposition. Hence, the road to amending the social distribution of ideals of the self is likely to be long and winding.

Any society concerned to streamline its moral and social progress cannot be blind to the potential barrier raised by false consciousness. The obvious remedy is to institutionalize discussion of ideals of the self, whenever they are unevenly distributed. If groups debarred from ideals allowed to and favoured by others *ever* contain members who regard those ideals as appropriate for themselves, and who, after serious reflection, volunteer for experiments to pattern their own lives after them, then the experiments should be carried out. Progressive societies need some institution through which they can uncover examples of false consciousness, and thus prepare the way for informed deliberations that might yield moral and social reform.

*

Let's suppose (implausibly?) that Dewey would endorse the (embryonic) methodology I have outlined. Recognizing the kinship between his own hopes for social advance and those articulated by several generations of brilliant Frankfurt intellectuals, he might contemplate a visit to the banks of the Main. After all, he has gifts to bring, pieces of practical method to complement the theoretical explorations of critical theory.

That is not, however, the principal reason for John Dewey to make the journey. Far more important is the fact that, in its Hegelian and Marxist roots, the Frankfurt School has found a style of critique that goes beyond the kinds of methods I have advocated. One way to put the point would be to recognize structural problems of societies, conditions giving rise to the aspects of social life that provoke the cries of the wounded.[17] The empirical search for method, it might be suggested, can only take us so far, enabling us to appreciate the more superficial properties that call for progressive social and moral change. Even taking false consciousness to be something that affects individuals when they are debarred from patterning their lives in ways available to others fails to penetrate to the social strata in which the deep causes of barriers to progress are to be found.

A different formulation of the point returns us to what I earlier dubbed the *ontological question*. The search for method, undertaken by the Deweyan pragmatist, can distill from the historical examples some obvious features – it might be seen as akin to the early stages in empirical sciences where patterns are discerned in the phenomena. At some stage, however, a deeper, more theoretical, approach is required. Classical genetics, pursued through experimentation on model organisms, made great strides. Yet eventually it was transformed by the attempt – the successful attempt – to discover the molecular structure of the genetic material. So too, method in moral and social inquiry can be refined and enhanced by seeking a theory of the sources of exclusion and of false consciousness. An account of what moral and social problems *are* can enable the aspiring methodologist to go further.

This line of argument strikes me not only as plausible, but as worth investigating. Pragmatists should recognize the power of theory in many fields of inquiry. Nor can critical theory be dismissed on the grounds that its deliverances are idle speculations, made from the comfort of an armchair. The tradition that extends from Hegel and Marx through Honneth and Jaeggi was informed, from the beginning, by extensive reflections on history and on the conditions of social life at various periods. Moreover, there is a significant link between critical theory's most recent efforts at answering the ontological question and the pragmatist analysis of the historical examples.[18] In both instances, the idea of increasing freedom – or, better, decreasing unfreedom – plays a crucial role.

To see this, it is useful to start with the oldest, most central, question of philosophy: How to live? Strictly speaking, this embraces two questions: How should *one* live? How should *we* live together? Both formulations encourage a venture undertaken in the ancient world, and revived after the Enlightenment, the search for a theory of "the good life" (or, in variant, non-equivalent, formulations: the happy life, the fully human life, the worthwhile life, and the meaningful life).[19] Pragmatists should be wary of this cluster of endeavours, with their suggestion of an ideal goal towards which efforts in human living aim. The comparative formulation is preferable: How could human lives go better than they currently do?

For anyone who adopts Dewey's social conception of the self, the two ancient questions are related. Discovering how individual lives might go better is simultaneously finding out how collective life might be improved. Proposals for advancing the quality of particular lives have implications for how living together would be enhanced. Whatever diminishes the life of a single person detracts from the community to which that person belongs – and conversely.[20] Ethical questions are social questions, as the closing chapter of *Human Nature and Conduct* declared.

Dewey's turn to biology, and to his idea of personhood as emerging through interactions between an organism and the environment[21] – an environment that is significantly social for members of our species – preserves the social conception of the self he originally acquired in his Hegelian youth. When the social environment is relatively benign, the developing person is supplied with resources for further growth. Improving that social environment tends to increase the prospects for the individuals whom it shapes; their healthy growth contributes to social progress. When the social environment declines, by contrast, it becomes more likely that those who inhabit it will become alienated from it, and that their lives will thus be stunted.

Critical theory understands these processes in more abstract terms. Honneth's treatment of freedom shows how the theoretical formulation can, nonetheless, be completely clear and precise.

> Because the individual's striving for freedom can thus be fulfilled only within – or with the aid of – institutions, the "intersubjective" concept of freedom expands once again into a "social" concept of freedom. A subject is only "free" if it encounters another subject, within the framework of institutional practices, to whom it is joined in a relationship of mutual recognition; only then can it regard the aims of the other as the condition for the realization of its own aims. (Honneth 2014, 45)

To expose the connection between this approach to freedom and the Deweyan pragmatism I've been trying to develop, it is useful to focus on the ways in which things go wrong. *Problems*, we might say, arise because the institutional framework fails to supply the conditions under which relationships of mutual recognition can develop. If my reading is correct, at the heart of Honneth's account is an answer to the ontological question. Structural problems, of a kind untouched by the Deweyan methodology I sketched earlier, are constituted by defects or pathologies of the institutional make-up of a society, thus confining the lives of individuals.

Return now to my three motivating examples. In each instance, moral and social progress consisted in responding to a source of confinement, something that prevented the lives of individuals from going as well as they might otherwise have done. The cries of the wounded were the evident symptoms of such problems. To recognize how the wounded might not even be aware of their own confinement, entrapped as they were within an institutional structure that debarred them from ideals of the self available to others, is to probe a little more deeply, identifying a particular way in which lives may be restricted and society may be pathological. But it doesn't penetrate deeply enough. Answering the ontological question, viewing problems as social configurations that limit freedom, enables pragmatists and critical theorists alike to make methodological progress.

John Dewey's trip to Frankfurt might reasonably close with a translation of the insight he has learned there into a pragmatist idiom. Our lives are lived in many domains, we work and play, enter into relationships of different types, learn skills and acquire information of highly diverse kinds, participate in rites and ceremonies, immerse ourselves in nature and in art, plan and build, buy and consume, and so forth. These domains are sites at which strands from institutional networks intersect, providing us with opportunities and restricting our choices. Some of the institutions, most notably those dominating initial socialization, growth, and education, play a decisive part in shaping the aspirations we come to see as expressing who we are. Throughout a human life, however, many institutions – legal, economic, political, religious, cultural, and intellectual – will channel, facilitate, and frustrate those aspirations. Once moral and social progress is understood in terms of removing or mitigating the sources of confinement, the search for methods of making progress is less chancy than it has hitherto been should not only focus on the partial consciousness of those who feel the pressure of the shackles. There should be a deliberate, self-conscious, effort to scrutinize those institutions and their effects.

Part of that is surely already recognized. Legal scholars review the existing framework of law, seeking out places at which it generates painful unintended consequences; medical research sometimes reflects on ways in which the practices of physicians and surgeons cause harm; to a lesser extent, economists and engineers study the commercial and financial arrangements of their societies, and worry about potential losses that popular new technologies may bring. In all of these domains, as well as in many others, the critical work can be aided if the efforts of the practitioners are supplemented by those of outsiders. Specific applications of philosophy can do, and have done, much good across a variety of fields, from philosophy of law, medical ethics, social philosophy, environmental philosophy, and philosophy of science. Yet, as critical theory sees clearly, a more general enterprise is also needed.[22]

For, as I noted, our lives are not shaped by one institution at a time, but by forces resulting from interactions among institutions. Once that is appreciated, the possibility of *institutional friction* should be evident. Viewed close up, in isolation from its connections to other parts of human life, an institution may appear to be in good order. It marches on triumphantly, solving problems and pushing back limits. Or, rather, it addresses what a perceptive, well-informed, observer, *focusing on it and on it alone*, would reasonably take to be problems, and expands what that same observer would take to be limits. ("Look," the brilliant entrepreneur from Silicon Valley declares, "and see how we've really increased the number of functions the apple watch can perform.") As we tour the principal institutions of a society, inspecting each on its own terms, the final report card might be overwhelmingly positive: all are progressing wonderfully. And yet, because of the interactions among the institutions, the society may suffer acute pathologies and the lives of its members may be diminished.

That possibility is understood by sceptics about progress, those who see no improvement in human life across the generations, or who even tell tales of decline.[23] They are right about the danger, but overly pessimistic in viewing it as unavoidable. The deepest insight of the tradition that unfolds from Hegel and Marx to the critical theory of the present is (in my outsider's view) its thought that the principal task of philosophy is to arrive at broad perspectives enabling those who reflect on the human condition in their own times to understand the general phenomenon, to identify the interacting forces that make up sources of confinement, and to take action to modify the problematic social constellation.

Although he does not make it explicit, Dewey has inklings of the crucial point. It underlies his varying attempts to specify the role of the philosopher.[24] Philosophy, according to his most fundamental conception of it, is not another discipline of the same kind as art history or economics or history or molecular genetics. Rather it works among all such disciplines, exploring them as they enter all areas of human life, with the aim of "liberating and clarifying meanings" (as he vaguely puts it) (LW1 307, see also the entire discussion, 306–9). The work of liberation and clarification is a crucial part of the critical method philosophy attempts to provide (ibid., 326. See also 318 and 325).

The Deweyan search for method can *begin* in the way I have suggested, but it can be aided by using insights from critical theory. Even with respect to my three main examples, it would be reasonable to judge that the *limits* of the progress made so far result from the response to symptoms, rather than to underlying causes. Structural racism, structural sexism, and (perhaps to a lesser extent?) structural prejudice against LGBTQ people persist – and their endurance cannot be attributed to the fact that the historical processes only *approximated* my proposed Deweyan method. Equally, the Deweyan attempt to go beyond ontology to formulate method can assist the enterprise of critical theory, offering ways to identify places at which specific diagnoses can be made, and the theoretical framework consequently refined. The Deweyan methodological project advances the unsystematic reflections on history and society on which Hegel, Marx, and their successors have typically relied. The flow of useful advice between New York and Frankfurt proceeds in both directions.

Manuel, the perceptive student who saw Axel and me as engaged in similar projects, glimpsed something along these lines. He hoped to make two superficially different enterprises mutually informative. I share that hope.

NOTES

1. In citing Dewey throughout, I shall follow the standard practice of referring to the edition of his writings published by the Southern Illinois University Press. Volumes of the Middle Works will be cited as "MW" followed by the volume number; volumes of the Later Works will be cited as "LW" followed by the volume number. Thus MW9 is the edition of *Democracy and Education*, and LW1 is the edition of *Experience and Nature*.

2. An alternative way to read the history would view the "transcendental framework" as introduced by Habermas and whittled away by his successors. The claim

in the text depends on reading "transcendental" quite broadly, in terms of framing assumptions derived from a historical tradition inaugurated by Kant, but not restricted to him. A priori presuppositions garnered from later figures in that tradition pervade the writings of Habermas' predecessors.

3. That appreciation seems clear in Honneth's Leibniz Lectures (Honneth 2017).

4. For much more detail on conceptions of progress, see my "On Progress" (Kitcher 2015); also in German (Kitcher 2016) and in Kitcher (2017). Similar views are advanced by Dewey (*Democracy and Education*, MW9, 231; *Logic: The Theory of Inquiry*, LW12, Chapter 3), by Thomas Kuhn (2000, 96ff.), by Richard Rorty (1998, 28), and by Amartya Sen (2008, 15–16, 101–2).

5. This is more fundamental, I believe, since problems are already formulated in language. Reacting to a problematic state by formulating a problem is itself an achievement.

6. *The Idea of Socialism* is also an important work, one which I take to extend the argument of *Freedom's Right* (a view perhaps shared by Honneth – see *Socialism* viii).

7. The Berkeley Lecture, "Philosophical Conceptions and Practical Results," delivered in 1898, is printed as Appendix 1 in this volume of the Harvard Edition of the Works of William James; compare p. 30 with the Appendix passage p. 260.

8. My late friend and colleague Isaac Levi attempted to convince me, over almost two decades, that ontological questions without methodological implications are empty. I have belatedly accepted at least part of his important insight.

9. The themes of these paragraphs and of the further discussion of method below are elaborated considerably in my *Moral Progress* (forthcoming).

10. Jaeggi's discussion of Dewey's approach to social change in *Critique of Life Forms* (274–86) offers an admirably sensitive account of the method presented in the *Logic*, but errs, I think, in assuming that that method would suffice for the moral/social domain. To my mind, it requires an elaboration comparable to that achieved by Darwin in the biological case.

11. This passage recalls James' discussion in "The Moral Philosopher and the Moral Life."

12. Philosophers brought up within the Anglophone tradition, in which the idea of negative freedom plays so potent a part, find it difficult to embrace a fully social conception of the self, even when they firmly believe that all worthwhile human projects have a social dimension. I am grateful to Dick Bernstein for his forceful corrections of my own inadequacies in this regard, during a highly constructive discussion at the New School. On the same occasion, Jay Bernstein and Axel Honneth helped me to understand how I might do better.

13. The language of the "assembly within the breast" resonates with themes from the ethical writings of Hume and Smith. I read Dewey as developing these themes in a distinctive fashion. See "The Hall of Mirrors," ch. 14 of my *Preludes to Pragmatism* (Kitcher 2013).

14. This book contains many similar passages.

15. The approach I develop was begun in *The Ethical Project* (Kitcher 2011; see especially ch. 9). It is extended and refined in *Moral Progress*.

16. Two prominent examples: the creation of Israel as a homeland for Jews, and the proposal, favoured by Lincoln at one stage, to relocate emancipated slaves to a

place outside continental North America. Whether consultation with those affected was adequate in the Palestinian case, or whether it would have been adequate if the once popular proposal for the former slaves had been adopted, are important questions for moral reflection.

17. I am indebted to Moishe Postone, whose reaction to an earlier version of some of the ideas I present here, offered this way of formulating the critique.

18. In the text, I focus on Honneth's approach to the ontological question. Jaeggi's rich and fascinating discussion – culminating in her proposal for understanding a particular dynamic of problem-solving social change (Jaeggi 2019, 290–296) – concurs with Honneth's in the return to Hegel and in the emphasis on freedom. She diverges, however, in taking "Freedom as a Principle, Not as a Goal" (293). I am not sure whether my Deweyan version, sketched in the text that follows, is closer to Honneth or to Jaeggi.

19. The differences in connotation among these terms ought to disturb those who use them interchangeably. I'm inclined to think that not all of the adjectives are aptly employed in all contexts of human life. Imagine, for example, asking late Paleolithic hunter-gatherers (or even early pastoralists) for their views of the meaningful life.

20. In a famous passage that inspired Ernest Hemingway, John Donne already appreciated the point: "No man is an *Iland*, intire of it selfe; every man is a peece of the *Continent*, a part of the maine; if a *Clod* bee washed away by the *Sea*, *Europe* is the lesse, as well as if a *Promontorie* were, as well as if a *Mannor* of thy *friends* or of *thine owne* were; any mans *death* diminishes *me*, because I am involved in *Mankinde*; And therefore never send to know for whom the *bell* tolls; It tolls for *thee*" (Donne 1962, 538).

21. See ch. 7 of *Experience and Nature*, LW 1. Dewey's approach avoids the difficulty tackled by Jaeggi in her deeply insightful study *Alienation* (2014). He can recognize a *biological* structure that interacts with the environment, without supposing some prior *person* whose character socialization ought to elicit.

22. For some reflections on what the philosophy of science can achieve, and on the need for a broad synthetic understanding of the "meanings" of our collective epistemic state, see my "So ... who *is* your audience?" (Kitcher 2019).

23. A recent brief for scepticism is given by John Gray *Seven Types of Atheism* (2018); among recent figures who see history in terms of decline, Alasdair Macintyre is a prominent figure; his approach to moral and social change is lucidly discussed in Jaeggi's *Critique of Forms of Life*.

24. I have defended this claim in Kitcher (forthcoming).

BIBLIOGRAPHY

Donne, John. 1962. *Devotions XVI*. In *Complete Poetry and Selected Prose*. London: Nonesuch Press.
Gray, John. 2018. *Seven Types of Atheism*. New York: Farrar, Straus, and Giroux.
Honneth, Axel. 2014. *Freedom's Right*. New York: Columbia University Press.
Honneth, Axel. 2017. *The Idea of Socialism*. Cambridge, UK: Polity.

Jaeggi, Rahel. 2014. *Alienation*. New York: Columbia University Press.
Jaeggi, Rahel. 2019. *Critique of Forms of Life*. Cambridge, MA: Harvard University Press.
James, William. 1975. *Pragmatism*. Cambridge, MA: Harvard University Press.
James, William. 1979. "The Moral Philosopher and the Moral Life." In *The Will to Believe*. Cambridge, MA: Harvard University Press.
Kitcher, Philip. 2011. *The Ethical Project*. Cambridge, MA: Harvard University Press.
Kitcher, Philip. 2013. *Preludes to Pragmatism*. New York: Oxford University Press.
Kitcher, Philip. 2015. "On Progress." In Subramanian Rangan (ed.), *Performance and Progress*. Oxford: Oxford University Press, 115–133.
Kitcher, Philip. 2016. "Über den Fortschritt." In *Deutsche Zeitschrift für Philosophie*, 64(2), 2016, 165–192.
Kitcher, Philip. 2017. "Social Progress." In *Social Philosophy and Policy*, 34(2), 46–65.
Kitcher, Philip. 2019. "So … Who *is* Your Audience?" In *European Journal for the Philosophy of Science*, 9(1), 1–15.
Kitcher, Philip. Forthcoming. "Dewey's Conception of Philosophy." In Stephen Fesmire (ed.), *The Oxford Handbook of John Dewey*. New York: Oxford University Press, 3–24.
Kuhn, Thomas. 2000. *The Road Since Structure*. Chicago: University of Chicago Press.
Mill, John Stuart. 2008. "The Subjection of Women." In Mill (ed.), *On Liberty and Other Essays*. Oxford: Oxford University Press, 471–582.
Rorty, Richard. 1998. *Achieving our Country*. Cambridge, MA: Harvard University Press.
Sen, Amartya. 2008. *The Idea of Justice*. Cambridge, MA: Harvard University Press.

Chapter 16

Political Progress

Piecemeal, Pragmatic, and Processual

Christopher F. Zurn

Are we witnessing progress or regress in the recent increasing popularity and electoral success of populist politicians and parties in consolidated democratic nations? On the one hand, populism could be seen as a progressive change in sclerotic democratic regimes run by popularly insulated elites who are themselves largely captured by major organs of social power. For flowering populism is associated both with increasing political participation among previously quietistic and apathetic citizens and with state policy reorientation away from the preferences and interests of the rich few and towards those of the many. On the other hand, we might take the rise of populism as a form of political regress, more specifically as a distinct pathological danger that representative democracies are endemically in danger of giving rise to. On this reading (my preferred reading), populism is inherently anti-pluralistic since populists politicians and parties claim to be the single and exclusive representative of the true will of the true demos, while denying any popular legitimacy for any political competitors or alternative views (Müller 2016; Zurn forthcoming). Populism is then a regressive use of electoral democracy to undermine pluralistic democracy.

Consider questions about changes in our political institutions, specifically in a direction towards increasingly democratic forms of constitutionalism. Is the innovative use of popular referendum in Great Britain to settle fundamental constitutional questions a progressive or regressive innovation? To be sure, it will be difficult to separate one's assessment here from one's take on the substance of Brexit, but there is a distinctive kind of institutional assessment involved here, one that we would like to be able to answer in order to understand and guide future changes in British political institutions and norms – as well as other representative democracies.[1] Similarly, is the increasing use of constituent assemblies to change constitutions across the world evidence of progress in democratic constitutionalism, or, a worryingly regressive change back towards unmediated popular majoritarianism? On the one hand, from the point of view of democratic theory, constituent assemblies appear to promise what other modes of constitutional change cannot: a way in which democratic citizens can best understand themselves as authors of the very laws they are subject to. On that account, they represent political progress in the long history of experimentation in the institutions of constitutional democracy. On the other hand, the performance of actual constituent assemblies have not always appeared to move democratic constitutionalism forward – quite the opposite in some cases. The leading example of such regression is of course Venezuela, where the Maduro regime has employed a constituent assembly to effectively bypass representative democracy and establish a one-party authoritarian regime. Other examples of constituent assemblies range from milder failures – for example, Bolivia from 2007 to 2009 – to successes in democratic constitutionalism – for example, Brazil in 1986–1988 and Iceland in 2009–2012. We might then say that the institutional innovation of contemporary constituent assemblies over the past thirty years is potentially progressive, but at the same time potentially regressive insofar as it risks being used in the service of democratic deconsolidation (Zurn 2016a).

This chapter reflects on some of the perils and promise of framing such questions with the conceptual couplet of progress and regress. It considers four compelling critiques of the use of "progress" and its cognates in socio-political theory, as well as arguing that such concepts are nevertheless ineliminable for our normative theories. The paper concludes by suggesting that we can avoid the most serious problems by employing only conceptions of political progress and regress that are piecemeal, pragmatic, and processual.

THREE KNOCKS ON PROGRESS

When we reflect on social and political changes the language of progress and regress is a familiar rhetoric, an easy idiom, for couching basic normative assessments of successive states of affairs as either better or worse. Perhaps more importantly, invocations of progress or regress also introduce into political discussions crucial affective and motivational content: we hope for progress and recoil from regress, and, we are spurred to action by both the promise of progress and the threat of regress. Thus to adopt this particular idiom is not merely to make anodyne and distanced normative comparisons between two different states of affairs. It is also simultaneously to urge needed change and impel progressive (or anti-regressive) political action, all in the light of the reasonable hope that the world can be changed for the better. In this register, progress is a concept tied closely to political hope: it is not just an evaluation of past developments but also a call to contribute to an improved future.² Despite quite divergent starting points and disparate accounts of the meaning and entailments of progress, recent literature has seen a minor explosion of philosophical theories of progress in the register of hope: a small sample includes Buchanan and Powell (2018), Kitcher (2011), and Singer (2011).

Right alongside this hopeful employment of the idiom of progress, however, is a contrasting set of discourses arguing that invocations of progress are fatally discredited factually, morally disreputable, and perniciously ideological in effect. First, appeals to progress appear to be intellectually discredited: musty remnants of grand nineteenth-century philosophies of history that were themselves foundationally grounded in grand metaphysical systems that are no longer convincing. From left to right, and from poststructuralists to philosophical anthropologists – and much in between – beliefs in or even hopes for progress are seen as fatally tied to quaint and rose-tinted misreadings of actual history, misreadings purportedly grounded in fundamental human nature and the lawlike tendencies of history. Yet such grand legitimating metanarratives of civilizational progress have been discredited along with their foundationalist justifications, thereby ceding both their cognitive believability and their morally orienting power (Lyotard 1984; Wagner 2016). Said otherwise, even as the notion of progress was put forward as an Enlightenment rebuttal of religious myths of history, belief in progress can itself be seen as a mythic secularization of teleological thinking. It is then no surprise that a general loss of the power of faith puts both forms of eschatological myths out to pasture simultaneously: traditional religions no less than the story of inevitable human improvement (Gray 2014).

Furthermore, the critique is not merely of the purported facts underlying the myth of progress, for many think talk of progress is, simply, morally disreputable in the light of the horrors witnessed in the twentieth and twenty-first centuries. "After Auschwitz ... not only every positive doctrine of progress but every assertion that history has *meaning* has become problematic and affirmative. ... Any appeal to the idea of progress would seem absurd given the scale of the catastrophe" (Adorno 2006, 4).³ The thought is that it is simply morally obscene to use the categories of progress when the very societies that have self-consciously thought of themselves as progressive have carried out mass atrocities on an unprecedented scale and thereby committed evils never before conceivable. The uncomfortableness is made particularly acute once we note that specific societies' self-congratulations in the form of progressivism – as the cultural heights of German *Bildung,* as the technological dynamism of liberal capitalism in the United States, and as the utopia of fully egalitarian communism in the Soviet Union – are all simultaneously directly pairable with unspeakable evils – the Holocaust, the use of nuclear weapons on civilians, and the gulag archipelago.

The third critique of the progress/regress couplet takes the thought of morally disreputable self-congratulation one step further, seeing myths of progress as not only fallacious and morally blind, but also as ideological rationalizations of and covers for institutional practices of exploitation, domination, and oppression. Well explored in critical social theory, the idea is that the high rhetoric of progress and especially human development have been repeatedly used by European and American nation-states to distract from or even positively rationalize their colonial and imperial exploits, particularly to cover over the brutal character of their racialized exploitation, oppression, and domination of non-Western peoples and resources (Allen 2016; Horkheimer and Adorno 2002; McCarthy 2009). "As James Tully has pithily put the point, the language of progress and development is the language of oppression and domination for two-thirds of the world's people" (Allen 2016, 3).[4]

THE INELIMINABILITY OF PROGRESS (AND A FOURTH KNOCK)

Despite these three critiques of progress as disreputable, discredited, and ideological, I would contend that progress is nevertheless an ineliminable concept for normative political thinking. To begin, there are examples of political change that, quite simply, are undeniably progressive. Consider the nineteenth-century demise of the various legal, social, and economic institutions of the race-based Atlantic chattel slave trade system. That system was ended through both violent and peaceful means in those nations that had themselves pioneered the imperial and colonial conquests that undergirded the international slave trade from the sixteenth through the nineteenth centuries. Surely the abolition of slavery counts as progress. Just as surely, we would not hesitate to condemn the reintroduction of slavery as political regress. Isn't it similarly obvious that the enfranchisement of women counts as political progress in those nations that had understood themselves as democracies and yet had limited the vote only to men? Indeed it is precisely cases like these that lie behind most of Buchanan and Powell's responses to historical pessimists, those who see only moral degeneration in Western societies over time. "With a little reflection, the denial of moral progress seems absurd ... [f]or shining examples of moral progress are not hard to come by" (2018, 2), including in their list not only emancipatory changes involving slavery and women's rights, but also the transformations in the treatment of non-human animals, cruelty in punishments, and citizen-responsive government.

Furthermore, progress is conceptually appealing, perhaps even unavoidable, for comprehending our normative orderings in general. If you have normative standards of any kind – values, norms, rules, principles, and so on – you invoke a measurement that reality can live up to or not. And once put into a temporal register, normative assessment of changes simply means measuring progress or regress. Like "good" and "bad" or "right" and "wrong," the couplet of "progress" and "regress" – along with its cognates and synonyms – is nearly unavoidable language when we are engaged in activities across a range of evaluative orders: morality, legality, ethics, self-understanding, politics, and even aesthetics. Of course, progress is ineliminable *for us,* we who have ineradicably taken on a modern time consciousness that understands change as non-cyclical and cumulative and so sees history as a meaningful sequence of transformations, where past, present, and future demarcate meaningfully different domains causally linking significant changes (Habermas 1987, 1–22). And this modern consciousness of linear time is fostered by the increasingly capacious achievements of scientific and technical endeavours, where changes over time seem best comprehended in terms of learning, of progress: the story of successive moments is a story of each cognitive accomplishment building onto and out of previous cognitive accomplishments. There are surely societies without modern time consciousness who have no need for the concept of progress – it is quite hard to make the case that progress was an *ineliminable* evaluative concept in Plato, Aristotle, or fifth-century BCE Athens more broadly. But given that we ourselves can't think historically without thinking of change and transformation, we also can't help but evaluate such changes with the language of whether we are moving forward or moving backward, whether that change is good or bad from the point of view of improvement or backsliding – that is, without the language of progress and regress.

Perhaps this is why some of the strongest critics of progress as discredited, disreputable, and ideological nevertheless pull their punches and, in the end, attempt to rehabilitate some chastened, modest, non-ideological, and thereby reputable concept of progress. For instance, after launching a rather withering attack on grand Enlightenment discourses celebrating inevitable human progress for being factually unbelievable discourses today – as thoroughly discredited – Peter Wagner suggests we ought nevertheless to retain a less grandiose conception of progress, one that is more granular in its judgements, that rejects claims of inevitability, that refuses to link together developments in different domains of social life, and that is more open to critique, agency, and imagination as motors of decent change. He recommends, in other words, that we both reject Enlightenment notions of progress and embrace a reconstructed notion of progress (Wagner 2016).

Thomas McCarthy's critique of progress brings together the charges of moral disrepute and ideology and yet still recommends recuperation. With case studies on Kant, Mill, social Darwinism, and modernization theory, he elegantly makes the case that the institutional realizations of racism and imperialism that have been central to the world order for the last four centuries are in fact conceptually linked to various discourses of progress. "From the settlement of the Americas and the formation of the East India and Royal African Companies in the seventeenth century to present-day neoimperialism, European (and later, American) dominion over non-Europeans has repeatedly been justified with conceptions of development, enlightenment, civilization and progress, which were deployed to reduce the cognitive dissonance between liberal universalism and liberal imperialism" (McCarthy 2009, 166). Yet McCarthy insists – rightly I think – that the family concepts of progress, development, and historical enlightenment are "both indispensable and dangerous," such that "there is no alternative to [their] ongoing deconstruction and reconstruction" (McCarthy 2009, 18). Progress on this account is what I have elsewhere called (inspired by McCarthy) an "illusionistic ideal": an ideal that is indispensable for normative reasons and yet deeply worthy of suspicion for empirical reasons of actual historical practice (Zurn 2013). Illusionistic ideals are systematically ambiguous, presenting with a Janus face: worthy of both endorsement and sceptical dismissal. Note that there are methodological entailments of taking illusionistic political ideals seriously: we then need sociopolitical theory that combines in a more or less systematic way normative analysis and empirical research. Just as it is not enough to simply examine the normativity of the ideal at issue, it is not enough to study the uses and abuses that concept has been put to in actual practice.

Such an idea of theory systematically combining empirical and normative elements – plus a firm commitment to human emancipation – is of course an identifying hallmark of critical social theory. Unsurprisingly, the progress/regress couplet has been virtually ineliminable from the core of critical social theory for the approximate century it has existed as a self-conscious theoretical tradition. For, in attempting a critical assessment of the present – aiming, as Marx had it, to capture the "struggles and wishes of the age in thought" – critical theory has always worried about assessing whether the present is in a mode of progress or regress, and in particular, exactly why that might be the case. Further, in undertaking the task of substantively coming to terms with modernity itself, critical theory has usually adopted the thesis, admittedly more or less forthrightly, that both the achievements and horrors of the current age are rooted in the same or similar developmental causes, most classically in (Horkheimer and Adorno 2002). Critical social theory has then sought to both normatively assess the substantive character of modernity as progressive or regressive and to explain the empirical causes of these changes, all in order to facilitate the project of human emancipation.

Beyond these substantive, empirical, and emancipatory interests, critical social theory also is invested in the question of progress for methodological reasons. Generally taking its bearings from left-Hegelian strategies for understanding normativity historically, various forms of critical social theory have adopted different versions of normative reconstruction. The basic idea of such reconstruction is to adduce normative standards for the critique of society out of the normally unthematized normative orders embedded historically in our actual practices, institutions, or social structures. Examples are Habermas's account of the normative rationality embedded in communicative uses of language (Habermas 1990) or Honneth's account of the normative ideals of social freedom embedded in our social institutions (Honneth 2014). To the extent these standards operate as empirical conditions of possibility for our ways of life together, the theorist can appeal to them in a critical assessment of the deficiencies of contemporary society. However, critical theory has generally reached for something stronger than mere appeals to the way we happen to do things around here, for such merely parochial appeals cannot answer to deep worries about ideological distortions or significant damages within our very form of life. Consider Adorno's dictum: "Wrong life cannot be lived rightly" (Adorno 1974, 39). As Allen has forcefully argued, here is where the idea of progress comes in to save the day in a perfectly left-Hegelian fashion: because certain of our standards are not only drawn out of our historical form of life but can also be shown to result from historical learning processes whereby better standards replaced less adequate earlier ones, our current standards are more than merely contingent accidents (Allen 2016). Though they are not alien deliverances of abstract ideal theory – since immanent to our social life – they are also justified as the outcomes of comprehensibly progressive processes, thereby representing improvements over previous ones. In short then, the concept of progress is ineliminable from critical social theory not only for substantive reasons – as part and parcel of the assessment of modernity itself – but also for methodological reasons – as the surety for the non-accidental character of our own normative standards.

Having argued that progress is methodologically ineliminable from the normative strategy of critical social theory, Allen then launches a two-pronged attack on the concept.[5] First, the rhetoric of progress and civilization has repeatedly been central to Eurocentric and racist rationalizations of colonial and imperialist depredations of non-Western countries by the West – in other words, progress is morally disreputable and ideological. Second – and this is a fourth knock on progress – Allen argues that the concept of progress cannot be used in the way left-Hegelianism envisages to strengthen immanent normative standards beyond mere parochialism. According to the dilemma she develops, either critical theory has a set of universal and timeless moral standards for judging progress in any and all societies – thus violating its commitment to immanent normativity – or it collapses into mere-self-congratulatory parochialism – thus violating its commitment to a fully critical interrogation of the present as possibly thoroughly damaged. Let me flag this as the dilemma of immanent progress; I will attempt to show how to steer around it with a processual concept of progress below. In the meantime, it is worth stressing that, after an extended critique of the concept of progress as employed in the work of Habermas, Honneth, Forst, Foucault, and Adorno, Allen herself is unwilling to entirely give up on the notion. Suggesting that we foreswear grand and justificatory backward-looking invocations of the progress we have supposedly achieved, Allen nevertheless allows room for modest and self-critical "locally and contextually grounded judgments about progress in history" (Allen 2016, 229). Furthermore, she is unwilling to give up on the aspirational, future-oriented characteristics of progress – what she calls "progress as a forward-looking moral-political imperative" (ibid.) – since, without hope for a better future, critical theory's emancipatory interests would wither, and we would be left only with the bitter taste of past calamities. In other words, like Wagner and McCarthy, Allen apparently understands progress as an ineliminable concept – one that needs to be recuperated in some suitably chastened and reconstructed manner, even after its thorough critique.[6]

PIECEMEAL, PRAGMATIC, AND PROCESSUAL

So then where does all of that leave us? Political progress is an illusionistic ideal: ambiguous and ambivalent; factually discredited and factually undeniable; morally disreputable and normatively ineliminable; ideologically pernicious and yet the ground of ideology critique. Ought we then use "progress" and its cognates in our thinking about contemporary political changes in established constitutional democracies such as those considered in the opening of the paper? If the ideal is illusionistic and yet ineliminable – as I've argued in general and for the particular case of critical social theory – then we'll need to employ a suitably qualified conception of that ideal in our sociopolitical thought. I'd like to conclude by recommending three modifications to, qualifications of, traditional notions of progress that we ought to employ, in concert, in order to fruitfully use the concept in our thinking. In short, assessments of political progress or regress ought to be piecemeal, pragmatic, and processual.

Piecemeal Progress

The first strategy is, simply, chastening claims for progress themselves. Rather than proffering grand judgements about overall progress – the majestic achievements of civilization simpliciter – we ought to limit ourselves to piecemeal and relatively constrained judgements about progress or regress in specific fields or domains: morality, political institutions and processes, economics, technology, science, personal realization, social relations, art and culture, and so on. More particularly, we ought to disambiguate what domain of social life we are talking about, and limit most claims to one domain at a time: we can talk about progress in computer chip technology or in genomic understanding or in the mechanisms of democratic accountability, but should resist more general claims about the grand march of truth and freedom simultaneously in all domains. And when we do make such claims that span more than one domain, we need to clearly show the causal dependence of changes in one domain on those in the other. For contrary to grand and woolly claims about "civilizational progress," we often witness progress in one domain simultaneously accompanying regress in another. In fact, these concurrent developments may be co-dependent, where the progress in one leads to regress in another and vice versa. Consider the rise of early capitalism: simultaneous cause of increases in material welfare and in the expansion of racial domination through slavery, among other effects (Buchanan and Powell 2018, 7). Furthermore, we need to be open to the possibility of focused, differentiated assessments even within one area of social transformation. For instance, in the domain of democratic politics, recent increases in populism may be simultaneously associated with progress on the register of participation – as more ordinary citizens become active – and regress on the register of inclusiveness – as this participatory energy may be driven by xenophobia or racism. Careful, focused, and piecemeal assessments allow us to acknowledge the ambivalent and complex nature of social changes. Along with domain specificity, piecemeal progress further resists attributions of historical necessity and linearity. That is to say, the metaphysical idea that history evinces some kind of inevitable, motoric, or necessary transformation is replaced by a frank acknowledgement of the contingency and non-inevitability of historical change. Likewise, the notion that progress is inherently linear, always moving forward and upward, is replaced by a full awareness of the possibility – and indeed the repeated reality – of stagnation or regress. There was no inevitability to women achieving the right to vote, and there are all too many examples of nations making progress towards more fully realized constitutional democracy only to regress into lawless authoritarianism, often with little hope for return to the progressive path.

The piecemeal concept of progress clearly responds directly to the critique of progress as factually discredited, since it avoids making sweeping and overly general truth claims which simply can't be redeemed – and the same goes for grand denunciations of social change as total and unmitigated degenerative regress. But it is also secondarily responsive to the worry about progress as morally disreputable, since with piecemeal assessments we are much less likely to gloss over injustices and calamities with abstract generalities about the forward march of civilization on a grand-scale – we should be thus less tempted towards teleological redemptions of the "slaughter-bench of history" through, says, the cunning of reason coming to know itself in the world. And it is partly responsive to worries about the ideological function of the rhetoric of progress, since it is harder to fulfil that function with respect to merely partially progressive changes, particularly where our assessments highlight simultaneous and often co-dependent instances of progressive and regressive changes. It is therefore not surprising that piecemeal modesty is a large part of the core of the chastened and reconstructed conceptions of progress that are offered by both contemporary defenders – Kitcher, Singer, Buchanann and Powell – and critics – Wagner, McCarthy, and Allen – of progress.

Pragmatic Learning

It is important at this juncture, once we have chastened theory against claims to grand, unfocused, linear, or automatic progress, not to liquidate the distinctive content of the concepts of progress/regress into generic synonyms of better/worse. For, as Buchanan and Powell rightly insist (2018, 45–53), progress cannot be applied to any and every change that we might judge to be superior, nor regress applied to every change for the worse. For instance, a fortuitous reduction in human disease rates due to climate change or a reduction in the crime rate due to depopulation within a territory would not count as instances of progress, since they did not result from some form of cognitive insight and corresponding deliberate changes in our practices. In other words, progress implies change for the better as a result of learning. The directionality evinced in progress is not just a fluke or contingency, but depends on some form of cognitively mediated awareness of a problem or a lack, combined with a more or less purposeful intervention that is intended to address that problem, and then some cognitive assessment of the intervention and its effects that, in turn, loops back into another cycle of awareness-intervention assessment. In Hegelian terms, progress constitutively involves determinate negation and sublation.[7] It is somewhat more complicated to say exactly what regress proper consists in, but at the least we can see that it might involve failures to maintain past progressive achievements, to acknowledge cognizable problems, to intervene appropriately, to responsibly assess failed or non-existent interventions – and any of this as a culpable result, somehow, of cognitive failures or deficits. This specification of progress/regress in terms of learning and unlearning is inspired by the basic pragmatist picture of problem-solving adumbrated clearly by Dewey (1984) and centrally employed by many theorists (Anderson 2014a, 2014b, 2016; Habermas 1984; Honneth 2014; Jaeggi 2018a, 2018b).

It may help to place this pragmatist account of change between two other ideal-typical models of learning: learning as accumulation and learning as stage-sequential development. For learning as the cumulative stockpiling of ever more information or knowledge – while surely important – appears too weak a notion to underwrite assessments of political progress. The state's increasing ability to gain knowledge of diverse agricultural markets may be an improvement, but it seems short of the type of transformative political change that we would want to label progress. On the other hand, the Piagetian conception of learning as linear development through a pre-set sequence of stages, where regress is only possible on pain of psychological or social pathology appears much too demanding a conception to be employed for gauging political changes as progressive or regressive. Though the analogy between cognitive ontogenesis and moral development is at least both theoretically tempting (see Kohlberg) and potentially empirically falsifiable, the further homology between stage-sequential ontogenesis and stage-sequential social learning (Habermas 1979) is likely several steps too far towards revising factually discredited grand Enlightenment theories of progress. In short, insisting on a problem-solving model of learning ensures that progress claims involve non-accidental changes, with cognitively directed and responsive interventions in the light of felt inadequacies, with a plurality of possibly progressive or regressive paths, yet without the discredited assumptions of linearity, unitary paths, or motoric necessity associated with hubristic philosophies of history.

Processual Progress

Finally, I would recommend we adopt a processual conception of progress rather than a substantialist conception, for as the problem-solving model at least suggests, we need not always have a determinate substantial normative standard for gauging progress. Often it is enough in attributing progress to note that the *process* of change itself embodied the requisite characteristics for learning. This is a significant move away from typical substantialist notions of progress as greater compliance with or approximation of some determinate normative content, where claims of progress need to be made in the light of some clearly articulated and antecedently known substantive goals, standards, norms, principles, social functions, or the like (Kitcher 2011; Singer 2011).

To be sure there are different processual models, all taking off from the Deweyan idea of progress through collective problem-solving. Most ambitiously – perhaps too ambitiously – there is a stage-sequential model of the relevant process, developed by Piaget and Kohlberg for ontogenesis and extended to phylogenesis by Habermas: progress as a process of moving through an invariant sequence of stages where, in response to crises that cannot be mastered at the current level, each subsequent stage effects an entire conceptual reorganization to a more cognitively adequate scheme and where regress is only possible on pain of serious pathology (Habermas 1979, 1984).[8] Other models are less ambitious and focus on different processes. Anderson focuses on those sociopolitical processes that are beneficial from the point of view of moral epistemology: when moral change happens due to social structures that counteract well-known sources of bias, confusion, oversight, and blindness in our moral thinking, those changes are likely to be progressive (Anderson 2014b, 2014a, 2016). Honneth focuses on processes of change in our major sociopolitical institutions of intimate life, the economy and politics, whereby social movements force experimentation in institutional design that reveal richer conceptions of the basic values integrating those institutions and those changed institutions more fully realize their animating values (Honneth 2014, 2017). Jaeggi's processual model of progress also attends to the dynamics of social movements, but with a focus specifically on changes in social practices and ethical forms of life overall and particularly highlighting the ability to successfully adapt to crises and potential regressions as criteria for progressive forms of life (Jaeggi 2018a, 2018b).

There are a number of advantages of processual over substantialist models. First, they allow for new normative discoveries and improvements through social innovations that cannot be anticipated.[9] Substantialist models, by contrast, posit some fixed content as the stable and unchanging metric of progress, itself measured only in increased compliance or approximation. Second, on processualist accounts, sociopolitical theory need articulate no abstract set of trans-historical and trans-contextual values nor more demandingly still fully adumbrate a utopian picture of ideal political institutions in order to gauge progress – it can avoid the arid and unmotivating heights of ideal theory. Third, processual theories can nevertheless secure a form of objectivity when they claim that a change is an instance of progress or regress. While substantialist models gain such objectivity by the ostensibly trans-contextual validity of their abstract standards, processual models posit that it is sufficient to show, for progress, that current arrangements solve problems that previous arrangements could not and, for regress, that current arrangements can no longer solve problems that earlier arrangements could. Consider this as analogous to non-realist but non-sceptical accounts of scientific progress. There is no need to claim that objective scientific progress is secured only by the ever greater approximation of a newer theory to an unmediated independent reality. There is enough objectivity in the cognitive character of the learning process itself: we show that a new theory solves the problems of the previous theory, solves other problems the old theory could not, and is able to explain why the previous theory was incapable of doing so (MacIntyre 1977). And, it is an objective instance of regress when we can show a process of unlearning, of falling back behind the problem-solving capacities of previous theories. Finally, at least for those forms of critical social theory that attempt to draw normativity immanently out of actual social phenomena while nevertheless retaining a critical distance from the present deliverances of social history, processualist models can avoid the dilemma posed by Allen: claims of progress must either invoke timeless, ideal, and transcendent normative criteria, or, collapse into mere self-congratulatory parochialism. Note that the dilemma depends on the assumption that claims of progress must advert to substantive standards for gauging better or worse. Once we drop that assumption, we can see that there is a third option: objectivity for critical standards achieved through demonstrating actual processes of learning or unlearning, even as those critical standards are drawn out of the world as we actually know it.[10]

REVISITING THE EXAMPLES

Let me suggest, in a very schematic way, how these qualifications of the progress/regress couplet might help make some headway in diagnosing the examples I started with. Consider first the rise of populism across consolidated democracies. First, we should be careful to disambiguate different components of the complex practices and institutions making up constitutional democracy. Thus in the domain of elections we can see populism as progressive in terms of increasing participation and political energy among ordinary citizens. Yet in the domain of governance populists have tended to perform quite poorly, and in the domain of democratic culture populism has tended to foster a fair amount of regressive unlearning of the hard-won achievements of egalitarian pluralism. Populism in general is neither progressive nor regressive; we need a more fine-grained and piecemeal approach. Second, populism appears regressive on the pragmatist register of problem-solving. While populism can easily be seen as responding to the twin problems of regime sclerosis and governmental capture by moneyed interests, it simply does not propose or implement cognizable solutions to those problems, let alone maintain past achievements of learning. Finally, the processual accounts of progress can likewise help us to see the regressive features of populism – without using any particular substantive standards valuing or disvaluing particular political policies or principles. For since populism rules only in the name of, and on behalf of, one of several sectors of the relevant demos – claiming to be the sole representative of the real or authentic people – it quite clearly does not fulfil any number of the felicity conditions for learning proposed by different accounts of progress. Consider, for instance, the widely endorsed condition that progressive processes of political change must include input from broad and diverse contestatory social movements into collective processes of opinion formation in order to facilitate the possibility of social and political learning itself (Anderson 2016; Habermas 1984; Honneth 2014; Jaeggi 2018a) – populism is regressive since it violates processual conditions required for political learning.

Rather than making any sweeping pronouncements about the character of the newer innovations in democratic constitutionalism, I'd like to conclude by recalling the cogent critiques of the rhetoric of progress as factually discredited, morally disreputable, and ideological, while suggesting that the qualified conceptions of progress can keep relevant ambiguities in view. For if we begin from ideal democratic theory, we would surely and simply celebrate both constitutional referendums and constituent assemblies as progressive, as better institutional realizations of the fundamental ideals of self-governance through law. Yet our chastened conception of progress counsels us first, to be sensitive to the facts: constitutional referendums are neither always exercises in high-quality self-rule (see the 2016 Brexit referendum) nor unambiguously democracy-enhancing, serving quite frequently rather to cement ongoing de-democratization (see the April 2019 constitutional referendum in Egypt). And such fact sensitivity is crucial to ensuring that democratic theory gloss over neither moral catastrophes nor ideological uses of the ideals of democratic progress – for example, the 2017 Venezuelan constituent assembly which not only ended democracy, but ideologically celebrated its demise with the exalted rhetoric of self-governance. Partial assessments of progress allow us to acknowledge the potentially illusionistic character of our political ideals in practice.

Let me nevertheless end by evoking the aspirational, future-oriented, and thereby hopeful and motivational registers of progress. Recent empirical scholarship has shown that constitution-making processes with wide, diverse, and early popular participation can have a beneficial impact on prospects for ongoing and long-lived democratic regimes, whereas elite-driven constitution-making processes are not as favourable for democratization (Eisenstadt et al. 2017). If we take seriously the pragmatic and processual elements of progress, there is reason for optimism that institutional experimentation with democratic forms of constitutionalism can be seen as democratically progressive: as potential solutions to problems that may increase our capacities for democratic authorship of our fundamental laws. Or at least that is the progressive hope.

NOTES

1. For interestingly contrasting takes on the advisability of constitutional referendums, see Tierney (2012) (largely in favour when properly run and in

suitable conditions) and Lenowitz (forthcoming) (largely against except under special conditions).

2. As different as their respective accounts of the political use of hope are, Ernst Bloch and Richard Rorty agree both that worthwhile politics is based in hope, and, that political hope is closely tied to invocations of political progress (Bloeser and Stahl 2017).

3. These words are from Adorno's notes for his Lecture 1, dated 10 November 1964. In Hilmar Tillack's notes from the lecture, Adorno associates the Holocaust and the atomic bomb, concluding with the thought: "What can it mean to say that the human race is making progress when millions are reduced to the level of objects?" (Adorno 2006, 8).

4. I am leaving aside here a critique frequently levelled at progress as an inherently chauvinistic discourse, specifically as an exercise in Eurocentric self-celebration that simultaneously entails invidious comparisons to non-Western cultures, peoples, and nation-states (e.g. Allen 2016). For it strikes me that this is not a critique of the concept of rhetoric of progress per se, but rather a perennial but generic danger for any and all normative concepts. For when those concepts are applied favourably to the practices of one's own group (society, nation, people, culture, etc.), there is always a possible inference that labelling our practices as better entails denigrating other groups' practices. It is surely a possibility that one's self-application of a positive normative concept is nothing more than a narcissistic or parochial prejudice dressed up in fancier clothes. But the same is just as true of progress as of other evaluative concepts: rational, just, moral, efficient, beautiful, and so on.

5. Elsewhere, I have considered at length Allen's critique of Honneth's strategy of normative reconstruction, and attempted to articulate the resources available in Honneth's theory of social freedom for responding to the critiques (Zurn 2015, 193–200). In this chapter, I am pulling back from the specifics of these two theorists and attempting to get a more general outlook on the problems and prospects of the concept of political progress.

6. Gray's relentless pessimism is an exception to this pattern of the critics of progress nevertheless endorsing some use of the concept. However, his work evinces a tendency to invoke the concepts of regress and decline, thereby refusing to break with the combination of normative standards and modern time consciousness that I adverted to above as ineliminably giving rise to the progress/regress doublet.

7. Actual political progress is, of course, a much more complex process of change, going well beyond mere free-standing cognitive insight, involving additionally political, institutional, economic, social, praxiological, psychological, and cultural factors. I am avoiding any specific explanatory theory of political change here; I mean merely to insist that learning is criterial for progress, to distinguish progress from lucky change for the better.

8. One might be concerned that Piaget's model of individual development is really a growth model rather than a problem-solving model, where moves from stage to stage are more or less automatically impelled by maturation. While I think this is a misreading of Piaget, it is certainly not the case for Habermas. For he sees ontogenetic and phylogenetic moves from stage to stage as impelled by crises in the current level of communicative rationality and thus the resolution of the problems at the next stage as explained by increases in communicative competences.

9. Buchanan and Powell (2018) argue that we ought reasonably infer from past moral failures that our current moral outlook will likewise be shown to be deficient in the future: "Human beings are not warranted in believing that they currently grasp all valid moral norms or that the norms they believe are valid will remain so under different institutional contexts" (107).

10. I've earlier argued that Honneth ought to adopt such a learning process model in order to better defend his claims for the superiority of certain forms of left-egalitarian economic structures (Zurn 2016b), but I think the point generalizes as a conceptual strategy that can be adopted by many different forms of critical social theory, with different processual models of progress and various methods of drawing on immanent normativity.

BIBLIOGRAPHY

Adorno, Theodor W. 1974. *Minima Moralia: Reflections from Damaged Life*. Translated by E.F.N. Jephcott. New York: Verso.
Adorno, Theodor W. 2006. *History and Freedom: Lectures 1964–1965*, edited by Rolf Tiedemann. Translated by Rodney Livingstone. Cambridge: Polity.
Allen, Amy. 2016. *The End of Progress: Decolonizing the Normative Foundations of Critical Theory*. New York: Columbia University Press.
Anderson, Elizabeth. 2014a. "Social Movements, Experiments in Living, and Moral Progress: Case Studies from Britain's Abolition of Slavery." *The Lindley Lecture*, 1–28. http://kuscholarworks.ku.edu/bitstream/handle/1808/14787/Anderson_Social_Movements.pdf.
Anderson, Elizabeth. 2014b. "The Quest for Free Labor: Pragmatism and Experiments in Emancipation." *The Amherst Lecture in Philosophy*, no. 9, 1–44. http://www.amherstlecture.org/anderson2014/anderson2014_ALP.pdf.
Anderson, Elizabeth. 2016. "The Social Epistemology of Morality: Learning from the Forgotten History of the Abolition of Slavery." In *The Epistemic Life of Groups: Essays in the Epistemology of Collectives*, edited by Miranda Fricker and Michael S. Brady, 75–94. New York: Oxford University Press.
Bloeser, Claudia and Titus Stahl. 2017. "Hope." In *The Stanford Encyclopedia of Philosophy*. Spring 2017 edition. https://plato.stanford.edu/archives/spr2017/entries/hope/.
Buchanan, Allen and Russell Powell. 2018. *The Evolution of Moral Progress: A Biocultural Theory*. New York: Oxford University Press.
Dewey, John. 2008. "The Public and Its Problems." In *The Later Works of John Dewey, 1925–1953, Vol 2: 1925–1927*, edited by Jo Ann Boydston, 235–372. Carbondale: Southern Illinois University Press.
Eisenstadt, Todd A., Carl A. LeVan, and Tofigh Maboudi. 2017. *Constituents Before Assembly: Participation, Deliberation, and Representation in the Crafting of New Constitutions*. New York: Cambridge University Press.
Gray, John. 2014. *The Silence of Animals: On Progress and Other Modern Myths*. New York: Farrar, Straus and Giroux.

Habermas, Jürgen. 1979. *Communication and the Evolution of Society*. Translated by Thomas McCarthy. Boston: Beacon Press.

Habermas, Jürgen. 1984. *The Theory of Communicative Action. Volume 1: Reason and the Rationalization of Society*. Translated by Thomas McCarthy. Boston: Beacon Press.

Habermas, Jürgen. 1987. *The Philosophical Discourse of Modernity: Twelve Lectures*. Translated by Frederick Lawrence. Cambridge, MA: The MIT Press.

Habermas, Jürgen. 1990. *Moral Consciousness and Communicative Action*. Translated by Christian Lenhardt and Shierry Weber Nicholsen. Cambridge, MA: The MIT Press.

Habermas, Jürgen. 2017. *The Idea of Socialism: Towards a Renewal*. Translated by Joseph Ganahal. Malden, MA: Polity Press.

Honneth, Axel. 2014. *Freedom's Right: The Social Foundations of Democratic Life*. Translated by Joseph Ganahal. Malden, MA: Polity Press.

Horkheimer, Max and Theodor W. Adorno. 2002. *Dialectic of Enlightenment: Philosophical Fragments*. Translated by Edmund Jephcott. Stanford, CA: Stanford University Press.

Jaeggi, Rahel. 2018a. *Critique of Forms of Life*. Translated by Ciaran Cronin. Cambridge, MA: Harvard University Press.

Jaeggi, Rahel. 2018b. "'Resistance to the Perpetual Danger of Relapse': Moral Progress and Social Change." In *From Alienation to Forms of Life: The Critical Theory of Rahel Jaeggi*, edited by Amy Allen and Eduardo Mendieta, 15–40. University Park, PA: The Pennsylvania State University Press.

Kitcher, Philip. 2011. *The Ethical Project*. Cambridge, MA: Harvard University Press.

Lenowitz, Jeffrey A. Forthcoming. *Why Ratification? Exploring an Unexamined Procedure*. Oxford University Press.

Lyotard, Jean-François. 1984. *The Postmodern Condition: A Report on Knowledge*. Translated by Geoff Bennington and Brian Massumi. Minneapolis: University of Minnesota Press.

MacIntyre, Alasdair. 1977. "Epistemological Crises, Dramatic Narrative and the Philosophy of Science." *The Monist* 60, no. 4: 453–72.

McCarthy, Thomas. 2009. *Race, Empire, and the Idea of Human Development*. New York: Cambridge University Press.

Müller, Jan-Werner. 2016. *What Is Populism?* Philadelphia, PA: University of Pennsylvania Press.

Singer, Peter. 2011. *The Expanding Circle: Ethics, Evolution, and Moral Progress*. Princeton, NJ: Princeton University Press.

Tierney, Stephen. 2012. *Constitutional Referendums: The Theory and Practice of Republican Deliberation*. Oxford: Oxford University Press.

Wagner, Peter. 2016. *Progress: A Reconstruction*. Malden, MA: Polity Press.

Zurn, Christopher F. 2013. "Political Civility: Another Idealistic Illusion." *Public Affairs Quarterly* 27, no. 4: 341–68.

Zurn, Christopher F. 2015. *Axel Honneth: A Critical Theory of the Social*. Cambridge: Polity Press.

Zurn, Christopher F. 2016a. "Democratic Constitutional Change: Assessing Institutional Possibilities." In *Democratizing Constitutional Law: Perspectives on Legal Theory and the Legitimacy of Constitutionalism*, edited by Thomas Bustamante and Bernardo Gonçalves Fernandes, 185–212. Cham, Switzerland: Springer Verlag.

Zurn, Christopher F. 2016b. "The Ends of Economic History: Alternative Teleologies and the Ambiguities of Normative Reconstruction." In *Die Philosophie des Marktes – The Philosophy of the Market*, edited by Hans-Christoph Schmidt am Busch, 289–323. Hamburg: Felix Meiner Verlag.

Zurn, Christopher F. Forthcoming. "Populism, Polarization, and Misrecognition." In *Recognition: Its Theory and Practice*, edited by Heikki Koskinen.

Chapter 17

Psychoanalysis and the Critique of Progress

Amy Allen

In his recent magisterial intellectual biography of Freud, Joel Whitebook distinguishes two strands of Freud's thinking, which he calls Freud's official and unofficial positions.[1] On Whitebook's interpretation, Freud's entire *oeuvre*, including his metapsychology and his contributions to social and cultural theory, is structured around the tension between these two positions. Whereas Freud's official position is Kantian, rationalist, pro-Enlightenment, and oriented towards the paternal and the Oedipal, his unofficial position is romantic, sceptical, Counter-Enlightenment, and oriented towards the maternal and the pre-Oedipal. Given the complex relationship between these two strands of Freud's thinking, Whitebook argues that Freud is best understood as a thinker of the "dark enlightenment," which he characterizes as a "deeper, conflicted, disconsolate, and even tragic yet still emancipatory tradition within the broader movement of the Enlightenment" (Whitebook 2017, 11). As a representative of this strand of the Enlightenment tradition, Freud took the claims of the Counter-Enlightenment seriously and, as Whitebook puts it, "attempted to integrate them into a chastened but radicalized defense of the Enlightenment" (ibid., 12).

Not surprisingly, given the centrality of the concept of progress to debates over the legacy of the Enlightenment, the question of progress is deeply implicated in this complex tension within Freud's thinking, although Whitebook doesn't fully draw out all of these implications. Freud's official position not only champions the Enlightenment virtues of rationality and autonomy, it also articulates a developmentalist story that links the ego's progressive mastery of the archaic forces of the id to the advance of civilization from "primitive" animism to scientific secularism. Moreover, these two stories are tightly linked via Freud's endorsement of the recapitulationist thesis developed by late nineteenth-century biologists working in the wake of Darwin: the claim that ontogeny – or the development of the individual – recapitulates phylogeny – the development of the species. As a result of Freud's endorsement of this thesis, his official position with regard to the psyche corresponds to a strong conception of civilizational development and progress. His unofficial position, by contrast, famously calls into question whether the ego can (or, more radically: should want to) be master of its own house and, relatedly, whether civilization is worth the high price that it necessarily exacts in the form of renunciation of instinct and resulting decrease in happiness.

However, the problem of progress cuts even deeper than this. Freud's official position is not only – arguably, at least – insufficiently tragic, it is also deeply implicated in racist modes of developmental thinking that were imported into Freudian theory through his reliance on the evolutionary anthropology and biology of his time, all of which crystallize in the problematic figure of "the primitive." Although Whitebook acknowledges and condemns the "Eurocentric Whiggishness" (ibid., 310) of Freud's social and cultural theory, he does not directly confront the developmental racism that pervades his official position.[2] Indeed, he insists that the core of Freud's developmental-historical claim – that Enlightenment secularism represents a civilizational advance – can be stripped of its Eurocentrism and ought to be defended, albeit in a modified form. Although I have no intention of suggesting that we should dismiss psychoanalysis on account of the undeniably racist elements of Freudian theory, I do want to argue that if psychoanalysis is to be a productive resource for critical theory, critical theorists will have to grapple with its residual developmental racism. Furthermore, I contend that this goal can be accomplished by drawing on and developing further the implications of what Whitebook calls Freud's unofficial position. However, this minor strand of Freud's thinking actually goes much further in subverting the notion of civilizational progress than Whitebook admits. Freud's unofficial position, as I reconstruct it, not only reminds us that what we think of as progress is always ambiguous inasmuch as it always comes at a cost, and one that we might well find too high to bear,[3] it ultimately undermines the very point of view from which judgements about civilizational progress could be made in the first place. Whereas Whitebook maintains that the core of Freud's developmentalism can be maintained while jettisoning its Eurocentric overtones, I argue: first, that, given the meaning of "the primitive" and the centrality of this figure to Freudian theory, this is significantly more difficult to accomplish than Whitebook realizes; and, second, that Whitebook's approach underplays the radicality of Freud's unofficial position, which is subversive of progressive, developmental models of the self and of civilization.

PSYCHE AND CIVILIZATION: OFFICIALLY AND UNOFFICIALLY

What Whitebook calls the official and unofficial positions are first and foremost ways of reading Freudian metapsychology. For the official position, the starting point for the development of the subject is a self-enclosed psyche governed solely by the logic of the pleasure principle.[4] Key to this conception of the psyche are the related distinctions between the pleasure and reality principles, on the one hand, and primary and secondary processes, on the other. Governed by the pleasure principle, primary processes are so called because they are the "residues of a phase of development in which they were the only kind of mental process" (Whitebook 2017, 219). In this phase, whatever needs may arise internally are satisfied, Freud explains, "in a hallucinatory manner, just as still happens to-day with our dream-thoughts every night" (ibid.). In other words, the psyche governed by primary process is monadic, self-contained, and capable of self-satisfaction. Although Freud acknowledges that this sounds like a fictitious construct, for any such creature could not survive for very long, if it could even come into being in the first place, he nevertheless maintains that the infant taken together with its primary caregiver – a significant caveat that I will return to below – can be understood in this way. Although (and on the condition that) the infant receives care and help in meeting its needs from its caregiver, it experiences the satisfaction of those needs as the result of its own activity – for example, its having screamed or kicked its arms and legs (ibid., 220). It is only when the infant's needs go unsatisfied, when it experiences disappointment and thus the failure of its hallucinatory sense of omnipotence, that the psyche begins the painful turn towards reality.

The official position is, then, a story of separation and opposition between a monadic, self-enclosed subject and the external reality whose demands he must learn, begrudgingly, to acknowledge and accept. On this conception, the primary functions of the ego are those of defence against the harsh demands of the reality principle and mediation between external reality and internal drive for pleasure. Given its focus on bringing the pleasure principle to heel under the demands of the reality principle, the official position conceives of psychological maturity or development as the progressive mastery or domination of instinctual demands. On this picture, as Whitebook explains, "the ego dominates the id, consciousness dominates the unconscious, realistic thinking dominates fantasy thinking, cognition dominates affect, activity dominates passivity, and the civilized part of the personality dominates the instincts" (ibid., 162).

Whitebook delineates three criticisms of Freud's official meta-psychological position. First, there is the conceptual worry that it is far from clear that

Freud can explain the turn to reality – and thus also to object-relatedness – given the starting point of a self-enclosed, monadic psyche.[5] If the psyche is really completely self-contained at the start, then how can it in fact experience the disappointment that motivates its turn to reality? How is disappointment able to pierce the subject's veil of monadic self-sufficiency? And insofar as the infant is able to experience disappointment, then can the psyche ever truly have been self-contained in the first place? The very fact that Freud notes that the infant can be viewed as a self-enclosed psyche *only when taken together with a maternal caregiver* suggests that there is a deep conceptual problem here. Second, the official position leads Freud to claim that the work of psychoanalysis (and also of civilization) can be likened to what he called the "draining of the Zuider Zee" (Freud [1933a] 2001, 80). This image suggests to Whitebook a highly unrealistic conception of psychic maturity understood as "a state where all the 'primitive' sludge of unconscious-instinctual life has been dredged out of mental life" (Whitebook 2017, 163). Third, the official position leads Freud to suggest that what he calls a "dictatorship of reason" represents a laudable, even if impossibly utopian, ideal (Freud (1933b) 2001, 213). Whitebook finds it remarkable that Freud would make such a claim – "as though he was totally unaware of the critique of reason to which he had made such a substantial contribution" (Whitebook 2017, 163). However, his official position presents an image of a monadic, isolated core of the psyche governed by the pleasure principle that must be progressively mastered and dominated by the ego. On this picture, the rational ego not only can but also should achieve a position of complete mastery over the unconscious, affective, irrational, instinctual, and "primitive" dimensions of psychic life, and the goal of psychoanalysis is to help individuals establish and maintain this dictatorship of reason.

However, as Freud himself famously argued in other parts of his work, the complete domination of inner nature – the ego's mastery of its own house – is not only impossible but perhaps even undesirable. And this insight brings us to Freud's unofficial position, which is already implicit in Whitebook's critique of the official position – indeed, it arguably serves as the tacit point of view from which that critique is launched. According to the unofficial position, psychic life begins in a state of unity or fusion with the primary caregiver (ibid., 163–164).[6] On the unofficial view, the function of the ego is not mastery and domination of the instincts but rather synthesis and integration. As Whitebook explains, the ego's function consists in "preserving the material of unconscious-instinctual life and holding it together, synthesizing it into larger and more differentiated unities" (ibid., 164).[7] The strength of the ego is thus measured not in terms of its ability to master, repress, and dominate, but rather as a function of its capacity for "expansion, greater integration, and differentiation of its associative web" (ibid., 154).

Although Whitebook's primary interest in sketching the outlines of the unofficial position is to analyse the role of the maternal and pre-Oedipal in Freud's thinking, along the way he gives some indication of how this distinction plays out in Freud's social and cultural theory, particularly with respect to the concept of progress. Whitebook never explicitly draws out the implications of Freud's unofficial position for his social theory, but he does note that the official position on psychic development finds its analogue in Freud's account of civilizational development as a process leading from "primitive" animistic cultures through religious societies to civilizations governed by secular, scientific views, a process that Freud explicitly links with the developmental trajectory from narcissism through object love to Oedipalization.[8] Here we can see the cultural analogues of the draining of the Zuider Zee and dictatorship of reason metaphors. According to Freud's official position, civilizational progress consists in a teleological development in which "primitive" stages are superseded and eliminated by more "advanced" stages. Through this process, the "primitive" sludge of animistic, magical, or illusory systems of thought are purged from cultures and mature, rational, secular science installed in their place.

As I indicated above, Whitebook acknowledges that this developmentalist picture is problematic not least for its "Eurocentric Whiggishness" and naivete (ibid., 310). In addition, he identifies two further problems with this conception of civilizational progress. First, Freud frequently displays the – deeply ironic – tendency to declare the triumph of science over omnipotence in a triumphalist, dogmatic, indeed, omnipotent fashion. In order to be internally consistent, Whitebook notes, Freud's opposition to magical thinking and the overcoming of omnipotence would have to be articulated in a non-omnipotent manner – that is, in a way that acknowledges the fallibilism, incompleteness, and perhaps even inevitable distortions of the scientific point of view (ibid., 400–401). Second, Whitebook wonders whether the demand that we overcome omnipotence by resigning ourselves to the painful reality of our finitude and insignificance might not itself be too demanding and thus, in a surprising twist, too utopian. Although resignation to our finitude is presented as the ultimate anti-utopian stance – as the clear-eyed rejection of the dangerous illusions of wishful thinking – perhaps it is just too difficult for creatures like us. Ironically, again, the very modesty of Freud's vision of how we should live, its emphasis on resignation and the acceptance of our finitude, is precisely what makes it so difficult for "creatures like us – with our incorrigible propensity for omnipotence, grandiosity, and magic – to realize this goal" (ibid., 401).

Nevertheless, Whitebook insists that there is a "valid kernel" to Freud's official position on civilizational progress that is worth defending and preserving. "When we strip away the Eurocentrism and the teleological philosophy of history," Whitebook writes, "this is what remains: For Freud, the goal – in science, life, and psychoanalytic treatment – is to master omnipotence and accept *Ananke* to the extent that is possible for finite creatures like us" (ibid., 310–311). The kernel of both civilizational and psychological maturity for Freud is the overcoming of omnipotence and the acceptance of our helplessness and insignificance (ibid., 394). Although Whitebook never quite states this claim explicitly, this demand that we accept our finitude and overcome omnipotence seems to entail a civilizational analogue to Whitebook's unofficial position on the psyche. If the unofficial position views psychic development not as a progressive process of rational mastery of the "primitive" instincts, but rather as the establishment of "free intercourse" between the more advanced and primitive layers of the psyche (ibid., 420), it views civilizational development in an analogous way. Without ceding any claim about the developmental superiority of secular, scientific, rationalized cultures, Whitebook's unofficial civilizational position suggests that more advanced societies should present their critique of "primitive" or religious cultures in a non-dominating and non-omnipotent – chastened, open-minded, non-dogmatic – way, one that facilitates "free intercourse" between advanced and "primitive" or "traditional" cultures.[9]

Notice, however, that this way of understanding the unofficial position retains the distinction between the advanced and primitive, implying a residual developmental claim. This, in turn, fits with Whitebook's defence of the core of Freud's civilizational argument, the part that he claims remains after the Whiggish Eurocentrism has been stripped away: namely, the idea that a culture of scientific secularism represents an important developmental advance over cultures animated by omnipotence, religious myth, and magical thinking. As such, we might well wonder whether Whitebook's – admittedly never fully articulated – account of the civilizational analogue of Freud's unofficial position goes far enough. After all, the problem with Freud's official position on civilizational development and progress is not *just* that it articulates the demand to overcome omnipotence in an omnipotent and unrealistic way. The problem is *also* that the very conception of civilizational maturity and development that Whitebook seeks to preserve and defend rests on a problematic conception of "the primitive" that is deeply embedded in a Eurocentric and racist developmental story. Although Whitebook condemns Freud's Eurocentric Whiggishness, he seems overly confident that a more modest and chastened model of civilizational development can, in fact, survive the attempt to strip Freud's official position of its Eurocentric racism. Contra Whitebook, I maintain *both* that actually stripping Freud's official position of its Eurocentric racism requires a more radical critique of progressive, developmental notions of civilization *and* that Freud's unofficial position on progress points in precisely this direction.

FREUD AND "THE PRIMITIVE"

As Celia Brickman has argued convincingly, the idea of "the primitive," far from being "a long-abandoned relic of anthropology's colonial ancestry," is in fact alive and well in psychoanalysis, where it refers first and foremost to "the raw and the rudimentary, the undeveloped, the archaic" that is, to "characteristics of infants and regressive episodes in adults" (Brickman 2002, 1–2). Although one might be tempted to dismiss this as an idiosyncratic usage that carries no racialized subtext, Brickman's work demonstrates exhaustively and in painstaking detail that this is not the case. The notion of "the primitive" in Freud's writings is deeply bound up with the racist and colonialist discourses of evolutionary anthropology on which he drew for his own social and cultural theory. For Freud, the term "primitive" refers *both* to the earliest and most basic stages of psychic development *and* to so-called savages taken to be, from a civilizational perspective, less mature or advanced than Europeans (ibid., 4–5). Indeed, Freud repeatedly ascribes the simplest, most rudimentary, and most archaic modes of psychological functioning not only to infants but also to "so-called primitive people of all ages" (ibid., 16). In virtue of this dual ascription, the term "primitive" functions as much more than a neutral psychoanalytic term that assesses levels or modes of psychic development; it simultaneously encodes a judgement about the developmental superiority of modern European subjects over what it takes to be "savage" or "primitive" cultural others (ibid.). Even when it is deployed in a purely psychoanalytic register to refer to a level of the psyche, the idea of the primitive thus carries this "covert racializing subtext" (ibid., 4).

At the core of Freud's conception of the primitive lies the recapitulation thesis: the claim that ontogeny recapitulates phylogeny. This thesis was propounded by Ernst Haeckel, a nineteenth-century German zoologist best known as a popularizer of Darwin, first and foremost as a (long since discredited) evolutionary-biological claim to the effect that the embryological development of the organism repeats the evolutionary history of the species. When taken up in the register of social theory, the recapitulationist thesis became a claim about individual and civilizational development, encapsulated in the idea that "the human child would recapitulate the history of the human race" (ibid., 45). According to this thesis, the development of the individual and the evolution of civilizations converge on the idea of the primitive, understood as that which stands at the beginning of both trajectories. Acceptance of this thesis produced two corollaries, both of which became fundamental premises of socio-evolutionary thinking: first, the belief that contemporary "primitives" or "savages" were living in the European past; and, second, the related methodological assumption that details about the prehistory of Europe could be ascertained through the study of contemporary indigenous peoples, and vice versa (ibid., 69).

The extensive influence of the recapitulation thesis on Freud's official position in social and cultural theory is most strikingly evident in the opening lines of *Totem and Taboo*, which are worth quoting in full:

> Prehistoric man, in the various stages of his development, is known to us through the inanimate monuments and implements which he has left behind, through the information about his art, his religion and his attitude towards life which has come to us either directly or by way of tradition handed down in legends, myths and fairy tales, and through the relics of his mode of thought which survive in our own manners and customs. But apart from this, in a certain sense he is still our contemporary. There are men still living who, as we believe, stand very near to primitive man, far nearer than we do, and whom we therefore regard as his direct heirs and representatives. Such is our view of those whom we describe as savages or half-savages; and their mental life must have a peculiar interest for us if we are right in seeing in it a well-preserved picture of an early stage of our own development. (Freud [1913] 2001, 1)

Here we have a clear statement of the first premise: that contemporary "savages" are "direct heirs or representatives" of "primitive man," and that as such they provide us with an image of "our" own prehistory. This claim, in turn, serves as the basis for Freud's adoption of the second premise, which is a version of what was known in anthropology as the comparative method (ibid.). Despite Freud's occasional methodological cautions regarding the possible distortions that might creep into our perceptions of "primitive" groups and our resulting interpretations of prehistory,[10] Freud puts the comparative method to expansive use. For example, famously resolving to focus on "the most backward and miserable of savages, the aborigines of Australia" (ibid.), Freud argues in the first essay of *Totem and Taboo* that the horror of incest among "primitives" is an infantile psychic state that is also commonly found in neurotics (ibid., 17). Similarly, in the second essay, he connects the operation of taboos in "primitive" cultures with the behaviour of obsessional neurotics, even going so far as to suggest that obsessional neurosis could just as easily be called "taboo sickness" (ibid.). The comparative method is deployed still more fully in the third essay, where Freud links the evolutionary anthropological thesis that the human race has developed through three stages or systems of thought – from animism (or myth) through religion to science – to the psychic development of the individual from infantile narcissism through Oedipal object choice to the resolution of the Oedipal crisis, the renunciation of the pleasure principle, and the resignation to an often painful reality (ibid., 90). In this way, as Brickman puts it, "libidinal development recapitulated the evolutionary scale" (Brickman 2003, 70).

Perhaps the most striking example of Freud's use of the comparative method is found in his account of the origin of totemism in the fourth essay of *Totem and Taboo*.[11] Based on his earlier analysis of animal phobias, which Freud had already concluded signal a fear of the father, Freud reasons via the comparative method that the father can be substituted for the totem animal in totemic systems of thought (Freud [1913] 2001, 131). This speculative assumption allows Freud to fill in crucial gaps in the existing social-anthropological research into the origins of totemism: if the totem animal and the father are functionally the same, then the two principal prohibitions that constitute the core of totemism – the prohibitions on killing the totem and on having sexual relations with women of the same totem clan – can be seen to coincide with "the two crimes of Oedipus" (ibid., 132). This in turn enables Freud to understand the rootedness of totemism, the origins of which are otherwise shrouded in an inaccessibly remote past, in the Oedipal situation. It is thus only by means of the comparative method that Freud is able to arrive at his famous hypothesis of the transition from the primal horde to the band of brothers via the murder of the primal father (ibid., 141–142). The basic argument of *Totem and Taboo* is repeated throughout most of Freud's contributions to social and cultural theory, from his major work of social psychology (*Group Psychology and the Analysis of the Ego*) which likens the group mind to that of children and "primitives" to his critique of religion (*The Future of an Illusion*), which offers arguably the most triumphalist and, in Whitebook's terms, omnipotent version of Freud's official position on civilizational development.

Although Brickman does not distinguish explicitly between Freud's official and unofficial positions on social and cultural development or progress, a version of this distinction hovers in the background of her discussion. Thus, as much effort as she devotes to tracking the influence of racialized models of civilizational development on Freud's account of the primitive, she also maintains that his account was more complex and ambivalent than the evolutionary anthropological model on which it was based. For Freud, unlike for the evolutionary anthropologists, "primitive stages along the evolutionary trajectory of the mind did not disappear as they were superseded but endured in the unconscious, capable of resurfacing at any moment in dreams or symptoms and of threatening to disturb the achievements of the civilized psyche" (Brickman 2003, 80). Thus, Brickman maintains, Freud's deployment of primitivity was highly ambivalent, both a universal feature of all human psyches and an evolutionarily prior and thus racially indexed category (ibid., 52). Contra Whitebook, for whom Freud's official position rests on not only the supersession but also the elimination of earlier, more "primitive" psychic and cultural forms, Brickman contends that even in his most developmentalist moments – and precisely as a result of the interlocking psychic and civilizational aspects of "primitivity" – Freud was mindful of the impossibility of this task. Thus, on her reading, even Freud's official position is less triumphalist than it might at first seem. On the flip side, however, she also reminds us that insofar as Freud's trenchant critique of European civilization consists in pointing out the persistence and ineliminability of "primitive" psychic and social forces in mature individuals and civilizations, it, too, rests on racially indexed notions of civilizational development. To the extent that this is the case, Brickman maintains that the "emancipatory intent of Freud's project" is "racially ambiguous" (ibid., 5).

Brickman's analysis not only complicates Whitebook's distinction between the official and unofficial positions – suggesting what we might call an "unofficial" aspect of the official story – it also reveals the degree to which Freud's Eurocentric Whiggishness pervades not just the official position but also Whitebook's version of the unofficial position as well. Inasmuch as the latter remains committed to defending the developmental model of civilization as the overcoming of omnipotence – in however chastened, modest, and fallibilist a manner – it remains mired in the racialized notions of primitivity that Brickman's work painstakingly exposes. Stripping away Freud's Eurocentric Whiggishness thus requires a much deeper and more radical challenge to his official position – perhaps even one that challenges the very interlocking of developmentalist conceptions of individual and civilization – than Whitebook seems to realize.

FREUD'S UNOFFICIAL POSITION ON CIVILIZATION AND PROGRESS

The foregoing discussion reveals a number of hurdles that a psychoanalytic critique of progress and civilizational development would need to clear. If it is to come to terms with its residual developmental racism discussed, such a critique would have to go beyond Whitebook's post-secular defence of the developmental, social-evolutionary model of civilization. It would also have to go beyond questioning whether or not civilization is worth the effort required to sustain it and pointing out that "primitive" modes of experience continue to exist alongside more mature developmental forms, at both the individual and the cultural levels. Why is this so? Because all of these critiques of the notion of civilizational progress retain, whether explicitly or implicitly, a commitment to the superiority of modern, secular, scientific, rational forms of life and subjectivity and the concomitant devaluation of "primitive" forms of life and experience. To truly break free of the racialized subtext of the notion of "the primitive," a psychoanalytic critique of progress would need to break with such developmental-historical modes of thinking altogether. As I see it, Freud's unofficial position on civilization and progress – which emerges in his late masterpiece, *Civilization and Its Discontents* – provides the outlines for just such a critique. Once the critique of progress in this text is reconstructed, we will be able to see that Freud's unofficial position on civilization is much more radical than Whitebook acknowledges, insofar as it entails not so much the cultural pessimism that is typically attributed to the late Freud but rather a radical epistemological challenge to the very idea of progress as a way of reading the history of societies and cultures.

The recently discovered the death drive, that "piece of unconquerable nature" that places us at odds with the demands and constraints of civilization and thus explains our persistent unhappiness (Freud [1930] 2001, 86), has profound implications for Freud's thinking about progress in *Civilization and Its Discontents*, but these emerge slowly over the course of Freud's discussion and are not fully visible until the closing pages. Indeed, the text opens with a definition of civilization that recalls Freud's official position. Civilization, Freud writes, refers to "the whole sum of the achievements and the regulations which distinguish our lives from those of our animal ancestors and which serve two purposes – namely to protect men against nature and to adjust their mutual relations" (ibid., 86). It is a human achievement that sets us apart from nature through the progressive mastery and control of nature – both inner and outer – and of each other. As a mechanism of control or mastery, civilization is antithetical to freedom or liberty, in particular the freedom to satisfy one's basic drives in an unimpeded manner. Because freedom of this sort inevitably leads to conflicts, civilization requires – indeed, to a large extent, consists in – submitting these drives to the control of the "higher psychical agencies, which have subjected themselves to the reality principle" (ibid., 79).

However, not all drives are created equal when it comes to their potential to create conflict and their need to be mastered by civilization. Although Freud starts his discussion with the conflict between the pleasure principle and the demands of civilization, as the discussion goes on, it becomes clear that the real problems arise *beyond* the pleasure principle. Love or Eros – defined by Freud as the drive to "preserve living substance and to join it into ever larger units" (ibid., 118) – is one of the foundations of civilization; insofar as its function is to bind people together into unities, Eros is pro-civilization, prosocial. To be sure, conflicts arise between particular sexual or family unions and the needs of the larger civilization; still, at the most basic level and in the broadest sense, there is no necessary conflict between Eros and civilization. The central conflict between the drives and the demands of civilization is rooted not in Eros but in the death drive. Civilization requires affective, even erotic, bonds and cooperative relationships between large groups of individuals, while the death drive constitutes an opposing force to Eros, perpetually disrupting our relations with other human being and threatening civilization with disintegration (ibid., 112).

To be sure, Freud maintains that civilization has means at its disposal to inhibit or at the very least redirect the aggressive instincts. By far the most effective of the means that it employs to this end is the development of the superego, which is formed through the introjection or internalization of aggression. Through this process, aggressiveness takes the form of "conscience," enacting "the same harsh aggressiveness that the ego would have liked to satisfy upon other, extraneous individuals" (ibid., 123). Through the constitution of the superego, civilization "obtains mastery over the individual's dangerous desire for aggression by weakening and disarming it and by setting up an agency within him to watch over it, like a garrison in a conquered city" (ibid., 123–124). With the development of the superego comes the sense of guilt; indeed, Freud goes so far as to identify "the sense of guilt as the most important problem in the development of civilization" and to conclude that "the price we pay for our advance in civilization is a loss of happiness through the heightening of the sense of guilt" (ibid., 134). This leads Freud to critique both the individual superego and the "cultural superego" of ethics and to suggest that the point of psychoanalysis is to work, both therapeutically and culturally, to loosen their excessive, unfulfillable demands (ibid., 142–143).

It is here, at the end of Freud's text, that the various scattered clues as to Freud's unofficial position on civilization and progress are gathered together into a coherent statement. Freud first notes that he has attempted to be impartial in his analysis of civilization, to be swayed neither by a prejudice of its favour, according to which civilization is viewed as the path to perfection, nor by the reverse assumption that civilization creates intolerable forms of constraint and is overall not worth the monumental effort required to hold it in place. "My impartiality," he notes wryly, "is made all the easier to me by my knowing very little about these things. One thing only do I know for certain and that is that man's judgments of value follow directly his wishes for happiness – that, accordingly, they are an attempt to support his illusions with arguments" (ibid., 144). To those who would find his analysis of civilization disheartening or devoid of solutions, Freud admits that he "can offer them no consolation" (ibid.). All that he can do is to pose what he calls "the fateful question for the human species," namely: "Whether and to what extent their cultural development will succeed in mastering the disturbance of their communal life by the human instinct of aggression and self-destruction" and, we might add, at what cost (ibid.).

What Freud sketches in these closing pages is a non-teleological, non-developmental, non-progressive way of reading history, a reading that remains agnostic not only on the question of whether the achievements of civilization are worth the repression and internalized domination necessary to achieve them, but also on the question of whether they constitute progress in any meaningful sense. In stark contrast not only to his official position but also to Whitebook's more chastened, humble, and post-secular version of the unofficial position, Freud here declines to offer any defence, however modest, of the achievements of civilization in general or of modern, secular, scientific, enlightenment rationalism in particular. Moreover, by taking this position, Freud is simply consistently following out the logic of his own argument. His conception of the death drive and its role in the generation of the superego leads him to locate the very foundation of morality in the aggressiveness of the superego. As such, for the late Freud as much as for Nietzsche, the roots of morality are "soaked in blood thoroughly and for a long time" (Nietzsche 1989, 65). With this conception of morality, Freud thus implicitly calls into question the very possibility of a context-transcendent normative point of view from which something could be identified as a civilizational or developmental advance at all – at least if advance is here understood in normative terms. As he says, we have to be "careful not to fall in line with the prejudice that civilization is synonymous with perfecting, that it is the road to perfection pre-ordained for men" (Freud [1930] 2001, 96). We have to be careful, too, of the extent to which our backward-looking, historical judgements about what constitutes progress and whether it has been achieved up to now, in the historical process that has led to our own civilization, are simply, as Freud might have said, an attempt to support our harmonistic illusions with arguments.

So, what then is Freud's unofficial stance towards civilization and progress? I agree with Whitebook that Freud is best understood as a thinker of the radical or dark enlightenment, but I would characterize the implications of this stance for his conception of progress differently. Freud's unofficial position as articulated in *Civilization and Its Discontents* consists in a tragic, unreconciled account of the conflicts between the death drive and the demands and constraints of civilization. This account is offered in the service of unsettling our harmonistic illusions by problematizing our own tendency towards complacent and self-congratulatory conceptions of progress. To say that Freud's late vision is tragic is not to say that he believes that moral or political progress is in principle impossible. Rather, it is tragic precisely because of its unreconciled reading of history, that is, its refusal to take sides with either the cheerleaders or the enemies of civilization, with either the defenders or the critics of Enlightenment. Freud's profession of impartiality on the question of whether civilization is the best thing that ever happened to us or not worth all the effort suggests precisely this: *any* attempt to read history as having a clear normative direction, whether that direction is construed progressively or regressively, constitutes an attempt to support one's illusions – be they optimistic or pessimistic – with arguments.

Insofar as Freud's unofficial position on civilization subverts or undermines the very idea of reading history in terms of progress, it entails a much more radical break from his official position than Whitebook imagines. However, precisely in virtue of its radical subversion of the progressive-developmental conception of history that undergirds theories of social evolution, Freud's unofficial position also points beyond the racialized conception of primitivity in which his official position – and Whitebook's formulation of the unofficial position – remains mired. More radically still, by undermining the conception of freestanding normativity from which judgements of civilizational progress would have to be made through his revelation of the rootedness of normativity in aggression, Freud's unofficial position provides the resources for a powerful psychoanalytic critique of the pernicious racialized legacy of the notion of historical progress. In his unofficial position, Freud not only reveals the source of the aggression and violence bottled up within judgements of relative civilizational value, he also holds up an unflattering mirror to the desire to sustain European modernity's self-congratulatory illusions of cultural superiority and progress with social-evolutionary arguments.[12]

CONCLUSION

Freud's unofficial position on civilization seems to many readers to come at the very high cost of leaving him mired in a conservative cultural pessimism that denies the possibility of any meaningful improvement in the human condition.[13] Although I don't think that this follows from his argument, I don't have time to pursue that thought here. For now, though, I want to focus on one complication that emerges in the course of Whitebook's discussion of this issue. Whitebook not only describes the late Freud as a cultural pessimist, he also attributes Freud's pessimism to his acceptance of the official position on the psyche (Whitebook 2016, 160). The thought here is that Freud's pessimism about progress is rooted in his conception of the psyche as founded on structures of repression and internalized domination made necessary by the deep, intractable conflict between the drives and the demands of civilization – that is, precisely, in his official position on the psyche. As I've already suggested, I think there is more motivating what I would characterize not as Freud's pessimism but rather as his scepticism about progress than simply the point about internalized domination, but there's no doubt that the latter is an important aspect of Freud's story, even as I've presented it. So, what gives?

Why would Freud present the clearest statement of his unofficial position on progress in the context of a staunch and uncompromising version of his official position on the psyche? Does this admission not undermine my reading of *Civilization and Its Discontents* as a statement of Freud's unofficial position on civilization? Not necessarily. At the risk of pointing out the obvious, the distinction between official and unofficial positions is not one that is explicit in Freud's work, and what Whitebook calls his unofficial position on the psyche is never worked out in the kind of depth and detail that marks his account of the official position. This is even more true of his unofficial position on civilizational progress, which is admittedly only a minor theme as compared to the bulk of his work in social and cultural theory. Perhaps, just as Freud struggled through much of his late work to incorporate his discovery of the death drive into his theory, he never fully realized the implications of his critique of civilizational progress, which, by undermining the phylogenetic logic that underpins the recapitulationist thesis, calls for a reconceptualization of the psyche that does away with developmental models altogether.[14]

NOTES

1. Earlier versions of this chapter were presented at Concordia University, the Oakley Center for the Humanities at Williams College, the Universidad Autónoma Metropolitana, Mexico City, and as the SPEP lecture at the Eastern APA. I am grateful to audiences on those occasions, and especially to Jana Sawicki, María Pía Lara, and Noëlle McAfee for their helpful comments and suggestions.

2. Indeed, although the issue of what to make of Freud's commitment to a racist and Eurocentric notion of civilizational progress and development has been widely discussed in the literature on psychoanalysis and race, it has been strikingly absent from Frankfurt School critical theorists' engagements with psychoanalysis. This chapter is the beginning of an attempt to correct for that silence.

3. On this point, see Whitebook's critique of *Moses and Monotheism*, in which, he argues, "The concept of Geistigkeit is too uncritical and affirmative – indeed, too un-analytic – and contains more than a whiff of sanctimony and self-satisfaction .... The 'third ear' of every self-respecting analyst should perk up at the mention of Fortschritt, for, as Freud taught us, there is no unambiguous progress in psychic life or in cultural history. Every advance exacts its price" (Whitebook 2017, 445–446). For a more positive assessment of Freud's argument in *Moses and Monotheism*, see Zaretsky (2015, ch. 3).

4. For a synoptic overview of this account of the psyche, see Freud ([1911] 2001).

5. See Whitebook (2017, 298); and Laplanche (1989, 75).

6. Whitebook tends to refer to this primary caregiver, a bit too unreflectively for my taste, as "the archaic mother." In order to avoid the essentializing and potentially ideological implications of the unproblematized use of such a term, and in recognition of the fact that the maternal function may be filled by a person who is neither a

biological parent nor a woman, I will strive to use the term "primary caregiver" when speaking in my own voice, though I will leave the terminology unchanged when quoting Whitebook and others.

7. In other words, the ego's function is essentially erotic – in the specific sense that Freud uses the term "Eros" in his late work to refer to the drive to bind things together into greater unities (see Freud [1930] 2001).

8. See, most infamously, Freud ([1913] 2001), (discussed further below).

9. As far as I can see, this brings Whitebook quite close to Habermas's recent work on post-secularism – which is surprising, given his trenchant critiques of Habermas. See, for example, Whitebook (1996). For critical discussion of Habermas's post-secular turn, see Calhoun/Mendieta/Van Antwerpen (2013).

10. For example, a footnote in the early pages of the first essay concludes with the line: "The difficulty ... is to decide whether we should regard the present state of things as a true picture of the significant features of the past or as a secondary distortion of them" (Freud [1913] 2001, 4). A similar caution appears in a later footnote: "It is never possible to decide without hesitation how far their present-day conditions and opinions preserve the primeval past in a petrified form and how far they are distortions and modifications of it" (ibid., 103).

11. Freud bases his account of the primal horde on his reading of Darwin, but the idea seems to be much more Freud's than Darwin's. See Richard Smith (2016, 838–843).

12. This might help to explain the otherwise apparently paradoxical conjunction of Freud's own embrace of developmental racism and the productivity of his theory for critical theories of race and racism, a conjunction that is noted repeatedly in the literature on psychoanalysis and race/colonialism. See Brickman (2003); Khanna (2003); and Lane (1998).

13. See, for example, Whitebook's contention that *Civilization and Its Discontents* "poses a seemingly insurmountable challenge to any progressivist desire to substantially transform modern society and ameliorate humanity's situation in modernity" because its primary lesson is that "the *telos* of modernity is a dead-end" (Whitebook 2016, 252).

14. As I argue in more detail elsewhere, in both of these respects, Melanie Klein represents Freud's most important successor. See Amy Allen, *Critique on the couch: Why Critical Theory Needs Psychoanalysis* (forthcoming).

BIBLIOGRAPHY

Allen, Amy. Forthcoming. Critique on the Couch: Why Critical Theory *Needs Psychoanalysis*. New York: Columbia University Press.

Brickman, Celia. 2003. *Aboriginal Populations in the Mind: Race and Primitivity in Psychoanalysis*. New York: Columbia University Press.

Calhoun, Craig, Eduardo Mendieta, and Jonathan Van Antwerpen, eds. 2013. *Habermas and Religion*. Cambridge: Polity Press.

Freud, Sigmund. 2001 (1911). "Formulations on the Two Principles of Mental Functioning," in *The Standard Edition of the Complete Psychological Works of Sigmund Freud*, volume XII (1911–1913), trans. James Strachey. London: Vintage.

———. 2001 (1913). *Totem and Taboo*, in *The Standard Edition of the Complete Psychological Works of Sigmund Freud*, volume XIV (1914–1916), trans. James Strachey. London: Vintage.

———. 2001 (1930). *Civilization and Its Discontents*, in *The Standard Edition of the Complete Psychological Works of Sigmund Freud*, volume XXI (1927–1931), trans. James Strachey. London: Vintage.

———. 2001 (1933a). *New Introductory Lectures on Psychoanalysis*, in *The Standard Edition of the Complete Psychological Works of Sigmund Freud*, volume XXII (1932–1936), trans. James Strachey. London: Vintage.

———. 2001 (1933b). "Why War?" in *The Standard Edition of the Complete Psychological Works of Sigmund Freud*, volume XXII (1932–1936), trans. James Strachey. London: Vintage.

Khanna, Ranjana. 2003. *Dark Continents: Psychoanalysis and Colonialism.* Durham, NC: Duke University Press.

Lane, Christopher, ed. 1998. *The Psychoanalysis of Race*. New York: Columbia University Press.

Laplanche, Jean. 1989. *New Foundations for Psychoanalysis*, trans. David Macey. New York: Basil Blackwell.

Nietzsche, Friedrich. 1989. *On the Genealogy of Morals* in *On the Genealogy of Morals and Ecce Homo*. New York: Vintage.

Smith, Richard. 2016. "Darwin, Freud, and the Continuing Misrepresentation of the Primal Horde." *Current Anthropology* 57, no. 6 (December 2016): 838–843.

Whitebook, Joel. 1996 *Perversion and Utopia: An Essay on Psychoanalysis and Critical Theory*. Cambridge: MIT Press.

———. 2017. *Freud: An Intellectual Biography*. Cambridge: Cambridge University Press.

Zaretsky, Eli. 2015. *Political Freud: A History*. New York: Columbia University Press.

About the Contributors and Editors

AUTHORS

Amy Allen is Liberal Arts Professor of Philosophy and Women's, Gender and Sexuality Studies at the Department of Philosophy of Pennsylvania State University.

Seyla Benhabib is Eugene Meyer Professor of Political Science and Professor of Philosophy at Yale University.

Robin Celikates is Professor of Practical Philosophy at Free University Berlin.

Didier Fassin is James D. Wolfensohn Professor of Social Science at the Institute for Advanced Studies in Princeton.

Rainer Forst is Professor of Political Theory and Philosophy at Goethe University Frankfurt.

Raymond Geuss is Emeritus Professor in the Faculty of Philosophy at Cambridge University.

Martin Hartmann is Professor of Philosophy at the University of Lucerne.

Sally Haslanger is Ford Professor of Philosophy and Women's & Gender Studies at the Massachusetts Institute of Technology.

Bruno Karsenti is Professor of Philosophy at the École des Hautes Études en Sciences Sociales in Paris.

Philip Kitcher is John Dewey Professor of Philosophy at Columbia University in New York.

Christoph Menke is Professor of Practical Philosophy at Goethe University Frankfurt.

David Miller is Professor of Political Theory at Oxford University.

Frederick Neuhouser is professor of Philosophy and Viola Manderfeld Professor of German at Barnard College of Columbia University in New York.

Beate Roessler is Professor of Ethics at the University of Amsterdam.

Martin Saar is Professor of Social Philosophy at Goethe University Frankfurt.

Joel Whitebook is a faculty member of the Columbia University Center for Psychoanalytic Training and Research.

Christopher F. Zurn is Professor of Philosophy at the University of Massachusetts in Boston.

EDITORS

Julia Christ is researcher in Philosophy at the French National Center for Scientifique Research (CNRS)/Ecole des Hautes Etudes en Sciences Sociales (EHESS) in Paris.

Kristina Lepold is Assistant Professor of Social Philosophy at Goethe University Frankfurt.

Daniel Loick is Associate Professor of Political and Social Philosophy at the University of Amsterdam.

Titus Stahl is Assistant Professor of Philosophy at the University of Groningen.

www.ingramcontent.com/pod-product-compliance
Lightning Source LLC
Chambersburg PA
CBHW020637230426

43665CB00008B/213